# 1 MONTH OF
# FREE
## READING

### at
## www.ForgottenBooks.com

By purchasing this book you are eligible for one month membership to ForgottenBooks.com, giving you unlimited access to our entire collection of over 700,000 titles via our web site and mobile apps.

To claim your free month visit:
www.forgottenbooks.com/free325331

ISBN 978-0-266-62052-5
PIBN 10325331

# Lessings

# Nathan der Weise

WITH

INTRODUCTION, NOTES, AND AN APPENDIX
OF PARALLEL PASSAGES

BY

## TOBIAS J. C. DIEKHOFF, Ph. D.

ASSISTANT PROFESSOR OF GERMAN IN THE UNIVERSITY OF MICHIGAN

---

NEW YORK-:-CINCINNATI-:-CHICAGO
AMERICAN BOOK COMPANY

Meinem lieben Vater
gewidmet

# CONTENTS

3

# PREFACE

To PUT another edition of *Nathan the Wise* on the market may need a word of justification. Without depreciating what other editors have done before me, I venture to hope that my work will not be entirely without merits of its own, which may give it a right to exist. The editions already accessible—both those of German and those of English or American origin—seem to be addressed to a class of students less mature in judgment than the ones with whom I have to deal, and whom I have had in mind in preparing the notes. To these I have endeavored to make accessible the most important material necessary for a critical study and a correct appreciation of *Nathan*.

The Introduction aims to make clear the historical setting, and to establish a view point from which *Nathan* can be seen advantageously. Particularly in the second part, dealing with *Nathan as a Work of Art*, I have been obliged to differ in several important instances from the current views. It is a safe literary principle to endeavor to justify the poet in what he chooses to make of his work—at least to give him credit for having good reasons for doing what he does, and then to try to discover what these reasons may be. Especially in dealing with a work so carefully elaborated in the minutest details this rule must be insisted upon.

The notes are more of a literary character, explaining linguistic points only where the ordinary grammar and dictionary fail.

An entirely new feature is the Appendix. It explains the views propounded in *Nathan* in relation to other works of Lessing, and from works which we may be reasonably sure he read. It condenses in a comparatively few pages the scattered parallels found in the reading of many weeks. A student with the inclination and time to do further work will find in the list of books mentioned a tolerably trustworthy guide; the ordinary reader who is not satisfied with a merely superficial understanding will find in the passages quoted some of the more striking parallels and references.

The text is based on Lachmann's edition of Lessing's works, newly revised by Franz Muncker. The punctuation has been faithfully preserved, even in a few instances where a change seemed desirable to me. The reasons are given in the notes. The orthography has been made to agree with the Prussian rules.

The literature bearing on *Nathan*, directly and indirectly, is very extensive. I have read a goodly number of works of the kind, but have directly made use of very few. To give a bibliography is of little purpose, inasmuch as one fairly complete is found in an Appendix to the *Life of G. E. Lessing* by T. W. Rolleston. The books which are, in my judgment, of most use to the average student are, besides the little Life of Lessing just mentioned, Erich Schmidt, *Lessing*, 2d edition, differing essentially from the first edition ; particularly chapters III, IV, V, and VI of Volume II ; C. Hebler, *Lessingstudien* ; C. R. Papst, *Vorlesungen über Lessings Nathan* ; Kuno Fischer, *Lessings Nathan der Weise* ; Willibald Beyschlag, *Lessings Nathan der Weise und das positive Christentum* ; Gustav Kettner, *Über den religiösen Gehalt von Lessings Nathan dem Weisen*. On the verse: Fr. Zarncke, *Über den fünffüssigen Jambus mit besonderer Rücksicht auf seine Behandlung durch Lessing, Schiller und Goethe*, in *Kleine Schriften* I. Many historical and other allusions are explained in Eduard Niemeyer's *Lessings Nathan der Weise*, etc.

I am greatly indebted to Professor Max Winkler of the University of Michigan for a careful manuscript reading of the Introduction, and a number of valuable suggestions. My friends Dr. E. C. Roedder, of the University of Wisconsin, Dr. J. A. C. Hildner, of the University of Michigan, and Mr. C. F. Weiser, of Detroit, have put me under obligation by reading the proof.

ANN ARBOR.                 TOBIAS DIEKHOFF.

# INTRODUCTION

CRITICS and commentators have freely bestowed their labor upon *Nathan the Wise*. But from the most humble of them up to Schiller (the pupil of Lessing destined to be greater than his master), they have been puzzled to decide upon the class of dramatic literature to which it belongs. Only of late years have scholars been content to recognize that it is a work totally of its own kind, a type for a new class.

It is also unique in being at the same time a work of art and a religious polemic; and, viewed from either standpoint, it is a very creditable production, in no way unworthy of its famous author. And yet, owing to the interrelation of the two sides, *Nathan*, as a polemic, is not as incisive and well-defined as other polemic works of its author; nor is it, as a work of art, pure, and free from non-artistic elements; the polemic digressions have not become wholly poetic at the same time. Accordingly, art critics have generally not been wholly satisfied with *Nathan*, while those looking at its religious content and meaning have been and are still divided.

To do justice to *Nathan*, the student must direct his attention with equal assiduity to both sides, and it is the place of an introduction to give the necessary guidance, as far as possible, without prejudice. Though the two sides are inseparably interwoven in the play, we shall, for the sake of clearness, separate them in the introduction, and consider

## I. NATHAN AS A RELIGIOUS POLEMIC

### I. The Genesis of Nathan

1. It has long been the fashion to speak of *Nathan* **Plea for** as the great plea for religious toleration. Its **Toleration?** relation to the polemic writings preceding it ought to suggest at least that it was not toleration about

which Lessing was primarily concerned. The same motive which guided him in the publication of the *Fragments* induced him also to write his *Nathan*. There are some elements in the play suggesting the idea of toleration, but even they do not stand for toleration in the noblest sense of the word. The toleration which *Nathan* does teach is, after all, the result of indifference rather than of that love which is the fulfillment of faith. None of the characters are at all fair representatives of their respective creeds. Creed differences they regard as merely external, as based on events which are all equally a matter of history, and as such equally open to doubt. Lessing himself seems to have overcome, to some extent, in his *Education of the Human Race*, this narrower, unhistorical attitude of *Nathan*.

2. And so we need not be surprised to find quite fre-**Change in** quently conservative Christians of our day looking **Religious** at *Nathan* with misgiving. They know that Lessing **Views.** avowedly wrote it against the orthodox Christianity of his time, and fail to take cognizance of the changes that have since taken place. Orthodoxy of Lessing's day and the orthodoxy of Protestant theology to-day are totally different matters. If orthodox Christians of our day were seriously confronted with the alternative of choosing between Lessing and his opponents, it may at least be considered doubtful with whom they would side.

It is both the privilege and the duty of every generation to work out its own ethical and religious ideals, and to determine what is orthodox and what is not. Conflicts are inevitable whenever this privilege is not felt as a duty, whenever people refuse to think for themselves, and are satisfied with the thoughts and ideals that were a quickening power in previous ages, but for them are nothing but dead symbols.

3. The principles for which the Reformation had stood, **Tenor of** the liberty which it had secured for the individual, **the Time.** had been lost. The champions of freedom had

themselves turned despots. Religion and morality had been divorced. Luther's "by faith alone" was interpreted to mean that a passive, indolent, intellectual subjection to the word of Scripture and dogma was the essence of Christianity. Thus religion had degenerated into speculative theology, and faith into superstition, which, with characteristic zeal, set no limits to its belief, and measured its righteousness by the multitude of things it took for granted. Whatever was contained between the two covers of the Bible was held to be true to the letter, not only in the domain of genuine religion, in which the Bible has its full value to-day and can never lose it, but also in all other matters incidentally mentioned and bearing evidently the signature of the times in which they originated. The reaction against this unnatural mental servitude expressed itself in two movements, which, though springing from the same source, soon became hostile to each other. The one is known as Pietism, the other as Enlightenment. Lessing was influenced by both, more deeply by the latter.

4. The nineteenth century has hardly been just in its estimate of the German Enlightenment. It was the **Enlightenment; its basic Principles.** outgrowth of the Renaissance, and shared with it as its fundamental principle the optimistic faith in man. But with the fantastic also the artistic tendencies of the Renaissance had been outgrown, and calm, studied, rigid reason held sway. Even for the highest representatives of the Renaissance, nature was in every part endowed with a soul. The hypothesis of the absoluteness of natural laws had not yet been postulated, and even men rightly numbered in the ranks of scientists recognized the influence and courted the favor of sprites and spirits, now friendly, now hostile to men. The entire chapter of astrology and alchemy is a record of superstition so gross, and, in its widely extending influence, so strange, that we can hardly reconcile it with its surroundings. The Enlightenment resolutely made an end of all this. Spirits and

magic charms fell into discredit, the gloom of witchcraft and heresy trials was dispersed by the new light. The Renaissance was still largely dependent for the sources of its development on the civilizations of the past. The Enlightenment cut loose from historical influences entirely, convinced that in his own intellect the individual has at hand a means quite adequate for an explanation of the world in all its phases. "There are, according to this system, in human nature constant conceptions, definite relations, a uniformity, from which there must everywhere be evolved with necessity the outlines of social life, of legal order, of moral law, aesthetic canons, faith in God, and worship of God. These natural tendencies, norms, and conceptions in our thought, our poetry, our faith and our social dealings are unchangeable and independent of the varying forms of civilization. They control all nations, are at work in all countries. Upon them depends the autonomy of man. In so far as men become conscious of them and make them the guide of their actions; in so far as they cite all creeds and all existing institutions before the tribunal of the system deduced from these inherent norms and tendencies, they enter upon the age of majority and enlightenment. And before this tribunal every institution of society and every dogma of the church is called into account. No greater and more prolonged trial has ever been conducted."

*a*) In philosophy, psychological consideration claims the In Philos- first place. Morality is based on psychology, not ophy. on theology or metaphysics. The motives of conduct are no longer external to man. Not punishment or reward to be expected in a world to come should be the stimuli to action, but the satisfaction and peace man feels in knowing that he acts rightly. And to act rightly means largely to act unselfishly in behalf of society.

*b*) In theology and religion the German Enlightenment was In especially influenced by English thinkers. The writ-Theology. ings of Hume, Gibbon, Toland, Locke and other

English philosophers, deists, and freethinkers were, partly
in translation, partly in the original, eagerly read and
readily assimilated in educated circles in Germany.  Still,
the German Enlightenment has its distinctive features, in
which it differs from the same movement in France and
England.  Two centuries before, the Italian Renaissance
had, under the influence of the German mind, developed
into the Reformation.  And the impulse given by this movement made the German Enlightenment predominantly theological.  Never doubting the reasonableness of his own
nature, the German *Aufklärer* proceeds to criticise existing ecclesiastical institutions.  His attacks, directed at first
against what is unreasonable, are soon leveled at everything
supernatural.  The human intellect, in the narrower sense,
is claimed to be coextensive with the human mind.  The
intellect, sufficient to itself, has no patience with any
historical element in religion.  The sole content of religion
is morality, the only reasonable worship is virtue.  This
implicit confidence in the all-sufficiency of the human intellect was shaken only by Kant's Critique.  To have overcome, in principle, the conflict thus inevitable between
religion and science, between faith and knowledge, "is, in
my opinion, the greatest and most general service of critical
philosophy.  It shows, that the discrepancy between the two
is only a phenomenon historically conditioned.  Conflicts
may arise between the statutory creed of some church or
other, and science; but with a purely ethical, practical,
rational faith, true philosophy and science can never conflict.
Scientific thinking which knows what knowledge is, and is
aware of the limits established by the nature of knowledge,
and religious faith, which knows what faith means, these
two, side by side, have ample room in the human mind;
indeed, the human mind requires both.  Conflicts arise only
when, on the one hand, science claims absoluteness, and
asserts that nothing exists in reality but what it can see; or
where, on the other hand, the church insists on the sub-

jection of reason to the tenets of its statutary dogma, which assumes authority not only regarding the things of faith, but also regarding the questions of knowledge."*

5. An ally of the Enlightenment in its struggle against **Pietism.** established religious institutions, notably against the orthodoxy of the time, was the other movement known as Pietism. It insisted, above all things, on practical religion. But the pietist, far from basing his creed on the declarations of reason, felt happy and secure and blessed in his religious, more or less mystical emotions and feelings, so much spurned by the Enlightenment. And Pietism was indeed productive of many noble, devoted Christian lives, and erected monuments to its earnestness and zeal in orphan asylums, schools for the poor, and other charitable institutions. Lessing pays a tribute to this movement in his Essay, *Gedanken über die Herrnhuter*, the Moravian Brethren, affiliated with the Pietists.

6. A third influence, finally, came from France, but **Storm and** gained its full strength only later. It is the **Stress.** beginning of the movement known in German thought and literature as the Storm and Stress Movement. The impulse was given by Rousseau, especially in his *Émile*. Here, too, the sources of right living and of consequent human happiness are found in man himself. But, instead of depending for the norms of life and conduct upon intellectual speculation, this new movement—agreeing in this respect with Pietism—laid the main stress upon *feeling*. Rousseau's demand, "Back to nature, back to the stage of humanity in which an exuberant civilization had not destroyed the mystic unity of feeling and intellect," is a manifesto against Enlightenment, which, while it made human life rigid and dutiful, had, by systematically making war upon all feeling, deprived it of many of its sweetest charms and rendered it poor and insipid.

* Paulsen, *Kants Verhältnis zur Metaphysik*, Vaihingers *Kant-studien*, vol. IV, p. 413 ff.

7. But, in their opposition to Orthodoxy, Pietism and
Storm and Stress united with the Enlightenment. It
**Opposition to Orthodoxy.** seems like the irony of fate that Orthodoxy should
have found its chief opponent in the Enlighten-
ment, when in reality both were suffering from the same
disease. The orthodox theologians had by strictly logical processes constructed a system, which was by no
means the work of bunglers and half-philosophers, as
Lessing himself confessed. They had used the same reason
from which the Enlighteners expected everything. They
were no less firmly convinced of its infallibility, and no less
successful in extirpating the more tender and delicate things
of life. Religion had died under their hands, and theology
flourished. The difference between the two movements of
thought consisted in the assumptions from which they started,
Orthodoxy basing its system upon certain dogmas externally
delivered through the Reformation ; the Enlightenment on
the other hand starting out with the assumption that,
independent of all history, man has within him the data
from which his intellect, by a formal logical process, can
produce the only right system of philosophy, ethics, and religion. The immediate reaction against Orthodoxy was Pietism ;
the immediate reaction against the Enlightenment was the
Storm and Stress movement.

8. Of course, it is not to be supposed that these various
**Blending of the Movements, and Gradations.** movements were kept clearly distinct, or that any
large number of men clearly represented any one
of them without being more or less affected by
the others also. Thus a large number of theologians, known as Neo-theologians at the time, were more
or less thoroughly in sympathy with the spirit of the Enlightenment. . Some were faithful adherents of the Lutheran
church, and only ventured to apply the apparatus of secular
philology to the text of the Bible. Others went one step
further ; they cut loose from every creed but still upheld the
Revelation, which, they claimed, never contradicts reason,

if only rightly construed. And, accordingly, they applied their construction. Still others regarded not only the creeds as contradictory to reason, and as being invented by ambitious priests, but also indulged in uncurbed criticism and denunciation of Revelation itself.

9. At a time when three such important movements **Represent-** were struggling with a system which had gained **ative** strength and influence in two centuries of almost **Men.** undisturbed peace, and, at the same time, each fighting for supremacy with little less than fanatic zeal, Lessing lived and worked. Frederic II.* was the model of potentates, Voltaire the idol of literary circles, and for a considerable time the idol of Lessing. What was more, theologians by profession began to make radical changes in the customary order of things. Ernesti in Leipzig, hardly equalled by any of his contemporaries in thorough and comprehensive knowledge of classic ancient literature, and a theologian of no mean repute, advocated the application of the whole apparatus of philological science to the books of the Bible. Michaelis, another theologian, was decidedly in sympathy with the Enlightenment, and made his doctrines popular' through the attractive form of his lectures at the University of Göttingen. Semler, agreeing with Spinoza in many of his views regarding the canonical books, whose inspiration he denied, published early in the seventies his *Freie Untersuchung des Kanons*, and thereby almost induced Lessing, as early as 1774 to issue under the title *Eine noch freiere Untersuchung des Kanons Alten und Neuen Testamentes*, a part of the *Fragments*, destined to play so conspicuous a part in Lessing's controversy afterward. Moses Mendelssohn,

---

* A few representative names are merely mentioned to serve as an index to further reading. Cf. Harold Höffding, *A History of Modern Philosophy*. Translated, London 1900, Macmillan. Or Wilh. Windelband, *A History of Philosophy*. Translated, Macmillan, N. Y. and London, and Isaac A. Dorner, *History of Protestant Theology*, Edinburgh, 1871.

one of the noblest leaders of the German Enlightenment and the greatest modern reformer of Judaism, was Lessing's bosom friend with whom he carried on philosophic discussions.

10. To these influences in Lessing's life may be added his **Lessing's** home training and his early education. His father **Environ-** was a pious Protestant clergyman, whose sincerity **ment.** and uprightness never failed to command the reverence of the son, though the slackness of the latter's correspondence, and the intervals between his visits at home, greater than even the imperfect means of travel at the time would seem to necessitate, might suggest at least a doubt as to the ardor of that filial devotion which has been ascribed to Lessing by many biographers. The influence of such a home was carefully fostered at the Cloister School of St. Afra. Lessing himself characterizes the time in which he lived, and the position he took in regard to some of its movements, in his *Bibliolatrie*. He says: "The better part of my life—whether for better or worse— belonged to a time when, in a sense, apologies for the truth of the Christian religion were the fashion . . . . No wonder that I, too, was occupied with this sort of reading and soon so engrossed that I found no peace until I had devoured every novelty appearing in this field . . . Not long, and I sought no less eagerly every article written against religion, and gave it the same patient, impartial hearing which I had hitherto considered due only to writings *in favor* of religion. I was tossed from one side to the other, wholly satisfied by neither. Both were dismissed from time to time with the resolution no sooner to pass final judgment *quam utrimque plenius fuerit peroratum*. So far probably the experience of many is similar to mine. In other respects I am more likely to be alone . . . . The more conclusive evidence one side meant to adduce in favor of the Christian faith, the more doubtful I became. The greater the effrontery and insolence with which the other side trampled it in

the dust, the more I was inclined to uphold it, at least in my heart."

11. Very early in life Lessing showed this interest in **Religious** religious matters. Even the New Year's letter, **Interest** which in 1743 the boy of fourteen addressed to **and Inde-** his father, gives fair promise of a character **pendence of** his father, gives fair promise of a character **Thought.** "which will not remain at ease where the accident of birth placed him, unless he remains for good reasons." And in 1749 Lessing wrote to his father, who was troubled, not entirely without cause, about his son's construction of his pious advice: "We will leave it for time to prove who is the better Christian: the one who has an apt memory for the tenets of Christianity, and parades them without much vital understanding, goes to church and complies with the ceremonial as a matter of custom; or the one who has at some time entertained reasonable doubt and by way of investigation reached conviction, or is, at least, making a fair attempt to reach it. The Christian religion is not a bequest to be accepted in good faith from the parents. As a matter of fact, most people do receive it as a paternal inheritance; and they plainly show in their conduct the genuineness of their confession. As long as I do not see observed one of the foremost injunctions of Christianity: *to love our enemies*, I cannot help doubting whether those are Christians indeed, who are Christians by profession." About the same time Lessing published a poem: *Die Religion.* In the preface he says: "The first canto is particularly devoted to the doubts which, owing to the internal and external misery of man, can be raised concerning everything divine. The poet expressed them in a soliloquy resulting from the quiet of a lonesome, troubled day. Do not imagine that he is losing sight of his subject when he seems to be straying in the labyrinths of introspection. Introspection, a realization of our own condition, has always been the nearest, and, I may add, the surest road to religion."

12. All through life Lessing kept up this interest in **Difficulties** theology, and wrote his thoughts quite exten-**in de-** sively particularly in connection with the con-**termining** **Lessing's** troversy from which *Nathan* sprang. He was **position. —** unusually well versed in ancient and modern **Change in** **his Views.** literatures, and had studied the Church Fathers with a thoroughness that challenged men professional in that particular field. But, an ardent friend of keen dialectics, he delighted, now and then, in speculations too venture-some for the average, and he took the part of the stigmat-ized sometimes to the extent of a fault. This may in some measure account for the diversity of opinion regarding his religious views. But this diversity is largely due to the peculiar shape which Lessing's theological writings assumed owing to the time, and more to the circumstances attend-ing their composition. Fortunately his letters have been preserved to a large extent, and furnish an excellent com-mentary on many of his works. One of them (to Moses Mendelssohn, Jan. 9, 1771) shows that Lessing himself was aware of a change in his views, of a return from an extreme radicalism which would have vied in denunciation of every-thing pertaining to the Christian dogma with the most radical of the Neo-theologians, to a more conservative, charitable position. He says: "I have been fearing, not only since yesterday, that in discarding certain prejudices I have cast away somewhat too much, which I shall have to recover. If I have not done so ere this, I have been prevented from it by the fear that gradually I should again drag into my house the whole rubbish."

13. This change in Lessing's views is one source of **Diplomacy.** confusion. Besides, he says many things not from conviction, but because his opponent cannot deny them, and must, admitting them, weaken his own posi-tion. As Lessing puts it himself, he makes many state-ments γυμναστικῶς, which he would not make δογματικῶς, or as he writes to his friend Elise Reimarus, the daughter

of the Fragmentist, who is to be mentioned later: "I am glad you so well understand the tactics of my last pamphlet. I shall resort to stratagems in my dealing with Goeze, of which he is surely not aware." In regard to the same matter Lessing writes to his brother Karl: "In a few days you will also receive a pamphlet against Goeze. With respect to him I have undoubtedly put myself in a position in which he cannot touch me as non-Christian." This, as well as a number of other utterances, are not exactly open declarations that Lessing personally did not regard himself a Christian, taking the word in any sense known at his time, but they certainly point very strongly in that direction.

14. If, in spite of all this, Lessing opposes the views of the new school of theologians more assiduously, if anything, than those of the Orthodox, it was owing to their inconsistency, and the discrepancies in their system. However little to Lessing's taste they might be, the views of the Orthodox were at least consistent. Orthodox theologians professedly did not try to adjust their doctrines to the canons of . human reason. They were an *open* enemy, as Lessing says on one occasion,—you knew where to find them. They had agreed to have a partition placed between philosophy and theology. The new school "tears down this partition, and under the pretense of making of us rational Christians, converts us into extremely unreasonable philosophers." Lessing openly agrees that the old system of theology is false, yet to him it is far more acceptable than the system which the new school intends to put in its place. He wishes with all his heart that every one might think rationally about religion, but prefers to pursue his own course in advancing rational religion. He has no desire whatever to maintain the old system, but neither is he anxious to do away with the old, as long as he sees no new one, worthy of the name, with which to replace it.

*Relative Position to Orthodox and Neo-theologians.*

15. **Doubtful Tactics.** This was his position with respect to the Orthodox and the Neo-theologians of his time, and it can easily be understood. But when, in his controversies, and notably in a letter to the Duke of Brunswick, he boasts of being considered the stanchest defender of the Lutheran doctrine in Germany, one finds it difficult not to condemn such a statement. Tactics of this kind, even though employed as strategic measures called for by the needs of the literary campaign, are hard to justify, particularly when one remembers Lessing's repeated charges of duplicity and hypocrisy leveled against Goeze and other opponents. It is not necessary blindly to worship a great man in order to prove our admiration. Lessing himself says in his *Dramaturgie*: "The true genius does not even believe that we recognize and appreciate his perfections, though we laud them extravagantly, unless he perceives that we have also eyes and appreciation for his weaknesses." And his brother Karl significantly suggests that the Neo-theologians might with equal justice, in view of their aims, lay claim to some forbearance regarding their methods.

It is quite plain, in spite of repeated statements to the contrary, that Lessing did not always contend solely in behalf of the principle at stake. He writes, June 9, 1766, to Klotz, with whom he was afterward involved in a bitter literary controversy: "Do we write merely for the sake of establishing our position? It seems to me I have done as much for truth if, through my failing to discover it, I induce some one else to find it, as if I had found it myself." How different Nov. 20, 1770, in a letter to Heyne: "It does not matter at all who of *us* two is in the right, so long as Klotz is not."

And thus it is, after all, not so easy to construe Lessing's creed from his own writings.

> "*Was ihr den Geist der Zeiten heisst,*
> *Das ist im Grund der Herren eigner Geist,*
> *In dem die Zeiten sich bespiegeln.*"

16. It is well for us also to heed this warning of Faust.
**Formula-** Lessing did not strictly belong to any class.
**tion of his** Like Schiller and Goethe, indeed like any man
**Views.** thinking at all for himself, he had a creed quite
**Pantheism.** 
**Spinoza's** his own. He indicated in a conversation with
**position.** Jacobi, a young philosopher and ardent admirer of
his, that he considered himself a pantheist. In trying
to be more exact, men have since called him a pan-en-
theist, indicating that for him everything was comprehended
in God. It is certain that he was influenced by Spinoza's
philosophy. But even if Jacobi's report of the conversation
with him is to be accepted as valid—about which there can
be little doubt—the fact that Lessing confessed to pantheism
would not necessarily stamp him as a follower of Spinoza.
"Pantheism * merely asserts that God is equivalent to an
eternal order. In what this eternal order consists, as far as
mere pantheism is concerned, is an open question. It may
be conceived of as a natural or a moral order, a mechanical
or a teleological, a material or a spiritual order, as nature,
or as creation. Pantheism does not involve anything beyond
this first equation; and it is apparent that it all depends
on the modifications under which this eternal order is conceived, whether freedom, teleological purpose, etc., are excluded or admitted. If we know that Spinoza conceived of
Substance as the one and only being besides which nothing
exists, the first sentence of his doctrine, *"substantia sive
deus,"* is sufficient to stamp it as pantheism.

"Moreover, Spinoza conceives of that eternal order, or
the interrelation of things, as a necessary consequence of
the nature of God, as a product, which the will can neither
create nor modify, as a world, from whose creative cause
reason and will, that is, the spiritual powers, are totally

* Cf. Kuno Fischer, *Geschichte der Philosophie* I 2, p. 533f.
Eduard Zeller, *Lessing als Theolog*, Von Sybels *Historische Zeit-
schrift*, vol. 23, p. 347ff. Johannes Hoops, *Lessing's Verhältnis zu
Spinoza*, Herrig's *Archiv*, vol. 86.

excluded. That is to say, he does not conceive of that eternal order of things as creation, but merely as *nature:* this modification comes second. The first declaration of his system is "*substantia sive deus,*" the second, "*deus sive natura.*" *Substantia sive deus* Spinoza says as a pantheist; *deus sive natura* he says as a naturalist (in the philosophic sense of the term).

17. "The Enlightenment of the eighteenth century, deistic in its nature, admitted of no revelation of God except that in the natural order of things. But it insisted on recognizing in this natural order the complete expression of divine wisdom and goodness . . . . Spinoza denies every purpose whatever, natural as well as moral, and admits in the total order of the universe of no other power and no other interrelation than solely that of causality."

Distinctive Views of the Enlightenment.

18. Much as Lessing may have been influenced by Spinoza in particulars, it seems tolerably certain that in the fundamental principles he did not agree with him. And so it is probably safe to say with Zeller that no other system so decidedly influenced the theological views of Lessing as that of Leibniz, this "great man," whom he mentions on every occasion with the greatest reverence, who, if he had his way, should not have written a solitary line in vain. "Extension, motion, thought—he says also to Jacobi—evidently have their source in a higher power, which in these attributes is by no means comprehended. And this power, he argues, must be infinitely more excellent than any of its actions (with Spinoza it equals the sum of its actions), and so it may be conceived as capable of a sort of enjoyment, which not only transcends all of our conceptions, but lies quite beyond our conception . . . . In his teleological view of the universe and in his faith in a providence, as well as in his individualism, Lessing differs as distinctly from Spinoza as he agrees in these points with Leibniz . . . . Of a personal,

Lessing — Spinoza — Leibniz.

extra-mundane deity he could not conceive: but for the very purpose of conceiving the deity as personal he was fond of considering it as the soul of the universe." Indeed, in his ethical individualism he seems to concede even more freedom to the individual than the monads of Leibniz, each with a steadily growing perfection peculiar to itself, could vouchsafe. A formula of this individualism we find in § 26 of his *Christentum der Vernunft*: "*Act* according to your individual perfection." He expresses this same law repeatedly, nowhere with more emphasis than in his *Gedanken über die Herrnhuter*: "*Der Mensch ist zum Thun nicht zum Vernünfteln geboren.*"—To ask of him belief in a son of God who is of the same essence with God he calls asking something against which all his reason revolts. If, therefore, in some of his treatises he speaks of the Son and the Spirit, these terms stand for philosophic conceptions: in one instance the Son for the world, the Spirit for a sort of harmony between God and the world. Nevertheless, after maturer thought he would not have subscribed to the monstrous insinuations against the Apostles and the early Christians in which he indulged in his uncompleted essay *Von der Art und Weise der Fortpflanzung und Ausbreitung der christlichen Religion.* He had learned to appreciate, in a measure at least, the significance of history. But, on the other hand, wherever he seemed to defend the dogma, he merely meant to show that it was logical, *starting from its assumptions.* He never attempted to establish its truths as absolutely valid for us, though he did not always avoid this appearance. His apologetics in his annotations to the *Fragments* were too evidently feigned to need very close consideration at this place.

19. He did not believe in any special revelation given **His View** at any one time with extraordinary clearness or em**of** phasis. But he did believe in "a continuous, univer**Revelation.** sal revelation of the divine spirit to the human, progressing according to the laws of inherent necessity" as

Schwarz * formulates it. That is to say, revelation for him amounted to nothing more than a natural, historical development of rational knowledge.

20. For him there are no miracles, nothing super-
**Of Miracles.** natural except the first great cause of things, still manifesting its wisdom and goodness in the orderly, purposeful course of events in the universe.

21. Man is no free moral agent, or better, there is no
**Freedom of the Will Denied.** freedom of the will. Lessing is, however, no fatalist of the vulgar kind. "Force and compulsion, constraining me to do what I conceive as best, how much do I prefer them to the bare ability to act, under the same circumstances, now one way, now another! I thank my creator that I *must*, that I *must* what is *best*. If within these limits I take so many false steps, what would I do if quite left to myself, if I were abandoned to a blind force, which is controlled by no law, and subjects me to chance, none the less chance because it has its origin within my own self."† Lessing's determinism may be defined in a few words thus: the more nearly a man attains to perfection, the more absolutely is he compelled to definite action. God *can not* be otherwise than perfect in his dealings. Man, in his conduct, is determined foremost by rational, moral causes tending to definite results. Where these causes are made non-effective, it is not by blind chance, but by certain irrational tendencies and psychological forces, feelings and emotions, which are stimulated partly by our physical nature.

22. He knows of no future reward or punishment in
**Metempsychosis.** their common meaning. He thinks of the world as steadily growing in perfection. In his plan no soul can be lost. If it could, every soul would have to fear this possibility, and even if itself saved, it would in its sympathy with the lost be forever wretched.

* Karl Schwarz, *Lessing als Theologe.*
† Lessing's Preface to *Jerusalem's Philosophic Essays.*

Every evil deed as well as every good deed must be of eternal consequence; but all men must approach perfection as their conceptions become clearer; every one is destined to develop continually toward perfection. "The ultimate aim of Christianity is not our eternal happiness coming whence it may, but our happiness by means of our enlightenment." Humanity at large is an organism which God is gradually educating to a higher plain, until it shall be ready for the new, eternal gospel, whose fundamental law will insist on virtue merely for virtue's sake. And parallel with the education of humanity as a whole goes the education of the individual. In both cases the process is exceedingly slow, so that man with his limited vision is apt to become impatient. "Go thy imperceptible pace, eternal Providence! Only let me not despair of thee on account of this imperceptibility! — Let me not despair of thee, even if thy steps should seem to me, sometimes, to retrograde. — It is not true that a straight line is always the shortest. Thou hast so much to take along in thy eternal course, so many digressions to make. And what if it were well-nigh established that the large, slow wheel, advancing the race to its perfection, were only set in motion by smaller, quicker wheels, of which each brings an individual to the same destiny? Just so! The very path on which the race arrives at its perfection must also be traversed by each individual, by one sooner, by another later. Traversed in one and the same life? Well, no! — But why could not every individual man have been in this world more than once? Why could not I, too, have taken at one time all the steps toward my perfection, to which temporal rewards and punishments alone can induce men? And why not at another time all those which the prospect of eternal reward aids us so strongly to take? Why should I not return as often as I am capable of attaining new knowledge, new accomplishments? Do I acquire so much at one coming that, possibly, it would not be worth while returning?"

23. After all, the elements entering into Lessing's the-
**Probable** ology are not so easily discernible. For our
**Creed.** purpose the question of just how much he owes
to Leibniz or Spinoza, to Hume and Bayle, or Tertullian
and St. Augustin, is of no great importance. It is certain
that he did not subscribe, without reserve, to the system of
any one of them, but had his own views, though he never
developed them into a well-defined, rounded system. He
openly declared his aversion to every sort of revealed or
positive religion, though he did not subscribe in his riper
years to the monstrous insinuations of men like Reimarus,
and some of his English predecessors, e. g. Gibbon. The
creed which he assigns to the so-called Natural Religion
was probably in the main also his creed, and his also the
relative position of natural religion to positive or revealed
religion. "To recognize a God; to form of him conceptions
most worthy of him; and to have due consideration of these
conceptions in all our actions and thoughts, is the complete
content of all natural religion. To this natural religion
every man is inclined and in duty bound, according to the
measure of his strength. This measure is different in different
men, and modifies accordingly the natural religion of every
man. On this account certain disadvantages arose, not
interfering with the natural liberty of man, but proving
cumbersome in his social relations with others. These disadvantages it was considered necessary to obviate." In
this attempt positive religions originated, differing according
to the various times, and the varying conditions of human
society, and receiving their sanction from their different
founders, who pretended that the conventional part came
from God as well as the essential, only indirectly. "That
which makes a positive religion necessary, and modifies
natural religion in every state according to the natural and
accidental peculiarities of each state, I call its inherent truth;
and this truth inherent in positive religions is as great in
one as in the other. Hence all positive and revealed

religions are equally true and equally false.  Equally true,
because it has been equally necessary among all peoples to
come to some agreement regarding some externals in order
to attain harmony and union in their public religion;
equally false, because the results of the compromise do not
exist merely alongside the essentials, but they weaken the
essentials and encroach upon them.  The *best* revealed or
positive religion is the one containing the least conventional
additions to natural religion, the one least interfering with
the beneficial effects of natural religion."

24.  The above is nearly the entire fragment entitled,
**Emphasis on Practical Religion.** *Über die Entstehung der geoffenbarten Religion,*
which together with another short one, called *Das
Christentum der Vernunft,* contains probably all
the germs of Lessing's speculative theology.  Directed more to the practical side are among other utterances his *Testament Johannis* and the *Gedanken über die
Herrnhuter.*

In his letter justifying him in his position with his
father, quoted in § 11, traces of his practical side are
apparent.  Schwarz says: "Morality is for Lessing always
a correlate of religion, and the capability of moral application and productivity is the criterion for the truth or
falseness of any religion."  Without investigating whether
Lessing carried out his principle in every point, in theory,
at least, he most emphatically advocated a sublime religion
of morality and mutual love.  Not only in the two essays
mentioned, but wherever he addresses himself to religious
subjects, the practical side of religion is emphasized.  One
quotation must serve for a multitude: "Little children, love ye
one another.  This was the last will and testament of St. John,
by which of yore a certain Salt of the Earth was want to
swear.  Nowadays this Salt of the Earth swears by the
Gospel of St. John, and I am told, that since this change
it hath somewhat lost its savor."  From the content we are
justified in substituting for the "Gospel of St. John" Dogma

in general, and, correspondingly, for the "Salt of the Earth" Orthodoxy.

25. In the *Fliegende Blätter aus dem Rauhen Hause zu Horn bei Hamburg*, the organ of the central committee for home missions of the German Evangelical Church, the following brief estimate of Lessing's character is given: "In true, genuine, chaste morality, indeed in heroism of real, self-denying love, not sensual passion, Lessing ranks far above all our great poets, and above most great men generally. As far as it is possible to be a Christian in deed without faith in Christianity, so far Lessing was a Christian, and in this he puts to shame the multitudes of those who, in spite of their name, in spite of what is Christian about them, are not Christians in deed and in truth, but often only in form."

26. From the preceding general sketch some idea can be obtained as to Lessing's relation to the *Fragments*, the controversy about which was the immediate cause of the publication of *Nathan the Wise*.

27. In the year 1770 Lessing had been appointed librarian in Wolfenbüttel, by the Duke of Brunswick. From Hamburg he brought with him a work of the learned professor Hermann Samuel Reimarus. The author, whose specialty had been oriental and classical philology, had, among his contemporaries, enjoyed the reputation of a great scholar, but his views were not considered discordant with the orthodoxy of his day. A number of his works which dealt with religious topics appeared in as many as four or more editions and were universally regarded as good and wholesome even for wider circles. Lessing was perfectly correct, when, in the controversy that followed, he pointed out to his opponents that the man they were now maligning had not very long before been regarded as a model scholar and a stanch defender of the faith. All of Reimarus' hostility to Christianity was subordinated to his greater enmity against Atheism and

Materialism. Brought up in a sturdy Christian family, he had long and earnestly struggled with his doubts as to the truth of Christianity, until he had finally resolved for himself to investigate its claims. The result was the work which Lessing published under the title of *Fragments of an Anonymous*. The first draft was completed early in the forties, and the author modified and improved it till his death in 1768. Reimarus' himself had called it "Apology or Defense of Reasonable Worshipers of God." Being of a retiring nature, and unable to speak his last word without endangering the reputation and social position of himself and his family, he had not intended his work for publication. He felt no desire to trouble the world with his views, or to be the cause of any disturbance. He says himself: "The work may remain in obscurity for the use of intelligent friends. With my consent it will not be published until the times are more enlightened. Rather let the common herd err a while longer, than that I, however innocently, should give them any offense, and provoke an outburst of mad religious fanaticism." The children of Reimarus, Lessing's intimate friends, intrusted the manuscript to him.

28. Why he felt called upon to publish the work, with *Manner of Publication, and probable Purpose* whose author he certainly did not, at this time, agree, without much reservation, is a question which cannot be answered with absolute certainty. He himself says, "I have drawn the author into the world, because I would no longer dwell under the same roof with him . . . A third party, I thought, must either more closely unite us, or separate us, and this third party can be no other than the public." He rightly expected from this publication a controversy, in which he would have an opportunity to express, and above all things to clarify, his own views. At any rate, in 1771 Jacobi and Mendelssohn in vain tried to dissuade him from publishing the manuscript. For the present, how-

ever, Lessing's project failed owing to the scruples of the publisher, who refused to undertake the publication as long as the official censors would not subscribe their "Vidi," which, according to the views of Nicolai, who was certainly most liberal, could hardly be expected from Christian theologians. But in the year 1774 Lessing found a way to carry out his plan. As librarian he had been editing since 1773 a periodical, *Contributions to History and Literature. — From the Treasures of the Ducal Library in Wolfenbüttel.* This periodical was exempt from the inspection of the censors, and thus a welcome medium for the publication of the Reimarus manuscript, which, accordingly, appeared as seven *Fragments of an Anonymous Author, Fragmente eines Ungenannten.*

29. It is of no advantage to give a detailed account of
**Content of the Fragments.** these *Fragments.* Most readers would find them tedious and uninteresting in spite of their great learning and intense zeal. A true disciple of his time, indeed by some considered to be the best exponent of the Enlightenment, Reimarus lacks all appreciation of historical development, ruthlessly condemns and himself lacks all poetic imagination, and adds to this an inveterate hatred against the Jewish race, whether ancient or contemporary. In general, he walks in the paths of the English Deists, of whom he mentions, among others, Bayle. With uncompromising frankness he denies the possibility of a divine revelation intended for all men, and credible in all ages. He accords to neither Old nor New Testament the character of Revelations or the divine origin claimed for them. The saints of the Bible, who are commonly regarded as models of piety and are represented as having enjoyed the special favor of God, he finds, in numberless cases, guilty of gross immorality. The belief in miracles in the Biblical sense is absurd, even dangerous, and wholly incompatible with any reverent view of God. And so he sees in the miracle accounts, notably that of the crossing of the

Red Sea by the Israelites, and that of the Resurrection, gross absurdities and irreconcilable contradictions. In a final *Fragment*, which Lessing did not publish, however, until 1778, when his campaign against Goeze was closed, Reimarus declares that even the establishment of the Christian religion was based on self-deception on the part of Christ (who was, however, in every respect a noble man), and on villainous imposture on the part of the disciples and the early missionaries.

30. It is significant that of all the other religions men-

Evident Unfairness of Reimarus to Christianity.

tioned not one is accused of such gross absurdity and intolerant bigotry as the Christian religion. Even the thoroughly hated Jews are said to have tolerated the *Proselites Portae* among them without molestation. Christians are unwilling to show this fairness to the Deists, though they are not separated from them by any greater gulf. Lessing himself points out in what respect the two cases are not parallel. The Proselytes were tolerated on condition: "the Deists demand unconditional toleration. They want the liberty of attacking the Christian religion, and yet expect to be tolerated. That is no doubt extravagant, and surely claiming more than was ever granted to their supposed predecessors in the ancient Jewish church."

31. The entire investigation is carried on in order to

Personal Element.

show the justness of the Deists in claiming the same toleration at the hands of enlightened men as is accorded to all sorts of heretics, Jews, Turks or heathen. Through all the bitter invectives, even through the frequent instances of frivolity with which the worst possible construction is put upon characters and events sacred to the hearts of many, there shines an austere morality, a cold reverence for the deity and a stoic trust in its providential guidance which command for the author a respect as cold as his for the feelings of his fellows.

**32.** That the *Fragments had at one time been*, in the main, an expression of Lessing's own views, we have little doubt. His *Origin of Revealed Religion* we have largely quoted, and need only refer to the ideas developed there. Even more to the point is the uncompleted essay *Von der Art und Weise der Fortpflanzung und Ausbreitung der chr. Religion*, in which a very plain parallel is drawn between the disciples of Christ and the immoral and intriguing Roman priests of Bacchus. *Much less closely* Lessing was in touch with the *Fragments* at the time of their publication. We have to remember the letter to Mendelssohn, mentioned above, in which he admits having gone too far in his renunciation. Possibly because he could no longer subscribe to the views expressed in the essay on the *Fortpflanzung und Ausbreitung der christlichen Religion*, it was not published while he lived, and can, in this case, serve only as an index to his views when they were most radical. When Lessing professed to have published the Reimarus manuscript with the purpose of ministering to the truth, we have indicated in what sense he might have really meant what he said. Herder, himself a theologian, and certainly a man whose testimony is not to be despised, says in 1781, the year of Lessing's death: "I, who knew Lessing personally, knew him at a time when the *Fragments* were probably in his hands, and were occupying his mind, as I must judge from a number of utterances; I, who also heard him express himself on matters of this nature, and think that I am sufficiently acquainted with his position as to what is manly love of truth,—I am, for myself, convinced (which may weigh little with others) that he undertook also the publication of these *Fragments solely and sincerely for the advancement of truth*, which he desired to see investigated, tested, and established from all sides, in a free and manly spirit. He himself has said this so often, so emphatically, so unequivocally; the whole manner in which he published the

*[Marginal note: Lessing's Attitude to the Fragments; Purpose in publishing them.]*

*Fragments* and, as a layman, at most ventured here and there a thought in refutation; and in general Lessing's character as it must be impressed on all who knew him (and others certainly ought to judge and speak of it cautiously): all this is for me a warrant of the *purity of his philosophic conviction*, that *in this also* he worked toward a good end, namely—I repeat—toward a freer investigation of the truth, and a truth so momentous as this history must be for every one believing in it. Now, if *this truth, this history, alone* of *all* truth and history, may not be investigated, or may not be investigated with reference to every doubt and every doubter, it was not Lessing's fault—but in our day no theologian, and no believer in religion would be likely to make any such assertion." And yet—when Lessing asks *orthodox*—not to say Christian—*theologians of his time* to consider the publication a deed intended for the glorification of the truth, he must certainly have been aware that the truth he meant, and the truth for which the theologians were contending, and with honest conviction, too, were wholly different matters.

33.   But two wholly different matters also were the

What Jus-<br>tification<br>for Pub-<br>lishing?<br>Purpose<br>and Tenor<br>of his<br>Comments. private convictions, the results of scholarly investigations of the foremost theologians — comparatively few in number — and the doctrines which were being disseminated from the pulpits. To this day the pulpits and the professorial chairs do not seem to accord entirely. And Lessing, having complained of this discrepancy with some success to the famous philologian and theologian Michaelis of Göttingen, may have intended to force men of learning to make public the secrets of their studies and their lecture rooms. The introduction and the notes which he appended to the *Fragments* were professedly intended to check the harm that might issue from them; at the same time they very skillfully opened up the controversy. They pointed out that the objections of the fragmentist were directed entirely against the theoretical side of the Christian religion, and might possibly alarm the learned theologian who sees his theories endangered, but surely not the Christian who feels in his heart the reality and force of his religion. They show in what way the objections, or some of them, might be met. Much of these notes is diplomacy on Lessing's part, surely not his honest conviction. He means to reassure a religious mind troubled by the assaults of the fragmentist, by pointing out that the entire historical foundation of Christianity might be undermined without detriment to his religion. What does it matter whether the *report about* Christianity will stand the test or not? For the believer Christianity is here, and in its possession he has a warrant of its reality. — Of course, the parallelism between Christianity and Mohammedanism or any other existing religion suggests itself, and it would be strange if Lessing had not seen it. He speaks from his heart when he points out that the belief in a verbal inspiration of the Bible is wholly untenable, and when he emphasizes the practical side of Christianity as over against the thoughtless and unfruitful confession of faith in the mysteries of the dogma.

34. But these notes really served to confine the attacks **Opponents.** made from all quarters of theologians entirely to the *Fragments* and their author; the publisher was practically unmolested.

35. Schumann had advanced as the best evidence of **Beweis des** the authenticity of the Revelation the ἀπόδειξις **Geistes und** πνεύματος καὶ δυνάμεως of Origen, the evidence of the **der Kraft;** **Testament** divine spirit and of divine power; the spirit's **Johannis.** working in the Old Testament being evident from the fact that its prophecies are fulfilled in the New; divine power is manifested in the miracles accompanying the teaching of Christ and believed in even by the heretics of the first centuries. Against him Lessing directed two answers: *Über den Beweis des Geistes und der Kraft*, and *Das Testament Johannis*. Prophecies ful-

filled, miracles accomplished in my own presence are one thing—mere reports of them are quite different things. "Accidental historical truth can never be made a proof of necessary rational truth." All we have of the miracles, or of Christ's own words, or of the inspiration of the authors of the Bible is a report. All these things are for us merely matters of history and can never be so well attested that, on them alone any one should be willing to rest his eternal welfare. "This, this is the ugly, wide gulf which I cannot cross, oft and earnestly as I have attempted the leap. If any one is able to help me across, let him do it, I beg, I implore him. He will be a Godsend to me."

36. Next in order came his *Duplik* in answer to an **Duplik.** attack by Pastor Ress upon the objections against the Resurrection. Lessing characterizes the respective position of the three parties involved thus: "The Fragmentist insists: The Resurrection of Christ is not to be believed, *also because* the reports of the various Evangelists are contradictory."

"I reply: The Resurrection of Christ may be a matter of fact, *although* the reports of the Evangelists are contradictory."

"Now a third party appears and says: The Resurrection of Christ is unquestionably to be believed, *because* the reports of the Evangelists are *not* contradictory."

"The reader will please notice this 'also because,' this 'although' and this 'because.' He will find that on these particles all but everything depends."

Lessing then proceeds to consider, one by one, the answers, which Ress proposed to the Fragmentist's objections. He proves every one of them to be absurd and insufficient, and "rather an accusation against the Evangelists than an answer to the Fragmentist," because Ress was not concerned about the credibility of each Evangelist, but about the validity of a certain harmony of the Gospels of his own creation, which, if it could be proved, would indict the Evangelists far more than the Fragmentist ever had any right or desire to do. Ress' argument was in the main that the Gospels are not to be considered as minutes of a case at hand, but as accounts written at later times under divine influence, with different purposes in view. And from this he draws the strange conclusion that there *can* be no contradictions in them, and the expositor merely needs to supplement the account of one Gospel by that of the others. — The good-natured tone in which Lessing had answered Schumann, and which prevails also in the opening pages of the *Duplik*, yields, in the end, to a passion and bitterness of which the cause seems hardly to lie in the discussion in hand. Lessing himself says in conclusion: "I am very well aware that my blood runs differently now that I end this *Duplik* than when I began it. I began so calm, so firmly determined to say everything I should have to say with calmness . . . . and I end with so much passion, can not deny that I have said many things with so much ardor and interest as I should be ashamed to display in a case where my neck was at stake." The great sorrow of his life had come upon him while at work on the rejoinder. Death had deprived him of wife and child. The happiness of his home life and the hope of greater happiness to come had enabled him to treat the follies of his opponents with the kindliness of a humorist. His hope had turned to despair, his joy to bitterness, his humor into the lash of scorn.

Numberless other opponents arose, nine to one in defense of the accounts of the Resurrection. To some of them answers are found, in more or less fragmentary form, in Lessing's posthumous works. Till the end of 1777 not a single attack had been directed against Lessing himself.

37. Only one man seems to have discovered the points in which orthodoxy might with perfect fairness attack Lessing as the publisher of the Fragments. And he pointed them out without any apparent

Goeze and his Position.

great bitterness.  This man was Johann Melchior Goeze,*
first pastor in the Church of St. Catherine in Hamburg, a
man to whom Lessing himself, in earlier years, ascribed
fair talents and considerable scholarship, a man whose
hospitality, if not whose friendship, Lessing had not deemed
it beneath him to accept.  That this man should attack
the *Fragments* and incidentally, also their publisher, can
fully be understood from the position he held as a minister
of the Gospel which had been maliciously slandered, and
need not be reduced to any petty personal feeling he may
have had against Lessing owing to a courtesy which Lessing
as librarian had unintentionally denied him.  In his controversy springing from the *Fragments*, Lessing had openly
declared that the theory of the verbal inspiration of the Bible
is untenable.  "Goeze is the last champion of orthodoxy
who rigidly and fiercely defends every tittle and iota of the
Biblical word,† and does not move an inch from the foundation of faith laid in the Augsburg confession, on which
the generations following had with arduous thought and
toil reared their dogmatic system . . . .  No one could expect
that he, who knew no fear of men, would tacitly allow the
anti-Christian anonymous Fragmentist and the agent inter-
ested in his behalf, to break into the fold.  For wherever, and
in whatever form, during these decades of great theological
reckoning, a challenge had been given to Christianity, Goeze
had taken up the gauntlet.  Should he now be silent, because
he had at one time been Lessing's 'sturdy Goeze,' and
because his brilliant former visitor, in spite of a trifling

* Of the more noted biographers of Lessing, Erich Schmidt, by far
the most thorough and scholarly, is also the only one who does justice
to Goeze without apologizing as if it were an injustice to Lessing.
Schmidt also published Goeze's Polemics against Lessing, under the
title of *Goeze's Streitschriften gegen Lessing* Göschen'sche Verlags-
handlung, Stuttgart.

† For a concise and lucid exposition of the whole question of Biblical
inspiration and the gradually changing attitude of the theologians
toward it, cf. Gennrich, *Der Kampf um die Schrift*, Berlin, 1898.

misunderstanding, still held a place in his heart? His whole past in the service of the church militant, and his impregnable conviction of his duties as a minister of the Gospel, in these times of danger, called him to arms."

38. Goeze *knows* he is standing for the large majority of contemporary orthodox theologians, and at the same time Lessing claims to be a stanch defender of the Lutheran church. If both mean what they say, they must certainly differ widely in their criteria of orthodoxy. Goeze had never hesitated to confess his faith, and thus plainly to state his position in the controversy. Can his repeated demand that Lessing as the defender of the *Fragmentist* should plainly state what religion he considered as the Christian religion, and what religion he himself confessed, justly be regarded inquisitorial as Lessing makes it to appear? Goeze says, for instance, on p. 66 of his *Polemics* as cited above: "If in this instance he plays again on the words *Christian Religion*, . . . if by *Christian Religion* he understands, with Tindal, Natural Religion, I grant his whole conclusion: but in that case, how about sincerity and honesty, which any honorable author owes to his readers, especially in dealing with a subject of so much moment?" If their controversy, for him at least, was to be more than a mere wrangling in words, it was not only desirable, but absolutely necessary to get a definite understanding of their relative points of view. It did not fit into Lessing's plan. The answer which Goeze received in the *Nötige Antwort auf eine sehr unnötige Frage* is in one sense Lessing's *definition* of the Christian faith and doctrines, but in no sense Lessing's confession of his own faith. It is only in one sense his definition, because he himself confesses in one of his letters that by his tactics he intended to set the Catholics against the Protestants, as Paul of old divided the Sanhedrim. And to Elise Reimarus he writes: "Since Goeze made the mistake of asking, not what of the Christ-

*Relative Position of Goeze and Lessing.*

ian religion I *believe* (but Goeze did ask this question), but what I consider *to be* the Christian religion, I have won the contest." And so he had. Goeze was silent.

39. Lessing had arrayed Catholic against Protestant

**Gist of Lessing's Argument.** in demanding recognition for ecclesiastical tradition. He asserted that the criterion of fellowship in the Christian church was the acceptance of the so-called *Regula Fidei*, the Rule of Faith, which, he insisted, and rightly, had been used in this capacity before the canon of Scripture had been established. "The letter is not the spirit, and the Bible is not religion. The Bible contains more than belongs to religion, and it is a mere hypothesis that the Bible is as infallible in this 'more' as it is in the rest. — Religion is not true because Evangelists and Apostles taught it, but they taught it because it is true. From their inherent truth the validity of written traditions must be established, and any possible amount of written tradition can give no inner truth to religion, if it has none in itself." These sentences were the bulwarks of Lessing's position. It seems strange to us that Goeze and his colleagues should have so violently opposed them. But they knew, on the one hand, that Lessing agreed with Reimarus particularly in his views regarding the origin of the Bible and the value of the miracles; to their minds, on the other hand, the verbal inspiration of the Bible was the only sure foundation for a creed, and, doubtless, Lessing's sentences were pregnant with danger to their theory.

40. Lessing had won the contest. Against his adroitness

**Character of the Controversy.** and skill at arms Goeze's heavy armor did not avail. "Victories decide wars, but they are very doubtful proofs of a just cause, or rather, they are no proof at all." With these words Lessing introduces his essay on the Moravians. Every one admits that the controversy was carried on from Lessing's side with a wealth of learning and brilliancy for which his opponent did not begin to be a match, but it is only fair to admit

also that his weapons were not entirely free from the poison
of malice and calumny.    Goeze was rather coarse and
clumsy, sometimes; Lessing answered with insinuations
derogatory to Goeze's character which.were wholly unnec-
essary and surely not worthy of him.    In his zeal for the
principle which he meant to establish he was wholly unjust
to the individual.    "He has for all time made Goeze the
type of narrowness and opposition to science," says Lessing's
biographer Stahr; — but he had no right to do so.    "He
needed just such an opponent, in whom theological bigotry,
with its rude superficiality, its unscrupulous distortion, its
logical clumsiness, its hypocritical solicitude for the souls of
others, was, as it were, personified," Schwarz, himself a
theologian, expatiates on Stahr; but Gross, editor of Lessing's theological writings, certainly with full justice questions his right indiscriminately to take any one for such an
opponent.

41. The inherent value of Lessing's polemic writings
**Outcome of** is not lessened on that account, and in their
**the** vivacity and beauty of style they are unexcelled
**Quarrel.** in German prose.    His work in the field of theology, as before that in the field of art, proved to be a most
powerful stimulus to professional theologians afterward,
and though few, if any, of his hypotheses stood the test
of more thorough research without some material modification, it is fair to say that also in the field of New
Testament criticism Lessing was a brave and fearless torch-
bearer.

42. It seems like a strange contradiction, the bitterness
**Occasion** of the quarrel and the gentleness and love breath-
**of the** ing from the *Last Will and Testament of St.*
**Publication**
**of Nathan.** *John,* which had shed its halo over the begin-
ning of the controversy, and in the end pronounced its
"Little children, love ye one another," from the mouth of
*Nathan the Wise.*    For the last polemic against Goeze is
*Nathan.*    The tenor of the *Fragments* and of Lessing's

own polemics, rather than some hints thrown out by Goeze, had induced the authorities to prohibit any further continuation of the controversy, and the publication of any theological matter from Lessing's side.  On the night of the tenth of August 1778, as he writes to his brother Karl, he conceived the idea of saying his last word in the matter from the stage.  Not, indeed, that he meant to yield entirely to the demands of the authorities.  For in spite of their prohibition he published a number of pamphlets against Goeze, and others.  But he had to be ready for the worst, as he says, and for emergencies one is never so well prepared as when one has money.  To procure money, of which he would be so much in need, in case he should lose his position as librarian, he took up an old dramatic subject, a part of which he had roughly sketched probably after his return from Italy 1776, and prepared to have his *Nathan* printed by subscription.  In a prospectus dated August 8 *, which was more or less privately circulated among friends, he says: "Inasmuch as it has been demanded that I should suddenly desist from a kind of labor which I have, doubtless, not carried on with that sort of pious craftiness with which alone it can successfully be carried on, circumstances rather than choice have caused me to take up an old theatrical attempt, which, I see, should long since have received the last finishing touches. For this purpose, it might be thought, I could not have chosen any more unsuitable moments than the moments of vexation, in which one should prefer to forget how the world really is.  Yet, not so.  The world of my speculation is by no means a less natural world, and I should not be surprised if it were not the fault of Providence alone that it is not just as real. — This attempt is of a somewhat unusual nature, and is called "*Nathan the Wise*,"

---

* This prospectus must have been dated back, if the statement in the letter to Karl of August 10th is correct.

in five acts.   Of the exact contents I can say nothing. Suffice it to say that it is well worthy of dramatic treatment, and that I shall do everything to be myself satisfied with this treatment."

43.   Some polemic disturbances, notably an attack by **Besetting** Professor Semler, and above all things dire pe- **Difficulties.** cuniary distress, made the labor very burdensome. To his sister, who had asked him for assistance, he wrote: "If you knew with what cares I have had to struggle since the death of my wife, and in how needy circumstances I have been living, you would rather pity than reproach me." Indeed, he was driven to accept a loan of two hundred and twenty-five dollars from a Jewish merchant, Wessely, in order to have the necessary means for the continuation of the work and the unavoidable expenses in publishing.

44.   On the 14th of November 1778 Lessing began to **Dates.** put the sketch into verse. The second act he began December 6th, the third December 28th, the fourth February 2d, 1779, and the fifth on March 7th. Not counting two or three predecessors, because they remained without any influence, *Nathan* is the first German drama in iambic pentameter.

45.   At this place as well as any other we may speak **How** briefly also of the reception accorded to *Nathan*. **Nathan** **was** Lessing himself professedly did not expect the **received.** play to be admitted to the stage, or at least not for a century to come. No place was sufficiently enlightened to receive *Nathan*. "But all hail to the place where this may first be done." The honor fell to Berlin. Only two years after Lessing's death, and hardly four after the completion of the play, April 14th, 1783, it was there produced, though with little or no success. Equally unsatisfactory were a few other early attempts. The play was first produced successfully on November 28, 1801, in Weimar, under the auspices of Schiller and Goethe, in the modified

version prepared by Schiller. Since then it has been translated into most of the languages of Europe. In 1842 it was produced in a modern Greek translation in Constantinople, and was received with great applause in this center of Mohammedanism. From time to time it still takes its place on German stages,* and less often in England. Its success depends in no small measure on the ability of the actors, whose rôles are anything but easy.

## II. The Religious Content of Nathan.

**46.** We have seen in the sketch of the genesis of **Nathan as a Jew an insult to Christianity?** *Nathan* what purpose the drama was to serve in connection with the theological troubles. It is not a mere plea for toleration. This purpose is served better in an earlier play of Lessing's, *Die Juden.* Neither can it be called an attack upon or an insult to Christianity. To be sure, the noblest character, Nathan, is a Jew, in name and ceremonial at least. But did not also Christ, preaching to the Jews, hold up the Publican and the Samaritan as models of the virtues which he missed in his hearers? Surely not because these virtues were not at all exemplified among his own people. But, choosing Publican and Samaritan, he implicitly says that their virtues could much more reasonably be expected from the Jews. A similar view we must take of *Nathan.*

**47.** But there is another reason why Lessing made **Nathan-Shylock.** Nathan a Jew. Not, indeed, the reason assigned by Kuno Fischer, namely that from Judaism as a religion to Nathan's free Humanity is a much longer step than from Christianity: Nathan is a Jew in name only. The reason lies in the social condition of the time. At the time of the crusades far more than even in Lessing's days, the Jew was without kingdom or nationality, nowhere

* During the twelve months ending July 1901, forty-five times.

equal with his fellow men, often not even tolerated. The legitimate product of indignities as those to which he was subjected is Shakespeare's Shylock. How noble the philosophy, the faith, that makes of Shylock a Nathan, a faith not impossible with a Jew of Nathan's time, and all the more to be expected from Christians, no matter how rarely found among them.

48. If, however, *Nathan* has often been regarded as an attack

**Nathan in Theory and Practice.** upon Christianity, it is in a large measure due to the fact that the interpretation has been almost wholly based upon the ring parable. Important as this is, it represents only the theoretical side of Nathan's faith, his *theology*. In theology, in externals, Nathan is still a Jew. The practical side, his *religion*, becomes apparent in the seventh scene of the fourth act, the great scene in which Nathan reveals his heart to the friar. Here we see Nathan in his life and vital principles. And they are Christian.

49. *a*) Lessing himself repeatedly referred to the *De-*

**THE PARABLE. Sources.** *camerone* of Boccaccio, First Day, Third Story, *Melchisedec the Jew*, as the source of his *Nathan*. "I believe I have invented a very interesting episode for it, so that the whole shall be very readable."— Years before he had found this story in Boccaccio, and had then made a rough plan for a drama, which he now carried out with a number of essential changes. — Besides the version of Boccaccio, Lessing knew two or three slightly different ones, found in the *Gesta Romanorum*, a mediaeval collection of short stories. The parable is older, however, than all of these versions. It was probably invented about the year 1100 by a Spanish Jew. About the history of the fable and its transformations, of which Lessing probably knew nothing, Erich Schmidt gives all necessary information in his *Lessing*, Vol. II, p. 327 f. Lessing followed seemingly in every detail the version of Boccaccio. The few innovations which he makes are, however, full of significance, and change the spirit and scope of the whole parable. They are worthy of our attention all the more because Lessing himself says in a letter to Ramler, who read a proof of his manuscript, that on the story especially he had spent much labor. Besides, we know what aim he pursued in the work.

50. Boccaccio starts in with the ring in possession of the man in the East: Lessing indicates also its origin: *"Aus lieber Hand."* It is fair to recognize with Kettner and Erich Schmidt as the original first giver God, and to assume that Lessing meant to indicate the divine origin of religion. To be remembered, however, that in his eyes the divine *in man* would be simply human, giving to this word its best and fullest significance. At all events, religion is not an arbitrary inn'ovation of an idle brain, and a religious consciousness may well believe it to be of divine origin.

*Differences between the parable and its source. — "Aus lieber Hand."*

51. Again, with Boccaccio the only advantage attaching to the ring is the primacy in the family. With Lessing the essential quality of the ring is the one which is also ascribed to it in one version of the *Gesta Romanorum:* it has the secret power of winning favor with God and men; on condition, however, that the owner wears it with this confidence. And this condition again is Lessing's own addition. It is possible that in giving his preference to the version of the *Gesta Romanorum* Lessing purposely meant to imply that any one implicitly confident of the love of God and men toward himself would, as a matter of fact, beside this religious confidence cultivate also religious love and its correlate, morality. If no human activity is called for beside that implied in the condition of faith in the efficacy of the ring (not necessarily in its genuineness), this is probably the case because it seems impossible to distinguish cause and effect: love of God and men and love to God and men, these two phases are inseparable.

*The Power of the Ring.*

**52.** It is a suggestive hypothesis of Kettner that in the man in the East, having received his ring "*aus lieber Hand*," we are to see not Judaism, or either of the other two religions considered, but rather a primary state of every religion. "The adherents of every religion," Lessing means to say, "consider themselves the chosen people, as long as they are unshaken in the belief that in their religion alone a revelation is transmitted. And accordingly they claim for their creed validity for the whole world." The making of two new rings is, then, not to signify the advent of two new religions, but rather the maturing of the consciousness that other religions make the same claim to universality. And this consciousness was certainly very strong with the persons acting in our play.

*The Man in the East.*

**53.** It is idle to speculate as to whom we are to see in the father of the three sons. A parable is not supposed to be applied in every insignificant detail. Accepting Kettner's hypothesis concerning the Man in the East, we might see in this father the representative of the consciousness matured to the stage of religious doubt. At all events, this father could not distinguish which one of the three religions had the better claims. And Nathan, too, does not venture to decide this, for the only ground on which, to his knowledge, religions might rest their claims are their respective revelations, which are all equally matters of history. Nathan, as we have seen of Lessing also, finds in the distinguishing features of the various positive religions only more or less harmless accessories to natural religion. The man of nature, and so also natural religion are *eo ipso* right, and it is assumed without questioning that the nucleus at least of this natural religion is contained in all positive religions. Historical development is so little appreciated, and the confidence in the correctness of the assumptions made *a priori* is so great, that all doctrinal differences are quite

*The Father of the three Sons disregarding the differences of creed.*

disregarded, both as to their significance and as to their effect on practical life and conduct.

54. In the advice of the judge, too, who is Lessing's **Emphasis upon Morality.** own creation and so independent of his model, the differences between the existing religions seem to be considered of no account. Attention is called to the fact that the virtue of the ring is to be made manifest in winning favor with God and men or — taking for granted that love begets love — in producing love for God and men in the owner. But of the three existing rings not one has the promised power, which must be due to one of two things: either, the genuine ring is not among the rings owned by the brothers, or the owner does not fulfill the condition on which the manifestation of its power depends, he does not wear the ring with the necessary confidence in its efficacy. The remedy suggested seems, in its first part, somewhat strange: each one of the brothers is to believe that his ring is the genuine one, and that it has the promised power. The more practical seems the additional advice that each one is to quicken this innate power

> "*mit Sanftmut,*
> *Mit herzlicher Verträglichkeit, mit Wohlthun,*
> *Mit innigster Ergebenheit in Gott.*"

And then, after thousands of years, the power of the stones — not of the one stone only — may show itself in their children's children's children. The present judge can not decide between the claims of the various owners; after thousands of years, another, wiser man will occupy his chair and judge. Indeed, it is suggested that possibly the wise father, who might here very well be Providence, made the three rings indistinguishable with a wise purpose, in order that one brother might not be favored above the others, but that rather all might have an incentive to realize the promised power. As a consequent result no decision would be necessary in the end, be-

cause if each loves the other, no one would ask for a
judgment. Here, as in other places, Lessing seems to
put the emphasis on morality, and, as in the *Duplik*,
esteems the effort in the search after the truth more
highly than the possession of the truth. Possession of
the truth, a religion with power, it seems, is to be attained after thousands of years by all the various con-
fessions, if they strive in that direction.

> *"Ein guter Mensch, in seinem dunkeln Drange,*
> *Ist sich des rechten Weges wohl bewusst."* *

Probably Lessing thought here of the new, eternal Gospel,
which, according to his *Education of the Human Race*, will
supersede the Christian Gospel, as this is an advance over
Judaism and Mohammedanism. But it may be reached
by the adherents of one creed as well as those of any other.
We have seen in another place what he considered to be
the best religion. Unimpeded development of so-called
Humanity, whatever that may mean for each successive
generation, is the end toward which the race is striving.

    55. *b*) It is fair to assume that in Nathan we are to
**NATHAN** see a representative of this perfect religion. We
**IN LIFE**
**AND** shall endeavor to do justice to his character in
**PRACTICE.** the second part. At this place we want to
cast a look at the scene mentioned at the beginning of
this chapter. It affords us a glance into Nathan's heart,
which he had modestly concealed from all but the pious,
single-hearted friar, because single-hearted piety alone can
appreciate deeds impossible for human nature, unless deeply
devoted to God, and completely resigned to his will and
purpose.

    And what do we find in his heart? He is human in
his tears, in his despair, in his vow of inveterate hatred:
he is almost more than human in his resignation to God's

* Cf. also Schiller's *Worte des Glaubens.*

will and ways: *"Und doch ist Gott, doch war auch Gottes Ratschluss das."* He is more than human in his consciousness of absolute dependence upon God: *"Ich will! Willst du nur, dass ich will!"* More than human in · his love for enemies :

> *"ich nahm*
> *Das Kind, trug's auf mein Lager, küsst' es, warf*
> *Mich auf die Knie und schluchzte: Gott! auf sieben*
> *Doch nun schon eines wieder!"*

And almost more than human he is, finally, in the acquiescence in God's counsels concerning him :

> *"Und ob mich siebenfache Liebe schon*
> *Bald an dies einz'ge fremde Mädchen band,*
> *Ob der Gedanke mich schon tötet, dass*
> *Ich meine sieben Söhn' in ihr aufs neue*
> *Verlieren soll: wenn sie von meinen Händen*
> *Die Vorsicht wieder fordert, — ich gehorche."*

It seems as if Lessing had reiterated and exemplified in this scene all the essentials of Nathan's religion. And whence are his principles? The good friar involuntarily ejaculates :

> *"Nathan, Nathan,*
> *Ihr seid ein Christ! — Bei Gott, Ihr seid ein Christ!*
> *Ein bess'rer Christ war nie!"*

To be sure, Nathan at once rejoins :

> *"Wohl uns! Denn was*
> *Mich Euch zum Christen macht, das macht Euch mir*
> *Zum Juden."*

But Beyschlag's objection to this rejoinder is well founded : the probability of such love for enemies is not given in Judaism, but it is given in Christianity. That is not saying that a Jew of to-day would not be capable of it ; but in so far as he practises it, he is realizing a Christian ideal. The Old Testament, the sacred document of Judaism and the truest exponent of its doctrines, nowhere, not even in the Psalms, in which personal piety finds its highest expression, commands love of enemies or exalts it as an ideal for which to strive. A reply to deeds such as the Christians are said to have perpetrated upon Nathan's wife and children is found in the pathos of the 137th Psalm: "By the rivers of Babylon, there we sat down, yea, we wept, when we remembered Zion." And it closes with the frightful prayer for vengeance upon Babylon which had committed such deeds: "O daughter of Babylon, who art to be destroyed; happy shall he be that rewardeth thee as thou hast served us. Happy shall he be that taketh and dasheth thy little ones against the stones." Words like these could not stand in the Psalms, if the religion of the Old Testament meant to educate men to that exalted love which Lessing ascribes to his Nathan. "This triumph of humanity, of love to God and men, was brought into the world by him who, dying on the cross, prayed for his murderers, and in virtue of his blood shed for his enemies wrote into the hearts of his followers the new commandment: 'Love your enemies, bless them that curse you, do good to them that hate you.'"—Mendelssohn practically made the same admission when he wrote: "When *Nathan* had made its appearance, it was rumored, that Lessing had slandered the Christian religion, although he had only ventured to find fault in some particulars with a few Christians, or at most with the Christian church. His *Nathan*, we must admit, is really an honor to the Christian church. On what a high plain of enlightenment and culture must the people be among whom a man can attain this height of sentiment, and develop this nice discernment of things human and divine." Possibly these words were not, and are not appreciated because coming from a Jew, and yet they seem to be directly to the point. Nathan is a Jew, "like whom there are few others," a Jew who has been willing to learn from Christianity and certainly lived by its principles more nearly than thousands of Christians in name and profession. His ethical principles bear the imprint of Christianity, though he did not seem to recognize it; but, though followed by a Jew, they remain Christian still.

56. Thus it appears that Nathan's — and Lessing's — *The Moral* ideal religion, as far as it goes, coincides with *of Nathan.* Christianity: ideal Christianity to be sure, but Christianity none the less. Lessing himself was probably aware of this. In the publication of his *Nathan* he promised "to play a worse trick on the theologians than he could by issuing ten more *Fragments*." He expected that in their hearts they would be full of anger, though none would venture to attack the play openly. Lessing's purpose in publishing his *Nathan*, accordingly, can hardly have been anything more or less than to represent ideal Christianity as a thing to be hoped for, possibly thousands of years hence, and to admonish the theologians of his day, as Christ admonished the Pharisee to whom he told the parable of the Good Samaritan: "Go ye and do likewise," implying that they had not yet so much as made an attempt to reach Nathan's perfection.

57. We have hinted that Lessing himself, even when *Lessing* he wrote his *Nathan*, had not reached the per*and his* fection of his hero. Above all things, there are *Ideal.* a number of features in the abominable character of the patriarch which are clearly intended to be travesties on Lessing's opponent, Pastor Goeze. The patriarch received even the outward physiognomy of Goeze. The passages in question are given in the Appendix, and we must here content ourselves with referring to them. — We are likely to judge too harshly, when we see that the poet, in point of whole-souled charity and nobleness of spirit could not rise to the creation of his mind and heart, the creation of the sacred hours of his life, hours sanctified by death and bereavement. In this instance, too, "He that is without sin, let him first cast a stone." Who

is he that would not humbly, and yet hopefully, confess that his own life has but rarely, if ever, come up to his ideal?

---

## II. NATHAN AS A WORK OF ART

58. *Nathan* was to be the last word in the quarrel **Nathan not** with Goeze, and it was not unnatural for Les- **a Satire.** sing's friends to expect that it would be bitter and satirical in its tone. Lessing disabused them of this notion, writing in a letter to his brother Karl: "It will be as touching a piece as ever I made." And in these words he characterized his work very well: it is touching; not, indeed, fostering a slovenly sentimentality, but a sturdy tenderness which `inspires and exalts us at the same time.

59. If the purpose and characteristic effect of tragedy* **Tragical in** is to make us appreciate the power of the good **its Effect.** in man, manifesting itself in defiance of evil and malice, *Nathan*, without being a tragedy, fulfills this primary requisite of tragedy. Indeed, more manifestly than in most of the species of this highest class of dramatic art, we find here genuine goodness celebrating a triumph.

60. The virtue which Nathan acquired in a life of **The Lead-** severe self-education and self-denial is exempli- **ing Idea of** fied in deeds, proves its power and efficiency in **the Play.** his dealings with men, and is unreservedly recognized and acknowledged by men, notwithstanding their prejudices and differences of creed. This is the leading idea of the play.

61. To appreciate *Nathan* as a work of art, which it **The proper** is primarily, we must be content to let the hero **Attitude to** act within the bounds prescribed for him by the **a Work of** **Art.** poet. The elements enlisting our interest in any work of art are not primarily Christian or sectarian, but

* Theodor Lipps, *Der Streit über die Tragödie.*

human.  In the instance at hand, we must above all things
disregard the polemic element, rise above our creeds, whatever they may be, in order that the names may not dis-
turb us, and so be prepared to estimate the life which
Nathan leads.  Taking him quite as the play presents him
to us, we can appreciate what a life like his demands and
what it gives.

> *"Und doch ist Gott!*
> *Doch war auch Gottes Ratschluss das! Wohlan!*
> *Komm! übe, was du längst begriffen hast,*
> *Was sicherlich zu üben schwerer nicht*
> *Als zu begreifen ist, wenn du nur willst."*

**62.**  This is the sum total of Nathan's experience, this is
**Nathan's** his wisdom.  This confidence enables him not only
**Character** to maintain that imperturbable equanimity in all
**and his Po-**
**sition in** the trials of his life, but is also the source of
**the Play.** his kindness, his charity and toleration.  And
these vicissitudes, in turn, were no doubt a means of
strengthening Nathan's faith, which is altogether too brave
and heroic to have been an inheritance which he accepted
from his ancestors without thought or trouble on his part.
He paid for it with the dearest treasures of his life.  His
wisdom is the truth which he had tested in his own experience; his rule of life and conduct, the love and forbearance of a heart ennobled, and softened, and tranquil-
lized in the joys and sorrows of an eventful life.  He had
seen the perverseness of the human heart, had felt its forti-
tude.  A Jew, mercilessly driven to the limits of human
endurance, he practised love toward his enemies, and con-
strained himself to obey the most exacting injunction of
Christianity. — No other character of our play has reached
anything like the perfection which Nathan attained in the
school of life.  And so they all serve as a background for
him; from the proud, youthful, unsettled Templar and the
mighty, charitable, but inconsiderate Sultan, to the naïve,
but well meaning nurse, and the hypocritical, intriguing

patriarch. The characters, individuals in themselves, none
the less serve to accentuate the extraordinary qualities in
Nathan, and it is worth while to make the comparison.

63. Between Nathan and Recha exists a most tender
**Nathan** relation. Having received her, as it were,
**and Recha.** from the hand of God as a compensation for
his seven sons, he is attached to her with sevenfold
love, and has taken the utmost pains with her education. Possibly in consideration of the position assigned
to man by his birth and kinship, he refrained from
perplexing the Christian child with dogmatic, sectarian
discussions, and emphasized the more the fundamental
tenet of his own special religion : he loved her and taught
her that God with more than fatherly care provides for
those who love Him, and even may work miracles in their
behalf. In what sense this is to be taken, he makes clear
at the first opportunity (cf. the note to ll. 210 ff.) emphasiz-
ing at the same time another important principle. After
her narrow escape from the fire, Recha had been spending
her hours in dreamy, grateful contemplation. Nathan
rouses her from her fantastic revery, and makes her ready
and anxious to express her gratitude to God in good deeds
toward his needy creatures. His view of gratitude takes the
place of Daja's vagaries. No friend of dead book learning, he has by word of mouth and by example educated
his daughter to be an ornament to any family, or any creed.
She, in turn, looks up to her father with reverential, loving confidence. All her angelic loveliness the Templar as
well as herself recognizes to be the creation of the artist
who imagined in the rejected block the divine form that he
released, and made it the most eloquent testimonial of all
the good and noble within himself.

64. Comparing Daja with Nathan, we find many good
**Nathan** and praiseworthy features in her, which have
**and Daja.** generally been quite disregarded. Kuno Fischer
finds fault with Lessing for allowing Nathan to commit the

pedagogical folly of making Daja Recha's companion. It
is well to remember the good friar's observation: children
above all else need love. And Daja devoted herself with
so much loving care to Recha that the orphaned child
hardly missed her mother. Possibly, Lessing meant to indicate that homely goodness also has its place in the world,
and that a man like Nathan could appreciate Daja in spite
of her evident limitations. Her solicitude for Recha's
eternal salvation never abates, and she is fully confident
that the dispensations of Heaven will eventually crown her
hopes and efforts in this direction with success, though, in
her judgment, the girl's relation to Nathan, the Jew, is
pregnant with danger. And, withal, she gratefully appre-
ciates Nathan's kindness and magnanimity toward her. In
her faith she differs most essentially from Nathan. His
foremost demand in matters of religion is truthfulness and
clearness, vital experience. Her faith is a matter of undefined feeling, fantastic devotion; and rigid truthfulness
and honesty with herself is so little her concern that she
does not shrink from fostering in Recha the fanciful angel
dream. In view of all this we can well excuse Nathan for
taking Daja's matters of conscience somewhat lightly.

65. If with Daja religion was a matter of undefined
**Nathan** feeling, it was naïve and generally harmless. The
**and the** patriarch, like his historic prototype, is, in a word,
**Patriarch.** a scoundrel, making of religion a cloak to shield
him from the legitimate results of his machinations. He
is forever prating about the welfare of the kingdom of God,
his resignation to God's will, and his devotion to the
church; and talks glibly of divine dispensations which proud
human reason should not attempt to fathom. But even
without his almost humorous grotesqueness, it would be
evident that all this is idle talk in his mouth. His das-
tardly plot against the life of the Sultan ought to have been
expiated on the gallows, and his crouching before the
Sultan's favorite, the Templar, to whom he had laid bare

his villainy, finds in contempt its only adequate return. The only God he knows is his own self, the welfare of the church is his own sordid advantage. He is at heart in every way the opposite of Nathan. Nathan's relation to God is that of reverential, childlike love. He proves in his life and conduct an unfaltering trust in the wisdom and goodness of God, a trust which, unlike Daja's blind faith, or the prelate's sanctimonious rascality, is not indeed content with flowery phrases, but is rational and contemplative, and yet humbly trusts without clear knowledge, wherever in the presence of the inscrutable ways of God the limits of human understanding forbid us to know.

66. Apparently Nathan and Saladin are alike in many
**Nathan and** ways : both equally generous, equally frugal, equally
**Saladin.** humble before God and tolerant toward men of different persuasion. And yet in this instance, too, the likeness is almost purely external. The virtues of the Sultan are rather spontaneous expressions of a noble, but uncultivated and untried natural inclination. Nathan's virtue is based on conviction, discernment, reasons, choice of the better. Regarding their generosity Al-Hafi distinguishes aptly, when he calls that of the Sultan prodigality; that of Nathan wise charity whose barns are ever filled. Saladin gives without consideration or discretion ; makes himself a carrion among vultures; is, in spite of his inexhaustible resources, reduced to pinching poverty, and allows subjects not within the range of his sight to be taxed and drained to the marrow, in order that he may have the means of satisfying lavishly the wants of those whom he sees. At the bottom his liberality is little more than refined selfishness. Similarly the toleration of the two men is of an entirely different nature. If Saladin does not insist on all trees having the same bark, it is with him not so much the expression of deeply rooted conviction as of indifference. With Nathan, on the contrary, tolerance is the legitimate result of the conviction that resignation to God's

will, the essence of his religion, does in no way depend upon our opinion concerning God. (On the import of this opinion, this *"Wähnen über Gott,"* cf. the Notes to 1589). As one accepts coin at the value stamped on its face and deposits it in a bag, so Saladin would fain gather truth into his head without reflection or investigation as to its real worth. Nathan is aware of the futility of this attempt. He knows at what price he acquired his wisdom, his conviction, his faith; knows also how severely life can put them to the test.

67. At first sight Sittah seems to reflect little light on
**Nathan and** Nathan's character. And yet she too accentuates
**Sittah.**    one side of his being. Good and lovable in other respects, she manifests a slyness and cunning, which is too unscrupulous to be commendable. She herself admits her fault, when, though frankly owning her inclination to cunning and sophistry, she at the same time deems it necessary to excuse it by reminding Saladin that he is no better, inasmuch as he is merely ashamed of the fox who suggests stealthy, wily tricks, while he does not hesitate to turn the tricks to his account. In Nathan we find the same cunning duly tempered: He is "wise as a serpent and guileless as a dove." Somewhat perplexed at the Sultan's question after truth, he wisely and cautiously clothes his answer in his famous parable, and he prudently restricts Saladin's encomium to the wise man who never conceals the truth, but cheerfully risks everything for it, by the condition: *"Ja, ja, wenn's nötig ist und nützt!"* — Though he need not be ashamed before God or men of having been the good Samaritan for Recha, and though he did not deny to the Templar, nor conceal from any one else who needed to know that she was a Christian and only his foster child; still he had found no one as yet whom he regarded entitled to the knowledge; and even Recha knows nothing of her relation to him. — Anxious to become more intimately acquainted with the Templar, he is unwilling to

reveal to the young knight the cause of his interest in his kinship.

> *"Denn wenn ich sie ihm sag', und der Verdacht*
> *Ist ohne Grund: so hab' ich ganz umsonst*
> *Den Vater auf das Spiel gesetzt . . . . . .*
> *. . . . . . . . Ich bliebe Rechas Vater*
> *Doch gar zu gern!"*

Thus he manifests everywhere wise, unobjectionable prudence, usually aiming at the welfare of others rather than at his own; nowhere does he, like Sittah, try to take advantage of others.

68. Toward his chess companion Nathan exhibits a **Nathan and** superior, self-conscious humor; but with playful **Al Hafi.** ease incidentally hints at momentous vital questions, and if at any time the light-footed desert philosopher is inclined to respond, his words assume an appropriate seriousness. Thus in the famous, ever misinterpreted words: *"Kein Mensch muss müssen; und ein Derwisch müsste? Was müsst' er denn?"* It is the same playful tone in which he had been conversing with Al-Hafi. The dervish wants to be, above all things, free, uncramped by circumstances and the artificial relations of civilized men; he had learned from Rousseau. On that account he is eager to resign his influential position at court, in which he has been obliged to do for others what he loathes from his inmost soul to do for himself. On the Ganges, where with bare feet and light heart he walks the burning sands together with his teachers, on the Ganges alone there are men. There no one knows of any constraint, but can take pleasure in acting from free choice: *"Kein Mensch muss müssen,"* least of all a dervish, who can without the least hesitation make up his mind to live for himself. This he has long since apprehended, and this fundamental tenet of his philosophy he no doubt often enough defended with all his extravagant one-sidedness against Nathan. In an unguarded moment he now excuses himself for having accepted the

hateful office at court with the words : *"Zwar, wenn man muss!"* And Nathan, discovering at once the exposure, cannot refrain from dealing a playful sarcastic thrust : *"Kein Mensch muss müssen"* has always been the Alpha and Omega of your philosophy, and now you mean to say that you have yielded to a constraint? *"Ein Derwisch müsste? Was müsst' er denn?"* — *"Warum man ihn recht bittet, und er für gut erkennt; das muss ein Derwisch."* — This answer of Al-Hafi quite unexpectedly turns out to be so serious, and above all things so apt, that Nathan for a moment involuntarily abandons his playful tone, and with his whole heart answers : *"Bei unserm Gott! Da sagst du wahr. — Lass' dich umarmen, Mensch. Du bist doch noch mein Freund?"* As if the last question were to be an apology for having for a moment seemed to trifle with considerations so vital in their influence on human life and conduct. — Really the practical agreement in this matter is the foundation of their friendship. *"Warum man ihn recht bittet, und er für gut erkennt; das muss ein Mensch."* On this principle they agree ; they differ in the manner in which each makes his principle count in his life and conduct. Al-Hafi sees the unreasonable and perverse in man and the world and is stimulated by it to flee the world and man, and to live a hermit's life. Nathan's eye is no less keen in this respect, but he is stimulated not to flight, but to action in the world. Whatever the dervish recognizes as good, that he feels bound to do ; but in order that he may not be bound to do something distasteful to his nature, he returns to the desert to a life of contemplative ease. Nathan stands unflinchingly in the midst of life and does his duty without taking much thought of his own pleasure or advantage.

69. Somewhat different is his relation to the good Nathan and friar. He too is "wise as a serpent, and harm-the Friar. less as a dove," and yet not in every sense. He is too closely bound by faith in authority to profess openly

what he believes in his heart, and to repudiate openly the power of the patriarch who through his never changing villainy has forfeited every claim to obedience. He sees the wrong, to be sure, but is not able to draw from it the only legitimate conclusion. Patriarch and church are for him the means without which he can not reach heaven. Though he loathes their mandates, yet he feels in duty bound to render external obedience at least, and, foregoing all speculation in the matter, he really seems to consider this obedience a meritorious deed. None the less he longs incessantly for his quiet retreat on Mount Tabor, where he will have no other care than that for his eternal salvation. Thus we find in him too a resignation longing to escape from a world in which numberless ills and evils annoy and oppress him. Nathan, on the other hand, can not be dissuaded by any human authority, or by the letter of the law from doing that which he considers good and right. He is a man whose conviction is a stimulus to courage and deeds.

70. Looking at the Templar superficially, we should **Nathan and** hardly find in him a feature reminding us of **the** Nathan. But Nathan detects at first sight: *"Die* **Templar.** *Schale kann nur bitter sein, der Kern ist's sicher nicht."* The Templar is young and impulsive: *"Wer weiss, was wir an seiner Stell'; in seinem Alter dächten!"* In time he promises to be like Nathan in many ways, though probably always more rash, more inconsiderate, . more violent, true in this respect to the traditions of the family, as they also assert themselves in Saladin and Assad. At least, he reflects upon himself and his relation to God and the world. And even his mistakes are of such a nature that with time and proper culture they may well be softened into virtues. With Nathan, this has been done. Life has smoothed the sharp, rough edges, and in the attractive, harmonious forms moral strength and beauty are blended.

71. We have tried, in the preceding paragraphs, to gain an advantageous point of view from which to appreciate the various characters, and particularly Nathan's relation to them. We might now proceed to a consideration of the more external means by which our play commands our interest and our admiration. But it is better to appreciate beauty face to face than from a description. The work may speak for itself. However, a few objections have so frequently been raised to the plot and execution of the drama, that it seems but fair to consider them here. We need to gain a point of view in this respect also.

72. Almost unanimously critics have found that *Nathan* **Wanting in** lacks in vividness of action. We can understand **Action.\*** why this objection should be raised, and yet, all

---

\* It is suggestive to compare two utterances of Lessing in this connection. In his *Dramaturgie,* L.-M. IX, 189, he says : *"Die erste Tragödie, die den Namen einer christlichen verdient, dürfte ohne Zweifel noch zu erwarten sein. Ich meine ein Stück, in welchem einzig der Christ als Christ uns interessiert.—Ist ein solches Stück aber auch wohl möglich? Ist der Charakter des wahren Christen nicht etwa ganz untheatralisch? Streiten nicht etwa die stille Gelassenheit, die unveränderliche Sanftmut, die seine wesentlichsten Züge sind, mit dem Geschäfte der Tragödie, welches Leidenschaften durch Leidenschaften zu reinigen sucht? Widerspricht nicht etwa seine Erwartung einer belohnenden Glückseligkeit nach diesem Leben der Uneigennützigkeit, mit welcher wir alle grosse und gute Handlungen auf der Bühne unternommen und vollzogen zu sehen wünschen?"*

*"Bis ein Werk des Genies, von dem man nur aus der Erfahrung lernen kann, wie viel Schwierigkeiten es zu übersteigen vermag, diese Bedenklichkeiten unwidersprechlich widerlegt, wäre also mein Rat: — man liesse alle bisherige christliche Trauerspiele unaufgeführt."*

It seems almost as if Lessing had attempted to produce this *Werk des Genies,* and was thinking of these words of the *Dramaturgie,* when he wrote in a preface to *Nathan:* *"Wenn man endlich sagen wird, dass ein Stück von so eigener Tendenz nicht reich genug an eigener Schönheit sei; — so werde ich schweigen, aber mich nicht schämen. Ich bin mir eines Zieles bewusst, unter dem man auch noch viel weiter mit allen Ehren bleiben darf."*

the circumstances considered, it is hardly justifiable.  A man who, like Nathan, has in every way rounded his character and so fully acquired the mastery of all his passions, cannot pursue a narrowed aim with wild, resistless impetuosity.   His goal is not a virtue, but virtue, and of virtue moderation is a part, if virtue is not, as Aristotle would have it, itself moderation.   In a drama, where Nathan is to be the main character, there can be no place for violent passion.   The calm, quiet tenor of the play is wholly in keeping with the character of Nathan as the hero.

73.   It has further been objected that the poet who in his *Dramaturgie* passed such severe judgment upon miracles and all incidents looking at all like chance should in his *Nathan* give such a wide range to this element.   And it must be admitted that the charge is not entirely without foundation, though the points in question can to some extent be explained.   We might bear in mind that in the creed of Nathan, as in that of Orsina in *Emilia Galotti*, nothing under the sun is to be regarded as chance, that the word chance or accident is a blasphemy.   But disregarding this, most of the events in *Nathan* that seem like chance are put into causal relation with fine acumen, and are psychologically quite possible. That the Templar was pardoned is explained by his similarity to Saladin's lost brother, though the deed itself was born of mere impulse.   The father of this Templar was a Mohammedan, joined in wedlock to a Christian lady, and he presented his children for Christian baptism.   He was, moreover, in every way a loving and loveable nature, and it is not at all strange that this man as a Christian knight * should have repeatedly saved Nathan from the sword, and

**Chance Happenings.**

* His being a brother of Saladin, and a Christian knight at the same time, is the strangest part about him.   But this, too, has its purpose : if it had been different, it would have been most natural to send Recha to Saladin, and not to Nathan.

should have learned to appreciate him as a Jew unlike
most other Jews. There was ample ground for confidence
and friendship between the two, and such a relation being
established, it was but natural for the father, face to face
with death, to intrust his little girl to the care of Nathan.
All this seems quite plausible. But it seems rather far-
fetched to make the dervish, that peculiar chess companion
of Nathan, the private treasurer of the sultan, in order to
establish the connection between Nathan, Saladin, and
Assad. And the pious, gentle recluse, the friar, is represented as having been, some twenty years before, the squire
of Recha's father, and is now a sort of factotum of the
patriarch. It seems, indeed, as if chance were playing
almost too prominent a part in all these intricacies.

74. The chief objection has from the start been di-
**Recha** rected against the relation between the Templar
**and the** and Recha. As to the Templar's love for Recha
**Templar.** there is no room for doubt; whether Recha returns his love is a matter of discussion. Certainly many
things point in that direction; Nathan thinks she does, so
do Daja, the Templar, Sittah, and Saladin; that is, all the
persons with whom she comes into contact; and we can
not very well assume that all of them are quite blind.
To be sure, her love is, particularly in its later stages, like
the love of most of Lessing's women, something like Emilia
Galotti's, cool and reserved; possibly more that of a sister
than that of a bride. We need not assume on that account
that the 'voice of nature,' to which Rousseau would have
us look for guidance, asserted itself in her. That would
probably be more Rousseauic than Rousseau himself. At
all events, the Templar loves Recha with all the ardor to
be desired; and it would have been an easy matter to in-
tensify her love also sufficiently to remove all doubt as to
its existence, granting there is room for doubt. Why then
make them turn out brother and sister in the end? An
easy solution is to make this ending a punishment for the

Templar's rashness and suspiciousness, as some have done. The Templar assures Nathan that by the exchange he gains rather than loses; there can therefore be no question of punishment. But even disregarding this, the explanation, an outgrowth of the determined effort to find everywhere the fateful "tragic guilt," is not worthy of serious consideration. Why, then, should the poet choose this ending after arousing our expectation of an entirely different one? He surely had a reason for his choice, for to end with a wedding would have been quite as easy. But would it also have satisfied the demands which the poet made on himself?

*a*) Let us first try to explain psychologically the fact that a lover suddenly finds in the lady who has won his affections his own sister, and yet declares that he gains rather than loses in the exchange. — If we might be permitted, in this connection to take cognizance of the poet's own experience, we should remember that he wrote his *Nathan* at the time when he had just returned from the funeral of his wife. His only comfort was that life could not have many similar experiences in store for him. Might not Lessing, when he made the Templar value a sister incomparably more than a wife, have remembered with sad heart his own short happiness and the maliciousness of fate, which after a short year robbed him of his wife and child? Though Lessing himself never evinced any deep affection for his sister, it was not an unnatural feature in the Templar. In every way like his father, who like Saladin, Sittah, and Lilla no doubt dearly loved his kin; he only needed to follow a natural inclination to love Recha as his sister too. To be sure, fraternal love as well as love between parent and child, on the origin of which the Templar speculates, is ordinarily based less on blood relationship than on community of interest, mutual accommodation, and self-sacrifice of each for the other's welfare. And did the

Templar so much as know of the existence of this sister of
his? His words:

> "*Ihr nehmt und gebt mir, Nathan!*
> *Mit vollen Händen beides! — Nein! Ihr gebt*
> *Mir mehr als Ihr mir nehmt! unendlich mehr!*"

these words, taken at their surface value, — and the
Templar does not ordinarily mince matters, and make a
virtue of necessity — are psychologically not easy to understand. But may we not assume that the Templar knew
something of the existence of this sister in Palestine, as he
also did of his relationship to Saladin? Might we not
even imagine that an undefinable longing for his relatives
turned his face to the Orient, when in his uncle, who had
been his second father, he had lost his last relative in
Germany? It would be by no means impossible, though
it is not directly indicated in the play. With this assumption, and as far as I can see, thus only, the words of the
Templar would find their explanation. The sister, from
whom an untoward fate had been separating him all his
life, and for whom he had learned to long all the more
fervently in total isolation, this sister he could embrace with
all ardor, even though he should meet her in the woman
whom he had already learned to love. All the more, when he
was perfectly aware that this love was not erotic, not based
on outward charms, but rather on nobility of soul, on such
qualities as only a Jew like Nathan was able to instil.
Was it without aim and purpose that Lessing makes the
Templar, in his long monologue (V. 3, ll. 3227 ff.) con-
template and express himself upon the reason for his love
for Recha?

*b*) But all this would still be no reason for choosing
this ending, it would only make this ending
psychologically justifiable, not necessary. The
necessity of the choice lies in the idea which
is to be represented in the play: the complete

The Nec-
essity for
Choosing
this
Ending.

and unconditional acknowledgment of the virtue incarnate in *Nathan*, in spite of personal prejudice due to differences of creed. It will be necessary to make a little digression in order to be clear.

1) The Templar had seemingly at first sight, when he **Love at** rescued Recha from the fire, been attracted to **First Sight** her. I am aware that this is not the generally **in Case of the** accepted opinion; I am also aware that this **Templar.** affection would have to undergo a change, if later the Templar is to account for his love for Recha on the ground of superior qualities of heart and intellect, as just mentioned. And yet I cannot avoid this view. How else are the verses in l. 766 ff., to be explained?

> "........ *Ich will von Euch an eine That*
> *Nicht fort und fort erinnert sein, bei der*
> *Ich nichts gedacht, die, wenn ich drüber denke,*
> *Zum Rätsel von mir selbst mir wird.*
> . . . . . . . . . . . . . . . . . . . . . . . . . . .
> ..... *Des Mädchens Bild*
> *Ist längst aus meiner Seele, wenn es je*
> *Da war.*"

The deed in itself certainly contained nothing at which a Templar, a knight, bound by vow and honor to come to the rescue of those in distress, would need to marvel. The marvel, the disquietude is due to the fact that the *Templar*, the *Christian knight*, who had of his own free choice pledged himself to celibacy, could not banish the image of the Jewess from his soul. Or should we take him at his word when he tells Daja, whose ready tongue he knows well enough, that Recha's image had long since disappeared from his soul? He knows, according to verse 3228 f., that heretofore they have been ready and even anxious to notice him under the palm trees near Nathan's house. Might not this very fact have been a reason for his being so fond of walking under these palms (V. 786), although he may have been unconscious of his motives? Daja's invitation he could not well accept, but if these little, comparatively harmless attentions of the lady and her maid had really displeased him so much, would it have been impossible to find other palms in Jerusalem affording a promenade for the annoyed young knight? —Verses 1636 f., seem to oppose this view.

> "........ Das war das Mädchen nicht,
> Nein, nein, das war es nicht, das aus dem Feuer
> Ich holte. — Denn wer hätte die gekannt
> Und aus dem Feuer nicht geholt, wer hätte
> Auf mich gewartet? Zwar — verstellt der Schreck."

This seems to indicate that the real appreciation of Recha's charms dates from the Templar's second meeting with her. But could it not as well mean that the image of the maiden which he harbored in his soul is far excelled by the reality? That the Templar did indeed not until then learn fully to prize her? Just what he meant to say after his *zwar*—, we do not know, but the dash indicates clearly that *verstellt der Schreck* is only an afterthought, an attempt to mislead his hearers. — Above all things, we can also, with this assumption, understand his persistent refusal to accept Recha's expression of her gratitude, for which we could otherwise assign no reason but senseless obstinacy. Not because he lacked all feeling and every vestige of courtesy did he refuse, but because he was still too thoroughly a Templar to be ensnared by any woman, especially by a Jewess. Is not that what he means to say in his monologue, verses 2111 f.:

> "*Ihm auszubeugen war der Streich zu schnell*
> *Gefallen, unter den zu kommen ich*
> *So lang und viel mich weigerte.*"

Does it not seem as if he had with conscious self-restraint avoided the blow? That he was for this reason so little anxious to see her? If later, (l. 2724) he tells the Sultan that he had refused to reap thanks where he had not sown them, we must bear in mind that even then, after his second meeting with Recha, he was ashamed before the Sultan to confess his love for her.

2) In this state of mind Nathan finds the Templar. His thanks are at first as rudely spurned as Daja's. The religious prejudice of the Templar is of little importance even now. He does not hate the Jews, but despises them on account of their pride, — and, it is not to be overlooked, a pride *which they transmitted to Christians and Mohammedans* — insisting that their God is the only God. To be consistent, the Templar must also *extend his contempt to Christian and Mohammedan.* And he does so ; as he indicates when he expects that Nathan will be amazed because he, a Christian, a Templar, should confess to such views. But as soon as he detects in Nathan a kindred soul, a man, who in the ordinary sense of the word is no more a Jew than he himself is a Christian, he offers his friendship, and now *burns with desire* to know Recha. He sees her. And soon he is not satisfied with Nathan's friendship : he wants also to call him father, but undoubtedly *only for Recha's sake.* For when Nathan, for reasons unintelligible to the young knight, hesitates to accept him, his ardor toward Nathan suddenly abates : he sees in him a man tolerant in words only, a Jewish wolf, making philosophy his sheep's clothing; intends without much ado to put him to the knife ; would not be surprised if the Jew would foist a brother upon Recha, as he had done a father.

*His Friendship with Nathan for Recha's Sake.*

3) Now, if in the face of all this Nathan once more proves his nobility; if now again, as in the great trial of his life, at Darun, he preserves in the midst of affliction his calmness, in the face of malice and slander, his love and forgiveness ; in short, if once more all the circumstances prove him to be not a mere babbler, but what he really is, — the Wise, the Good ; and if in consequence *now* the Templar asks him again to

*Reverence of Nathan's Character.*

remain Recha's father, and manifests in the tone of his words how much he too desires to be his child — now in a different relation — it is done this time not for Recha's sake, with whom any father might be an acceptable accessory, but *for Nathan's own sake, for the sake of the virtue* for which he stands.

c) And this, it seems to me, is the reason for the **Objections** peculiar relationship between Recha and the **to the** Templar. Another explanation has found con-**Usual** siderable favor, by which the ending is interpreted **Allegorical** **Interpreta-** allegorically. The family which was separated **tion.** by religious prejudice, intolerance, is said to be united again by the humane liberality of Nathan and the other characters concerned. The family is to rèpresent the whole human race, separated by creeds, united by creed-less, ethical, natural religion. But several considerations militate against the view. There is nothing in the characters as we have them to necessitate any separation of the family in the first place. Saladin and his sisters, as well as Assad, *if liberal enough to unite*, were also liberal enough *not to separate* on account of differences of creed. ·But if we accept the separation as an accomplished fact, the family circle would have been as much established through a wedding as through a recognition, and, besides, there would have been an excellent opportunity to exemplify Saladin's and Sittah's liberal ideas about marriage between members of different creeds. Finally it seems forced to interpret the ending allegorically, as representative of the relations and hopes of races and creeds.

75. Now we can understand the Templar's position. **The Final** You give me more than you take from me — he **Harmony.** means to say — infinitely more, — the sister for whom I had been longing in my hours of isolation ; you restore to me my father, who called you his friend ere I was born, and made you father of my sister; you were his most trusted friend on earth, and are most fit to meet him

in his heaven. — More than that. Nathan restores to the Templar his own self, his peace of mind, an unsullied conscience. For who could not detect from the long argumentation, the sophistical pros and cons regarding the right which he thinks he has to Recha (l. 2130 ff.), in spite of his being a Templar, that in his inmost soul he still feels bound by his vow to celibacy? Though wedlock with Recha would be "a falling with men" ("*mit Männern fallen*"), a fall it would be none the less. This too can now be obviated. He need not live without Recha: she is bound to him by sacred ties; and the charms of other women with their fascination for other men had ever been lost on him. He remains what he has ever been, and pledged his honor to be, — a Christian, a Templar, — of a peculiar kind, to be sure, as Nathan continues to be a Jew, whom the pious friar would welcome as a brother in his Lord; and as Saladin remains a Mohammedan. As a professed Christian, though merely in name, he chooses of his own free will, without ulterior motives, the Jew as his father, for the sake of his virtue alone; as a Christian, he remains the nephew of Saladin and Sittah. To these he is bound by the ties of blood, to Nathan with bonds woven by virtue and nobility of soul, to Recha by both.

In conclusion a few lines from Dilthey's biography of Schleiermacher, p. 59 : "*Nathan entstand. Wer ihn las, der empfand nicht nur um sich, unsichtbar, den Atem der neuen Zeit; er lernte sie begreifen, ja lernte ihr Mitbürger zu sein. In diesem Menschen ist der Gedanke der Aufklärung zur vollendeten Schönheit verklärt. Und um ihn ist eine dichterische Welt gebildet, in welcher, was Lessing in bittrem, unverständigem Kampfe sah, tiefverstehend eins das andere auf Grund der höchsten sittlichen Ideen, geschwisterlich heiter, sich die Hände reicht.*"

## III. THE SOURCES OF NATHAN.

76. Just a word remains to be said about the sources of *Nathan*. The origin of the parable has been mentioned. The data concerning the history of the time, and especially concerning Saladin, Lessing found largely in Marin's *History of Saladin*. — Two other novels, or stories, from *Boccaccio* are supposed to have furnished, besides the name *Nathan*, who might, however, also be a namesake of the prophet, some details, namely *Decamerone* X, 3, and V, 5. The resemblance seems less striking. (Erich Schmidt, II, 349 f., gives the content of the stories.) — The enthusiasm with which Marin describes Saladin and his position in the crusades had been kindled by Voltaire's writings. Traces of some influence exercised by Voltaire's *Le fanatisme ou Mahomet le prophète*, his *Zaïre*, and his *Les Guèbres, ou la tolérance* have been found in *Nathan*.

---

## IV. HISTORICAL FOUNDATION.

77. It needs hardly to be mentioned that Lessing was
*Summary of the His-torical Sit-uation as-sumed in the Play.* wholly independent in the use of these sources, and managed historical dates and events also with the sovereignty unquestionably belonging to the dramatist. He himself says: "Regarding the historical facts lying at the basis of the drama, I have quite disregarded all chronology, and have even made use of the names quite as it best suited my purpose."

The nearest we can get to the date of the play is the year 1192; the place, Jerusalem. — The Christian Kingdom of Jerusalem had been established in the year 1100 by Baldwin I., a brother of the pious Godfrey of Bouillon who had been too humble to wear a crown during his life,

though valiant enough to conquer and protect the Holy
Sepulcher. But the kingdom was not of long duration.
The conquerors were jealous of each other; the enthusiasm
of European knights had to some extent subsided; the
orders of the Knights of St. John and of the Templars were,
partly owing to their increasing worldliness and consequent
moral decadence, unable at length to prevent the gradual
decay of the state. In the year 1146 Sultan Nureddin had
conquered Edessa, the bulwark of the Christian empire in
the East, and forty years later Jerusalem itself was engulfed
in the ruin.

"While the Christian occupants were giving themselves
up more and more to the softening influences of the cli-
mate and the loosened responsibilities of life far away from
their proper homes, the Mohammedan power in the South
had been gaining a new impulse from the career of the
most remarkable leader of the whole crusading period.
Saladin was the subordinate governor of Egypt under the
rule of the Turks in Asia, but through personal talent and
ambition rose to the practically independent control of the
whole of Syria as well. His personal uprightness of character, his devotion to his cause and his cultivation of learning and the arts of life stand out in favorable contrast to
the barbarism of most of the leading princes of the crusading army. His policy seems to have been at first to get on
with the Christian occupants, if possible, by treating with
them on equal terms, and allowing them liberty to maintain their settlement, if they would in turn let him alone.
This reasonable policy was, however, in direct contrast to
the intolerant spirit of the crusaders. Repeated treaties were
violated with impunity by individual Christians, who in the
year 1178 won their last victory over the formidable enemy
in the battle of Ramla, near Ascalon, and thus postponed
the fall of Jerusalem by the space of a few years. — In
this battle the Christian knight Wolf von Filnek, represented
to be Saladin's brother Assad, of whom history knows

nothing, however, finds his death. — At last, in despair of keeping the peace on these terms, Saladin sounded the crusading note among the excited Mohammedan population of Syria and Egypt. The result was a fair and open fight near Tiberias, in which the Christian army was totally defeated, and the king and the chief leaders captured. The power of life and death was in Saladin's hands, but he used it only against those who had openly violated their faith with him." Among them were many of the Templars. On the third of October 1187, Saladin marched in triumph into Jerusalem. The symbols of Christianity disappeared, but the Christians themselves and the pilgrims from Europe were treated kindly — quite in contrast with the example they had given on previous occasions. The office of the Patriarch of Jerusalem was henceforth vacant — contrary to our play.

The news of the fall of Jerusalem kindled anew the crusading zeal of all Europe. Frederic Barbarossa, Philip August II. of France, and Richard the Lion-hearted started each on a new expedition. Frederic had successfully led his army, after the customary battles and adventures on the way with their attendant losses, to the boundaries of Syria, when on the tenth of June 1190 he lost his life in the endeavor to cross the Saleph river in Cilicia. Here Daja's husband, one of the many knights attempting a rescue, was drowned also. As Daja, according to her account, accompanied her husband, she could hardly have reached Jerusalem before the end of 1190, and could at the time of our play not have been Recha's nurse for more than a year or two, which, again, does not agree with other statements.

The remnants of Frederic's army were led on to Palestine by his son Frederic of Suabia and Leopold of Austria. They joined the dethroned king Guido de Lusignan, who after having been released from his imprisonment by the magnanimity of Saladin, was besieging Ptolemais (or Acre).

Richard and Philip reënforced them and Acre was won. Richard particularly distinguished himself, and his fame spread throughout the Orient, but at the same time enkindled the jealousy of the allies who withdrew with their troops and started on the homeward march. Richard and Saladin mutually respected and esteemed each other, and soon a truce was made (verse 647 f.). Indeed, projects of a union between Saladin's brother Malek el Adel (Lessing's Melek) with Richard's sister, the widow of William of Sicily, were fostered. The prospective marriage between Sittah and a brother of Richard is an invention of the poet. While these negotiations are under way, our play opens. An attack of the Templars upon the fortress of Tebnin had just been repulsed by Saladin. As Philip had returned, and there was no Patriarch of Jerusalem, the negotiations going on between them, according to verses 670 ff., are unhistorical. — Also Saladin's father as treasurer (verse 403) is unknown to history.

The presentiments of death which Saladin entertains in our play (2635 and 3175), were soon fulfilled. He died the third day of May 1193, loved by his friends and his people, respected, and even idealized by his foes.

# Nathan der Weise.

---

## Ein dramatisches Gedicht

### in fünf Aufzügen.

*Introite, nam et hic dii sunt!*
—Apud Gellium.

Von

## Gotthold Ephraim Lessing.

1779.

# Perſonen.

**Sultan Saladin.**

**Sittah,** deſſen Schweſter.

**Nathan,** ein reicher Jude in Jeruſalem.

**Recha,** deſſen angenommene Tochter.

**Daja,** eine Chriſtin, aber in dem Hauſe des Juden, als Geſell-
    ſchafterin der Recha.

**Ein junger Tempelherr.**

**Ein Derwiſch.**

**Der Patriarch von Jeruſalem.**

**Ein Kloſterbruder.**

**Ein Emir** nebſt verſchiedenen Mamelucken des Saladin.

Die Scene iſt in Jeruſalem.

# Erster Aufzug.

## Erster Auftritt.

(Scene: Flur in Nathans Hause.)

Nathan von der Reise kommend. Daja ihm entgegen.

### Daja.

Er ist es! Nathan! — Gott sei ewig Dank,
Daß Ihr doch endlich einmal wiederkommt.

### Nathan.

Ja, Daja; Gott sei Dank! Doch warum endlich?
Hab' ich denn eher wiederkommen wollen?
5 Und wiederkommen können? Babylon
Ist von Jerusalem, wie ich den Weg,
Seitab bald rechts, bald links, zu nehmen bin
Genötigt worden, gut zweihundert Meilen;
Und Schulden einkassieren, ist gewiß
10 Auch kein Geschäft, das merklich fördert, das
So von der Hand sich schlagen läßt.

### Daja.

             O Nathan,
Wie elend, elend hättet Ihr indes
Hier werden können! Euer Haus...

### Nathan.

             Das brannte.
So hab' ich schon vernommen. — Gebe Gott,
15 Daß ich nur alles schon vernommen habe!

77

**Daja.**

Und wäre leicht von Grund aus abgebrannt.

**Nathan.**

Dann, Daja, hätten wir ein neues uns
Gebaut; und ein bequemeres.

**Daja.**

          Schon wahr! —
Doch Recha wär' bei einem Haare mit
20 Verbrannt.

**Nathan.**

        Verbrannt? Wer? meine Recha? sie? —
Das hab' ich nicht gehört. — Nun dann! So hätte
Ich keines Hauses mehr bedurft. — Verbrannt
Bei einem Haare! — Ha! sie ist es wohl!
Ist wirklich wohl verbrannt! — Sag' nur heraus!
25 Heraus nur! — Töte mich: und martre mich
Nicht länger. — Ja, sie ist verbrannt.

**Daja.**

             Wenn sie
Es wäre, würdet Ihr von mir es hören?

**Nathan.**

Warum erschreckest du mich denn? — O Recha!
O meine Recha!

**Daja.**

        Eure? Eure Recha?

**Nathan.**

30 Wenn ich mich wieder je entwöhnen müßte,
Dies Kind mein Kind zu nennen! .

**Daja.**

          Nennt Ihr alles,

Was Ihr besitzt, mit eben so viel Rechte
Das Eure?

**Nathan.**

Nichts mit größerm! Alles, was
Ich sonst besitze, hat Natur und Glück
35 Mir zugeteilt. Dies Eigentum allein
Dank' ich der Tugend.

**Daja.**

O wie teuer laßt
Ihr Eure Güte, Nathan, mich bezahlen!
Wenn Güt', in solcher Absicht ausgeübt,
Noch Güte heißen kann!

**Nathan.**

In solcher Absicht?
40 In welcher?

**Daja.**

Mein Gewissen . . .

**Nathan.**

Daja, laß
Vor allen Dingen dir erzählen . . .

**Daja.**

Mein
Gewissen, sag' ich . . .

**Nathan.**

Was in Babylon
Für einen schönen Stoff ich dir gekauft.
So reich, und mit Geschmack so reich! Ich bringe
45 Für Recha selbst kaum einen schönern mit.

**Daja.**

Was hilft's? Denn mein Gewissen, muß ich Euch
Nur sagen, läßt sich länger nicht betäuben.

### Nathan.

Und wie die Spangen, wie die Ohrgehenke,
Wie Ring und Kette dir gefallen werden,
50 Die in Damaskus ich dir ausgesucht:
Verlanget mich zu sehn.

### Daja.

So seid Ihr nun!
Wenn Ihr nur schenken könnt! nur schenken könnt!

### Nathan.

Nimm du so gern, als ich dir geb': — und schweig!

### Daja.

Und schweig! — Wer zweifelt, Nathan, daß Ihr nicht
55 Die Ehrlichkeit, die Großmut selber seid?
Und doch . . .

### Nathan.

Doch bin ich nur ein Jude. — Gelt,
Das willst du sagen?

### Daja.

Was ich sagen will,
Das wißt Ihr besser.

### Nathan.

Nun so schweig!

### Daja.

Ich schweige.
Was Sträfliches vor Gott hierbei geschieht,
60 Und ich nicht hindern kann, nicht ändern kann, —
Nicht kann, — komm' über Euch!

### Nathan.

Komm' über mich! —
Wo aber ist sie denn? wo bleibt sie? — Daja,
Wenn du mich hintergehst! — Weiß sie es denn,
Daß ich gekommen bin?

**Daja.**

Das frag' ich Euch!
65 Noch zittert ihr der Schreck durch jede Nerve.
Noch malet Feuer ihre Phantasie
Zu allem, was sie malt. Im Schlafe wacht,
Im Wachen schläft ihr Geist: bald weniger
Als Tier, bald mehr als Engel.

**Nathan.**

Armes Kind!
70 Was sind wir Menschen!

**Daja.**

Diesen Morgen lag
Sie lange mit verschloßnem Aug', und war
Wie tot. Schnell fuhr sie auf, und rief: „Horch! horch!
Da kommen die Kamele meines Vaters!
Horch! seine sanfte Stimme selbst!" — Indem
75 Brach sich ihr Auge wieder: und ihr Haupt,
Dem seines Armes Stütze sich entzog,
Stürzt' auf das Kissen. — Ich, zur Pfort' hinaus!
Und sieh: da kommt Ihr wahrlich! kommt Ihr
wahrlich! —
Was Wunder! ihre ganze Seele war
80 Die Zeit her nur bei Euch — und ihm. —

**Nathan.**

Bei ihm?
Bei welchem Ihm?

**Daja.**

Bei ihm, der aus dem Feuer
Sie rettete.

**Nathan.**

Wer war das? wer? — Wo ist er?
Wer rettete mir meine Recha? wer?

### Daja.

Ein junger Tempelherr, den, wenig Tage
85 Zuvor, man hier gefangen eingebracht,
Und Saladin begnadigt hatte.

### Nathan.

                              Wie?
Ein Tempelherr, dem Sultan Saladin
Das Leben ließ? durch ein gering'res Wunder
War Recha nicht zu retten? Gott!

### Daja.

                         Ohn' ihn,
90 Der seinen unvermuteten Gewinst
Frisch wieder wagte, war es aus mit ihr.

### Nathan.

Wo ist er, Daja, dieser edle Mann? —
Wo ist er? Führe mich zu seinen Füßen.
Ihr gabt ihm doch fürs erste, was an Schätzen
95 Ich Euch gelassen hatte? gabt ihm alles?
Verspracht ihm mehr? weit mehr?

### Daja.

                         Wie konnten wir?

### Nathan.

Nicht? Nicht?

### Daja.

                    Er kam, und niemand weiß woher.
Er ging, und niemand weiß wohin. — Ohn' alle
Des Hauses Kundschaft, nur von seinem Ohr
100 Geleitet, drang, mit vorgespreiztem Mantel,
Er kühn durch Flamm' und Rauch der Stimme nach,
Die uns um Hülfe rief. Schon hielten wir
Ihn für verloren, als aus Rauch und Flamme
Mit eins er vor uns stand, im starken Arm
105 Empor sie tragend. Kalt und ungerührt

Vom Jauchzen unsers Danks, setzt seine Beute
Er nieder, drängt sich unters Volk und ist —
Verschwunden!

### Nathan.

Nicht auf immer, will ich hoffen.

### Daja.

Nachher die ersten Tage sahen wir
110 Ihn untern Palmen auf und nieder wandeln,
Die dort des Auferstandnen Grab umschatten.
Ich nahte mich ihm mit Entzücken, dankte,
Erhob, entbot, beschwor, — nur einmal noch
Die fromme Kreatur zu sehen, die
115 Nicht ruhen könne, bis sie ihren Dank
Zu seinen Füßen ausgeweinet.

### Nathan.
### Nun?

### Daja.

Umsonst! Er war zu unsrer Bitte taub;
Und goß so bittern Spott auf mich besonders ...

### Nathan.

Bis dadurch abgeschreckt ...

### Daja.
### Nichts weniger!

120 Ich trat ihn jeden Tag von neuem an;
Ließ jeden Tag von neuem mich verhöhnen.
Was litt ich nicht von ihm! Was hätt' ich nicht
Noch gern ertragen! — Aber lange schon
Kommt er nicht mehr, die Palmen zu besuchen,
125 Die unsers Auferstandnen Grab umschatten;
Und niemand weiß, wo er geblieben ist. —
Ihr staunt? Ihr sinnt?

### Nathan.

Ich überdenke mir,
Was das auf einen Geist, wie Rechas, wohl
für Eindruck machen muß. Sich so verschmäht
130 Von dem zu finden, den man hochzuschätzen
Sich so gezwungen fühlt; so weggestoßen,
Und doch so angezogen werden; — traun,
Da müssen Herz und Kopf sich lange zanken,
Ob Menschenhaß, ob Schwermut siegen soll.
135 Oft siegt auch keines; und die Phantasie,
Die in den Streit sich mengt, macht Schwärmer,
Bei welchen bald der Kopf das Herz, und bald
Das Herz den Kopf muß spielen. — Schlimmer Tausch! —
Das letztere, verkenn' ich Recha nicht,
140 Ist Rechas Fall: sie schwärmt.

### Daja.

Allein so fromm,
So liebenswürdig!

### Nathan.

Ist doch auch geschwärmt!

### Daja.

Vornehmlich e i n e — Grille, wenn Ihr wollt,
Ist ihr sehr wert. Es sei ihr Tempelherr
Kein Irdischer und keines Irdischen;
145 Der Engel einer, deren Schutze sich
Ihr kleines Herz, von Kindheit auf, so gern
Vertrauet glaubte, sei aus seiner Wolke,
In die er sonst verhüllt, auch noch im Feuer,
Um sie geschwebt, mit eins als Tempelherr
150 Hervorgetreten. — Lächelt nicht! — Wer weiß!
Laßt lächelnd wenigstens ihr einen Wahn,
In dem sich Jud' und Christ und Muselmann
Vereinigen; — so einen süßen Wahn!

**Nathan.**

Auch mir so süß! — Geh, wackre Daja, geh;
155 Sieh, was sie macht; ob ich sie sprechen kann. —
Sodann such' ich den wilden, launigen
Schutzengel auf. Und wenn ihm noch beliebt,
Hienieden unter uns zu wallen; noch
Beliebt, so ungesittet Ritterschaft
160 Zu treiben: find' ich ihn gewiß; und bring'
Ihn her.

**Daja.**

Ihr unternehmet viel.

**Nathan.**

Macht dann
Der süße Wahn der süßern Wahrheit Platz: —
Denn, Daja, glaube mir; dem Menschen ist
Ein Mensch noch immer lieber, als ein Engel —
165 So wirst du doch auf mich, auf mich nicht zürnen,
Die Engelschwärmerin geheilt zu sehn?

**Daja.**

Ihr seid so gut, und seid zugleich so schlimm!
Ich geh'! — Doch hört! doch seht! — Da kommt sie selbst.

————

**Zweiter Auftritt.**

Recha, und die Vorigen.

**Recha.**

So seid Ihr es doch ganz und gar, mein Vater?
170 Ich glaubt', Ihr hättet Eure Stimme nur
Vorausgeschickt. Wo bleibt Ihr? Was für Berge,
Für Wüsten, was für Ströme trennen uns
Denn noch? Ihr atmet Wand an Wand mit ihr,
Und eilt nicht, Eure Recha zu umarmen?

175 Die arme Recha, die indes verbrannte! —
Fast, fast verbrannte! fast nur. Schaudert nicht!
Es ist ein garst'ger Tod, verbrennen. O!

### Nathan.

Mein Kind! mein liebes Kind!

### Recha.

Ihr mußtet über
Den Euphrat, Tigris, Jordan; über — wer
180 Weiß was für Wasser all? — Wie oft hab' ich
Um Euch gezittert, eh' das Feuer mir
So nahe kam! Denn seit das Feuer mir
So nahe kam: dünkt mich im Wasser sterben
Erquickung, Labsal, Rettung. — Doch Ihr seid
185 Ja nicht ertrunken: ich, ich bin ja nicht
Verbrannt. Wie wollen wir uns freu'n, und Gott,
Gott loben! Er, er trug Euch und den Nachen
Auf Flügeln seiner unsichtbaren Engel
Die ungetreuen Ström' hinüber. Er,
190 Er winkte meinem Engel, daß er sichtbar
Auf seinem weißen Fittiche, mich durch
Das Feuer trüge —

### Nathan.

(Weißem Fittiche!
Ja, ja! der weiße vorgespreizte Mantel
Des Tempelherrn.)

### Recha.

Er sichtbar, sichtbar mich
195 Durchs Feuer trüg', von seinem Fittiche
Verweht. — Ich also, ich hab' einen Engel
Von Angesicht zu Angesicht gesehn;
Und meinen Engel.

**Nathan.**

Recha wär' es wert;
Und würd' an ihm nichts Schön'res sehn, als er
200 An ihr.

**Recha** (lächelnd).

Wem schmeichelt Ihr, mein Vater? wem?
Dem Engel, oder Euch?

**Nathan.**

Doch hätt' auch nur
Ein Mensch — ein Mensch, wie die Natur sie täglich
Gewährt, dir diesen Dienst erzeigt: er müßte
Für dich ein Engel sein. Er müßt' und würde.

**Recha.**

205 Nicht so ein Engel; nein! ein wirklicher;
Es war gewiß ein wirklicher! — Habt Ihr,
Ihr selbst die Möglichkeit, daß Engel sind,
Daß Gott zum Besten derer, die ihn lieben,
Auch Wunder könne thun, mich nicht gelehrt?
210 Ich lieb' ihn ja.

**Nathan.**

Und er liebt dich; und thut
Für dich, und deinesgleichen, stündlich Wunder;
Ja, hat sie schon von aller Ewigkeit
Für euch gethan.

**Recha.**

Das hör' ich gern.

**Nathan.**

Wie? Weil
Es ganz natürlich, ganz alltäglich klänge,
215 Wenn dich ein eigentlicher Tempelherr
Gerettet hätte: sollt' es darum weniger
Ein Wunder sein? — Der Wunder höchstes ist,

Daß uns die wahren, echten Wunder so
Alltäglich werden können, werden sollen.
220 Ohn' dieses allgemeine Wunder, hätte
Ein Denkender wohl schwerlich Wunder je
Genannt, was Kindern bloß so heißen müßte,
Die gaffend nur das Ungewöhnlichste,
Das Neuste nur verfolgen.

**Daja** (zu Nathan).

Wollt Ihr denn
225 Ihr ohnedem schon überspanntes Hirn
Durch solcherlei Subtilitäten ganz
Zersprengen?

**Nathan.**

Laß mich! — Meiner Recha wär'
Es Wunders nicht genug, daß sie ein Mensch
Gerettet, welchen selbst kein kleines Wunder
230 Erst retten müssen? Ja, kein kleines Wunder!
Denn wer hat schon gehört, daß Saladin
Je eines Tempelherrn verschont? Daß je
Ein Tempelherr von ihm verschont zu werden
Verlangt? gehofft? ihm je für seine Freiheit
235 Mehr als den ledern Gurt geboten, der
Sein Eisen schleppt; und höchstens seinen Dolch?

**Recha.**

Das schließt für mich, mein Vater. — Darum eben
War das kein Tempelherr; er schien es nur. —
Kommt kein gefangner Tempelherr je anders
240 Als zum gewissen Tode nach Jerusalem;
Geht keiner in Jerusalem so frei
Umher: wie hätte mich des Nachts freiwillig
Denn einer retten können?

**Nathan.**

Sieh! wie sinnreich.

Jetzt, Daja, nimm das Wort. Ich hab' es ja
245 Von dir, daß er gefangen hergeschickt
Ist worden. Ohne Zweifel weißt du mehr.

**Daja.**

Nun ja. — So sagt man freilich; — doch man sagt
Zugleich, daß Saladin den Tempelherrn
Begnadigt, weil er seiner Brüder einem,
250 Den er besonders lieb gehabt, so ähnlich sehe.
Doch da es viele zwanzig Jahre her,
Daß dieser Bruder nicht mehr lebt, — er hieß,
Ich weiß nicht wie; — er blieb, ich weiß nicht wo: —
So klingt das ja so gar — so gar unglaublich,
255 Daß an der ganzen Sache wohl nichts ist.

**Nathan.**

Ei, Daja! Warum wäre denn das so
Unglaublich? Doch wohl nicht — wie's wohl geschieht —
Um lieber etwas noch Unglaublichers
Zu glauben? — Warum hätte Saladin,
260 Der sein Geschwister insgesamt so liebt,
In jüngern Jahren einen Bruder nicht
Noch ganz besonders lieben können? — Pflegen
Sich zwei Gesichter nicht zu ähneln? — Ist
Ein alter Eindruck ein verlorener? — Wirkt
265 Das nämliche nicht mehr das nämliche? —
Seit wann? — Wo steckt hier das Unglaubliche? —
Ei freilich, weise Daja, wär's für dich
Kein Wunder mehr; und deine Wunder nur
Bedürf . . . verdienen, will ich sagen, Glauben.

**Daja.**

270 Ihr spottet.

**Nathan.**

Weil du meiner spottest. — Doch
Auch so noch, Recha, bleibet deine Rettung

Ein Wunder, dem nur möglich, der die ſtrengſten
Entſchlüſſe, die unbändigſten Entwürfe
Der Könige, ſein Spiel — wenn nicht ſein Spott —
275 Gern an den ſchwächſten Fäden lenkt.

Recha.

                            Mein Vater!
Mein Vater, wenn ich irr', Ihr wißt, ich irre
Nicht gern.

Nathan.

          Vielmehr, du läßt dich gern belehren. —
Sieh! eine Stirn, ſo oder ſo gewölbt;
Der Rücken einer Naſe, ſo vielmehr
280 Als ſo geführet; Augenbrauen, die
Auf einem ſcharfen oder ſtumpfen Knochen
So oder ſo ſich ſchlängeln; eine Linie,
Ein Bug, ein Winkel, eine Falt', ein Mal,
Ein Nichts, auf eines wilden Europäers
285 Geſicht: — und du entkommſt dem Feu'r, in Aſien!
Das wär' kein Wunder, wunderſücht'ges Volk?
Warum bemüht ihr denn noch einen Engel?

Daja.

Was ſchadet's — Nathan, wenn ich ſprechen darf —
Bei alledem, von einem Engel lieber
290 Als einem Menſchen ſich gerettet denken?
Fühlt man der erſten unbegreiflichen
Urſache ſeiner Rettung nicht ſich ſo
Viel näher?

Nathan.

          Stolz! und nichts als Stolz! Der Topf
Von Eiſen will mit einer ſilbern Zange
295 Gern aus der Glut gehoben ſein, um ſelbſt
Ein Topf von Silber ſich zu dünken. — Pah! —
Und was es ſchadet, fragſt du? was es ſchadet?

Was hilft es? dürft' ich nur hinwieder fragen. —
Denn dein „Sich Gott um so viel näher fühlen",
300 Ist Unsinn oder Gotteslästerung. —
Allein es schadet; ja, es schadet allerdings. —
Kommt! hört mir zu. — Nicht wahr? dem Wesen, das
Dich rettete, — es sei ein Engel oder
Ein Mensch, — dem möchtet ihr, und du besonders,
305 Gern wieder viele große Dienste thun? —
Nicht wahr? — Nun, einem Engel, was für Dienste,
für große Dienste könnt ihr dem wohl thun?
Ihr könnt ihm danken; zu ihm seufzen, beten;
Könnt in Entzückung über ihn zerschmelzen;
310 Könnt an dem Tage seiner Feier fasten,
Almosen spenden. — Alles nichts. — Denn mich
Däucht immer, daß ihr selbst und euer Nächster
Hierbei weit mehr gewinnt als er. Er wird
Nicht sett durch euer Fasten; wird nicht reich
315 Durch eure Spenden; wird nicht herrlicher
Durch eu'r Entzücken; wird nicht mächtiger
Durch eu'r Vertrau'n. Nicht wahr? Allein ein Mensch!

### Daja.

Ei freilich hätt' ein Mensch, etwas für ihn
Zu thun, uns mehr Gelegenheit verschafft.
320 Und Gott weiß, wie bereit wir dazu waren!
Allein er wollte ja, bedurfte ja
So völlig nichts; war in sich, mit sich so
Vergnügsam, als nur Engel sind, nur Engel
Sein können.

### Recha.

Endlich, als er gar verschwand . . .

### Nathan.

325 Verschwand? — Wie denn verschwand? — Sich untern
Palmen

Nicht ferner sehen ließ? — Wie? oder habt
Ihr wirklich schon ihn weiter aufgesucht?

**Daja.**

Das nun wohl nicht.

**Nathan.**

                    Nicht, Daja? nicht? — Da sieh
Nun was es schad't! — Grausame Schwärmerinnen! —
330 Wenn dieser Engel nun — nun krank geworden!...

**Recha.**

Krank!

**Daja.**

    Krank! Er wird doch nicht!

**Recha.**

                    Welch kalter Schauer
Befällt mich! — Daja! — Meine Stirne, sonst
So warm, fühl'! ist auf einmal Eis.

**Nathan.**

                    Er ist
Ein franke, dieses Klimas ungewohnt;
335 Ist jung; der harten Arbeit seines Standes,
Des Hungerns, Wachens ungewohnt.

**Recha.**

                    Krank! krank!

**Daja.**

Das wäre möglich, meint ja Nathan nur.

**Nathan.**

Nun liegt er da! hat weder Freund, noch Geld
Sich freunde zu besolden.

**Recha.**

    Ah, mein Vater!

**Nathan.**

340 Liegt ohne Wartung, ohne Rat und Zuſprach',
Ein Raub der Schmerzen und des Todes da!

**Recha.**

Wo? wo?

**Nathan.**

Er, der für eine, die er nie
Gekannt, geſehn — genug, es war ein Menſch —
Ins Feu'r ſich ſtürzte . . .

**Daja.**

Nathan, ſchonet ihrer!

**Nathan.**

345 Der, was er rettete, nicht näher kennen,
Nicht weiter ſehen mocht', — um ihm den Dank
Zu ſparen . . .

**Daja.**

Schonet ihrer, Nathan!

**Nathan**

Weiter
Auch nicht zu ſehn verlangt', — es wäre denn,
Daß er zum zweitenmal es retten ſollte —
350 Denn g'nug, es iſt ein Menſch . . .

**Daja.**

Hört auf, und ſeht!

**Nathan.**

Der, der hat ſterbend ſich zu laben, nichts —
Als das Bewußtſein dieſer That!

**Daja.**

Hört auf!

Ihr tötet ſie!

### Nathan.

Und du haſt ihn getötet! —
Hätt'ſt ſo ihn töten können. — Recha! Recha!
355 Es iſt Arznei, nicht Gift, was ich dir reiche.
Er lebt! — komm zu dir! — iſt auch wohl nicht krank;
Nicht einmal krank!

### Recha.

Gewiß? — nicht tot? nicht krank?

### Nathan.

Gewiß, nicht tot! — Denn Gott lohnt Gutes, hier
Gethan, auch hier noch. — Geh! — Begreifſt du aber,
360 Wie viel andächtig ſchwärmen leichter, als
Gut handeln iſt? Wie gern der ſchlaffſte Menſch
Andächtig ſchwärmt, um nur, — iſt er zuzeiten
Sich ſchon der Abſicht deutlich nicht bewußt —
Um nur gut handeln nicht zu dürfen?

### Recha.

                                        Ah,
365 Mein Vater! laßt, laßt Eure Recha doch
Nie wiederum allein! — Nicht wahr, er kann
Auch wohl verreiſt nur ſein? —

### Nathan.

                          Geht! — Allerdings. —
Ich ſeh', dort muſtert mit neugier'gem Blick
Ein Muſelmann mir die beladenen
370 Kamele. Kennt ihr ihn?

### Daja.

              Ha! Euer Derwiſch.

### Nathan.

Wer?

**Daja.**

Euer Derwisch; Euer Schachgesell!

**Nathan.**

Al-Hafi? das Al-Hafi?

**Daja.**

Jetzt des Sultans

Schatzmeister.

**Nathan.**

Wie? Al-Hafi? Träumst du wieder? —
Er ist's! — wahrhaftig, ist's! — kommt auf uns zu.
375 Hinein mit euch, geschwind! — Was werd' ich hören!

---

### Dritter Auftritt.

Nathan und der Derwisch.

**Derwisch.**

Reißt nur die Augen auf, soweit Ihr könnt!

**Nathan.**

Bist du's? Bist du es nicht? — In dieser Pracht,
Ein Derwisch! . . .

**Derwisch.**

Nun? Warum denn nicht? Läßt sich
Aus einem Derwisch denn nichts, gar nichts machen?

**Nathan.**

380 Ei wohl, genug! — Ich dachte mir nur immer,
Der Derwisch — so der rechte Derwisch — woll'
Aus sich nichts machen lassen.

**Derwisch.**

Beim Propheten!

Daß ich kein rechter bin, mag auch wohl wahr sein.
Zwar wenn man muß —

#### Nathan.

Muß! Derwisch! — Derwisch muß?
385 Kein Mensch muß müssen, und ein Derwisch müßte?
Was müßt' er denn?

#### Derwisch.

Warum man ihn recht bittet,
Und er für gut erkennt: das muß ein Derwisch.

#### Nathan.

Bei unserm Gott! da sagst du wahr. — Laß dich
Umarmen, Mensch. — Du bist doch noch mein Freund?

#### Derwisch.

390 Und fragt nicht erst, was ich geworden bin?

#### Nathan.

Trotz dem, was du geworden!

#### Derwisch.

Könnt' ich nicht
Ein Kerl im Staat geworden sein, des Freundschaft
Euch ungelegen wäre?

#### Nathan.

Wenn dein Herz
Noch Derwisch ist, so wag' ich's drauf. Der Kerl
395 Im Staat ist nur dein Kleid.

#### Derwisch.

Das auch geehrt
Will sein. — Was meint Ihr? ratet! — Was wär' ich
An Eurem Hofe?

**Nathan.**

Derwisch; weiter nichts.
Doch nebenher, wahrscheinlich — Koch.

**Derwisch.**

Nun ja!
Mein Handwerk bei Euch zu verlernen. — Koch!
400 Nicht Kellner auch? — Gesteht, daß Saladin
Mich besser kennt. — Schatzmeister bin ich bei
Ihm worden.

**Nathan.**

Du? — bei ihm?

**Derwisch.**

Versteht:
Des kleinern Schatzes, — denn des größern waltet
Sein Vater noch — des Schatzes für sein Haus.

**Nathan.**

405 Sein Haus ist groß.

**Derwisch.**

Und größer, als Ihr glaubt;
Denn jeder Bettler ist von seinem Hause.

**Nathan.**

Doch ist den Bettlern Saladin so feind —

**Derwisch.**

Daß er mit Stumpf und Stiel sie zu vertilgen
Sich vorgesetzt, — und sollt' er selbst darüber
410 Zum Bettler werden.

**Nathan.**

Brav! — So mein' ich's eben.

**Derwisch.**

Er ist's auch schon, trotz einem! — Denn sein Schatz

Ist jeden Tag mit Sonnenuntergang
Viel leerer noch, als leer. Die Flut, so hoch
Sie morgens eintritt, ist des Mittags längst
415 Verlaufen —

Nathan.

Weil Kanäle sie zum Teil
Verschlingen, die zu füllen oder zu
Verstopfen, gleich unmöglich ist.

Derwisch.

Getroffen!

Nathan.

Ich kenne das!

Derwisch.

Es taugt nun freilich nichts,
Wenn Fürsten Geier unter Äsern sind.
420 Doch sind sie Äser unter Geiern, taugt's
Noch zehnmal weniger.

Nathan.

O nicht doch, Derwisch!
Nicht doch!

Derwisch.

Ihr habt gut reden, Ihr! — Kommt an:
Was gebt Ihr mir? so tret' ich meine Stell'
Euch ab.

Nathan.

Was bringt dir deine Stelle?

Derwisch.

Mir?
425 Nicht viel. Doch Euch, Euch kann sie trefflich wuchern.
Denn ist es Ebb' im Schatz, — wie öfters ist, —
So zieht Ihr Eure Schleusen auf: schießt vor,
Und nehmt an Zinsen, was Euch nur gefällt.

**Nathan.**

Auch Zins vom Zins der Zinsen?

**Derwisch.**

Freilich!

**Nathan.**

Bis

430 Mein Kapital zu lauter Zinsen wird.

**Derwisch.**

Das lockt Euch nicht? — So schreibet unsrer freund-
schaft
Nur gleich den Scheidebrief! Denn wahrlich hab'
Ich sehr auf Euch gerechnet.

**Nathan.**

Wahrlich? Wie
Denn so? wie so denn?

**Derwisch.**

Daß Ihr mir mein Amt
435 Mit Ehren würdet führen helfen; daß
Ich allzeit offne Kasse bei Euch hätte. —
Ihr schüttelt?

**Nathan.**

Nun, verstehn wir uns nur recht!
Hier giebt's zu unterscheiden. — Du? warum
Nicht du? Al-Hafi Derwisch ist zu allem,
440 Was ich vermag, mir stets willkommen. — Aber
Al-Hafi Defterdar des Saladin,
Der — dem —

**Derwisch.**

Erriet ich's nicht? Daß Ihr doch immer
So gut als klug, so klug als weise seid! —
Geduld! Was Ihr am Hafi unterscheidet,

445 Soll bald geschieden wieder sein. — Seht da
Das Ehrenkleid, das Saladin mir gab.
Eh es verschossen ist, eh es zu Lumpen
Geworden, wie sie einen Derwisch kleiden,
Hängt's in Jerusalem am Nagel, und
450 Ich bin am Ganges, wo ich leicht und barfuß
Den heißen Sand mit meinen Lehrern trete.

### Nathan.

Dir ähnlich g'nug!

### Derwisch.

Und Schach mit ihnen spiele.

### Nathan.

Dein höchstes Gut!

### Derwisch.

Denkt nur, was mich verführte! —
Damit ich selbst nicht länger betteln dürfte?
455 Den reichen Mann mit Bettlern spielen könnte?
Vermögend wär' im Hui den reichsten Bettler
In einen armen Reichen zu verwandeln?

### Nathan.

Das nun wohl nicht.

### Derwisch.

Weit etwas Abgeschmackters!
Ich fühlte mich zum erstenmal geschmeichelt;
460 Durch Saladins gutherz'gen Wahn geschmeichelt —

### Nathan.

Der war?

### Derwisch.

Ein Bettler wisse nur, wie Bettlern
Zu Mute sei; ein Bettler habe nur
Gelernt, mit guter Weise Bettlern geben.

„Dein Vorfahr," sprach er, „war mir viel zu kalt,
465 Zu rauh. Er gab so unhold, wenn er gab;
Erkundigte so ungestüm sich erst
Nach dem Empfänger; nie zufrieden, daß
Er nur den Mangel kenne, wollt' er auch
Des Mangels Ursach' wissen, um die Gabe
470 Nach dieser Ursach' filzig abzuwägen.
Das wird Al-Hafi nicht! So unmild mild
Wird Saladin im Hafi nicht erscheinen!
Al-Hafi gleicht verstopften Röhren nicht,
Die ihre klar und still empfangnen Wasser
475 So unrein und so sprudelnd wiedergeben.
Al-Hafi denkt; Al-Hafi fühlt wie ich!" —
So lieblich klang des Voglers Pfeife, bis
Der Gimpel in dem Netze war. — Ich Geck!
Ich eines Gecken Geck!

#### Nathan.

               Gemach, mein Derwisch,
480 Gemach!

#### Derwisch.

         Ei was! — Es wär' nicht Geckerei,
Bei Hunderttausenden die Menschen drücken,
Ausmergeln, plündern, martern, würgen; und
Ein Menschenfreund an einzeln scheinen wollen?
Es wär' nicht Geckerei, des Höchsten Milde,
485 Die sonder Auswahl über Bös' und Gute
Und flur und Wüstenei, in Sonnenschein
Und Regen sich verbreitet, — nachzuäffen,
Und nicht des Höchsten immer volle Hand
Zu haben? Was? es wär' nicht Geckerei...

#### Nathan.

490 Genug! hör' auf!

#### Derwisch.

          Laßt meiner Geckerei

Mich doch nur auch erwähnen! — Was? es wäre
Nicht Geckerei, an solchen Geckereien
Die gute Seite dennoch auszuspüren,
Um Anteil, dieser guten Seite wegen,
495 An dieser Geckerei zu nehmen? He?
Das nicht?

Nathan.

Al-Hafi, mache, daß du bald
In deine Wüste wieder kommst. Ich fürchte,
Grad' unter Menschen möchtest du ein Mensch
Zu sein verlernen.

Derwisch.

Recht, das fürcht' ich auch.
500 Lebt wohl!

Nathan.

So hastig? — Warte doch, Al-Hafi.
Entläuft dir denn die Wüste? — Warte doch! —
Daß er mich hörte! — He, Al-Hafi! hier! —
Weg ist er; und ich hätt' ihn noch so gern
Nach unserm Tempelherrn gefragt. Vermutlich,
505 Daß er ihn kennt.

Vierter Auftritt.

Daja eilt herbei. Nathan.

Daja.
O Nathan, Nathan!

Nathan.

Nun?
Was giebt's?
Daja.

Er läßt sich wieder sehn! Er läßt
Sich wieder sehn!

**Nathan.**

Wer, Daja? wer?

**Daja.**

Er! er!

**Nathan.**

Er? er? — Wann läßt sich der nicht sehn! — Ja so,
Nur euer Er heißt er. — Das sollt' er nicht!
510 Und wenn er auch ein Engel wäre, nicht!

**Daja.**

Er wandelt untern Palmen wieder auf
Und ab; und bricht von Zeit zu Zeit sich Datteln.

**Nathan.**

Sie essend? — und als Tempelherr?

**Daja.**

Was quält
Ihr mich? — Ihr gierig Aug' erriet ihn hinter
515 Den dicht verschränkten Palmen schon; und folgt
Ihm unverrückt. Sie läßt Euch bitten, — Euch
Beschwören, — ungesäumt ihn anzugehn.
O eilt! Sie wird Euch aus dem Fenster winken,
Ob er hinauf geht oder weiter ab
520 Sich schlägt. O eilt!

**Nathan.**

So wie ich vom Kamele
Gestiegen? — Schickt sich das? — Geh, eile du
Ihm zu; und meld' ihm meine Wiederkunft.
Gieb acht, der Biedermann hat nur mein Haus
In meinem Absein nicht betreten wollen;
525 Und kommt nicht ungern, wenn der Vater selbst
Ihn laden läßt. Geh, sag', ich laß' ihn bitten,
Ihn herzlich bitten ...

### Daja.

All umsonst! Er kommt
Euch nicht. — Denn kurz; er kommt zu keinem Juden.

### Nathan.

So geh, geh wenigstens ihn anzuhalten;
530 Ihn wenigstens mit deinen Augen zu
Begleiten. — Geh, ich komme gleich dir nach.

(Nathan eilt hinein, und Daja heraus.)

---

## Fünfter Auftritt.

(Scene: ein Platz mit Palmen, unter welchen der Tempelherr
auf und nieder geht. Ein Klosterbruder folgt ihm in einiger
Entfernung von der Seite, immer als ob er ihn anreden wolle.)

### Tempelherr.

Der folgt mir nicht vor langer Weile! — Sieh,
Wie schielt er nach den Händen! — Guter Bruder, ...
Ich kann Euch auch wohl Vater nennen; nicht?

### Klosterbruder.

Nur Bruder — Laienbruder nur; zu dienen.

### Tempelherr.

535 Ja, guter Bruder, wer nur selbst was hätte!
Bei Gott! bei Gott! ich habe nichts —

### Klosterbruder.

Und doch
Recht warmen Dank! Gott geb' Euch tausendfach
Was Ihr gern geben wolltet. Denn der Wille
540 Und nicht die Gabe macht den Geber. — Auch
Ward ich dem Herrn Almosens wegen gar
Nicht nachgeschickt.

### Tempelherr.
Doch aber nachgeschickt?

### Klofterbruder.
Ja; aus dem Klofter.

### Tempelherr.
Wo ich eben jetzt
Ein kleines Pilgermahl zu finden hoffte?

### Klofterbruder.
545 Die Tifche waren fchon befetzt: komm' aber
Der Herr nur wieder mit zurück.

### Tempelherr.
Wozu?
Ich habe Fleifch wohl lange nicht gegeffen:
Allein was thut's?  Die Datteln find ja reif.

### Klofterbruder.
Nehm' fich der Herr in acht mit diefer Frucht.
550 Zu viel genoffen taugt fie nicht; verftopft
Die Milz; macht melancholifches Geblüt.

### Tempelherr.
Wenn ich nun melancholifch gern mich fühlte? —
Doch diefer Warnung wegen wurdet Ihr
Mir doch nicht nachgefchickt?

### Klofterbruder.
O nein! — Ich foll
555 Mich nur nach Euch erkunden; auf den Zahn
Euch fühlen.

### Tempelherr.
Und das fagt Ihr mir fo felbft?

**Klosterbruder.**

Warum nicht?

**Tempelherr.**

(Ein verschmitzter Bruder!) — Hat
Das Kloster Euresgleichen mehr?

**Klosterbruder.**

Weiß nicht.
Ich muß gehorchen, lieber Herr.

**Tempelherr.**

Und da
560 Gehorcht Ihr denn auch ohne viel zu klügeln?

**Klosterbruder.**

Wär's sonst gehorchen, lieber Herr?

**Tempelherr.**

(Daß doch
Die Einfalt immer Recht behält!) — Ihr dürft
Mir doch auch wohl vertrauen, wer mich gern
Genauer kennen möchte? — Daß Ihr's selbst
565 Nicht seid, will ich wohl schwören.

**Klosterbruder.**

Ziemte mir's?
Und frommte mir's?

**Tempelherr.**

Wem ziemt und frommt es denn,
Daß er so neubegierig ist? Wem denn?

**Klosterbruder.**

Dem Patriarchen; muß ich glauben. — Denn
Der sandte mich Euch nach.

**Tempelherr.**

Der Patriarch?

570 Kennt der das rote Kreuz auf weißem Mantel
Nicht besser?

#### Klosterbruder.

Kenn' ja ich's!

#### Tempelherr.

Nun, Bruder? Nun? —
Ich bin ein Tempelherr; und ein gefangner. —
Setz' ich hinzu: gefangen bei Tebnin,
Der Burg, die mit des Stillstands letzter Stunde
575 Wir gern erstiegen hätten, um sodann
Auf Sidon los zu gehn; — setz' ich hinzu:
Selbzwanzigster gefangen und allein
Vom Saladin begnadiget: so weiß
Der Patriarch, was er zu wissen braucht; —
580 Mehr, als er braucht.

#### Klosterbruder.

Wohl aber schwerlich mehr,
Als er schon weiß. — Er wüßt' auch gern, warum
Der Herr von Saladin begnadigt worden;
Er ganz allein.

#### Tempelherr.

Weiß ich das selber? — Schon
Den Hals entblößt, kniet' ich auf meinem Mantel,
585 Den Streich erwartend: als mich schärfer Saladin
Ins Auge faßt, mir näher springt, und winkt.
Man hebt mich auf; ich bin entfesselt; will
Ihm danken; seh' sein Aug' in Thränen: stumm
Ist er, bin ich; er geht, ich bleibe. — Wie
590 Nun das zusammenhängt, enträtsle sich
Der Patriarche selbst.

#### Klosterbruder.

Er schließt daraus,

Daß Gott zu großen, großen Dingen Euch
Müss' aufbehalten haben.

### Tempelherr.

Ja, zu großen!
Ein Judenmädchen aus dem Feu'r zu retten;
595 Auf Sinai neugier'ge Pilger zu
Geleiten; und dergleichen mehr.

### Klosterbruder.

Wird schon
Noch kommen! — Ist inzwischen auch nicht übel. —
Vielleicht hat selbst der Patriarch bereits
Weit wicht'gere Geschäfte für den Herrn.

### Tempelherr.

600 So? meint Ihr, Bruder? — Hat er gar Euch schon
Was merken lassen?

### Klosterbruder.

Ei, ja wohl! — Ich soll
Den Herrn nur erst ergründen, ob er so
Der Mann wohl ist.

### Tempelherr.

Nun ja; ergründet nur!
(Ich will doch sehn, wie der ergründet!) — Nun?

### Klosterbruder.

605 Das kürz'ste wird wohl sein, daß ich dem Herrn
Ganz gradezu des Patriarchen Wunsch
Eröffne.

### Tempelherr.
Wohl!

### Klosterbruder.

Er hätte durch den Herrn

Ein Briefchen gern bestellt.

### Tempelherr.

Durch mich? Ich bin
Kein Bote. — Das, das wäre das Geschäft,
610 Das weit glorreicher sei, als Judenmädchen
Dem Feu'r entreißen?

### Klosterbruder.

Muß doch wohl! Denn — sagt
Der Patriarch — an diesem Briefchen sei
Der ganzen Christenheit sehr viel gelegen.
Dies Briefchen wohl bestellt zu haben, — sagt
615 Der Patriarch, — werd' einst im Himmel Gott
Mit einer ganz besondern Krone lohnen.
Und dieser Krone, — sagt der Patriarch, —
Sei niemand würd'ger, als mein Herr.

### Tempelherr.

Als ich?

### Klosterbruder.

Denn diese Krone zu verdienen, — sagt
620 Der Patriarch, — sei schwerlich jemand auch
Geschickter, als mein Herr.

### Tempelherr.

Als ich?

### Klosterbruder.

Er sei
Hier frei; könn' überall sich hier besehn;
Versteh', wie eine Stadt zu stürmen und
Zu schirmen; könne, — sagt der Patriarch, —
625 Die Stärk' und Schwäche der von Saladin
Neu aufgeführten, innern, zweiten Mauer

Am besten schätzen, sie am deutlichsten
Den Streitern Gottes, — sagt der Patriarch, —
Beschreiben.

### Tempelherr.

Guter Bruder, wenn ich doch
Nun auch des Briefchens nähern Inhalt wüßte.

### Klosterbruder.

Ja ben, — den weiß ich nun wohl nicht so recht.
Das Briefchen aber ist an König Philipp. —
Der Patriarch . . . Ich hab' mich oft gewundert,
Wie doch ein Heiliger, der sonst so ganz
635 Im Himmel lebt, zugleich so unterrichtet
Von Dingen dieser Welt zu sein herab
Sich lassen kann. Es muß ihm sauer werden.

### Tempelherr.

Nun denn? Der Patriarch? —

### Klosterbruder.

Weiß ganz genau,
Ganz zuverlässig, wie und wo, wie stark,
640 Von welcher Seite Saladin, im Fall
Es völlig wieder losgeht, seinen Feldzug
Eröffnen wird.

### Tempelherr.

Das weiß er?

### Klosterbruder.

Ja, und möcht'
Es gern den König Philipp wissen lassen:
Damit der ungefähr ermessen könne,
645 Ob die Gefahr denn gar so schrecklich, um
Mit Saladin den Waffenstillestand,

Den Euer Orden schon so brav gebrochen,
Es koste was es wolle, wieder her
Zu stellen.

### Tempelherr.

Welch ein Patriarch! — Ja so!
650 Der liebe tapfre Mann will mich zu keinem
Gemeinen Boten; will mich — zum Spion. —
Sagt Euerm Patriarchen, guter Bruder,
So viel Ihr mich ergründen können, wär'
Das meine Sache nicht. — Ich müsse mich
655 Noch als Gefangenen betrachten; und
Der Tempelherren einziger Beruf
Sei mit dem Schwerte drein zu schlagen, nicht
Kundschafterei zu treiben.

### Klosterbruder.

Dacht' ich's doch! —
Will's auch dem Herrn nicht eben sehr verübeln. —
660 Zwar kommt das Beste noch. — Der Patriarch
Hiernächst hat ausgegattert, wie die Feste
Sich nennt, und wo auf Libanon sie liegt,
In der die ungeheuern Summen stecken,
Mit welchen Saladins vorsicht'ger Vater
665 Das Heer besoldet, und die Zurüstungen
Des Kriegs bestreitet. Saladin verfügt
Von Zeit zu Zeit auf abgelegnen Wegen
Nach dieser Feste sich, nur kaum begleitet. —
Ihr merkt doch?

### Tempelherr.

Nimmermehr!

### Klosterbruder.

Was wäre da
670 Wohl leichter, als des Saladin sich zu

Bemächtigen? den Garaus ihm zu machen? —
Ihr schaudert? — O es haben schon ein paar
Gott'sfürcht'ge Maroniten sich erboten,
Wenn nur ein wackrer Mann sie führen wolle,
675 Das Stück zu wagen.

**Tempelherr.**

Und der Patriarch
Hätt' auch zu diesem wackern Manne mich
Ersehn?

**Klosterbruder.**

Er glaubt, daß König Philipp wohl
Von Ptolemais aus die Hand hierzu
Am besten bieten könne.

**Tempelherr.**

Mir? mir, Bruder?
680 Mir? Habt Ihr nicht gehört? nur erst gehört,
Was für Verbindlichkeit dem Saladin
Ich habe?

**Klosterbruder.**

Wohl hab' ich's gehört.

**Tempelherr.**

Und doch?

**Klosterbruder.**

Ja, — meint der Patriarch, — das wär' schon gut:
Gott aber und der Orden . . .

**Tempelherr.**

Ändern nichts!
685 Gebieten mir kein Bubenstück!

**Klosterbruder.**

Gewiß nicht! —
Nur, — meint der Patriarch, — sei Bubenstück
Vor Menschen, nicht auch Bubenstück vor Gott.

**Tempelherr.**

Ich wär' dem Saladin mein Leben schuldig:
Und raubt' ihm seines?

**Klosterbruder.**

Pfui! — Doch bliebe, — meint
690 Der Patriarch, — noch immer Saladin
Ein Feind der Christenheit, der Euer Freund
Zu sein, kein Recht erwerben könne.

**Tempelherr.**

Freund?
An dem ich bloß nicht will zum Schurken werden;
Zum undankbaren Schurken?

**Klosterbruder.**

Allerdings! —
695 Zwar, — meint der Patriarch, — des Dankes sei
Man quitt, vor Gott und Menschen quitt, wenu uns
Der Dienst um unsertwillen nicht geschehen.
Und da verlauten wolle, — meint der Patriarch, —
Daß Euch nur darum Saladin begnadet,
700 Weil ihm in Eurer Mien', in Euerm Wesen,
So was von seinem Bruder eingeleuchtet ...

**Tempelherr.**

Auch dieses weiß der Patriarch; und doch? —
Ah! wäre das gewiß! Ah, Saladin! —
Wie? die Natur hätt' auch nur e i n e n Zug
705 Von mir in deines Bruders Form gebildet:
Und dem entspräche nichts in meiner Seele?
Was dem entspräche, könnt' ich unterdrücken,
Um einem Patriarchen zu gefallen? —
Natur, so lügst du nicht! So widerspricht
710 Sich Gott in seinen Werken nicht! — Geht Bruder! —
Erregt mir meine Galle nicht! — Geht! geht!

### Klosterbruder.

Ich geh'; und geh' vergnügter, als ich kam.
Verzeihe mir der Herr. Wir Klosterleute
Sind schuldig, unsern Obern zu gehorchen.

---

### Sechster Auftritt.

Der Tempelherr und Daja, die den Tempelherrn schon eine
Zeitlang von weitem beobachtet hatte, und sich nun ihm nähert.

### Daja.

715 Der Klosterbruder, wie mich dünkt, ließ in
Der besten Laun' ihn nicht. — Doch muß ich mein
Paket nur wagen.

### Tempelherr.

                Nun, vortrefflich! — Lügt
Das Sprichwort wohl: daß Mönch und Weib, und Weib
Und Mönch des Teufels beide Krallen sind? ·
720 Er wirft mich heut aus einer in die andre.

### Daja.

Was seh' ich? — Edler Ritter, Euch? — Gott Dank!
Gott tausend Dank! — Wo habt Ihr denn
Die ganze Zeit gesteckt? — Ihr seid doch wohl
Nicht krank gewesen?

### Tempelherr.
Nein.

### Daja.
        Gesund doch?

### Tempelherr
                            Ja.
### Daja.

725 Wir waren Euretwegen wahrlich ganz
Bekümmert.

**Tempelherr.**

So?

**Daja.**

Ihr wart gewiß verreist?

**Tempelherr.**

Erraten!

**Daja.**

Und kamt heut erst wieder?

**Tempelherr.**

Gestern.

**Daja.**

Auch Rechas Vater ist heut angekommen.
Und nun darf Recha doch wohl hoffen?

**Tempelherr.**

Was?

**Daja.**

Warum sie Euch so öfters bitten lassen.
730 Ihr Vater ladet Euch nun selber bald
Aufs dringlichste. Er kommt von Babylon;
Mit zwanzig hochbeladenen Kamelen,
Und allem, was an edeln Spezereien,
735 An Steinen und an Stoffen, Indien
Und Persien und Syrien, gar Sina,
Kostbares nur gewähren.

**Tempelherr.**

Kaufe nichts.

**Daja.**

Sein Volk verehret ihn als einen Fürsten.
Doch daß es ihn den weisen Nathan nennt,

740 Und nicht vielmehr den Reichen, hat mich oft
Gewundert.

### Tempelherr.

Seinem Volk ist reich und weise
Vielleicht das nämliche.

### Daja.

Vor allem aber
Hätt's ihn den Guten nennen müssen. Denn
Ihr stellt Euch gar nicht vor, wie gut er ist.
745 Als er erfuhr, wie viel Euch Recha schuldig:
Was hätt', in diesem Augenblicke, nicht
Er alles Euch gethan, gegeben!

### Tempelherr.

Ei!

### Daja.

Versucht's und kommt und seht!

### Tempelherr.

Was denn? wie schnell
Ein Augenblick vorüber ist?

### Daja.

Hätt' ich,
750 Wenn er so gut nicht wär', es mir so lange
Bei ihm gefallen lassen? meint Ihr etwa,
Ich fühle meinen Wert als Christin nicht?
Auch mir ward's vor der Wiege nicht gesungen,
Daß ich nur darum meinem Eh'gemahl
755 Nach Palästina folgen würd', um da
Ein Judenmädchen zu erziehn. Es war
Mein lieber Eh'gemahl ein edler Knecht
In Kaiser Friedrichs Heere —

**Tempelherr.**

Von Geburt
Ein Schweizer, dem die Ehr' und Gnade ward
760 Mit Seiner Kaiserlichen Majestät
In einem Flusse zu ersaufen. — Weib!
Wie vielmal habt Ihr mir das schon erzählt?
Hört Ihr denn gar nicht auf mich zu verfolgen?

**Daja.**

Verfolgen! lieber Gott!

**Tempelherr.**

Ja, ja, verfolgen.
765 Ich will nun einmal Euch nicht weiter sehn!
Nicht hören! Will von Euch an eine That
Nicht fort und fort erinnert sein, bei der
Ich nichts gedacht; die, wenn ich drüber denke,
Zum Rätsel von mir selbst mir wird. Zwar möcht'
770 Ich sie nicht gern bereuen. Aber seht;
Ereignet so ein Fall sich wieder: Ihr
Seid schuld, wenn ich so rasch nicht handle; wenn
Ich mich vorher erkund', — und brennen lasse,
Was brennt.

**Daja.**

Bewahre Gott!

**Tempelherr.**

Von heut an thut
775 Mir den Gefallen wenigstens, und kennt
Mich weiter nicht. Ich bitt' Euch drum. Auch laßt
Den Vater mir vom Halse. Jud' ist Jude.
Ich bin ein plumper Schwab'. Des Mädchens Bild
Ist längst aus meiner Seele; wenn es je
780 Da war.

**Daja.**

Doch Eures ist aus ihrer nicht.

**Tempelherr.**

Was soll's nun aber da? was soll's?

**Daja.**

　　　　　　　　　　Wer weiß!
Die Menschen sind nicht immer, was sie scheinen.

**Tempelherr.**

Doch selten etwas Bessers. Er geht.

**Daja.**

　　　　　Wartet doch!
Wo so ... ihr?

**Tempelherr.**

　　　Weib, macht mir der Palmen nicht
so viele, weiget ... ihr so gern fort mendle!

**Daja.**

So sich die hurtige Sie ... geht. — Und doch
... ich die Spur des Tores nicht verliere.

*Sie geht ihm zu weiten nach.*

# Zweiter Aufzug.

## Erster Auftritt.

Die Scene: des Sultans Palast.

Saladin und Sittah spielen Schach.

**Sittah.**

Wo bist du, Saladin? Wie spielst du heut?

**Saladin.**

Nicht gut? Ich dächte doch.

**Sittah.**

für mich; und kaum.

790 Nimm diesen Zug zurück.

**Saladin.**

Warum?

**Sittah.**

Der Springer

Wird unbedeckt.

**Saladin.**

Ist wahr. Nun so!

**Sittah.**

So zieh'

Ich in die Gabel.

**Saladin.**

Wieder wahr. — Schach denn!

**Sittah.**

Was hilft dir das? Ich setze vor: und du
Bist, wie du warst.

**Saladin.**

Aus dieser Klemme, seh'
795 Ich wohl, ist ohne Buße nicht zu kommen.
Mag's! Nimm den Springer nur.

**Sittah.**

Ich will ihn nicht.

Ich geh' vorbei.

**Saladin.**

Du schenkst mir nichts. Dir liegt
An diesem Platze mehr, als an dem Springer.

**Sittah.**

Kann sein.

**Saladin.**

Mach' deine Rechnung nur nicht ohne
800 Den Wirt. Denn sieh! Was gilt's, das warst du nicht
Vermuten?

**Sittah.**

Freilich nicht. Wie konnt' ich auch
Vermuten, daß du deiner Königin
So müde wärst?

**Saladin.**

Ich meiner Königin?

**Sittah.**

Ich seh nun schon: ich soll heut' meine tausend
805 Dinar', kein Naserinchen mehr gewinnen.

**Saladin.**

Wie so?

### Sittah.

Frag' noch! — Weil du mit Fleiß, mit aller
Gewalt verlieren willst. — Doch dabei find'
Ich meine Rechnung nicht.  Denn außer, daß
Ein solches Spiel das unterhaltendste
810 Nicht ist: gewann ich immer nicht am meisten
Mit dir, wenn ich verlor? Wann hast du mir
Den Satz, mich des verlornen Spieles wegen
Zu trösten, doppelt nicht hernach geschenkt?

### Saladin.

Ei sieh! so hättest du ja wohl, wenn du
815 Verlorst, mit Fleiß verloren, Schwesterchen?

### Sittah.

Zum wenigsten kann gar wohl sein, daß deine
Freigebigkeit, mein liebes Brüderchen,
Schuld ist, daß ich nicht besser spielen lernen.

### Saladin.

Wir kommen ab vom Spiele.  Mach' ein Ende!

### Sittah.

So bleibt es? Nun denn: Schach! und doppelt Schach!

### Saladin.

Nun freilich; dieses Abschach hab' ich nicht
Gesehn, das meine Königin zugleich
Mit niederwirft.

### Sittah.

                War dem noch abzuhelfen?
Laß sehn.

### Saladin.

            Nein, nein; nimm nur die Königin.
825 Ich war mit diesem Steine nie recht glücklich.

#### Sittah.

Bloß mit dem Steine?

#### Saladin.

fort damit! — Das thut
Mir nichts. Denn so ist alles wiederum
Geschützt.

#### Sittah.

Wie höflich man mit Königinnen
Verfahren müsse: hat mein Bruder mich
830 Zu wohl gelehrt. (Sie läßt sie stehen.)

#### Saladin.

Nimm, oder nimm sie nicht!
Ich habe keine mehr.

#### Sittah.

Wozu sie nehmen?
Schach! — Schach!

#### Saladin.

Nur weiter.

#### Sittah.

Schach! — und Schach! — und Schach! —

#### Saladin.

Und matt!

#### Sittah.

Nicht ganz! du ziehst den Springer noch
Dazwischen; oder was du machen willst.
835 Gleichviel!

#### Saladin.

Ganz recht! — Du hast gewonnen: und
Al-Hafi zahlt. — Man laß' ihn rufen! gleich! —
Du hattest, Sittah, nicht so unrecht; ich

War nicht so ganz beim Spiele; war zerstreut.
Und dann: wer giebt uns denn die glatten Steine
840 Beständig? die an nichts erinnern, nichts
Bezeichnen. Hab' ich mit dem Imam denn
Gespielt? — Doch was? Verlust will Vorwand. Nicht
Die ungeformten Steine, Sittah, sind's,
Die mich verlieren machten: deine Kunst,
845 Dein ruhiger und schneller Blick ...

### Sittah.

                  Auch so
Willst Du den Stachel des Verlusts nur stumpfen.
Genug, du warst zerstreut; und mehr als ich.

### Saladin.

Als du? Was hätte dich zerstreuet?

### Sittah.

                 Deine
Zerstreuung freilich nicht! — O Saladin,
850 Wann werden wir so fleißig wieder spielen!

### Saladin.

So spielen wir um soviel gieriger! —
Ah! weil es wieder losgeht, meinst du? — Mag's! —
Nur zu! — Ich habe nicht zuerst gezogen;
Ich hätte gern den Stillestand aufs neue
855 Verlängert; hätte meiner Sittah gern,
Gern einen guten Mann zugleich verschafft.
Und das muß Richards Bruder sein: er ist
Ja Richards Bruder.

### Sittah.

          Wenn du deinen Richard
Nur loben kannst!

### Saladin.

Wenn unserm Bruder Melek
860 Dann Richards Schwester wär' zu teile worden:
Ha! welch ein Haus zusammen! Ha, der ersten,
Der besten Häuser in der Welt das beste! —
Du hörst, ich bin mich selbst zu loben, auch
Nicht faul. Ich dünk' mich meiner Freunde wert. —
865 Das hätte Menschen geben sollen! das!

### Sittah.

Hab' ich des schönen Traums nicht gleich gelacht?
Du kennst die Christen nicht, willst sie nicht kennen.
Ihr Stolz ist: Christen sein; nicht Menschen. Denn
Selbst das, was, noch von ihrem Stifter her,
870 Mit Menschlichkeit den Aberglauben würzt,
Das lieben sie, nicht weil es menschlich ist:
Weil's Christus lehrt; weil's Christus hat gethan. —
Wohl ihnen, daß er so ein guter Mensch
Noch war! Wohl ihnen, daß sie seine Tugend
875 Auf Treu' und Glauben nehmen können! — Doch
Was Tugend? — Seine Tugend nicht; sein Name
Soll überall verbreitet werden; soll
Die Namen aller guten Menschen schänden,
Verschlingen. Um den Namen, um den Namen
880 Ist ihnen nur zu thun.

### Saladin.

Du meinst: warum
Sie sonst verlangen würden, daß auch ihr,
Auch du und Melek, Christen hießet, eh'
Als Eh'gemahl ihr Christen lieben wolltet?

### Sittah.

Ja wohl! Als wär' von Christen nur, als Christen,

885 Die Liebe zu gewärtigen, womit
Der Schöpfer Mann und Männin ausgestattet!

### Saladin.

Die Christen glauben mehr Armseligkeiten,
Als daß sie die nicht auch noch glauben könnten! —
Und gleichwohl irrst du dich. — Die Tempelherren,
890 Die Christen nicht, sind schuld: sind nicht, als Christen,
Als Tempelherren schuld. Durch die allein
Wird aus der Sache nichts. Sie wollen Akka,
Das Richards Schwester unserm Bruder Melek
Zum Brautschatz bringen müßte, schlechterdings
895 Nicht fahren lassen. Daß des Ritters Vorteil
Gefahr nicht laufe, spielen sie den Mönch,
Den albern Mönch. Und ob vielleicht im Fluge
Ein guter Streich gelänge: haben sie
Des Waffenstillestandes Ablauf kaum
900 Erwarten können. — Lustig! Nur so weiter!
Ihr Herren, nur so weiter! — Mir schon recht! —
Wär' alles sonst nur, wie es müßte.

### Sittah.

Nun?
Was irrte dich denn sonst? Was könnte sonst
Dich aus der Fassung bringen?

### Saladin.

Was von je
905 Mich immer aus der Fassung hat gebracht. —
Ich war auf Libanon, bei unserm Vater.
Er unterliegt den Sorgen noch . . .

### Sittah.

O weh!

### Saladin.

Er kann nicht durch; es klemmt sich allerorten;
Es fehlt bald da, bald dort —

### Sittah.

Was klemmt? was fehlt?

### Saladin.

910 Was sonst, als was ich kaum zu nennen würd'ge?
Was, wenn ich's habe, mir so überflüssig,
Und hab' ich's nicht, so unentbehrlich scheint. —
Wo bleibt Al-Hafi denn? Ist niemand nach
Ihm aus? — Das leidige, verwünschte Geld! —
915 Gut, Hafi, daß du kommst.

---

### Zweiter Auftritt.

#### Der Derwisch Al-Hafi. Saladin. Sittah.

### Al-Hafi.

Die Gelder aus
Ägypten sind vermutlich angelangt.
Wenn's nur fein viel ist.

### Saladin.

Hast du Nachricht?

### Al-Hafi.

Ich?
Ich nicht. Ich denke, daß ich hier sie in
Empfang soll nehmen.

### Saladin.

Zahl' an Sittah tausend
920 Dinare! (In Gedanken hin- und hergehend.)

**Al-Hafi.**

Zahl'! anstatt, empfang! O schön!
Das ist für was noch weniger als nichts. —
An Sittah? — wiederum an Sittah? Und
Verloren? — wiederum im Schach verloren? —
Da steht es noch das Spiel!

**Sittah.**

Du gönnst mir doch

925 Mein Glück?

**Al-Hafi** (das Spiel betrachtend).

Was gönnen? Wenn — Ihr wißt ja wohl.

**Sittah** (ihm winkend).

Bst! Hafi! bst!

**Al-Hafi** (noch auf das Spiel gerichtet).

Gönnt's Euch nur selber erst!

**Sittah.**

Al-Hafi! bst!

**Al-Hafi** (zu Sittah).

Die Weißen waren Euer?
Ihr bietet Schach?

**Sittah.**

Gut, daß er nichts gehört!

**Al-Hafi.**

Nun ist der Zug an ihm?

**Sittah** (ihm näher tretend).

So sage doch,
930 Daß ich mein Geld bekommen kann.

**Al-Hafi** (noch auf das Spiel geheftet).

Nun ja;
Ihr sollt's bekommen, wie Ihr's stets bekommen.

**Sittah.**

Wie? bist du toll?

**Al-Hafi.**

Das Spiel ist ja nicht aus.
Ihr habt ja nicht verloren, Saladin.

**Saladin** (kaum hinhörend).

Doch! doch! Bezahl'! bezahl'!

**Al-Hafi.**

Bezahl'! bezahl'!
935 Da steht ja Eure Königin.

**Saladin** (noch so).

Gilt nicht;
Gehört nicht mehr ins Spiel.

**Sittah.**

So mach' und sag',
Daß ich das Geld mir nur kann holen laffen!

**Al-Hafi** (noch immer in das Spiel vertieft).

Versteht sich, so wie immer. — Wenn auch schon;
Wenn auch die Königin nichts gilt: Ihr seid
940 Doch darum noch nicht matt.

**Saladin** (tritt hinzu und wirft das Spiel um).

Ich bin es; will
Es sein.

**Al-Hafi.**

Ja so! — Spiel wie Gewinst! So wie
Gewonnen, so bezahlt.

**Saladin** (zu Sittah).

Was sagt er? was?

**Sittah** (von Zeit zu Zeit dem Hafi winkend).

Du kennst ihn ja. Er sträubt sich gern; läßt gern
Sich bitten; ist wohl gar ein wenig neidisch. —

**Saladin.**

945 Auf dich doch nicht? Auf meine Schwester nicht? —
Was hör' ich, Hafi? Neidisch? du?

**Al-Hafi.**

Kann sein!
Kann sein! — Ich hätt' ihr Hirn wohl lieber selbst;
Wär' lieber selbst so gut, als sie.

**Sittah.**

Indes
Hat er doch immer richtig noch bezahlt.
950 Und wird auch heut bezahlen. Laß ihn nur! —
Geh nur, Al-Hafi, geh! Ich will das Geld
Schon holen lassen.

**Al-Hafi.**

Nein; ich spiele länger
Die Mummerei nicht mit. Er muß es doch
Einmal erfahren.

**Saladin.**

Wer? und was?

**Sittah.**

Al-Hafi!

955 Iſt dieſes dein Verſprechen? Hältſt du ſo
Mir Wort?

### Al-Hafi.

Wie konnt' ich glauben, daß es ſo
Weit gehen würde.

### Saladin.

Nun? erfahr' ich nichts?

### Sittah.

Ich bitte dich, Al-Hafi; ſei beſcheiden.

### Saladin.

Das iſt doch ſonderbar! Was könnte Sittah
960 So feierlich, ſo warm bei einem Fremden,
Bei einem Derwiſch lieber, als bei mir,
Bei ihrem Bruder ſich verbitten wollen.
Al-Hafi, nun befehl' ich. — Rede, Derwiſch!

### Sittah.

Laß eine Kleinigkeit, mein Bruder, dir
965 Nicht näher treten, als ſie würdig iſt.
Du weißt, ich habe zu verſchiednen Malen
Dieſelbe Summ' im Schach von dir gewonnen.
Und weil ich jetzt das Geld nicht nötig habe;
Weil jetzt in Hafis Kaſſe doch das Geld
970 Nicht eben allzuhäufig iſt: ſo ſind
Die Poſten ſtehn geblieben. Aber ſorgt
Nur nicht! Ich will ſie weder dir, mein Bruder,
Noch Hafi, noch der Kaſſe ſchenken.

### Al-Hafi.

Ja,
Wenn's das nur wäre! das!

### Sittah.

Und mehr dergleichen. —

975 Auch das ist in der Kasse stehn geblieben,
Was du mir einmal ausgeworfen; ist
Seit wenig Monden stehn geblieben.

**Al-Hafi.**
Noch

Nicht alles.

**Saladin.**

Noch nicht? — Wirst du reden?

**Al-Hafi.**

Seit aus Ägypten wir das Geld erwarten,
980 Hat sie . . .

**Sittah** (zu Saladin).

Wozu ihn hören?

**Al-Hafi.**
Nicht nur nichts

Bekommen . . .

**Saladin.**
Gutes Mädchen! — Auch beiher
Mit vorgeschossen. Nicht?

**Al-Hafi.**
Den ganzen Hof
Erhalten; Euern Aufwand ganz allein
Bestritten.

**Saladin.**

Ha! das, das ist meine Schwester! (sie umarmend).

**Sittah.**

985 Wer hatte, dies zu können, mich so reich
Gemacht, als du, mein Bruder?

**Al-Hafi.**
Wird schon auch

So bettelarm sie wieder machen, als
Er selber ist.

### Saladin.

Ich arm? der Bruder arm?
Wann hab' ich mehr? wann weniger gehabt? —
990 Ein Kleid, ein Schwert, ein Pferd, — und einen Gott!
Was brauch' ich mehr? Wann kann's an dem mir
fehlen?
Und doch, Al-Hafi, könnt' ich mit dir schelten.

### Sittah.

Schilt nicht, mein Bruder. Wenn ich unserm Vater
Auch seine Sorgen so erleichtern könnte!

### Saladin.

995 Ah! Ah! Nun schlägst du meine Freudigkeit
Auf einmal wieder nieder! — Mir, für mich
Fehlt nichts, und kann nichts fehlen. Aber ihm,
Ihm fehlet; und in ihm uns allen. — Sagt,
Was soll ich machen? — Aus Ägypten kommt
1000 Vielleicht noch lange nichts. Woran das liegt,
Weiß Gott. Es ist doch da noch alles ruhig. —
Abbrechen, einziehn, sparen, will ich gern,
Mir gern gefallen lassen; wenn es mich,
Bloß mich betrifft; bloß mich, und niemand sonst
1005 Darunter leidet. — Doch was kann das machen?
Ein Pferd, ein Kleid, ein Schwert, muß ich doch
haben.
Und meinem Gott ist auch nichts abzudingen.
Ihm g'nügt schon so mit wenigem genug;
Mit meinem Herzen. — Auf den Überschuß
1010 Von deiner Kasse, Hafi, hatt' ich sehr
Gerechnet.

### Al-Hafi.

Überschuß? — Sagt selber, ob

Ihr mich nicht hättet spießen, wenigstens
Mich drosseln lassen, wenn auf Überschuß
Ich von Euch wär' ergriffen worden. Ja,
1015 Auf Unterschleif! das war zu wagen.

### Saladin.

Nun,
Was machen wir denn aber? — Konntest du
Vorerst bei niemand anderm borgen, als
Bei Sittah?

### Sittah.

Würd' ich dieses Vorrecht, Bruder,
1020 Mir haben nehmen lassen? Mir von ihm?
Auch noch besteh' ich drauf. Noch bin ich auf
Dem Trocknen völlig nicht.

### Saladin.

Nur völlig nicht!
Das fehlte noch! — Geh gleich, mach' Anstalt, Hafi!
Nimm auf bei wem du kannst! und wie du kannst!
1025 Geh, borg', versprich. — Nur, Hafi, borge nicht
Bei denen, die ich reich gemacht. Denn borgen
Von diesen, möchte wiederfordern heißen.
Geh zu den Geizigsten; die werden mir
Am liebsten leihen. Denn sie wissen wohl,
1030 Wie gut ihr Geld in meinen Händen wuchert.

### Al-Hafi.

Ich kenne deren keine.

### Sittah.

Eben fällt
Mir ein, gehört zu haben, Hafi, daß
Dein Freund zurückgekommen.

**Al-Hafi** (betroffen).

freund? mein freund?

Wer wär' denn das?

**Sittah.**

Dein hochgeprief'ner Jude.

**Al-Hafi.**

Geprief'ner Jude? hoch von mir?

**Sittah.**

Dem Gott, —

1035 Mich denkt des Ausdrucks noch recht wohl, des einst

Du felber dich von ihm bedienteft, — dem

Sein Gott von allen Gütern diefer Welt

Das kleinft' und größte fo in vollem Maß

Erteilet habe. —

**Al-Hafi.**

Sagt' ich fo? — Was meint'

1040 Ich denn damit?

**Sittah.**

Das kleinfte: Reichtum. Und

Das größte: Weisheit.

**Al-Hafi.**

Wie? von einem Juden?

Von einem Juben hätt' ich das gefagt?

**Sittah.**

Das hätteft du von deinem Nathan nicht

Gefagt?

**Al-Hafi.**

Ja fo! von dem! vom Nathan! — fiel

1045 Mir der doch gar nicht bei. — Wahrhaftig? Der

Ist endlich wieder heimgekommen? Ei!
So mag's doch gar so schlecht mit ihm nicht stehn. —
Ganz recht: den nannt' einmal das Volk den Weisen!
Den Reichen auch.

### Sittah.

Den Reichen nennt es ihn
1050 Jetzt mehr als je. Die gauze Stadt erschallt,
Was er für Kostbarkeiten, was für Schätze,
Er mitgebracht.

### Al-Hafi.

Nun, ist's der Reiche wieder:
So wird's auch wohl der Weise wieder sein.

### Sittah.

Was meinst du, Hafi, wenn du diesen angingst?

### Al-Hafi.

1055 Und was bei ihm? — Doch wohl nicht borgen? — Ja,
Da kennt Ihr ihn. — Er borgen! — Seine Weisheit
Ist eben, daß er niemand borgt.

### Sittah.

Du hast
Mir sonst doch ganz ein ander Bild von ihm
Gemacht.

### Al-Hafi.

Zur Not wird er Euch Waren borgen.
1060 Geld aber, Geld? Geld nimmermehr! — Es ist
Ein Jude freilich übrigens, wie's nicht
Viel Juden giebt. Er hat Verstand; er weiß
Zu leben; spielt gut Schach. Doch zeichnet er
Im Schlechten sich nicht minder, als im Guten
1065 Von allen andern Juden aus. — Auf den,
Auf den nur rechnet nicht. — Den Armen giebt

Er zwar; und giebt vielleicht trotz Saladin.
Wenn schon nicht ganz so viel: doch ganz so gern;
Doch ganz so sonder Ansehn.   Jud' und Christ
1070 Und Muselmann und Parsi, alles ist
Ihm eins.

### Sittah.

Und so ein Mann . . .

### Saladin.

                              Wie kommt es denn,
Daß ich von diesem Manne nie gehört? . . .

### Sittah.

Der sollte Saladin nicht borgen? nicht
Dem Saladin, der nur für andre braucht,
1075 Nicht sich?

### Al-Hafi.

                Da seht nun gleich den Juden wieder;
Den ganz gemeinen Juden! — Glaubt mir's doch! —
Er ist aufs Geben Euch so eifersüchtig,
So neidisch! Jedes Lohn von Gott, das in
Der Welt gesagt wird, zög' er lieber ganz
1080 Allein. Nur darum eben leiht er keinem,
Damit er stets zu geben habe. Weil
Die Mild' ihm im Gesetz geboten; die
Gefälligkeit ihm aber nicht geboten: macht
Die Mild' ihn zu dem ungefälligsten
1085 Gesellen auf der Welt. Zwar bin ich seit
Geraumer Zeit ein wenig übern Fuß
Mit ihm gespannt; doch denkt nur nicht, daß ich
Ihm darum nicht Gerechtigkeit erzeige.
Er ist zu allem gut: bloß dazu nicht;
1090 Bloß dazu wahrlich nicht. Ich will auch gleich
Nur gehn, an andre Thüren klopfen . . . Da

Besinn' ich mich soeben eines Mohren,
Der reich und geizig ist. — Ich geh'; ich geh'.

### Sittah.

Was eilst du, Hafi?

### Saladin.

Laß ihn! Laß ihn!

---

### Dritter Auftritt.

#### Sittah. Saladin.

#### Sittah.

       Eilt
1095 Er doch, als ob er mir nur gern entkäme! —
Was heißt das? — Hat er wirklich sich in ihm
Betrogen, oder — möcht' er uns nur gern
Betrügen?

#### Saladin.

    Wie? das fragst du mich? Ich weiß
Ja kaum, von wem die Rede war; und höre
1100 Von euerm Juden, euerm Nathan, heut
Zum erstenmal.

#### Sittah.

      Ist's möglich? daß ein Mann
Dir so verborgen blieb, von dem es heißt,
Er habe Salomons und Davids Gräber
Erforscht, und wisse deren Siegel durch
1105 Ein mächtiges geheimes Wort zu lösen?
Aus ihnen bring' er dann von Zeit zu Zeit
Die unermeßlichen Reichtümer an
Den Tag, die keinen mindern Quell verrieten.

### Saladin.

Hat seinen Reichtum dieser Mann aus Gräbern,
1110 So waren's sicherlich nicht Salomons,
Nicht Davids Gräber. Narren lagen da
Begraben!

### Sittah.

Oder Bösewichter! — Auch
Ist seines Reichtums Quelle weit ergiebiger
Weit unerschöpflicher, als so ein Grab
1115 Voll Mammon.

### Saladin.

Denn er handelt; wie ich hörte.

### Sittah.

Sein Saumtier treibt auf allen Straßen, zieht
Durch alle Wüsten; seine Schiffe liegen
In allen Häfen. Das hat mir wohl eh
Al-Hafi selbst gesagt; und voll Entzücken
1120 Hinzugefügt, wie groß, wie edel dieser
Sein Freund anwende, was so klug und emsig
Er zu erwerben für zu klein nicht achte:
Hinzugefügt, wie frei von Vorurteilen
Sein Geist; sein Herz wie offen jeder Tugend,
1125 Wie eingestimmt mit jeder Schönheit sei.

### Saladin.

Und jetzt sprach Hafi doch so ungewiß,
So kalt von ihm.

### Sittah.

Kalt nun wohl nicht; verlegen.
Als halt' er's für gefährlich, ihn zu loben,
Und woll' ihn unverdient doch auch nicht tadeln. —
1130 Wie? oder wär' es wirklich so, daß selbst

Der Beſte ſeines Volkes ſeinem Volke
Nicht ganz entfliehen kann? daß wirklich ſich
Al-Hafi ſeines Freunds von dieſer Seite
Zu ſchämen hätte? — Sei dem, wie ihm wolle! —
1135 Der Jude ſei mehr oder weniger
Als Jud', iſt er nur reich: genug für uns!

#### Saladin.

Du willſt ihm aber doch das Seine mit
Gewalt nicht nehmen, Schweſter?

#### Sittah.

              Ja, was heißt
Bei dir Gewalt? Mit feu'r und Schwert? Nein, nein,
1140 Was braucht es mit den Schwachen für Gewalt,
Als ihre Schwäche? — Komm für jetzt nur mit
In meinen Haram, eine Sängerin
Zu hören, die ich geſtern erſt gekauft.
Es reift indes bei mir vielleicht ein Anſchlag,
1145 Den ich auf dieſen Nathan habe. — Komm!

---

#### Vierter Auftritt.

(Scene: vor dem Hauſe des Nathan, wo es an die Palmen ſtößt.)
Recha und Nathan kommen heraus. Zu ihnen Daja.

#### Recha.

Ihr habt Euch ſehr verweilt, mein Vater. Er
Wird kaum noch mehr zu treffen ſein.

#### Nathan.

              Nun, nun;
Wenn hier, hier untern Palmen ſchon nicht mehr:
Doch anderwärts. — Sei jetzt nur ruhig. — Sieh!
1150 Kommt dort nicht Daja auf uns zu?

### Recha.

Ihn ganz gewiß verloren haben.          Sie wird

### Nathan.

                    Auch
Wohl nicht.

### Recha.

          Sie würde sonst geschwinder kommen.

### Nathan.

Sie hat uns wohl noch nicht gesehn ...

### Recha.

                    Nun sieht
Sie uns.

### Nathan.

          Und doppelt ihre Schritte.  Sieh! —
1155 Sei doch nur ruhig! ruhig!

### Recha.

                    Wolltet Ihr
Wohl eine Tochter, die hier ruhig wäre?
Sich unbekümmert ließe, wessen Wohlthat
Ihr Leben sei? Ihr Leben, — das ihr nur
So lieb, weil sie es Euch zuerst verdanket.

### Nathan.

1160 Ich möchte dich nicht anders, als du bist:
Auch wenn ich wüßte, daß in deiner Seele
Ganz etwas anders noch sich rege.

### Recha.

                    Was,
Mein Vater?

### Nathan.

Fragst du mich? so schüchtern mich?
Was auch in deinem Innern vorgeht, ist
1165 Natur und Unschuld. Laß es keine Sorge
Dir machen. Mir, mir macht es keine. Nur
Versprich mir: wenn dein Herz vernehmlicher
Sich einst erklärt, mir seiner Wünsche keinen
Zu bergen.

### Recha.

Schon die Möglichkeit, mein Herz
1170 Euch lieber zu verhüllen, macht mich zittern.

### Nathan.

Nichts mehr hiervon! Das ein= für allemal
Ist abgethan. — Da ist ja Daja. — Nun?

### Daja.

Noch wandelt er hier untern Palmen; und
Wird gleich um jene Mauer kommen. — Seht,
1175 Da kommt er!

### Recha.

Ah! und scheinet unentschlossen,
Wohin? ob weiter? ob hinab? ob rechts?
Ob links?

### Daja.

Nein, nein; er macht den Weg ums Kloster
Gewiß noch öfter; und dann muß er hier
Vorbei. — Was gilt's?

### Recha.

Recht! recht! — Hast du ihn schon
1180 Gesprochen? Und wie ist er heut?

### Daja.

Wie immer.

### Nathan.

So macht nur, daß er euch hier nicht gewahr
Wird. Tretet mehr zurück. Geht lieber ganz
Hinein.

### Recha.

Nur einen Blick noch! — Ah! die Hecke,
Die mir ihn stiehlt.

### Daja.

Kommt! kommt! der Vater hat
1185 Ganz recht. Ihr lauft Gefahr, wenn er Euch sieht,
Daß auf der Stell' er umkehrt.

### Recha.

Ah! die Hecke!

### Nathan.

Und kommt er plötzlich dort aus ihr hervor:
So kann er anders nicht, er muß euch sehn.
Drum geht doch nur!

### Daja.

Kommt! kommt! Ich weiß ein
Fenster,
1190 Aus dem wir sie bemerken können.

### Recha.

Ja? (Beide hinein.)

### Fünfter Auftritt.

Nathan und bald darauf der Tempelherr.

#### Nathan.

Fast scheu' ich mich des Sonderlings. Fast macht
Mich seine rauhe Tugend stutzen. Daß
Ein Mensch doch einen Menschen so verlegen
Soll machen können! — Ha! er kommt. — Bei Gott!
1195 Ein Jüngling wie ein Mann. Ich mag ihn wohl
Den guten, trotz'gen Blick! den drallen Gang!
Die Schale kann nur bitter sein: der Kern
Ist's sicher nicht. — Wo sah ich doch dergleichen? —
Verzeihet, edler Franke . . .

#### Tempelherr.

Was?

#### Nathan.

Erlaubt . . .

#### Tempelherr.

1200 Was, Jude? was?

#### Nathan.

Daß ich mich untersteh',
Euch anzureden.

#### Tempelherr.

Kann ich's wehren? Doch
Nur kurz.

#### Nathan.

Verzieht, und eilet nicht so stolz,
Nicht so verächtlich einem Mann vorüber,
Den Ihr auf ewig Euch verbunden habt.

### Tempelherr.

1205 Wie das? — Ah, faſt errat' ich's. Nicht? Ihr ſeid...

### Nathan.

Ich heiße Nathan; bin des Mädchens Vater,
Das Eure Großmut aus dem Feu'r gerettet;
Und komme ...

### Tempelherr.

        Wenn zu danken: — ſpart's! Ich hab'
Um dieſe Kleinigkeit des Dankes ſchon
1210 Zu viel erdulden müſſen. — Vollends Ihr,
Ihr ſeid mir gar nichts ſchuldig. Wußt' ich denn,
Daß dieſes Mädchen Eure Tochter war?
Es iſt der Tempelherren Pflicht, dem erſten
Dem beſten beizuſpringen, deſſen Not
1215 Sie ſehn. Mein Leben war mir ohnedem
In dieſem Augenblicke läſtig. Gern,
Sehr gern ergriff ich die Gelegenheit,
Es für ein andres Leben in die Schanze
Zu ſchlagen: für ein andres — wenn's auch nur
1220 Das Leben einer Jüdin wäre.

### Nathan.

        Groß!
Groß und abſcheulich! — Doch die Wendung läßt
Sich denken. Die beſcheidne Größe flüchtet
Sich hinter das Abſcheuliche, um der
Bewundrung auszuweichen. — Aber wenn
1225 Sie ſo das Opfer der Bewunderung
Verſchmäht: was für ein Opfer denn verſchmäht
Sie minder? — Ritter, wenn Ihr hier nicht fremd,
Und nicht gefangen wäret, würd' ich Euch
So dreiſt nicht fragen. Sagt, befehlt: womit
1230 Kann man Euch dienen?

**Tempelherr.**

Ihr? Mit nichts.

**Nathan.**

Ich bin

Ein reicher Mann.

**Tempelherr.**

Der reich're Jude war
Mir nie der beff're Jude.

**Nathan.**

Dürft Ihr denn
Darum nicht nützen, was dem ungeachtet
Er Beff'res hat? nicht seinen Reichtum nützen?

**Tempelherr.**

1235 Nun gut, das will ich auch nicht ganz verreden;
Um meines Mantels willen nicht. Sobald
Der ganz und gar verschlissen; weder Stich
Noch Fetze länger halten will: komm' ich
Und borge mir bei Euch zu einem neuen,
1240 Tuch oder Geld. — Seht nicht mit eins so finster!
Noch seid Ihr sicher; noch ist's nicht so weit
Mit ihm. Ihr seht; er ist so ziemlich noch
Im stande. Nur der eine Zipfel da
Hat einen garst'gen Fleck; er ist versengt.
1245 Und das bekam er, als ich Eure Tochter
Durchs Feuer trug.

**Nathan** (der nach dem Zipfel greift und ihn betrachtet).

Es ist doch sonderbar,
Daß so ein böser Fleck, daß so ein Brandmal
Dem Mann ein beff'res Zeugnis redet, als
Sein eigner Mund. Ich möcht' ihn küssen gleich —
1250 Den Flecken! — Ah, verzeiht! — Ich that es ungern.

**Tempelherr.**

Was?

**Nathan.**

Eine Thräne fiel darauf.

**Tempelherr.**

Thut nichts!
Er hat der Tropfen mehr. — (Bald aber fängt
Mich dieser Jud' an zu verwirren.)

**Nathan.**

Wär't
Ihr wohl so gut, und schicktet Euern Mantel
1255 Auch einmal meinem Mädchen?

**Tempelherr.**

Was damit?

**Nathan.**

Auch ihren Mund an diesen Fleck zu drücken.
Denn Eure Kniee selber zu umfassen,
Wünscht sie nun wohl vergebens.

**Tempelherr.**

Aber, Jude —
Ihr heißet Nathan? — Aber, Nathan — Ihr
1260 Setzt Eure Worte sehr — sehr gut — sehr spitz —
Ich bin betreten — Allerdings — ich hätte . . .

**Nathan.**

Stellt und verstellt Euch, wie Ihr wollt. Ich find'
Auch hier Euch aus. Ihr wart zu gut, zu bieder,
Um höflicher zu sein. — Das Mädchen, ganz
1265 Gefühl; der weibliche Gesandte, ganz
Dienstfertigkeit; der Vater weit entfernt —

Ihr trugt für ihren guten Namen Sorge;
floht ihre Prüfung; floht, um nicht zu siegen.
Auch dafür dank ich Euch —

### Tempelherr.

Ich muß gestehn,
1270 Ihr wißt, wie Tempelherren denken sollten.

### Nathan.

Nur Tempelherren? sollten bloß? und bloß
Weil es die Ordensregeln so gebieten?
Ich weiß, wie gute Menschen denken; weiß,
Daß alle Länder gute Menschen tragen.

### Tempelherr.

1275 Mit Unterschied, doch hoffentlich?

### Nathan.

Ja wohl;
An Farb', an Kleidung, an Gestalt verschieden.

### Tempelherr.

Auch hier bald mehr, bald weniger, als dort.

### Nathan.

Mit diesem Unterschied ist's nicht weit her.
Der große Mann braucht überall viel Boden;
1280 Und mehrere, zu nah' gepflanzt, zerschlagen
Sich nur die Äste. Mittelgut, wie wir,
Find't sich hingegen überall in Menge.
Nur muß der eine nicht den andern mäkeln.
Nur muß der Knorr den Knubben hübsch vertragen.
1285 Nur muß ein Gipfelchen sich nicht vermessen,
Daß es allein der Erde nicht entschossen.

**Tempelherr.**

Sehr wohl gesagt! — Doch kennt Ihr auch das Volk,
Das diese Menschenmäkelei zuerst
Getrieben? Wißt Ihr, Nathan, welches Volk
1290 Zuerst das auserwählte Volk sich nannte?
Wie? wenn ich dieses Volk nun, zwar nicht haßte,
Doch wegen seines Stolzes zu verachten,
Mich nicht entbrechen könnte? seines Stolzes;
Den es auf Christ und Muselmann vererbte,
1295 Nur sein Gott sei der rechte Gott! — Ihr stutzt,
Daß ich, ein Christ, ein Tempelherr, so rede?
Wann hat, und wo die fromme Raserei,
Den bessern Gott zu haben, diesen bessern
Der ganzen Welt als besten aufzudringen,
1300 In ihrer schwärzesten Gestalt sich mehr
Gezeigt, als hier, als jetzt? Wem hier, wem jetzt
Die Schuppen nicht vom Auge fallen . . . Doch
Sei blind, wer will! — Vergeßt, was ich gesagt;
Und laßt mich! (Will gehen).

**Nathan.**

Ha! Ihr wißt nicht, wie viel fester
1305 Ich nun mich an Euch drängen werde. — Kommt,
Wir müssen, müssen Freunde sein! — Verachtet
Mein Volk so sehr Ihr wollt. Wir haben beide
Uns unser Volk nicht auserlesen. Sind
Wir unser Volk? Was heißt denn Volk?
1310 Sind Christ und Jude eher Christ und Jude
Als Mensch? Ah! wenn ich einen mehr in Euch
Gefunden hätte, dem es g'nügt, ein Mensch
Zu heißen!

**Tempelherr.**

Ja, bei Gott, das habt Ihr, Nathan!

Das habt Ihr! — Eure Hand! — Ich schäme mich
1315 Euch einen Augenblick verkannt zu haben.

### Nathan.

Und ich bin stolz darauf. Nur das Gemeine
Verkennt man selten.

### Tempelherr.

Und das Seltene
Vergißt man schwerlich. — Nathan, ja;
Wir müssen, müssen Freunde werden.

### Nathan.

Sind
1320 Es schon. — Wie wird sich meine Recha freuen! —
Und ah! welch eine heitre Ferne schließt
Sich meinen Blicken auf! — Kennt sie nur erst!

### Tempelherr.

Ich brenne vor Verlangen — Wer stürzt dort
Aus Euerm Hause? Ist's nicht ihre Daja?

### Nathan.

1325 Ja wohl. So ängstlich?

### Tempelherr.

Unsrer Recha ist
Doch nichts begegnet?

### Sechster Auftritt.

**Die Vorigen und Daja eilig.**

**Daja.**

Nathan! Nathan!

**Nathan.**

Nun?

**Daja.**

Verzeihet, edler Ritter, daß ich Euch
Muß unterbrechen.

**Nathan.**

Nun, was ist's?

**Tempelherr.**

Was ist's?

**Daja.**

Der Sultan hat geschickt. Der Sultan will
1330 Euch sprechen. Gott, der Sultan!

**Nathan.**

Mich? der Sultan?
Er wird begierig sein, zu sehen, was
Ich Neues mitgebracht. Sag' nur, es sei
Noch wenig oder gar nichts ausgepackt.

**Daja.**

Nein, nein; er will nichts sehen; will Euch sprechen,
1335 Euch in Person, und bald; sobald Ihr könnt.

**Nathan.**

Ich werde kommen. — Geh nur wieder, geh!

**Daja.**

Nehmt ja nicht übel auf, gestrenger Ritter. —
Gott, wir sind so bekümmert, was der Sultan
Doch will.

**Nathan.**

Das wird sich zeigen. Geh nur, geh!

———

## Siebenter Auftritt.

Nathan und der Tempelherr.

**Tempelherr.**

1340 So kennt Ihr ihn noch nicht? — ich meine, von
Person.

**Nathan.**

Den Saladin? Noch nicht. Ich habe
Ihn nicht vermieden, nicht gesucht zu kennen.
Der allgemeine Ruf sprach viel zu gut
Von ihm, daß ich nicht lieber glauben wollte,
1345 Als sehn. Doch nun, — wenn anders dem so ist, —
Hat er durch Sparung Eures Lebens ...

**Tempelherr.**

Ja;

Dem allerdings ist so. Das Leben, das
Ich leb', ist sein Geschenk.

**Nathan.**

Durch das er mir
Ein doppelt, dreifach Leben schenkte. Dies
1350 Hat alles zwischen uns verändert; hat
Mit eins ein Seil mir umgeworfen, das
Mich seinem Dienst auf ewig fesselt. Kaum,

Und kaum, kann ich es nun erwarten, was
Er mir zuerst befehlen wird.  Ich bin
1355 Bereit zu allem; bin bereit ihm zu
Gestehn, daß ich es Euertwegen bin.

### Tempelherr.

Noch hab' ich selber ihm nicht danken können:
So oft ich auch ihm in den Weg getreten.
Der Eindruck, den ich auf ihn machte, kam
1360 So schnell, als schnell er wiederum verschwunden.
Wer weiß, ob er sich meiner gar erinnert.
Und dennoch muß er, einmal wenigstens,
Sich meiner noch erinnern, um mein Schicksal
Ganz zu entscheiden.  Nicht genug, daß ich
1365 Auf sein Geheiß noch bin, m i t seinem Willen
Noch leb': ich muß nun auch von ihm erwarten,
N a c h wessen Willen ich zu leben habe.

### Nathan.

Nicht anders; um so mehr will ich nicht säumen. —
Es fällt vielleicht ein Wort, das mir, auf Euch
1370 Zu kommen, Anlaß giebt. — Erlaubt, verzeiht —
Ich eile — Wann, wann aber sehn wir Euch
Bei uns?

### Tempelherr.

Sobald ich darf.

### Nathan.

Sobald Ihr wollt.

### Tempelherr.

Noch heut.

### Nathan.

Und Euer Name? — muß ich bitten.

**Tempelherr.**

Mein Name war — ist Kurt von Stauffen. — Kurt!

**Nathan.**

1375 Von Stauffen? — Stauffen? — Stauffen?

**Tempelherr.**
Warum fällt

Euch das so auf?

**Nathan.**
Von Stauffen? — Des Geschlechts

Sind wohl schon mehrere . . .

**Tempelherr.**
O ja! hier waren,

Hier faulen des Geschlechts schon mehrere.
Mein Oheim selbst, — mein Vater will ich sagen, —
1380 Doch warum schärft sich Euer Blick auf mich
Je mehr und mehr?

**Nathan.**
O nichts! o nichts! Wie kann

Ich Euch zu sehn ermüden?

**Tempelherr.**
Drum verlaß'

Ich Euch zuerst. Der Blick des Forschers fand
Nicht selten mehr, als er zu finden wünschte.
1385 Ich fürcht' ihn, Nathan. Laßt die Zeit allmählich,
Und nicht die Neugier, unsre Kundschaft machen.
(Er geht).

**Nathan** (der ihm mit Erstaunen nachsieht).

„Der Forscher fand nicht selten mehr, als er
„Zu finden wünschte." — Ist es doch, als ob

In meiner Seel' er lese! — Wahrlich ja;
1390 Das könnt' auch mir begegnen. — Nicht allein
Wolfs Wuchs, Wolfs Gang: auch seine Stimme. So,
Vollkommen so, warf Wolf sogar den Kopf;
Trug Wolf sogar das Schwert im Arm; strich Wolf
Sogar die Augenbrauen mit der Hand,
1395 Gleichsam das Feuer seines Blicks zu bergen. —
Wie solche tiefgeprägte Bilder doch
Zuzeiten in uns schlafen können, bis
Ein Wort, ein Laut sie weckt. — Von Stauffen! —
Ganz recht, ganz recht; Filnek und Stauffen. —
1400 Ich will das bald genauer wissen; bald.
Nur erst zum Saladin. — Doch wie? lauscht dort
Nicht Daja? — Nun so komm nur näher, Daja.

---

## Achter Auftritt.

### Daja. Nathan.

#### Nathan.

Was gilt's? nun drückt's euch beiden schon das Herz,
Noch ganz was anders zu erfahren, als
1405 Was Saladin mir will.

#### Daja.

Verdenkt Ihr's ihr?
Ihr fingt soeben an, vertraulicher
Mit ihm zu sprechen: als des Sultans Botschaft
Uns von dem Fenster scheuchte.

#### Nathan.

Nun so sag'
Ihr nur, daß sie ihn jeden Augenblick
1410 Erwarten darf.

#### Daja.

Gewiß? gewiß?

### Nathan.

Ich kann
Mich doch auf dich verlassen, Daja? Sei
Auf deiner Hut; ich bitte dich. Es soll
Dich nicht gereuen. Dein Gewissen selbst
Soll seine Rechnung dabei finden. Nur
1415 Verdirb mir nichts in meinem Plane. Nur
Erzähl' und frage mit Bescheidenheit,
Mit Rückhalt ...

### Daja.

Daß Ihr doch noch erst, so was
Erinnern könnt! — Ich geh'; geht Ihr nur auch.
Denn seht! ich glaube gar, da kommt vom Sultan
1420 Ein zweiter Bot', Al-Hafi, Euer Derwisch. (Geht ab.)

---

### Neunter Auftritt.

#### Nathan. Al-Hafi.

### Al-Hafi.

Ha! ha! zu Euch wollt' ich nun eben wieder.

### Nathan.

Ist's denn so eilig? Was verlangt er denn
Von mir?

### Al-Hafi.

Wer?

### Nathan.

Saladin. — Ich komm', ich komme.

### Al-Hafi.

Zu wem? Zum Saladin?

### Nathan.

Schickt Saladin
1425 Dich nicht?

### Al-Hafi.

Mich? nein.    Hat er denn ſchon geſchickt?

### Nathan.

Ja freilich hat er.

### Al-Hafi.

Nun, ſo iſt es richtig.

### Nathan.

Was? was iſt richtig?

### Al-Hafi.

Daß . . . ich bin nicht ſchuld;
Gott weiß, ich bin nicht ſchuld. — Was hab' ich nicht
Von Euch geſagt, gelogen, um es abzuwenden!

### Nathan.

1430 Was abzuwenden? Was iſt richtig?

### Al-Hafi.

Daß
Nun Ihr ſein Defterdar geworden.   Ich
Bedaur' Euch.   Doch mit anſehn will ich's nicht.
Ich geh' von Stund' an; geh', Ihr habt es ſchon
Gehört, wohin; und wißt den Weg. — Habt Ihr
1435 Des Wegs was zu beſtellen, ſagt: ich bin
Zu Dienſten.   Freilich muß es mehr nicht ſein,
Als was ein Nackter mit ſich ſchleppen kann.
Ich geh', ſagt bald.

### Nathan.

Beſinn dich doch, Al-Hafi.
Beſinn dich, daß ich noch von gar nichts weiß.
1440 Was plauderſt du denn da?

**Al-Hafi.**

Ihr bringt sie doch
Gleich mit, die Beutel?

**Nathan.**

Beutel?

**Al-Hafi.**

Nun, das Geld,
Das Ihr dem Saladin vorschießen sollt.

**Nathan.**

Und weiter ist es nichts?

**Al-Hafi.**

Ich sollt' es wohl
Mit ansehn, wie er Euch von Tag zu Tag
1445 Aushöhlen wird bis auf die Zehen? Sollt'
Es wohl mit ansehn, daß Verschwendung aus
Der weisen Milde sonst nie leeren Scheuern
So lange borgt, und borgt, und borgt, bis auch
Die armen eingebornen Mäuschen drin
1450 Verhungern? — Bildet Ihr vielleicht Euch ein,
Wer Euers Gelds bedürftig sei, der werde
Doch Euerm Rate wohl auch folgen? — Ja;
Er Rate folgen! Wann hat Saladin
Sich raten lassen? — Denkt nur, Nathan, was
1455 Mir eben jetzt mit ihm begegnet.

**Nathan.**

Nun?

**Al-Hafi.**

Da komm' ich zu ihm, eben daß er Schach
Gespielt mit seiner Schwester. Sittah spielt

Nicht übel; und das Spiel, das Saladin
Verloren glaubte, schon gegeben hatte,
1460 Das stand noch ganz so da.    Ich seh' Euch hin,
Und sehe, daß das Spiel noch lange nicht
Verloren.

#### Nathan.

Ei! das war für dich ein Fund!

#### Al-Hafi.

Er durfte mit dem König an den Bauer
Nur rücken, auf ihr Schach — wenn ich's Euch gleich
1465 Nur zeigen könnte!

#### Nathan.

O ich traue dir!

#### Al-Hafi.

Denn so bekam der Roche Feld: und sie
War hin. — Das alles will ich ihm nun weisen
Und ruf' ihn. — Denkt! ...

#### Nathan.

Er ist nicht deiner Meinung?

#### Al-Hafi.

Er hört mich gar nicht an, und wirft verächtlich
1470 Das ganze Spiel in Klumpen.

#### Nathan.

Ist das möglich?

#### Al-Hafi.

Und sagt: er wolle matt nun einmal sein;
Er wolle! Heißt das spielen?

#### Nathan.

Schwerlich wohl;
Heißt mit dem Spiele spielen.

**Al-Hafi.**

Gleichwohl galt
Es keine taube Nuß.

**Nathan.**

Geld hin, Geld her!
1475 Das ist das wenigste. Allein dich gar
Nicht anzuhören! über einen Punkt
Von solcher Wichtigkeit dich nicht einmal
Zu hören! Deinen Adlerblick nicht zu
Bewundern! das, das schreit um Rache; nicht?

**Al-Hafi.**

1480 Ach was? Ich sag' Euch das nur so, damit
Ihr sehen könnt, was für ein Kopf er ist.
Kurz, ich, ich halt's mit ihm nicht länger aus.
Da lauf' ich nun bei allen schmutz'gen Mohren
Herum, und frage, wer ihm borgen will.
1485 Ich, der ich nie für mich gebettelt habe,
Soll nun für andre borgen. Borgen ist
Viel besser nicht als betteln: so wie leihen,
Auf Wucher leihen, nicht viel besser ist,
Als stehlen. Unter meinen Ghebern, an
1490 Dem Ganges, brauch' ich beides nicht, und brauche
Das Werkzeug beider nicht zu sein. Am Ganges,
Am Ganges nur giebt's Menschen. Hier seid Ihr
Der einzige, der noch so würdig wäre,
Daß er am Ganges lebte. — Wollt Ihr mit? —
1495 Laßt ihm mit eins den Plunder ganz im Stiche,
Um den es ihm zu thun. Er bringt Euch nach
Und nach doch drum. So wär' die Plackerei
Auf einmal aus. Ich schaff' Euch einen Delk.
Kommt! kommt!

**Nathan.**

Ich dächte zwar, das blieb' uns ja

1500 Noch immer übrig. Doch, Al-Hafi, will
Ich's überlegen. Warte...

#### Al-Hafi.

Überlegen?
Nein, so was überlegt sich nicht.

#### Nathan.

Nur bis
Ich von dem Sultan wiederkomme; bis
Ich Abschied erst ...

#### Al-Hafi.

Wer überlegt, der sucht
1505 Bewegungsgründe, nicht zu dürfen. Wer
Sich Knall und Fall, ihm selbst zu leben, nicht
Entschließen kann, der lebet andrer Sklav'
Auf immer. — Wie Ihr wollt! — Lebt wohl! wie's Euch
Wohl dünkt. — Mein Weg liegt dort; und Eurer da.

#### Nathan.

1510 Al-Hafi! Du wirst selbst doch erst das Deine
Berichtigen?

#### Al-Hafi.

Ach Possen! Der Bestand
Von meiner Kaff' ist nicht des Zählens wert;
Und meine Rechnung bürgt — Ihr oder Sittah.
Lebt wohl! (Ab.)

#### Nathan (ihm nachsehend).

Die bürg' ich! — Wilder, guter, edler —
1515 Wie nenn' ich ihn? — Der wahre Bettler ist
Doch einzig und allein der wahre König!

(Von einer andern Seite ab.)

# Dritter Aufzug.

## Erster Auftritt.

(Scene: in Nathans Hause.)

Recha und Daja.

### Recha.

Wie, Daja, drückte sich mein Vater aus?
„Ich dürf' ihn jeden Augenblick erwarten?"
Das klingt — nicht wahr? — als ob er noch so bald
1520 Erscheinen werde. — Wie viel Augenblicke
Sind aber schon vorbei! — Ah nun: wer denkt
An die verflossenen? — Ich will allein
In jedem nächsten Augenblicke leben.
Er wird doch einmal kommen, der ihn bringt.

### Daja.

1525 O der verwünschten Botschaft von dem Sultan!
Denn Nathan hätte sicher ohne sie
Ihn gleich mit hergebracht.

### Recha.

　　　　　　　　Und wenn er nun
Gekommen dieser Augenblick; wenn dann
Nun meiner Wünsche wärmster, innigster
1530 Erfüllet ist: was dann? — was dann?

### Daja.

　　　　　　　　Was dann?
Dann hoff' ich, daß auch meiner Wünsche wärmster
Soll in Erfüllung gehen.

### Recha.

　　　　Was wird dann

In meiner Brust an dessen Stelle treten,
Die schon verlernt, ohn' einen herrschenden
1535 Wunsch aller Wünsche sich zu dehnen? — Nichts?
Ah, ich erschrecke! ...

### Daja.

Mein, mein Wunsch wird dann
An des erfüllten Stelle treten; meiner.
Mein Wunsch, dich in Europa, dich in Händen
Zu wissen, welche deiner würdig sind.

### Recha.

1540 Du irrst. — Was diesen Wunsch zu deinem macht,
Das nämliche verhindert, daß er meiner
Je werden kann.    Dich zieht dein Vaterland:
Und meines, meines sollte mich nicht halten?
Ein Bild der Deinen, das in Deiner Seele
1545 Noch nicht verloschen, sollte mehr vermögen,
Als die ich sehn, und greifen kann, und hören,
Die Meinen?

### Daja.

Sperre dich, so viel du willst!
Des Himmels Wege sind des Himmels Wege.
Und wenn es nun dein Retter selber wäre,
1550 Durch den sein Gott, für den er kämpft, dich in
Das Land, dich zu dem Volke führen wollte,
Für welche du geboren wurdest?

### Recha.

Daja!
Was sprichst du da nun wieder, liebe Daja!
Du hast doch wahrlich deine sonderbaren
1555 Begriffe! „Sein, sein Gott! für den er kämpft!“
Wem eignet Gott? was ist das für ein Gott,
Der einem Menschen eignet? der für sich

Muß kämpfen laffen? — Und wie weiß
Man denn, für welchen Erdkloß man geboren,
1560 Wenn man's für den nicht ift, auf welchem man
Geboren? — Wenn mein Vater dich fo hörte! —
Was that er dir, mir immer nur mein Glück
So weit von ihm als möglich vorzufpiegeln?
Was that er dir, den Samen der Vernunft,
1565 Den er fo rein in meine Seele ftreute,
Mit deines Landes Unkraut oder Blumen
So gern zu mifchen? — Liebe, liebe Daja,
Er will nun deine bunten Blumen nicht
Auf meinem Boden! — Und ich muß dir fagen,
1570 Ich felber fühle meinen Boden, wenn
Sie noch fo fchön ihn kleiden, fo entkräftet,
So ausgezehrt durch deine Blumen; fühle
In ihrem Dufte, fauerfüßem Dufte,
Mich fo betäubt, fo fchwindelnd! — Dein Gehirn
1575 Ift deffen mehr gewohnt. Ich tadle drum
Die ftärkern Nerven nicht, die ihn vertragen.
Nur fchlägt er mir nicht zu; und fchon dein Engel,
Wie wenig fehlte, daß er mich zur Närrin
Gemacht? — Noch fchäm' ich mich vor meinem Vater
1580 Der Poffe!

**Daja.**

Poffe! — Als ob der Verftand
Nur hier zu Haufe wäre! Poffe! Poffe!
Wenn ich nur reden dürfte!

**Recha.**

Darfft du nicht?
Wann war ich nicht ganz Ohr, fo oft es dir
Gefiel, von deinen Glaubenshelden mich
1585 Zu unterhalten? Hab' ich ihren Thaten
Nicht ftets Bewunderung; und ihren Leiden
Nicht immer Thränen gern gezollt? Ihr Glaube

Schien freilich mir das Heldenmäßigste
An ihnen nie. Doch so viel tröstender
1590 War mir die Lehre, daß Ergebenheit
In Gott von unserm Wähnen über Gott
So ganz und gar nicht abhängt. — Liebe Daja,
Das hat mein Vater uns so oft gesagt;
Darüber haft du selbst mit ihm so oft
1595 Dich einverstanden: warum untergräbst
Du denn allein, was du mit ihm zugleich
Gebauet? — Liebe Daja, das ist kein
Gespräch, womit wir unserm Freund am besten
Entgegensehn. Für mich zwar, ja! Denn mir,
1600 Mir liegt daran unendlich, ob auch er...
Horch, Daja! — Kommt es nicht an unsre Thüre?
Wenn er es wäre! Horch!

---

### Zweiter Auftritt.

Recha, Daja und der Tempelherr, dem jemand von außen die
Thüre öffnet mit den Worten:

Nur hier herein!

#### Recha
(fährt zusammen, faßt sich, und will ihm zu Füßen fallen).

Er ist's! — Mein Retter, ah!

#### Tempelherr.

Dies zu vermeiden
Erschien ich bloß so spät: und doch —

#### Recha.

Ich will
1605 Ja zu den Füßen dieses stolzen Mannes
Nur Gott noch einmal danken; nicht dem Manne.

Der Mann will keinen Dank; will ihn so wenig
Als ihn der Waffereimer will, der bei
Dem Löschen so geschäftig sich erwiesen.
1610 Der ließ sich füllen, ließ sich leeren, mir
Nichts, dir nichts: also auch der Mann.    Auch der
Ward nur so in die Glut hineingestoßen;
Da fiel ich ungefähr ihm in den Arm;
Da blieb ich ungefähr, so wie ein Funken
1615 Auf seinem Mantel, ihm in seinen Armen;
Bis wiederum, ich weiß nicht was, uns beide
Herausschmiß aus der Glut. — Was giebt es da
Zu danken? — In Europa treibt der Wein
Zu noch weit andern Thaten. — Tempelherren,
1620 Die müssen einmal nun so handeln; müssen
Wie etwas beffer zugelernte Hunde,
Sowohl aus Feuer, als aus Waffer holen.

### Tempelherr
(der sie mit Erstaunen und Unruhe die ganze Zeit über betrachtet).

O Daja, Daja! Wenn in Augenblicken
Des Kummers und der Galle, meine Laune
1625 Dich übel anließ, warum jede Thorheit,
Die meiner Zung' entfuhr, ihr hinterbringen?
Das hieß sich zu empfindlich rächen, Daja!
Doch wenn du nur von nun an, beffer mich
Bei ihr vertreten willst.

### Daja.
          Ich denke, Ritter,
1630 Ich denke nicht, daß diese kleinen Stacheln,
Ihr an das Herz geworfen, Euch da sehr
Geschadet haben.

### Recha.
Wie? Ihr hattet Kummer?

Und wart mit Enerm Kummer geiziger
Als Euerm Leben?

### Tempelherr.

Gutes, holdes Kind! —
1635 Wie ist doch meine Seele zwischen Auge
Und Ohr geteilt! — Das war das Mädchen nicht,
Nein, nein, das war es nicht, das aus dem Feuer
Ich holte. — Denn wer hätte die gekannt,
Und aus dem Feuer nicht geholt? Wer hätte
1640 Auf mich gewartet? — Zwar — verstellt — der Schreck.

(Pause, unter der er, in Anschauung ihrer, sich wie verliert.)

### Recha.

Ich aber find' Euch noch den nämlichen. —

(Dergleichen; bis sie fortfährt, um ihn in seinem Anstaunen
zu unterbrechen.)

Nun, Ritter, sagt uns doch, wo Ihr so lange
Gewesen? — Fast dürft' ich auch fragen: wo
Ihr jetzo seid?

### Tempelherr.

Ich bin, — wo ich vielleicht
1645 Nicht sollte sein. —

### Recha.

Wo Ihr gewesen? — Auch
Wo Ihr vielleicht nicht solltet sein gewesen?
Das ist nicht gut.

### Tempelherr.

Auf — auf — wie heißt der Berg?
Auf Sinai.

### Recha.

Auf Sinai? — Ah schön!

Nun kann ich zuverlässig doch einmal
1650 Erfahren, ob es wahr ...

### Tempelherr.

Was? was? Ob's wahr,
Daß noch daselbst der Ort zu sehn, wo Moses
Vor Gott gestanden, als ...

### Recha.

Nun das wohl nicht.
Denn wo er stand, stand er vor Gott. Und davon
Ist mir zur G'nüge schon bekannt. — Ob's wahr,
1655 Möcht' ich nur gern von Euch erfahren, daß —
Daß es bei weitem nicht so mühsam sei,
Auf diesen Berg hinauf zu steigen, als
Herab? — Denn seht; so viel ich Berge noch
Gestiegen bin, war's just das Gegenteil. —
1660 Nun, Ritter? — Was? — Ihr kehrt Euch von mir ab?
Wollt mich nicht sehn?

### Tempelherr.

Weil ich Euch hören will.

### Recha.

Weil Ihr mich nicht wollt merken lassen, daß
Ihr meiner Einfalt lächelt; daß Ihr lächelt,
Wie ich Euch doch so gar nichts Wichtigers
1665 Von diesem heiligen Berg aller Berge
Zu fragen weiß? Nicht wahr?

### Tempelherr.

So muß
Ich doch Euch wieder in die Augen sehn. —
Was? Nun schlagt Ihr sie nieder? nun verbeißt
Das Lächeln Ihr? wie ich noch erst in Mienen,

1670 In zweifelhaften Mienen lesen will,
Was ich so deutlich hör', Ihr so vernehmlich
Mir sagt — verschweigt? — Ah Recha! Recha! Wie
Hat er so wahr gesagt: „Kennt sie nur erst!"

##### Recha.

Wer hat? — von wem? — Euch das gesagt?

##### Tempelherr.

„Kennt sie
1675 Nur erst!" hat Euer Vater mir gesagt;
Von Euch gesagt.

##### Daja.

Und ich nicht etwa auch?
Ich denn nicht auch?

##### Tempelherr.

Allein wo ist er denn?
Wo ist denn Euer Vater? Ist er noch
Beim Sultan?

##### Recha.

Ohne Zweifel.

##### Tempelherr.

Noch, noch da? —
1680 O mich Vergeßlichen! Nein, nein; da ist
Er schwerlich mehr. — Er wird dort unten bei
Dem Kloster meiner warten; ganz gewiß.
So red'ten, mein' ich, wir es ab. Erlaubt!
Ich geh', ich hol' ihn ...

##### Daja.

Das ist meine Sache.
1685 Bleibt, Ritter, bleibt. Ich bring' ihn unverzüglich.

##### Tempelherr.

Nicht so, nicht so! Er sieht mir selbst entgegen;

Nicht Euch. Dazu, er könnte leicht ... wer weiß? ...
Er könnte bei dem Sultan leicht, ... Ihr kennt
Den Sultan nicht! ... leicht in Verlegenheit
1690 Gekommen sein. — Glaubt mir; es hat Gefahr,
Wenn ich nicht geh'.

Recha.

Gefahr? was für Gefahr?

Tempelherr.

Gefahr für mich, für Euch, für ihn: wenn ich
Nicht schleunig, schleunig geh'.     (Ab.)

Dritter Auftritt.

Recha und Daja.

Recha.

Was ist das, Daja? —
So schnell? — Was kommt ihm an? Was fiel ihm auf?
1695 Was jagt ihn?

Daja.

Laßt nur, laßt.   Ich denk', es ist
Kein schlimmes Zeichen.

Recha.

Zeichen? und wovon?

Daja.

Daß etwas vorgeht innerhalb.   Es kocht,
Und soll nicht überkochen.   Laßt ihn nur.
Nun ist's an Euch.

Recha.

Was ist an mir? Du wirst,
1700 Wie er, mir unbegreiflich.

**Daja.**

Bald nun könnt
Ihr ihm die Unruh' all vergelten, die
Er Euch gemacht hat. Seid nur aber auch
Nicht allzu streng, nicht allzu rachbegierig.

**Recha.**

Wovon du sprichst, das magst du selber wissen.

**Daja.**

1705 Und seid denn Ihr bereits so ruhig wieder?

**Recha.**

Das bin ich; ja das bin ich . . .

**Daja.**

Wenigstens
Gesteht, daß Ihr Euch seiner Unruh' freut;
Und seiner Unruh' danket, was Ihr jetzt
Von Ruh' genießt.

**Recha.**

Mir völlig unbewußt!
1710 Denn was ich höchstens dir gestehen könnte,
Wär', daß es mich — mich selbst befremdet, wie
Auf einen solchen Sturm in meinem Herzen
So eine Stille plötzlich folgen können.
Sein voller Anblick, sein Gespräch, sein Thun
1715 Hat mich . . .

**Daja.**

Gesättigt schon?

**Recha.**

Gesättigt, will
Ich nun nicht sagen; nein — bei weitem nicht —

**Daja.**

Den heißen Hunger nur gestillt.

**Recha.**

Nun ja;
Wenn du so willst.

**Daja.**

Ich eben nicht.

**Recha.**

Er wird
Mir ewig wert; mir ewig werter, als
1720 Mein Leben bleiben: wenu auch schon mein Puls
Nicht mehr bei seinem bloßen Namen wechselt;
Nicht mehr mein Herz, so oft ich an ihn denke,
Geschwinder, stärker schlägt.—Was schwatz' ich? Komm,
Komm, liebe Daja, wieder an das Fenster,
1725 Das auf die Palmen sieht.

**Daja.**

So ist er doch
Wohl noch nicht ganz gestillt, der heiße Hunger.

**Recha.**

Nun werd' ich auch die Palmen wieder sehn:
Nicht ihn bloß untern Palmen.

**Daja.**

Diese Kälte
Beginnt auch wohl ein neues Fieber nur.

**Recha.**

1730 Was Kält'? Ich bin nicht kalt. Ich sehe wahrlich
Nicht minder gern, was ich mit Ruhe sehe.

## Vierter Auftritt.

(Scene: Ein Audienzsaal in dem Palaste des Saladin.)
Saladin und Sittah.

**Saladin** (im Hereintreten, gegen die Thüre).

Hier bringt den Juden her, sobald er kommt.
Er scheint sich eben nicht zu übereilen.

**Sittah.**

Er war auch wohl nicht bei der Hand; nicht gleich
1735 Zu finden.

**Saladin.**

Schwester! Schwester!

**Sittah.**

Thust du doch
Als stünde dir ein Treffen vor.

**Saladin.**

Und das
Mit Waffen, die ich nicht gelernt zu führen.
Ich soll mich stellen; soll besorgen lassen;
Soll fallen legen; soll auf Glatteis führen.
1740 Wann hätt' ich das gekonnt? Wo hätt' ich das
Gelernt? — Und soll das alles, ah, wozu?
Wozu? — Um Geld zu fischen; Geld! — Um Geld,
Geld einem Juden abzubangen; Geld!
Zu solchen kleinen Listen wär' ich endlich
1745 Gebracht, der Kleinigkeiten kleinste mir
Zu schaffen?

**Sittah.**

Jede Kleinigkeit, zu sehr
Verschmäht, die rächt sich, Bruder.

**Saladin.**

Leider wahr. —

Und wenn nun dieſer Jude gar der gute,
Vernünft'ge Mann iſt, wie der Derwiſch dir
1750 Ihn ehedem beſchrieben?

**Sittah.**

O nun dann!
Was hat es dann für Not! Die Schlinge liegt
Ja nur dem geizigen, beſorglichen,
Furchtſamen Juden: nicht dem guten, nicht
Dem weiſen Manne.    Dieſer iſt ja ſo
1755 Schon unſer, ohne Schlinge.    Das Vergnügen
Zu hören, wie ein ſolcher Mann ſich ausred't;
Mit welcher dreiſten Stärk' entweder, er
Die Stricke kurz zerreißet; oder auch
Mit welcher ſchlauen Vorſicht er die Netze
1760 Vorbei ſich windet: dies Vergnügen haſt
Du obendrein.

**Saladin.**

Nun, das iſt wahr.    Gewiß;
Ich freue mich darauf.

**Sittah.**

So kann dich ja
Auch weiter nichts verlegen machen.    Denn
Iſt's einer aus der Menge bloß; iſt's bloß
1765 Ein Jude, wie ein Jude: gegen den
Wirſt du dich doch nicht ſchämen, ſo zu ſcheinen
Wie er die Menſchen all ſich denkt? Vielmehr;
Wer ſich ihm beſſer zeigt, der zeigt ſich ihm
Als Geck, als Narr.

**Saladin.**

So muß ich ja wohl gar
1770 Schlecht handeln, daß von mir der Schlechte nicht
Schlecht denke?

### Sittah.

Traun! wenn du schlecht handeln nennst,
Ein jedes Ding nach seiner Art zu brauchen.

### Saladin.

Was hätt' ein Weiberkopf erdacht, das er
Nicht zu beschönen wüßte!

### Sittah.

Zu beschönen!

### Saladin.

1775 Das feine, spitze Ding, besorg' ich nur,
In meiner plumpen Hand zerbricht! — So was
Will ausgeführt sein, wie's erfunden ist:
Mit aller Pfiffigkeit, Gewandtheit. — Doch,
Mag's doch nur, mag's! Ich tanze, wie ich kann;
1780 Und könnt' es freilich, lieber — schlechter noch
Als besser.

### Sittah.

Trau' dir auch nur nicht zu wenig!
Ich stehe dir für dich! Wenn du nur willst. —
Daß uns die Männer deinesgleichen doch
So gern bereden möchten, nur ihr Schwert,
1785 Ihr Schwert nur habe sie so weit gebracht.
Der Löwe schämt sich freilich, wenn er mit
Dem Fuchse jagt: — des Fuchses, nicht der List.

### Saladin.

Und daß die Weiber doch so gern den Mann
Zu sich herunter hätten! — Geh nur, geh! —
1790 Ich glaube meine Lektion zu können.

### Sittah.

Was? ich soll gehn?

**Saladin.**

Du wolltest doch nicht bleiben?

**Sittah.**

Wenn auch nicht bleiben ... im Gesicht euch bleiben —
Doch hier im Nebenzimmer —

**Saladin.**

Da zu horchen?
Auch das nicht, Schwester; wenn ich soll bestehn. —
1795 Fort, fort! der Vorhang rauscht; er kommt! — doch daß
Du ja nicht da verweilst! Ich sehe nach.

(Indem sie sich durch die eine Thür entfernt, tritt Nathan zu der
andern herein; und Saladin hat sich gesetzt.)

---

### Fünfter Auftritt.

Saladin und Nathan.

**Saladin.**

Tritt näher, Jude! — Näher! — Nur ganz her! —
Nur ohne Furcht!

**Nathan.**

Die bleibe deinem Feinde!

**Saladin.**

Du nennst dich Nathan?

**Nathan.**

Ja.

**Saladin.**

Den weisen Nathan?

**Nathan.**

1800 Nein.

Saladin.

Wohl! nennst du dich nicht; nennt dich das Volk.

Nathan.

Kann sein; das Volk!

Saladin.

Du glaubst doch nicht, daß ich
Verächtlich von des Volkes Stimme denke? —
Ich habe längst gewünscht, den Mann zu kennen,
Den es den Weisen nennt.

Nathan.

Und wenn es ihn
1805 Zum Spott so nennte? Wenn dem Volke weise
Nichts weiter wär' als klug? und klug nur der,
Der sich auf seinen Vorteil gut versteht?

Saladin.

Auf seinen wahren Vorteil, meinst du doch?

Nathan.

Dann freilich wär' der Eigennützigste
1810 Der Klügste. Dann wär' freilich klug und weise
Nur eins.

Saladin.

Ich höre dich erweisen, was
Du widersprechen willst. — Des Menschen wahre
Vorteile, die das Volk nicht kennt, kennst du.
Hast du zu kennen wenigstens gesucht;
1815 Hast drüber nachgedacht: das auch allein
Macht schon den Weisen.

Nathan.

Der sich jeder dünkt
Zu sein.

**Saladin.**

Nun der Bescheidenheit genug!
Denn sie nur immerdar zu hören, wo
Man trockene Vernunst erwartet, ekelt. (Er springt auf.)
1820 Laß uns zur Sache kommen! Aber, aber
Aufrichtig, Jud', aufrichtig!

**Nathan.**

Sultan, ich
Will sicherlich dich so bedienen, daß
Ich deiner fernern Kundschaft würdig bleibe.

**Saladin.**

Bedienen? wie?

**Nathan.**

Du sollst das Beste haben
1825 Von allem; sollst es um den billigsten
Preis haben.

**Saladin.**

Wovon sprichst du? doch wohl nicht
Von deinen Waren? — Schachern wird mit dir
Schon meine Schwester. (Das der Horcherin!) —
Ich habe mit dem Kaufmann nichts zu thun.

**Nathan.**

1830 So wirst du ohne Zweifel wissen wollen,
Was ich auf meinem Wege von dem Feinde,
Der allerdings sich wieder reget, etwa
Bemerkt, getroffen? — Wenn ich unverhohlen ...

**Saladin.**

Auch darauf bin ich eben nicht mit dir
1835 Gesteuert. Davon weiß ich schon, so viel
Ich nötig habe. — Kurz; —

**Nathan.**

Gebiete, Sultan.

### Saladin.

Ich heische deinen Unterricht in ganz
Was anderm; ganz was anderm. — Da du nun
So weise bist: so sage mir doch einmal —
1840 Was für ein Glaube, was für ein Gesetz
Hat dir am meisten eingeleuchtet?

### Nathan.

                           Sultan,
Ich bin ein Jud'.

### Saladin.

           Und ich ein Muselmann.
Der Christ ist zwischen uns. — Von diesen drei
Religionen kann doch eine nur
1845 Die wahre sein. — Ein Mann, wie du, bleibt da
Nicht stehen, wo der Zufall der Geburt
Ihn hingeworfen: oder wenn er bleibt,
Bleibt er aus Einsicht, Gründen, Wahl des Bessern.
Wohlan! so teile deine Einsicht mir
1850 Denn mit.  Laß mich die Gründe hören, denen
Ich selber nachzugrübeln, nicht die Zeit
Gehabt.  Laß mich die Wahl, die diese Gründe
Bestimmt, — versteht sich, im Vertrauen — wissen,
Damit ich sie zu meiner mache. — Wie?
1855 Du stutzest? wägst mich mit dem Auge? — Kann
Wohl sein, daß ich der erste Sultan bin,
Der eine solche Grille hat; die mich
Doch eines Sultans eben nicht so ganz
Unwürdig dünkt. — Nicht wahr? — So rede doch!
1860 Sprich! — Oder willst du einen Augenblick,
Dich zu bedenken? Gut; ich geb' ihn dir. —
(Ob sie wohl horcht? Ich will sie doch belauschen;
Will hören, ob ich's recht gemacht. —) Denk' nach!
Geschwind denk' nach! Ich säume nicht, zurück
1865 Zu kommen. (Er geht in das Nebenzimmer, nach welchem sich
              Sittah begeben.)

### Sechster Auftritt.

Nathan allein.

#### Nathan.

Hm! hm! — wunderlich! — Wie ist
Mir denn? — Was will der Sultan? was? — Ich bin
Auf Geld gefaßt; und er will — Wahrheit. Wahrheit!
Und will sie so, — so bar, so blank, — als ob
Die Wahrheit Münze wäre! — Ja, wenn noch
1870 Uralte Münze, die gewogen ward! —
Das ginge noch! Allein so neue Münze,
Die nur der Stempel macht, die man aufs Brett
Nur zählen darf, das ist sie doch nun nicht!
Wie Geld in Sack, so striche man in Kopf
1875 Auch Wahrheit ein? Wer ist denn hier der Jude?
Ich oder er? — Doch wie? Sollt' er auch wohl
Die Wahrheit nicht in Wahrheit fordern? — Zwar,
Zwar der Verdacht, daß er die Wahrheit nur
Als Falle brauche, wär' auch gar zu klein! —
1880 Zu klein? — Was ist für einen Großen denn
Zu klein? — Gewiß, gewiß: er stürzte mit
Der Thüre so ins Haus! Man pocht doch, hört
Doch erst, wenn man als Freund sich naht. — Ich muß
Behutsam gehn! — Und wie? wie das? — So ganz
1885 Stockjude sein zu wollen, geht schon nicht. —
Und ganz und gar nicht Jude, geht noch minder.
Denn, wenn kein Jude, dürft' er mich nur fragen,
Warum kein Muselmann? — Das war's! Das kann
Mich retten! — Nicht die Kinder bloß, speist man
1890 Mit Märchen ab. — Er kommt. Er komme nur!

### Siebenter Auftritt.

#### Saladin und Nathan.

#### Saladin.

(So iſt das Feld hier rein!) — Ich komm' dir doch
Nicht zu geſchwind zurück? Du biſt zu Rande
Mit deiner Überlegung. — Nun ſo rede!
Es hört uns keine Seele.

#### Nathan.

         Möcht' auch doch
1895 Die ganze Welt uns hören.

#### Saladin.

          So gewiß
Iſt Nathan ſeiner Sache? Ha! das nenn'
Ich einen Weiſen! Nie die Wahrheit zu
Verhehlen! für ſie alles auf das Spiel
Zu ſetzen! Leib und Leben! Gut und Blut!

#### Nathan.

1900 Ja! ja! wenn's nötig iſt und nützt.

#### Saladin.

            Von nun
An darf ich hoffen, einen meiner Titel,
Verbeſſerer der Welt und des Geſetzes,
Mit Recht zu führen.

#### Nathan.

        Traun, ein ſchöner Titel!
Doch, Sultan, eh' ich mich dir ganz vertraue,
1905 Erlaubſt du wohl, dir ein Geſchichtchen zu
Erzählen?

**Saladin.**

Warum das nicht? Ich bin stets
Ein Freund gewesen von Geschichtchen, gut
Erzählt.

**Nathan.**

Ja, gut erzählen, das ist nun
Wohl eben meine Sache nicht.

**Saladin.**

Schon wieder
1910 So stolz bescheiden? — Mach'! erzähl', erzähle!

**Nathan.**

Vor grauen Jahren lebt' ein Mann in Osten,
Der einen Ring von unschätzbarem Wert
Aus lieber Hand besaß. Der Stein war ein
Opal, der hundert schöne Farben spielte,
1915 Und hatte die geheime Kraft, vor Gott
Und Menschen angenehm zu machen, wer
In dieser Zuversicht ihn trug. Was Wunder,
Daß ihn der Mann in Osten darum nie
Vom Finger ließ; und die Verfügung traf,
1920 Auf ewig ihn bei seinem Hause zu
Erhalten? Nämlich so. Er ließ den Ring
Von seinen Söhnen dem geliebtesten;
Und setzte fest, daß dieser wiederum
Den Ring von seinen Söhnen dem vermache,
1925 Der ihm der liebste sei; und stets der liebste,
Ohn' Ansehn der Geburt, in Kraft allein
Des Rings, das Haupt, der Fürst des Hauses werde. —
Versteh mich, Sultan.

**Saladin.**

Ich versteh' dich. Weiter!

## Nathan.

So kam nun dieser Ring, von Sohn zu Sohn,
1930 Auf einen Vater endlich von drei Söhnen;
Die alle drei ihm gleich gehorsam waren,
Die alle drei er folglich gleich zu lieben
Sich nicht entbrechen konnte. Nur von Zeit
Zu Zeit schien ihm bald der, bald dieser, bald
1935 Der dritte, — so wie jeder sich mit ihm
Allein befand, und sein ergießend Herz
Die andern zwei nicht teilten, — würdiger
Des Ringes; den er denn auch einem jeden
Die fromme Schwachheit hatte, zu versprechen.
1940 Das ging nun so, folang' es ging. — Allein
Es kam zum Sterben, und der gute Vater
Kommt in Verlegenheit. Es schmerzt ihn, zwei
Von seinen Söhnen, die sich auf sein Wort
Verlaffen, so zu kränken. — Was zu thun? —
1945 Er sendet in geheim zu einem Künstler,
Bei dem er, nach dem Muster seines Ringes,
Zwei andere bestellt, und weder Kosten
Noch Mühe sparen heißt, sie jenem gleich,
Vollkommen gleich zu machen. Das gelingt
1950 Dem Künstler. Da er ihm die Ringe bringt,
Kann selbst der Vater seinen Musterring
Nicht unterscheiden. Froh und freudig ruft
Er seine Söhne, jeden insbesondre;
Giebt jedem insbesondre seinen Segen, —
1955 Und seinen Ring, — unb stirbt. — Du hörst doch, Sultan?

### Saladin (der sich betroffen von ihm gewandt).

Ich hör', ich höre! — Komm mit deinem Märchen
Nur bald zu Ende. — Wird's?

### Nathan.

Ich bin zu Ende.

Denn was noch folgt, versteht sich ja von selbst. —
Kaum war der Vater tot, so kommt ein jeder
1960 Mit seinem Ring, und jeder will der Fürst
Des Hauses sein. Man untersucht, man zankt,
Man klagt. Umsonst; der rechte Ring war nicht
Erweislich; —

(nach einer Pause, in welcher er des Sultans Antwort erwartet)

        fast so unerweislich, als
Uns jetzt — der rechte Glaube.

#### Saladin.

                Wie? das soll
1965 Die Antwort sein auf meine Frage? . . .

#### Nathan.

                  Soll
Mich bloß entschuldigen, wenn ich die Ringe,
Mir nicht getrau' zu unterscheiden, die
Der Vater in der Absicht machen ließ,
Damit sie nicht zu unterscheiden wären.

#### Saladin.

1970 Die Ringe! — Spiele nicht mit mir! — Ich dächte,
Daß die Religionen, die ich dir
Genannt, doch wohl zu unterscheiden wären.
Bis auf die Kleidung; bis auf Speis' und Trank!

#### Nathan.

Und nur von Seiten ihrer Gründe nicht. —
1975 Denn gründen alle sich nicht auf Geschichte?
Geschrieben oder überliefert! — Und
Geschichte muß doch wohl allein auf Treu'
Und Glauben angenommen werden? — Nicht? —
Nun wessen Treu' und Glauben zieht man denn
1980 Am wenigsten in Zweifel? Doch der Seinen?
Doch deren Blut wir sind? doch deren, die

Von Kindheit an uns Proben ihrer Liebe
Gegeben? die uns nie getäuscht, als wo
Getäuscht zu werden uns heilsamer war? —
1985 Wie kann ich meinen Vätern weniger,
Als du den deinen glauben? Oder umgekehrt. —
Kann ich von dir verlangen, daß du deine
Vorfahren Lügen strafst, um meinen nicht
Zu widersprechen? Oder umgekehrt.
1990 Das nämliche gilt von den Christen. Nicht? —

### Saladin.

(Bei dem Lebendigen! Der Mann hat recht.
Ich muß verstummen.)

### Nathan.

Laß auf unsre Ring'
Uns wieder kommen. Wie gesagt: die Söhne
Verklagten sich; und jeder schwur dem Richter,
1995 Unmittelbar aus seines Vaters Hand
Den Ring zu haben. — Wie auch wahr! — Nachdem
Er von ihm lange das Versprechen schon
Gehabt, des Ringes Vorrecht einmal zu
Genießen. — Wie nicht minder wahr! — Der Vater,
2000 Beteu'rte jeder, könne gegen ihn
Nicht falsch gewesen sein; und eh' er dieses
Von ihm, von einem solchen lieben Vater,
Argwohnen laß': eh' müss' er seine Brüder,
So gern er sonst von ihnen nur das Beste
2005 Bereit zu glauben sei, des falschen Spiels
Bezeihen; und er wolle die Verräter
Schon auszufinden wissen; sich schon rächen.

### Saladin.

Und nun, der Richter? — Mich verlangt zu hören,
Was du den Richter sagen lässest. Sprich!

### Nathan.

2010 Der Richter sprach: Wenn ihr mir nun den Vater
Nicht bald zur Stelle schafft, so weiß' ich euch
Von meinem Stuhle. Denkt ihr, daß ich Rätsel
Zu lösen da bin? Oder harret ihr,
Bis daß der rechte Ring den Mund eröffne? —
2015 Doch halt! Ich höre ja, der rechte Ring
Besitzt die Wunderkraft, beliebt zu machen;
Vor Gott und Menschen angenehm. Das muß
Entscheiden! Denn die falschen Ringe werden
Doch das nicht können! — Nun; wen lieben zwei
2020 Von euch am meisten?—Macht, sagt an! Ihr schweigt?
Die Ringe wirken nur zurück? und nicht
Nach außen? Jeder liebt sich selber nur
Am meisten? — O so seid Ihr alle drei
Betrogene Betrüger! Eure Ringe
2025 Sind alle drei nicht echt. Der echte Ring
Vermutlich ging verloren. Den Verlust
Zu bergen, zu ersetzen, ließ der Vater
Die drei für einen machen.

### Saladin.

Herrlich! herrlich!

### Nathan.

Und also; fuhr der Richter fort, wenn ihr
2030 Nicht meinen Rat, statt meines Spruches, wollt:
Geht nur! — Mein Rat ist aber der: ihr nehmt
Die Sache völlig wie sie liegt. Hat von
Euch jeder seinen Ring von seinem Vater:
So glaube jeder sicher seinen Ring
2035 Den echten. — Möglich; daß der Vater nun
Die Tyrannei des einen Rings nicht länger
In seinem Hause dulden wollen! — Und gewiß;
Daß er euch alle drei geliebt, und gleich

Geliebt: indem er zwei nicht drücken mögen,
2040 Um einen zu begünstigen. — Wohlan!
Es eifre jeder seiner unbestochnen
Von Vorurteilen freien Liebe nach!
Es strebe von euch jeder um die Wette,
Die Kraft des Steins in seinem Ring an Tag
2045 Zu legen! komme dieser Kraft mit Sanftmut,
Mit herzlicher Verträglichkeit, mit Wohlthun,
Mit innigster Ergebenheit in Gott,
Zu Hilf'! Und wenn sich dann der Steine Kräfte
Bei euern Kindes-Kindeskindern äußern:
2050 So lad' ich über tausend tausend Jahre,
Sie wiederum vor diesen Stuhl.    Da wird
Ein weis'rer Mann auf diesem Stuhle sitzen,
Als ich; und sprechen.    Geht! — So sagte der
Bescheidne Richter.

### Saladin.

Gott! Gott!

### Nathan.

Saladin,
2055 Wenn du dich fühlest, dieser weisere
Versprochne Mann zu sein: ...

### Saladin
(der auf ihn zustürzt und seine Hand ergreift, die er bis
zu Ende nicht wieder fahren läßt).

Ich Staub? Ich Nichts?
O Gott!

### Nathan.

Was ist dir, Sultan?

### Saladin.

Nathan! lieber Nathan! —
Die tausend tausend Jahre deines Richters

Sind noch nicht um. — Sein Richterstuhl ist nicht
2060 Der meine. — Geh! — Geh! — Aber sei mein Freund.

### Nathan.

Und weiter hätte Saladin mir nichts
Zu sagen?

### Saladin.
   Nichts.

### Nathan.
   Nichts?

### Saladin.

   Gar nichts. — Und warum?

### Nathan.

Ich hätte noch Gelegenheit gewünscht,
Dir eine Bitte vorzutragen.

### Saladin.

   Braucht's
2065 Gelegenheit zu einer Bitte? — Rede!

### Nathan.

Ich komm' von einer weiten Reis', auf welcher
Ich Schulden eingetrieben. — Fast hab' ich
Des baren Gelds zu viel. — Die Zeit beginnt
Bedenklich wiederum zu werden; — und
2070 Ich weiß nicht recht, wo sicher damit hin. —
Da dacht' ich, ob nicht du vielleicht, — weil doch
Ein naher Krieg des Geldes immer mehr
Erfordert, — etwas brauchen könntest.

### Saladin (ihm steif in die Augen sehend).

      Nathan! —
Ich will nicht fragen, ob Al-Hafi schon

2075 Bei dir gewesen; — will nicht unterfuchen,
Ob dich nicht fonft ein Argwohn treibt, mir diefes
Erbieten freierdings zu thun: ...

#### Nathan.

Ein Argwohn?

#### Saladin.

Ich bin ihn wert. — Verzeih mir! — Denn was hilft's?
Ich muß dir nur geftehen, — daß ich im
2080 Begriffe war —

#### Nathan.

Doch nicht, das nämliche
An mich zu fuchen?

#### Saladin.

Allerdings.

#### Nathan.

So wär'
Uns beiden ja geholfen! — Daß ich aber
Dir alle meine Barfchaft nicht kann fchicken,
Das macht der junge Tempelherr. — Du kennft
2085 Ihn ja. — Ihm hab' ich eine große Poft
Vorher noch zu bezahlen.

#### Saladin.

Tempelherr?
Du wirft doch meine fchlimmften Feinde nicht
Mit deinem Geld auch unterftützen wollen?

#### Nathan.

Ich fpreche von dem einen nur, dem du
2090 Das Leben fparteft ...

#### Saladin.

Ah! woran erinnerft

Du mich! — Hab' ich doch diesen Jüngling ganz
Vergessen! — Kennst du ihn? — Wo ist er?

### Nathan.

Wie?

So weißt du nicht, wieviel von deiner Gnade
für ihn, durch ihn auf mich geflossen? Er,
2095 Er mit Gefahr des neu erhaltnen Lebens,
Hat meine Tochter aus dem Feu'r gerettet.

### Saladin.

Er? Hat er das? — Ha! darnach sah er aus.
Das hätte traun mein Bruder auch gethan,
Dem er so ähnelt! — Ist er denn noch hier?
2100 So bring' ihn her! — Ich habe meiner Schwester
Von diesem ihrem Bruder, den sie nicht
Gekannt, so viel erzählet, daß ich sie
Sein Ebenbild doch auch muß sehen lassen! —
Geh, hol' ihn! — Wie aus einer guten That,
2105 Gebar sie auch schon bloße Leidenschaft,
Doch so viel andre gute Thaten fließen!
Geh, hol' ihn!

### Nathan (indem er Saladins Hand fahren läßt).

Augenblicks! Und bei dem andern
Bleibt es doch auch? (Ab.)

### Saladin.

Ah! daß ich meine Schwester
Nicht horchen lassen! — Zu ihr! zu ihr! — Denn
2110 Wie soll ich alles das ihr nun erzählen?

(Ab von der andern Seite.)

## Achter Auftritt.

(Die Scene: unter den Palmen, in der Nähe des Klosters, wo
der Tempelherr Nathans wartet.)

**Tempelherr**
(geht, mit sich selbst kämpfend, auf und ab; bis er losbricht).

— Hier hält das Opfertier ermüdet still. —
Nun gut! Ich mag nicht, mag nicht näher wissen,
Was in mir vorgeht; mag voraus nicht wittern,
Was vorgehn wird. — Genug, ich bin umsonst
2115 Geflohn! umsonst. — Und weiter konnt' ich doch
Auch nichts, als fliehn! — Nun komm', was kommen soll! —
Ihm auszubeugen, war der Streich zu schnell
Gefallen; unter den zu kommen, ich
So lang' und viel mich weigerte. — Sie sehn,
2120 Die ich zu sehn so wenig lüstern war, —
Sie sehn, und der Entschluß, sie wieder aus
Den Augen nie zu lassen — Was Entschluß?
Entschluß ist Vorsatz, That: und ich, ich litt,
Ich litte bloß.   Sie sehn, und das Gefühl,
2125 An sie verstrickt, in sie verwebt zu sein,
War eins. — Bleibt eins. — Von ihr getrennt
Zu leben, ist mir ganz undenkbar; wär'
Mein Tod, — und wo wir immer nach dem Tode
Noch sind, auch da mein Tod. — Ist das nun Liebe:
2130 So — liebt der Tempelritter freilich, — liebt
Der Christ das Judenmädchen freilich. — Hm!
Was thut's? — Ich hab' in dem gelobten Lande, —
Und drum auch mir gelobt auf immerdar! —
Der Vorurteile mehr schon abgelegt. —
2135 Was will mein Orden auch? Ich Tempelherr
Bin tot; war von dem Augenblick ihm tot,
Der mich zu Saladins Gefangnen machte.

Der Kopf, den Saladin mir schenkte, wär'
Mein alter? — Ist ein neuer; der von allem
2140 Nichts weiß, was jenem eingeplaudert ward,
Was jenen band. — Und ist ein beſſ'rer; für
Den väterlichen Himmel mehr gemacht.
Das ſpür' ich ja.   Denn erſt mit ihm beginn'
Ich ſo zu denken, wie mein Vater hier
2145 Gedacht muß haben; wenn man Märchen nicht
Von ihm mir vorgelogen. — Märchen? — doch
Ganz glaubliche; die glaublicher mir nie,
Als jetzt geſchienen, da ich nur Geſahr
Zu ſtraucheln laufe, wo er fiel. — Er fiel?
2150 Ich will mit Männern lieber fallen, als
Mit Kindern ſtehn. — Sein Beiſpiel bürget mir
für ſeinen Beifall.   Und an weſſen Beiſall
Liegt mir denn ſonſt? — An Nathans? — O an deſſen
Ermuntrung mehr, als Beifall, kann es mir
2155 Noch weniger gebrechen. — Welch ein Jude! —
Und der ſo ganz nur Jude ſcheinen will!
Da kommt er; kommt mit Haſt; glüht heitre Freude.
Wer kam vom Saladin je anders? — He!
He, Nathan!

––––––

### Neunter Auftritt.

#### Nathan und der Tempelherr.

**Nathan.**

Wie? ſeid Ihr's?

**Tempelherr.**

Ihr habt
2160 Sehr lang' Euch bei dem Sultan aufgehalten.

**Nathan.**

So lange nun wohl nicht.   Ich ward im Hingehn

Zu viel verweilt. — Ah, wahrlich Kurt; der Mann
Steht seinen Ruhm. — Sein Ruhm ist bloß sein Schatten. —
Doch laßt vor allen Dingen Euch geschwind
2165 Nur sagen ...

### Tempelherr.

Was?

### Nathan.

Er will Euch sprechen; will,
Daß ungesäumt Ihr zu ihm kommt. Begleitet
Mich nur nach Hause, wo ich noch für ihn
Erst etwas anders zu verfügen habe:
Und dann, so gehn wir.

### Tempelherr.

Nathan, Euer Haus
2170 Betret' ich wieder eher nicht ...

### Nathan.

So seid
Ihr doch indes schon da gewesen? habt
Indes sie doch gesprochen? — Nun? — Sagt: wie
Gefällt Euch Recha?

### Tempelherr.

Über allen Ausdruck! —
Allein, — sie wiedersehn — das werd' ich nie!
2175 Nie! nie! — Ihr müßtet mir zur Stelle denn
Versprechen: — daß ich sie auf immer, immer —
Soll können sehn.

### Nathan.

Wie wollt Ihr, daß ich das
Versteh'?

### Tempelherr
(nach einer kurzen Pause ihm plötzlich um den Hals fallend).

Mein Vater!

**Nathan.**

— Junger Mann!

**Tempelherr** (ihn ebenso plötzlich wieder lassend).

Nicht Sohn? —

Ich bitt' Euch, Nathan!

**Nathan.**

Lieber junger Mann!

**Tempelherr.**

2180 Nicht Sohn? — Ich bitt' Euch, Nathan! — Ich beschwör'
Euch bei den ersten Banden der Natur! —
Zieht ihnen spätre Fesseln doch nicht vor! —
Begnügt Euch doch ein Mensch zu sein! — Stoßt mich
Nicht von Euch!

**Nathan.**

Lieber, lieber Freund! . . .

**Tempelherr.**

Und Sohn?

2185 Sohn nicht? — Auch dann nicht, dann nicht einmal, wenn
Erkenntlichkeit zum Herzen Eurer Tochter
Der Liebe schon den Weg gebahnet hätte?
Auch dann nicht einmal, wenn in eins zu schmelzen
Auf Euern Wink nur beide warteten? —
2190 Ihr schweigt?

**Nathan.**

Ihr überrascht mich, junger Ritter.

**Tempelherr.**

Ich überrasch' Euch? — überrasch' Euch, Nathan,
Mit Euern eigenen Gedanken? — Ihr
Verkennt sie doch in meinem Munde nicht? —
Ich überrasch' Euch?

### Nathan.

Eh ich einmal weiß,
2195 Was für ein Stauffen Euer Vater denn
Gewesen ist!

### Tempelherr.

Was sagt Ihr, Nathan? was? —
In diesem Augenblicke fühlt Ihr nichts,
Als Neubegier?

### Nathan.

Denn seht! Ich habe selbst
Wohl einen Stauffen ehedem gekannt,
2200 Der Konrad hieß.

### Tempelherr.

Nun — wenn mein Vater denn
Nun ebenso geheißen hätte?

### Nathan.

Wahrlich?

### Tempelherr.

Ich heiße selber ja nach meinem Vater: Kurt
Ist Konrad.

### Nathan.

Nun — so war mein Konrad doch
Nicht Euer Vater. Denn mein Konrad war,
2205 Was Ihr; war Tempelherr; war nie vermählt.

### Tempelherr.

O darum!

### Nathan.

Wie?

### Tempelherr.

O darum könnt' er doch
Mein Vater wohl gewesen sein.

**Nathan.**

Ihr scherzt.

**Tempelherr.**

Und Ihr nehmt's wahrlich zu genau! — Was wär's
Denn nun? So was von Bastard oder Bankert!
2210 Der Schlag ist auch nicht zu verachten. — Doch
Entlaßt mich immer meiner Ahnenprobe.
Ich will Euch Eurer wiederum entlassen.
Nicht zwar, als ob ich den geringsten Zweifel
In Euern Stammbaum setzte. Gott behüte!
2215 Ihr könnt ihn Blatt vor Blatt bis Abraham
Hinauf belegen. Und von da so weiter,
Weiß ich ihn selbst; will ich ihn selbst beschwören.

**Nathan.**

Ihr werdet bitter. — Doch verdien' ich's? — Schlug
Ich denn Euch schon was ab? — Ich will Euch ja
2220 Nur bei dem Worte nicht den Augenblick
So fassen. — Weiter nichts.

**Tempelherr.**

Gewiß? — Nichts weiter?
O so vergebt! ...

**Nathan.**

Nun kommt nur, kommt!

**Tempelherr.**

Wohin?
Nein! — Mit in Euer Haus? — Das nicht! Das nicht! —
Da brennt's! — Ich will Euch hier erwarten. Geht! —
2225 Soll ich sie wiedersehn: so seh' ich sie
Noch oft genug. Wo nicht: so sah ich sie
Schon viel zu viel ...

**Nathan.**

Ich will mich möglichst eilen.

### Zehnter Auftritt.

**Der Tempelherr und bald darauf Daja.**

#### Tempelherr.

Schon mehr als g'nug! — Des Menschen Hirn faßt so
Unendlich viel; und ist doch manchmal auch
2230 So plötzlich voll! von einer Kleinigkeit
So plötzlich voll! — Taugt nichts, taugt nichts; es sei
Auch voll wovon es will. — Doch nur Geduld!
Die Seele wirkt den aufgedunf'nen Stoff
Bald ineinander, schafft sich Raum, und Licht
2235 Und Ordnung kommen wieder. — Lieb' ich denn
Zum erstenmale? — Oder war, was ich
Als Liebe kenne, Liebe nicht? — Ist Liebe
Nur was ich jetzt empfinde? ...

**Daja** (die sich von der Seite herbeigeschlichen).

Ritter! Ritter!

#### Tempelherr.

Wer ruft? — Ha, Daja, Ihr?

#### Daja.

Ich habe mich
2240 Bei ihm vorbei geschlichen. Aber noch
Könnt' er uns sehn, wo Ihr da steht. — Drum kommt
Doch näher zu mir, hinter diesen Baum.

#### Tempelherr.

Was giebt's denn? — So geheimnisvoll? — Was ist's?

#### Daja.

Ja wohl betrifft es ein Geheimnis, was
2245 Mich zu Euch bringt; und zwar ein doppeltes.

Das eine weiß nur ich; das andre wißt
Nur Ihr. — Wie wär' es, wenn wir tauschten?
Vertraut mir Euers: so vertrau' ich Euch
Das meine.

### Tempelherr.

Mit Vergnügen. — Wenn ich nur
2250 Erst weiß, was Ihr für meines achtet. Doch
Das wird aus Euerm wohl erhellen. — Fangt
Nur immer an.

### Daja.

Ei denkt doch! — Nein, Herr Ritter:
Erst Ihr; ich folge. — Denn versichert, mein
Geheimnis kann Euch gar nichts nützen, wenn
2255 Ich nicht zuvor das Eure habe. — Nur
Geschwind! — Denn frag' ich's Euch erst ab: so habt
Ihr nichts vertrauet. Mein Geheimnis dann
Bleibt mein Geheimnis; und das Eure seid
Ihr los. — Doch armer Ritter! — Daß ihr Männer
2260 Ein solch Geheimnis vor uns Weibern haben
Zu können, auch nur glaubt!

### Tempelherr.

Das wir zu haben
Oft selbst nicht wissen.

### Daja.

Kann wohl sein. Drum muß
Ich freilich erst, Euch selbst damit bekannt
Zu machen, schon die Freundschaft haben. — Sagt:
2265 Was hieß denn das, daß Ihr so Knall und Fall
Euch aus dem Staube machtet? daß Ihr uns
So sitzen ließet? — daß Ihr nun mit Nathan
Nicht wiederkommt? — Hat Recha denn so wenig
Auf Euch gewirkt? wie? oder auch, so viel? —
2270 So viel! so viel! — Lehrt Ihr des armen Vogels,

Der an der Rute klebt, Geflattre mich
Doch kennen! — Kurz: gesteht es mir nur gleich,
Daß Ihr sie liebt, liebt bis zum Unsinn; und
Ich sag' Euch was ...

### Tempelherr.

Zum Unsinn? Wahrlich; Ihr
2275 Versteht Euch trefflich drauf.

### Daja.

Nun gebt mir nur
Die Liebe zu; den Unsinn will ich Euch
Erlassen.

### Tempelherr.

Weil er sich von selbst versteht? —
Ein Tempelherr ein Judenmädchen lieben! ...

### Daja.

Scheint freilich wenig Sinn zu haben. — Doch
2280 Zuweilen ist des Sinns in einer Sache
Auch mehr, als wir vermuten; und es wäre
So unerhört doch nicht, daß uns der Heiland
Auf Wegen zu sich zöge, die der Kluge
Von selbst nicht leicht betreten würde.

### Tempelherr.

Das
2285 So feierlich? — (Und setz' ich statt des Heilands
Die Vorsicht: hat sie dann nicht recht? —) Ihr macht
Mich neubegieriger, als ich wohl sonst
Zu sein gewohnt bin.

### Daja.

O! das ist das Land
Der Wunder!

### Tempelherr.

(Nun! — des Wunderbaren. Kann

2290 Es auch wohl anders fein? Die gauze Welt
Drängt fich ja hier zusammen.) — Liebe Daja,
Nehmt für geftanden an, was Ihr verlangt:
Daß ich fie liebe; daß ich nicht begreife,
Wie ohne fie ich leben werde; daß . . .

### Daja.

2295 Gewiß? Gewiß? — So fchwört mir, Ritter, fie
Zur Eurigen zu machen; fie zu retten;
Sie zeitlich hier, fie ewig dort zu retten.

### Cempelherr.

Und wie? — Wie kann ich? — Kann ich fchwören, was
In meiner Macht nicht fteht?

### Daja.

In Eurer Macht
2300 Steht es. Ich bring' es durch ein einzig Wort
In Eure Macht.

### Cempelherr.

Daß felbft der Vater nichts
Dawider hätte?

### Daja.

Ei, was Vater! Vater!
Der Vater foll fchon müffen.

### Cempelherr.

Müffen, Daja? —
Noch ift er unter Räuber nicht gefallen. —
2305 Er muß nicht müffen.

### Daja.

Nun, fo muß er wollen;
Muß gern am Ende wollen.

### Cempelherr.

Muß und gern! —

Doch, Daja, wenn ich Euch nun sage, daß
Ich selber diese Sait' ihm anzuschlagen
Bereits versucht?

### Daja.

Was? und er fiel nicht ein?

### Tempelherr.

2310 Er fiel mit einem Mißlaut ein, der mich —
Beleidigte.

### Daja.

Was sagt Ihr? — Wie? Ihr hättet
Den Schatten eines Wunsches nur nach Recha
Ihm blicken lassen: und er wär' vor Freuden
Nicht aufgesprungen? hätte frostig sich
2315 Zurückgezogen? hätte Schwierigkeiten
Gemacht?

### Tempelherr.

So ungefähr.

### Daja.

So will ich denn
Mich länger keinen Augenblick bedenken — (Pause).

### Tempelherr.

Und Ihr bedenkt Euch doch?

### Daja.

Der Mann ist sonst
So gut! — Ich selber bin so viel ihm schuldig! —
2320 Daß er doch gar nicht hören will! — Gott weiß,
Das Herze blutet mir, ihn so zu zwingen.

### Tempelherr.

Ich bitt' Euch, Daja, setzt mich kurz und gut

Aus dieser Ungewißheit.   Seid Ihr aber
Noch selber ungewiß; ob, was Ihr vorhabt,
2325 Gut oder böse, schändlich oder löblich
Zu nennen: — schweigt! Ich will vergessen, daß
Ihr etwas zu verschweigen habt.

#### Daja.
Das spornt
Anstatt zu halten.   Nun; so wißt denn: Recha
Ist keine Jüdin; ist — ist eine Christin.

#### Tempelherr (kalt).

2330 So? Wünsch' Euch Glück! Hat's schwer gehalten? Laßt
Euch nicht die Wehen schrecken! — Fahret ja
Mit Eifer fort, den Himmel zu bevölkern,
Wenn Ihr die Erde nicht mehr könnt!

#### Daja.
Wie, Ritter?
Verdienet meine Nachricht diesen Spott?
2335 Daß Recha eine Christin ist: das freuet
Euch, einen Christen, einen Tempelherrn,
Der Ihr sie liebt, nicht mehr?

#### Tempelherr.
Besonders, da
Sie eine Christin ist von Eurer Mache.

#### Daja.

Ah! so versteht Ihr's? So mag's gelten! — Nein!
2340 Den will ich sehn, der die bekehren soll!
Ihr Glück ist, längst zu sein, was sie zu werden
Verdorben ist.

#### Tempelherr.

Erklärt Euch, oder — geht!

**Daja.**

Sie ist ein Christenkind; von Christeneltern
Geboren; ist getauft ...

**Tempelherr** (hastig).

Und Nathan?

**Daja.**

Nicht

2345 Ihr Vater!

**Tempelherr.**

Nathan nicht ihr Vater? — Wißt
Ihr, was Ihr sagt?

**Daja.**

Die Wahrheit, die so oft
Mich blut'ge Thränen weinen machen. — Nein,
Er ist ihr Vater nicht ...

**Tempelherr.**

Und hätte sie,
Als seine Tochter nur erzogen? hätte
2350 Das Christenkind als eine Jüdin sich
Erzogen?

**Daja.**

Ganz gewiß.

**Tempelherr.**

Sie wüßte nicht,
Was sie geboren sei? — Sie hätt' es nie
Von ihm erfahren, daß sie eine Christin
Geboren sei, und keine Jüdin?

**Daja.**

Nie!

**Tempelherr.**

2355 Er hätt' in diesem Wahne nicht das Kind
Bloß auferzogen? ließ' das Mädchen noch
In diesem Wahne?

**Daja.**

Leider!

**Tempelherr.**

Nathan — Wie? —
Der weise gute Nathan hätte sich
Erlaubt, die Stimme der Natur so zu
2360 Verfälschen? — Die Ergießung eines Herzens
So zu verlenken, die, sich selbst gelassen,
Ganz andre Wege nehmen würde? — Daja,
Ihr habt mir allerdings etwas vertraut —
Von Wichtigkeit, — was folgen haben kann, —
2365 Was mich verwirrt, — worauf ich gleich nicht weiß,
Was mir zu thun. — Drum laßt mir Zeit. — Drum geht!
Er kommt hier wiederum vorbei. Er möcht'
Uns überfallen! Geht!

**Daja.**

Ich wär' des Todes!

**Tempelherr.**

Ich bin ihn jetzt zu sprechen ganz und gar
2370 Nicht fähig. Wenn Ihr ihm begegnet, sagt
Ihm nur, daß wir einander bei dem Sultan
Schon finden würden.

**Daja.**

Aber laßt Euch ja
Nichts merken gegen ihn. — Das soll nur so
Den letzten Druck dem Dinge geben; soll
2375 Euch, Recha's wegen, alle Skrupel nur
Benehmen! — Wenn Ihr aber dann, sie nach

Europa führt: so laßt Jhr doch mich nicht
Zurück?

**Tempelherr.**

Das wird sich finden.　Geht nur, geht!

---

## Vierter Aufzug.

### Erster Auftritt.

(Scene: in den Kreuzgängen des Klosters.)

Der Klosterbruder und bald darauf der Tempelherr.

**Klosterbruder.**

Ja, ja! er hat schon recht, der Patriarch!
2380 Es hat mir freilich noch von alle dem
Nicht viel gelingen wollen, was er mir
So aufgetragen. — Warum trägt er mir
Auch lauter solche Sachen auf? — Jch mag
Nicht fein sein; mag nicht überreden; mag
2385 Mein Näschen nicht in alles stecken; mag
Mein Händchen nicht in allem haben. — Bin
Jch darum aus der Welt geschieden, ich
Für mich; um mich für andre mit der Welt
Noch erst recht zu verwickeln?

**Tempelherr** (mit Hast auf ihn zukommend).

Guter Bruder!
2390 Da seid Jhr ja.　Jch hab' Euch lange schon
Gesucht.

**Klosterbruder.**

Mich, Herr?

**Tempelherr.**

Jhr kennt mich schon nicht mehr?

### Klofterbruder.

Doch, doch! Ich glaubte nur, daß ich den Herrn
In meinem Leben wieder nie zu fehn
Bekommen würde.    Denn ich hofft' es zu
2395 Dem lieben Gott. — Der liebe Gott, der weiß
Wie fauer mir der Antrag ward, den ich
Dem Herrn zu thun verbunden war.    Er weiß,
Ob ich gewünfcht, ein offnes Ohr bei Euch
Zu finden; weiß, wie fehr ich mich gefreut,
2400 Im Innerften gefreut, daß Ihr fo rund
Das alles, ohne viel Bedenken, von
Euch wieft, was einem Ritter nicht geziemt. —
Nun kommt Ihr doch; nun hat's doch nachgewirkt!

### Tempelherr.

Ihr wißt es fchon, warum ich komme? Kaum
2405 Weiß ich es felbft.

### Klofterbruder.

              Ihr habt's nun überlegt;
Habt nun gefunden, daß der Patriarch
So unrecht doch nicht hat; daß Ehr' und Geld
Durch feinen Anfchlag zu gewinnen; daß
Ein Feind ein Feind ift, wenn er unfer Engel
2410 Auch fiebenmal gewefen wäre.    Das,
Das habt Ihr nun mit Fleifch und Blut erwogen,
Und kommt, und tragt Euch wieder an. — Ach Gott!

### Tempelherr.

Mein frommer, lieber Mann! Gebt Euch zufrieden.
Deswegen komm' ich nicht; deswegen will
2415 Ich nicht den Patriarchen fprechen.    Noch,
Noch denk' ich über jenen Punkt, wie ich
Gedacht, und wollt' um alles in der Welt
Die gute Meinung nicht verlieren, deren

Mich ein so grader, frommer, lieber Mann
2420 Einmal gewürdiget. — Ich komme bloß,
Den Patriarchen über eine Sache
Um Rat zu fragen ...

#### Klosterbruder.

          Ihr den Patriarchen?
Ein Ritter, einen — Pfaffen? (Sich schüchtern umsehend.)

#### Tempelherr.

          Ja; — die Sach'
Ist ziemlich pfäffisch.

#### Klosterbruder.

          Gleichwohl fragt der Pfaffe
2425 Den Ritter nie, die Sache sei auch noch
So ritterlich.

#### Tempelherr.

          Weil er das Vorrecht hat,
Sich zu vergehn; das unsereiner ihm
Nicht sehr beneidet. — Freilich, wenn ich nur
Für mich zu handeln hätte; freilich, wenn
2430 Ich Rechenschaft nur mir zu geben hätte:
Was braucht' ich Euers Patriarchen? Aber
Gewisse Dinge will ich lieber schlecht,
Nach andrer Willen, machen; als allein
Nach meinem, gut. — Zudem, ich seh' nun wohl,
2435 Religion ist auch Partei; und wer
Sich drob auch noch so unparteiisch glaubt,
Hält, ohn' es selbst zu wissen, doch nur seiner
Die Stange.   Weil das einmal nun so ist:
Wird's so wohl recht sein.

#### Klosterbruder.

          Dazu schweig' ich lieber.
2440 Denn ich versteh' den Herrn nicht recht.

### Tempelherr.

Und doch! —

(Laß sehn, warum mir eigentlich zu thun!
Um Machtspruch oder Rat? — Um lautern, oder
Gelehrten Rat?) — Ich dank' Euch, Bruder; dank'
Euch für den guten Wink. — Was Patriarch? —
2445 Seid Ihr mein Patriarch! Ich will ja doch
Den Christen mehr im Patriarchen, als
Den Patriarchen in dem Christen fragen. —
Die Sach' ist die . . .

### Klosterbruder.

Nicht weiter, Herr, nicht weiter!
Wozu? — Der Herr verkennt mich. — Wer viel weiß,
2450 Hat viel zu sorgen; und ich habe ja
Mich e i n e r Sorge nur gelobt. — O gut!
Hört! seht! Dort kommt, zu meinem Glück, er selbst.
Bleibt hier nur stehn. Er hat Euch schon erblickt.

––––––––––

### Zweiter Auftritt.

Der Patriarch, welcher mit allem geistlichen Pomp den einen
Kreuzgang heraufkommt, und die Vorigen.

### Tempelherr.

Ich wich' ihm lieber aus. — Wär' nicht mein Mann! —
2455 Ein dicker, roter, freundlicher Prälat!
Und welcher Prunk!

### Klosterbruder.

Ihr solltet ihn erst sehn,
Nach Hofe sich erheben. Jetzo kommt
Er nur von einem Kranken. •

### Tempelherr.

Wie sich da
Nicht Saladin wird schämen müssen!

### Patriarch (indem er näher kommt, winkt dem Bruder).

Hier! —
2460 Das ist ja wohl der Tempelherr. Was will
Er?

### Klosterbruder.

Weiß nicht.

### Patriarch
(auf ihn zugehend, indem der Bruder und das Gefolge zurücktreten).

Nun, Herr Ritter! — Sehr erfreut
Den braven jungen Mann zu sehn! — Ei, noch
So gar jung! — Nun, mit Gottes Hilfe, daraus
Kann etwas werden.

### Tempelherr.

Mehr, ehrwürd'ger Herr,
2465 Wohl schwerlich, als schon ist. Und eher noch,
Was weniger.

### Patriarch.

Ich wünsche wenigstens,
Daß so ein frommer Ritter lange noch
Der lieben Christenheit, der Sache Gottes
Zu Ehr' und Frommen blühn und grünen möge!
2470 Das wird denn auch nicht fehlen, wenn nur sein
Die junge Tapferkeit dem reifen Rate
Des Alters folgen will! — Womit wär' sonst
Dem Herrn zu dienen?

### Tempelherr.

Mit dem nämlichen,
Woran es meiner Jugend fehlt: mit Rat.

**Patriarch.**

2475 Recht gern! — Nur ist der Rat auch anzunehmen.

**Tempelherr.**

Doch blindlings nicht?

**Patriarch.**

Wer sagt denn das? — Ei freilich
Muß niemand die Vernunft, die Gott ihm gab,
Zu brauchen unterlassen, — wo sie hin
Gehört. — Gehört sie aber überall
2480 Denn hin? — O nein! — Zum Beispiel: wenn uns Gott
Durch einen seiner Engel, — ist zu sagen,
Durch einen Diener seines Worts, — ein Mittel
Bekannt zu machen würdiget, das Wohl
Der ganzen Christenheit, das Heil der Kirche,
2485 Auf irgend eine ganz besondre Weise
Zu fördern, zu befestigen: wer darf
Sich da noch unterstehn, die Willkür bes,
Der die Vernunft erschaffen, nach Vernunft
Zu untersuchen? und das ewige
2490 Gesetz der Herrlichkeit des Himmels, nach
Den kleinen Regeln einer eiteln Ehre
Zu prüfen? — Doch hiervon genug. — Was ist
Es benn, worüber unsern Rat für jetzt
Der Herr verlangt?

**Tempelherr.**

Gesetzt, ehrwürd'ger Vater,
2495 Ein Jude hätt' ein einzig Kind, — es sei
Ein Mädchen, — das er mit der größten Sorgfalt
Zu allem Guten auferzogen, das
Er liebe mehr als seine Seele, das
Ihn wieder mit der frömmsten Liebe liebe.

2500 Und nun würd' unfereinem hinterbracht,
Dies Mädchen fei des Juden Tochter nicht;
Er hab' es in der Kindheit aufgelefen,
Gekauft, geftohlen, — was Ihr wollt; man wiffe,
Das Mädchen fei ein Chriftenkind, und fei
2505 Getauft; der Jude hab' es nur als Jüdin
Erzogen; laff' es nur als Jüdin und
Als feine Tochter fo verharren: — fagt,
Ehrwürd'ger Vater, was wär' hierbei wohl
Zu thun?

#### Patriarch.

Mich schaudert! — Doch zu allererft
2510 Erkläre fich der Herr, ob fo ein Fall
Ein Faktum oder eine Hypothef'.
Das ift zu fagen: ob der Herr fich das
Nur bloß fo dichtet, oder ob's gefchehn,
Und fortfährt zu gefchehn.

#### Tempelherr.

Ich glaubte, das
2515 Sei eins, um Euer Hochehrwürden Meinung
Bloß zu vernehmen.

#### Patriarch.

Eins? — da feh' der Herr
Wie fich die ftolze menfchliche Vernunft
Im Geiftlichen doch irren kann. — Mit nichten!
Denn ift der vorgetragne Fall nur fo
2520 Ein Spiel des Witzes: fo verlohnt es fich
Der Mühe nicht, im Ernft ihn durchzudenken.
Ich will den Herrn damit auf das Theater
Verwiefen haben, wo dergleichen pro
Et contra fich mit vielem Beifall könnte
2525 Behandeln laffen. — Hat der Herr mich aber
Nicht bloß mit einer theatral'fchen Schnurre

Zum beſten; iſt der Fall ein Faktum; hätt'
Er ſich wohl gar in unſrer Diöceſ',
In unſrer lieben Stadt Jeruſalem,
2530 Ereignet: — ja alsdann —

### Tempelherr.

Und was alsdann?

### Patriarch.

Dann wäre mit dem Juden förderſamſt
Die Strafe zu vollziehn, die päpſtliches
Und kaiſerliches Recht ſo einem Frevel,
So einer Laſterthat beſtimmen.

### Tempelherr.

So?

### Patriarch.

2535 Und zwar beſtimmen obbeſagte Rechte
Dem Juden, welcher einen Chriſten zur
Apoſtaſie verführt, — den Scheiterhaufen, —
Den Holzſtoß —

### Tempelherr.

So?

### Patriarch.

Und wie vielmehr dem Juden,
Der mit Gewalt ein armes Chriſtenkind
2540 Dem Bunde ſeiner Tauf' entreißt! Denn iſt
Nicht alles, was man Kindern thut, Gewalt? —
Zu ſagen: — ausgenommen, was die Kirch'
An Kindern thut.

### Tempelherr.

Wenn aber nun das Kind,
Erbarmte ſeiner ſich der Jude nicht,
2545 Vielleicht im Elend umgekommen wäre?

### Patriarch.

Thut nichts! Der Jude wird verbrannt. — Denn beſſer,
Es wäre hier im Elend umgekommen,
Als daß zu ſeinem ewigen Verderben
Es ſo gerettet ward. — Zudem, was hat
2550 Der Jude Gott denn vorzugreifen? Gott
Kann, wen er retten will, ſchon ohn' ihn retten.

### Tempelherr.

Auch trotz ihm, ſollt' ich meinen, — ſelig machen.

### Patriarch.

Thut nichts! der Jude wird verbrannt.

### Tempelherr.

                          Das geht
Mir nah'! Beſonders, da man ſagt, er habe
2555 Das Mädchen nicht ſowohl in ſeinem, als
Vielmehr in keinem Glauben auferzogen,
Und ſie von Gott nicht mehr, nicht weniger
Gelehrt, als der Vernunft genügt.

### Patriarch.

                          Thut nichts!
Der Jude wird verbrannt ... Ja, wär' allein
2560 Schon dieſerwegen wert, dreimal verbrannt
Zu werden! — Was? ein Kind ohn' allen Glauben
Erwachſen laſſen? — Wie? die große Pflicht,
Zu glauben, ganz und gar ein Kind nicht lehren?
Das iſt zu arg! — Mich wundert ſehr, Herr Ritter,
2565 Euch ſelbſt ...

### Tempelherr.

          Ehrwürd'ger Herr, das übrige,
Wenn Gott will, in der Beichte.   (Will gehn.)

### Patriarch.

                          Was? mir nun

Nicht einmal Rede stehn? — Den Bösewicht,
Den Juden mir nicht nennen? — mir ihn nicht
Zur Stelle schaffen? — O da weiß ich Rat!
2570 Ich geh' sogleich zum Sultan. — Saladin,
Vermöge der Kapitulation,
Die er beschworen, muß uns, muß uns schützen;
Bei allen Rechten, allen Lehren schützen,
Die wir zu unsrer allerheiligsten
2575 Religion nur immer rechnen dürfen!
Gottlob! wir haben das Original.
Wir haben seine Hand, sein Siegel.   Wir! —
Auch mach' ich ihm gar leicht begreiflich, wie
Gefährlich selber für den Staat es ist,
2580 Nichts glauben! Alle bürgerliche Bande
Sind aufgelöset, sind zerrissen, wenn
Der Mensch nichts glauben darf. — Hinweg! hinweg
Mit solchem Frevel!...

### Tempelherr.

Schade, daß ich nicht
Den trefflichen Sermon mit beßrer Muße
2585 Genießen kann! Ich bin zum Saladin
Gerufen.

### Patriarch.

Ja? — Nun so — Nun freilich — Dann —

### Tempelherr.

Ich will den Sultan vorbereiten, wenn
Es Euer Hochehrwürden so gefällt.

### Patriarch.

O, oh! — Ich weiß, der Herr hat Gnade funden
2590 Vor Saladin! — Ich bitte meiner nur
Im besten bei ihm eingedenk zu sein. —
Mich treibt der Eifer Gottes lediglich.

Was ich zu viel thu', thu' ich ihm. — Das wolle
Doch ja der Herr erwägen! — Und nicht wahr,
2595 Herr Ritter? das vorhin Erwähnte von
Dem Juden, war nur ein Problema? — ist
Zu sagen —

Tempelherr.

Ein Problema.    (Geht ab.)

Patriarch.

                    (Dem ich tiefer
Doch auf den Grund zu kommen suchen muß.
Das wär' so wiederum ein Auftrag für
2600 Den Bruder Bonafides.) — Hier, mein Sohn!

(Er spricht im Abgehn mit dem Klosterbruder.)

———

Dritter Auftritt.

(Scene: ein Zimmer im Palaste des Saladin, in welches von
Sklaven eine Menge Beutel getragen, und auf dem Boden neben
einander gestellt werden.)

Saladin und bald darauf Sittah.

Saladin (der dazu kommt).

Nun wahrlich! das hat noch kein Ende. — Ist
Des Dings noch viel zurück?

Ein Sklave.

                    Wohl noch die Hälfte.

Saladin.

So tragt das übrige zu Sittah. — Und
Wo bleibt Al-Hafi? Das hier soll sogleich
2605 Al-Hafi zu sich nehmen. — Oder ob

Ich's nicht vielmehr dem Vater schicke? Hier
Fällt mir es doch nur durch die Finger. — Zwar
Man wird wohl endlich hart; und nun gewiß
Soll's Künste kosten, mir viel abzuzwacken.
2610 Bis wenigstens die Gelder aus Ägypten
Zur Stelle kommen, mag das Armut sehn
Wie's fertig wird! — Die Spenden bei dem Grabe,
Wenn die nur fortgehn! Wenn die Christenpilger
Mit leeren Händen nur nicht abziehn dürfen!
2615 Wenn nur —

**Sittah.**

   Was soll nun das? Was soll das Geld
Bei mir?

**Saladin.**

  Mach' dich davon bezahlt; und leg'
Auf Vorrat, wenn was übrig bleibt!

**Sittah.**

      Ist Nathan
Noch mit dem Tempelherrn nicht da?

**Saladin.**

      Er sucht
Ihn allerorten.

**Sittah.**

   Sieh doch, was ich hier,
2620 Indem mir so mein alt Geschmeide durch
Die Hände geht, gefunden. (Ihm ein klein Gemälde zeigend.)

**Saladin.**

    Ha! mein Bruder!
Das ist er, ist er! — War er! war er! ah! —
Ah wackrer lieber Junge, daß ich dich
So früh verlor! Was hätt' ich erst mit dir,
2625 An deiner Seit' erst unternommen! — Sittah,
Laß mir das Bild. Auch kenn' ich's schon: er gab

Es deiner ältern Schwester, feiner Lilla,
Die eines Morgens ihn fo ganz und gar
Nicht aus den Armen laffen wollt'.  Es war
2630 Der letzte, den er ausritt. — Ah, ich ließ
Ihn reiten, und allein! — Ah, Lilla ftarb
Vor Gram, und hat mir's nie vergeben, daß
Ich fo allein ihn reiten laffen. — Er
Blieb weg!

Sittah.

Der 'arme Bruder!

Saladin.

Laß nur gut
2635 Sein! — Einmal bleiben wir doch alle weg! —
Zudem, — wer weiß? Der Tod ift's nicht allein,
Der einem Jüngling feiner Art das Ziel
Verrückt.  Er hat der Feinde mehr; und oft
Erliegt der Stärkfte gleich dem Schwächften. — Nun,
2640 Sei wie ihm fei! — Ich muß das Bild doch mit
Dem jungen Tempelherrn vergleichen; muß
Doch fehn, wie viel mich meine Phantafie
Getäufcht.

Sittah.

Nur darum bring' ich's.  Aber gieb
Doch, gieb! Ich will dir das wohl fagen; das
2645 Verfteht ein weiblich Aug' am beften.

Saladin (zu einem Thürfteher, der hereintritt).

Wer
Ift da? — der Tempelherr? — Er komm'!

Sittah.

Euch nicht
Zu ftören: ihn mit meiner Neugier nicht
Zu irren —
(Sie fetzt fich feitwärts auf ein Sofa und läßt den Schleier fallen.)

### Saladin.

Gut so! gut! — (Und nun sein Ton!
Wie der wohl sein wird! — Assads Ton
2650 Schläft auch wohl wo in meiner Seele noch!)

---

### Vierter Auftritt.

#### Der Tempelherr und Saladin.

### Tempelherr.

Ich, dein Gefangner, Sultan...

### Saladin.

Mein Gefangner?
Wem ich das Leben schenke, werd' ich dem
Nicht auch die Freiheit schenken?

### Tempelherr.

Was dir ziemt
Zu thun, ziemt mir, erst zu vernehmen, nicht
2655 Vorauszusetzen.  Aber, Sultan, — Dank,
Besondern Dank dir für mein Leben zu
Beteuern, stimmt mit meinem Stand' und meinem
Charakter nicht. — Es steht in allen Fällen
Zu deinen Diensten wieder.

### Saladin.

Brauch' es nur
2660 Nicht wider mich! — Zwar ein paar Hände mehr,
Die gönnt' ich meinem Feinde gern.  Allein
Ihm so ein Herz auch mehr zu gönnen, fällt
Mir schwer. — Ich habe mich mit dir in nichts
Betrogen, braver junger Mann!  Du bist
2665 Mit Seel' und Leib mein Assad.  Sieh! ich könnte

Dich fragen: wo du denn die ganze Zeit
Gesteckt? in welcher Höhle du geschlafen?
In welchem Ginnistan, von welcher guten
Div diese Blume fort und fort so frisch
2670 Erhalten worden? Sieh! ich könnte dich
Erinnern wollen, was wir dort und dort
Zusammen ausgeführt. Ich könnte mit
Dir zanken, daß du ein Geheimnis doch
Vor mir gehabt! Ein Abenteuer mir
2675 Doch unterschlagen: — Ja, das könnt' ich; wenn
Ich dich nur säh', und nicht auch mich. — Nun, mag's!
Von dieser süßen Träumerei ist immer
Doch so viel wahr, daß mir in meinem Herbst
Ein Assad wieder blühen soll. — Du bist
2680 Es doch zufrieden, Ritter?

### Tempelherr.

Alles, was
Von dir mir kommt, — sei was es will — das lag
Als Wunsch in meiner Seele.

### Saladin.

Laß uns das
Sogleich versuchen. — Bliebst du wohl bei mir?
Um mir? — Als Christ, als Muselmann: gleich viel!
2685 Im weißen Mantel, oder Jamerlonk;
Im Tulban, oder deinem Filze: wie
Du willst! Gleich viel! Ich habe nie verlangt,
Daß allen Bäumen eine Rinde wachse.

### Tempelherr.

Sonst wärst du wohl auch schwerlich, der du bist:
2690 Der Held, der lieber Gottes Gärtner wäre.

**Saladin.**

Nun dann; wenn du nicht schlechter von mir denkst:
So wären wir ja halb schon richtig?

**Tempelherr.**

Ganz!

**Saladin** (ihm die Hand bietend).

Ein Wort?

**Tempelherr** (einschlagend).

Ein Mann! — Hiermit empfange mehr
Als du mir nehmen konntest.   Ganz der Deine!

**Saladin.**

2695 Zuviel Gewinn für einen Tag! zuviel! —
Kam er nicht mit!

**Tempelherr.**

Wer?

**Saladin.**

Nathan.

**Tempelherr** (frostig).

Nein.   Ich kam
Allein.

**Saladin.**

Welch eine That von dir! Und welch
Ein weises Glück, daß eine solche That
Zum Besten eines solchen Mannes ausschlug.

**Tempelherr.**

2700 Ja, ja!

**Saladin.**

So kalt? — Nein, junger Mann! wenn Gott

Was Gutes durch uns thut, muß man so kalt
Nicht sein! — selbst aus Bescheidenheit so kalt
Nicht scheinen wollen!

### Tempelherr.

                    Daß doch in der Welt
Ein jedes Ding so manche Seiten hat! —
2705 Von denen oft sich gar nicht denken läßt,
Wie sie zusammenpassen!

### Saladin.

                    Halte dich
Nur immer an die best', und preise Gott!
Der weiß, wie sie zusammenpassen. — Aber,
Wenn du so schwierig sein willst, junger Mann:
2710 So werd' auch ich ja wohl auf meiner Hut
Mich mit dir halten müssen? Leider bin
Auch ich ein Ding von vielen Seiten, die
Oft nicht so recht zu passen scheinen mögen.

### Tempelherr.

Das schmerzt! — Denn Argwohn ist so wenig sonst
2715 Mein Fehler —

### Saladin.

                    Nun, so sage doch, mit wem
Du's hast? — Es schien ja gar, mit Nathan. Wie?
Auf Nathan Argwohn? du? — Erklär' dich! sprich!
Komm, gieb mir deines Zutrau'ns erste Probe.

### Tempelherr.

Ich habe wider Nathan nichts. Ich zürn'
2720 Allein mit mir —

### Saladin.

                    Und über was?

**Tempelherr.**

Daß mir
Geträumt, ein Jude könn' auch wohl ein Jude
Zu sein verlernen; daß mir wachend so
Geträumt.

**Saladin.**

Heraus mit diesem wachen Traume!

**Tempelherr.**

Du weißt von Nathans Tochter, Sultan.   Was
2725 Ich für sie that, das that ich, — weil ich's that.
Zu stolz, Dank einzuernten, wo ich ihn
Nicht säete, verschmäht' ich Tag für Tag
Das Mädchen noch einmal zu sehn.   Der Vater
War fern; er kommt; er hört; er sucht mich auf;
2730 Er dankt; er wünscht, daß seine Tochter mir
Gefallen möge; spricht von Aussicht, spricht
Von heitern Fernen. — Nun, ich lasse mich
Beschwatzen, komme, sehe, finde wirklich
Ein Mädchen ... Ah, ich muß mich schämen, Sultan! —

**Saladin.**

2735 Dich schämen? — daß ein Judenmädchen auf
Dich Eindruck machte: doch wohl nimmermehr?

**Tempelherr.**

Daß diesem Eindruck, auf das liebliche
Geschwätz des Vaters hin, mein rasches Herz
So wenig Widerstand entgegensetzte! —
2740 Ich Tropf! ich sprang zum zweitenmal ins Feuer. —
Denn nun warb ich, und nun ward ich verschmäht.

**Saladin.**

Verschmäht?

**Tempelherr.**

Der weise Vater schlägt nun wohl

Mich platterdings nicht aus.   Der weise Vater
Muß aber doch sich erst erkunden, erst
2745 Besinnen.   Allerdings!  That ich denn das
Nicht auch?  Erkundete, besann ich denn
Mich erst nicht auch, als sie im Feuer schrie? —
Fürwahr! bei Gott! Es ist doch gar was Schönes,
So weise, so bedächtig sein!

### Saladin.
                              Nun, nun!
2750 So sieh doch einem Alten etwas nach!
Wie lange können seine Weigerungen
Denn dauern?  Wird er denn von dir verlangen,
Daß du erst Jude werden sollst?

### Tempelherr.
                              Wer weiß!
### Saladin.
Wer weiß? — der diesen Nathan besser kennt.

### Tempelherr.
2755 Der Aberglaub', in dem wir aufgewachsen,
Verliert, auch wenn wir ihn erkennen, darum
Doch seine Macht nicht über uns. — Es sind
Nicht alle frei, die ihrer Ketten spotten.

### Saladin.
Sehr reif bemerkt!  Doch Nathan wahrlich, Nathan . . .

### Tempelherr.
2760 Der Aberglauben schlimmster ist, den seinen
Für den erträglichern zu halten .

### Saladin.
                              Mag
Wohl sein! Doch Nathan . . . .

**Tempelherr.**

Dem allein
Die blöde Menschheit zu vertrauen, bis
Sie hellern Wahrheitstag gewöhne; dem
2765 Allein ...

**Saladin.**

Gut! Aber Nathan! — Nathaus Los
Ist diese Schwachheit nicht.

**Tempelherr.**

So dacht' ich auch! ...
Wenn gleichwohl dieser Ausbund aller Menschen
So ein gemeiner Jude wäre, daß
Er Christenkinder zu bekommen suchte,
2770 Um sie als Juden aufzuziehn: — wie dann?

**Saladin.**

Wer sagt ihm so was nach?

**Tempelherr.**

Das Mädchen selbst,
Mit welcher er mich körnt, mit deren Hoffnung
Er gern mir zu bezahlen schiene, was
Ich nicht umsonst für sie gethan soll haben: —
2775 Dies Mädchen selbst, ist seine Tochter — nicht;
Ist ein verzettelt Christenkind.

**Saladin.**

Das er
Dem ungeachtet dir nicht geben wollte?

**Tempelherr** (heftig).

Woll' oder wolle nicht! Er ist entdeckt.
Der tolerante Schwätzer ist entdeckt!
2780 Ich werde hinter diesen jüd'schen Wolf

Im philosoph'schen Schafspelz, Hunde schon
Zu bringen wissen, die ihn zausen sollen!

#### Saladin (ernst).

Sei ruhig, Christ!

#### Tempelherr.

Was? ruhig Christ? — Wenn Jud'
Und Muselmann, auf Jud', auf Muselmann
2785 Bestehen: soll allein der Christ den Christen
Nicht machen dürfen?

#### Saladin (noch ernster).

Ruhig, Christ!

#### Tempelherr (gelassen).

Ich fühle
Des Vorwurfs ganze Last, — die Saladin
In diese Silbe preßt! Ah, wenn ich wüßte,
Wie Assad, — Assad sich an meiner Stelle
2790 Hierbei genommen hätte!

#### Saladin.

Nicht viel besser! —
Vermutlich, ganz so brausend! — Doch, wer hat
Denn dich auch schon gelehrt, mich so wie er
Mit einem Worte zu bestechen? Freilich
Wenn alles sich verhält, wie du mir sagest:
2795 Kann ich mich selber kaum in Nathan finden. —
Indes, er ist mein Freund, und meiner Freunde
Muß keiner mit dem andern hadern. — Laß
Dich weisen! Geh behutsam! Gieb ihn nicht
Sofort den Schwärmern deines Pöbels preis!
2800 Verschweig, was deine Geistlichkeit, an ihm
Zu rächen, mir so nahe legen würde!

Sei keinem Juden, keinem Muselmanne
Zum Trotz ein Christ!

### Tempelherr.

                    Bald wär's damit zu spät!
Doch Dank der Blutbegier des Patriarchen,
2805 Des Werkzeug mir zu werden graute!

### Saladin.
                                        Wie?
Du kamst zum Patriarchen eher, als
Zu mir?

### Tempelherr.

        Im Sturm der Leidenschaft, im Wirbel
Der Unentschlossenheit! — Verzeih! — Du wirst
Von deinem Assad, fürcht' ich, ferner nun
2810 Nichts mehr in mir erkennen wollen.

### Saladin.
                                Wär'
Es diese Furcht nicht selbst! Mich dünkt, ich weiß,
Aus welchen Fehlern unsre Tugend keimt.
Pfleg' diese ferner nur, und jene sollen
Bei mir dir wenig schaden. — Aber geh!
2815 Such' du nun Nathan, wie er dich gesucht;
Und bring' ihn her.   Ich muß euch doch zusammen
Verständigen. — Wär' um das Mädchen dir
Im Ernst zu thun: sei ruhig.   Sie ist dein!
Auch soll es Nathan schon empfinden, daß
2820 Er ohne Schweinefleisch ein Christenkind
Erziehen dürfen! — Geh!

(Der Tempelherr geht ab, und Sittah verläßt das Sofa.)

### Fünfter Auftritt.

Saladin und Sittah.

#### Sittah.

Ganz ſonderbar!

#### Saladin.

Gelt, Sittah? Muß mein Aſſad nicht ein braver,
Ein ſchöner jnnger Mann geweſen ſein?

#### Sittah.

Wenn er ſo war, und nicht zu dieſem Bilde
2825 Der Tempelherr vielmehr geſeſſen! — Aber
Wie haſt du doch vergeſſen können dich
Nach ſeinen Eltern zu erkundigen?

#### Saladin.

Und insbeſondere wohl nach ſeiner Mutter?
Ob ſeine Mutter hier zu Lande nie
2830 Geweſen ſei? — Nicht wahr?

#### Sittah.

Das machſt du gut!

#### Saladin.

O, möglicher wär' nichts! Denn Aſſad war
Bei hübſchen Chriſtendamen ſo willkommen,
Auf hübſche Chriſtendamen ſo erpicht,
Daß einmal gar die Rede ging — Nun, nun;
2835 Man ſpricht nicht gern davon. — Genug; ich hab'
Ihn wieder! — will mit allen ſeinen Fehlern,
Mit allen Launen feines weichen Herzens
Ihn wieder haben! — Oh! das Mädchen muß
Ihm Nathan geben. Meinſt du nicht?

**Sittah.**

Ihm geben?

2840 Ihm laffen!

**Saladin.**

Allerdings! Was hätte Nathan,
Sobald er nicht ihr Vater ift, für Recht
Auf fie? Wer ihr das Leben fo erhielt,
Tritt einzig in die Rechte des, der ihr
Es gab.

**Sittah.**

Wie alfo, Saladin? wenn du
2845 Nur gleich das Mädchen zu dir nähmft? Sie nur
Dem unrechtmäßigen Befitzer gleich
Entzögeft?

**Saladin.**

Thäte das wohl not?

**Sittah.**

Not nun
Wohl eben nicht! — Die liebe Neubegier
Treibt mich allein, dir diefen Rat zu geben.
2850 Denn von gewiffen Männern mag ich gar
Zu gern, fo bald wie möglich, wiffen, was
Sie für ein Mädchen lieben können.

**Saladin.**

Nun,
So fchick' und laß fie holen.

**Sittah.**

Darf ich, Bruder?

**Saladin.**

Nur fchone Nathans! Nathan muß durchaus
2855 Nicht glauben, daß man mit Gewalt ihn von
Ihr trennen wolle.

### Sittah.

Sorge nicht.

### Saladin.

Und ich,
Ich muß schon selbst sehn, wo Al-Hafi bleibt.

———

### Sechster Auftritt.

(Scene: die offne Flur in Nathans Hause, gegen die Palmen zu;
wie im ersten Auftritte des ersten Aufzugs. Ein Teil der
Waren und Kostbarkeiten liegt ausgekramt, deren ebendaselbst gedacht wird.)

Nathan und Daja.

### Daja.

O, alles herrlich! alles auserlesen!
O, alles — wie nur Ihr es geben könnt.
2860 Wo wird der Silberstoff mit goldnen Ranken
Gemacht? Was kostet er? — Das nenn' ich noch
Ein Brautkleid! Keine Königin verlangt
Es besser.

### Nathan.

Brautkleid? Warum Brautkleid eben?

### Daja.

Je nun! Ihr dachtet daran freilich nicht,
2865 Als Ihr ihn kauftet. — Aber wahrlich, Nathan,
Der und kein andrer muß es sein! Er ist
Zum Brautkleid wie bestellt. Der weiße Grund;
Ein Bild der Unschuld: und die goldnen Ströme,
Die allerorten diesen Grund durchschlängeln;
2870 Ein Bild des Reichtums. Seht Ihr? Allerliebst!

**Nathan.**

Was witzelst du mir da? Von wessen Brautkleid
Sinnbilderst du mir so gelehrt? — Bist du
Denn Braut?

**Daja.**

Ich?

**Nathan.**

Nun wer denn?

**Daja.**

Ich? — lieber Gott!

**Nathan.**

Wer denn? Von wessen Brautkleid sprichst du denn? —
2875 Das alles ist ja dein, und keiner andern.

**Daja.**

Ist mein? Soll mein sein? — Ist für Recha nicht?

**Nathan.**

Was ich für Recha mitgebracht, das liegt
In einem andern Ballen. Mach'! nimm weg!
Trag deine Siebensachen fort!

**Daja.**

Versucher!
2880 Nein, wären es die Kostbarkeiten auch
Der ganzen Welt! Nicht rühr' an! wenn Ihr mir
Vorher nicht schwört, von dieser einzigen
Gelegenheit, dergleichen Euch der Himmel
Nicht zweimal schicken wird, Gebrauch zu machen.

**Nathan.**

2885 Gebrauch? von was? — Gelegenheit? wozu?

**Daja.**

O stellt Euch nicht so fremd! — Mit kurzen Worten!

Der Tempelherr liebt Recha: gebt sie ihm,
So hat doch einmal Eure Sünde, die
Ich länger nicht verschweigen kann, ein Ende.
2890 So kommt das Mädchen wieder unter Christen;
Wird wieder was sie ist; ist wieder, was
Sie ward: und Ihr, Ihr habt mit all dem Guten,
Das wir Euch nicht genug verdanken können,
Nicht feuerkohlen bloß auf Euer Haupt
2895 Gesammelt.

#### Nathan.

            Doch die alte Leier wieder? —
Mit einer neuen Saite nur bezogen,
Die, fürcht' ich, weder stimmt noch hält.

#### Daja.

                              Wie so?

#### Nathan.

Mir wär' der Tempelherr schon recht.   Ihm gönnt'
Ich Recha mehr als einem in der Welt.
2900 Allein ... Nun, habe nur Geduld.

#### Daja.

                              Geduld?
Geduld, ist Eure alte Leier nun
Wohl nicht?

#### Nathan.

            Nur wenig Tage noch Geduld! ...
Sieh doch! — Wer kommt denn dort? Ein Klosterbruder?
Geh, frag' ihn was er will.

#### Daja.

                  Was wird er wollen?
(Sie geht auf ihn zu und fragt.)

#### Nathan.

2905 So gieb! — und eh er bittet. — (Wüßt' ich nur

Dem Tempelherrn erst beizukommen, ohne
Die Ursach' meiner Neugier ihm zu sagen!
Denn wenn ich sie ihm sag', und der Verdacht
Ist ohne Grund: so hab' ich ganz umsonst
2910 Den Vater auf das Spiel gesetzt.) — Was ist's?

### Daja.

Er will Euch sprechen.

### Nathan.

Nun, so laß ihn kommen;
Und geh indes.

———

### Siebenter Auftritt.

### Nathan und der Klosterbruder.

### Nathan.

(Ich bliebe Rechas Vater
Doch gar zu gern! — Zwar kann ich's denn nicht bleiben,
Auch wenn ich aufhör', es zu heißen? — Ihr,
2915 Ihr selbst werd' ich's doch immer auch noch heißen,
Wenn sie erkennt, wie gern ich's wäre.) — Geh! —
Was ist zu Euern Diensten, frommer Bruder?

### Klosterbruder.

Nicht eben viel. — Ich freue mich, Herr Nathan,
Euch annoch wohl zu sehn.

### Nathan.

So kennt Ihr mich?

### Klosterbruder.

2920 Je nu; wer kennt Euch nicht? Ihr habt so manchem

Ja Euern Namen in die Hand gedrückt.
Er steht in meiner auch, seit vielen Jahren.

**Nathan** (nach seinem Beutel langend).

Kommt, Bruder, kommt; ich frisch' ihn auf.

**Klosterbruder.**

Habt Dank!
Ich würd' es Ärmern stehlen; nehme nichts. —
2925 Wenn Ihr mir nur erlauben wollt, ein wenig
Euch meinen Namen aufzufrischen. Denn
Ich kann mich rühmen, auch in Eure Hand
Etwas gelegt zu haben, was nicht zu
Verachten war.

**Nathan.**

Verzeiht! — Ich schäme mich —
2930 Sagt, was? — und nehmt zur Buße siebenfach
Den Wert desselben von mir an.

**Klosterbruder.**

Hört doch
Vor allen Dingen, wie ich selber nur
Erst heut an dies mein Euch vertrautes Pfand
Erinnert worden!

**Nathan.**

Mir vertrautes Pfand?

**Klosterbruder.**

2935 Vor kurzem saß ich noch als Eremit
Auf Quarantana, unweit Jericho.
Da kam arabisch Raubgesindel, brach
Mein Gotteshäuschen ab und meine Zelle,
Und schleppte mich mit fort. Zum Glück entkam
2940 Ich noch, und floh hierher zum Patriarchen,
Um mir ein ander Plätzchen auszubitten,

Allwo ich meinem Gott in Einsamkeit
Bis an mein selig Ende dienen könne.

### Nathan.

Ich steh' auf Kohlen, guter Bruder. Macht
2945 Es kurz. Das Pfand! das mir vertraute Pfand!

### Klosterbruder.

Sogleich, Herr Nathan. — Nun, der Patriarch
Versprach mir eine Siedelei auf Tabor,
Sobald als eine leer; und hieß inzwischen
Im Kloster mich als Laienbruder bleiben.
2950 Da bin ich jetzt, Herr Nathan; und verlange
Des Tags wohl hundertmal auf Tabor. Denn
Der Patriarch braucht mich zu allerlei,
Wovor ich großen Ekel habe. Zum
Exempel:

### Nathan.

Macht, ich bitt' Euch!

### Klosterbruder.

Nun, es kommt! —
2955 Da hat ihm jemand heut ins Ohr gesetzt:
Es lebe hier herum ein Jude, der
Ein Christenkind als seine Tochter sich
Erzöge.

### Nathan.

Wie? (Betroffen.)

### Klosterbruder.

Hört mich nur aus! — Indem
Er mir nun aufträgt, diesem Juden stracks,
2960 Wo möglich, auf die Spur zu kommen, und
Gewaltig sich ob eines solchen Frevels
Erzürnt, der ihm die wahre Sünde wider

Den heil'gen Geist bedünkt; — das ist, die Sünde,
Die aller Sünden größte Sünd' uns gilt,
2965 Nur daß' wir, Gott sei Dank, so recht nicht wissen,
Worin sie eigentlich besteht: — da wacht
Mit einmal mein Gewissen auf; und mir
Fällt bei, ich könnte selber wohl vorzeiten
Zu dieser unverzeihlich großen Sünde
2970 Gelegenheit gegeben haben. — Sagt:
Hat Euch ein Reitknecht nicht vor achtzehn Jahren
Ein Töchterchen gebracht von wenig Wochen?

#### Nathan.

Wie das? — Nun freilich — allerdings —

#### Klosterbruder.

Ei, seht
Mich doch recht an! — Der Reitknecht, der bin ich.

#### Nathan.

2975 Seid Ihr?

#### Klosterbruder.

Der Herr, von welchem ich's Euch brachte,
War — ist mir recht — ein Herr von Filnek. — Wolf
Von Filnek!

#### Nathan.

Richtig!

#### Klosterbruder.

Weil die Mutter kurz
Vorher gestorben war; und sich der Vater
Nach — mein' ich — Gazza plötzlich werfen mußte,
2980 Wohin das Würmchen ihm nicht folgen konnte:
So sandt' er's Euch. Und traf ich Euch damit
Nicht in Darun?

#### Nathan.

Ganz recht!

**Klosterbruder.**

Es wär' kein Wunder,
Wenn mein Gedächtnis mich betrög'. Ich habe
Der braven Herrn so viel gehabt; und diesem
2985 Hab' ich nur gar zu kurze Zeit gedient.
Er blieb bald drauf bei Askalon; und war
Wohl sonst ein lieber Herr.

**Nathan.**

Ja wohl! ja wohl!
Dem ich so viel, so viel zu danken habe!
Der mehr als einmal mich dem Schwert entrissen!

**Klosterbruder.**

2990 O schön! So werd't Ihr seines Töchterchens
Euch um so lieber angenommen haben.

**Nathan.**

Das könnt Ihr denken.

**Klosterbruder.**

Nun, wo ist es denn?
Es ist doch wohl nicht etwa gar gestorben? —
Laßt's lieber nicht gestorben sein! — Wenn sonst
2995 Nur niemand um die Sache weiß: so hat
Es gute Wege.

**Nathan.**

Hat es?

**Klosterbruder.**

Traut mir, Nathan!
Denn seht, ich denke so! Wenn an das Gute,
Das ich zu thun vermeine, gar zu nah
Was gar zu Schlimmes grenzt: so thu' ich lieber
3000 Das Gute nicht; weil wir das Schlimme zwar
So ziemlich zuverlässig kennen, aber
Bei weitem nicht das Gute. — War ja wohl

Natürlich; wenn das Christentöchterchen
Recht gut von Euch erzogen werden sollte:
3005 Daß Ihr's als Euer eigen Töchterchen
Erzögt. — Das hättet Ihr mit aller Lieb'
Und Treue nun gethan, und müßtet so
Belohnet werden? Das will mir nicht ein.
Ei freilich, klüger hättet Ihr gethan;
3010 Wenn Ihr die Christin durch die zweite Hand
Als Christin auferziehen lassen: aber
So hättet Ihr das Kindchen Eures Freunds
Auch nicht geliebt. Und Kinder brauchen Liebe,
Wär's eines wilden Tieres Lieb' auch nur,
3015 In solchen Jahren mehr, als Christentum.
Zum Christentume hat's noch immer Zeit.
Wenn nur das Mädchen sonst gesund und fromm
Vor Euern Augen aufgewachsen ist,
So blieb's vor Gottes Augen, was es war.
3020 Und ist denn nicht das gauze Christentum
Aufs Judentum gebaut? Es hat mich oft
Geärgert, hat mir Thränen g'nug gekostet,
Wenn Christen gar so sehr vergessen konnten,
Daß unser Herr ja selbst ein Jude war.

### Nathan.

3025 Ihr, guter Bruder, müßt mein Fürsprach sein,
Wenn Haß und Gleisnerei sich gegen mich
Erheben sollten, — wegen einer That —
Ah, wegen einer That! — Nur Ihr, Ihr sollt
Sie wissen! — Nehmt sie aber mit ins Grab!
3030 Noch hat mich nie die Eitelkeit versucht,
Sie jemand anderm zu erzählen. Euch
Allein erzähl' ich sie. Der frommen Einfalt
Allein erzähl' ich sie. Weil die allein
Versteht, was sich der gottergebne Mensch
3035 Für Thaten abgewinnen kann.

**Klosterbruder.**

Ihr seid

Gerührt, und Euer Auge steht voll Wasser?

**Nathan.**

Ihr traft mich mit dem Kinde zu Darun.
Ihr wißt wohl aber nicht, daß wenig Tage
Zuvor, in Gath die Christen alle Juden
3040 Mit Weib und Kind ermordet hatten; wißt
Wohl nicht, daß unter diesen meine Frau
Mit sieben hoffnungsvollen Söhnen sich
Befunden, die in meines Bruders Hause,
Zu dem ich sie geflüchtet, insgesamt
3045 Verbrennen müssen.

**Klosterbruder.**

Allgerechter!

**Nathan.**

Als

Ihr kamt, hatt' ich drei Tag' und Nächt' in Asch'
Und Staub vor Gott gelegen, und geweint. —
Geweint? Beiher mit Gott auch wohl gerechtet,
Gezürnt, getobt, mich und die Welt verwünscht;
3050 Der Christenheit den unversöhnlichsten
Haß zugeschworen —

**Klosterbruder.**

Ach! Ich glaub's Euch wohl!

**Nathan.**

Doch nun kam die Vernunft allmählich wieder.
Sie sprach mit sanfter Stimm': „Und doch ist Gott!
Doch war auch Gottes Ratschluß das! Wohlan!
3055 Komm! übe, was du längst begriffen hast;
Was sicherlich zu üben schwerer nicht
Als zu begreifen ist, wenn du nur willst.

Steh auf!" — Ich stand! und rief zu Gott: ich will!
Willst du nur, daß ich will! — Indem stiegt Ihr
3060 Vom Pferd, und überreichtet mir das Kind,
In Euern Mantel eingehüllt. — Was Ihr
Mir damals sagtet; was ich Euch: hab' ich
Vergessen. So viel weiß ich nur; ich nahm
Das Kind, trug's auf mein Lager, küßt' es, warf
3065 Mich auf die Knie und schluchzte: Gott! auf sieben
Doch nun schon eines wieder!

### Klosterbruder.

Nathan! Nathan!
Ihr seid ein Christ! — Bei Gott, Ihr seid ein Christ!
Ein beff'rer Christ war nie!

### Nathan.

Wohl uns! Denn was
Mich Euch zum Christen macht, das macht Euch mir
3070 Zum Juden! — Aber laßt uns länger nicht
Einander nur erweichen. Hier braucht's That!
Und ob mich siebenfache Liebe schon
Bald an dies einz'ge fremde Mädchen band;
Ob der Gedanke mich schon tötet, daß
3075 Ich meine sieben Söhn' in ihr auf's neue
Verlieren soll: — wenn sie von meinen Händen
Die Vorsicht wieder fordert, — ich gehorche!

### Klosterbruder.

Nun vollends! — Eben das bedacht' ich mich
So viel, Euch anzuraten! Und so hat's
3080 Euch Euer guter Geist schon angeraten!

### Nathan.

Nur muß der erste beste mir sie nicht
Entreißen wollen!

**Klosterbruder.**

Nein, gewiß nicht!

**Nathan.**

Wer

Auf sie nicht größre Rechte hat, als ich;
Muß frühere zum mind'sten haben —

**Klosterbruder.**

Freilich!

**Nathan.**

3085 Die ihm Natur und Blut erteilen.

**Klosterbruder.**

So

Mein' ich es auch!

**Nathan.**

Drum nennt mir nur geschwind
Den Mann, der ihr als Bruder oder Ohm,
Als Vetter oder sonst als Sipp' verwandt:
Ihm will ich sie nicht vorenthalten — Sie,
3090 Die jedes Hauses, jedes Glaubens Zierde
Zu sein erschaffen und erzogen ward. —
Ich hoff', Ihr wißt von diesem Euerm Herrn
Und dem Geschlechte dessen, mehr als ich.

**Klosterbruder.**

Das, guter Nathan, wohl nun schwerlich! — Denn
3095 Ihr habt ja schon gehört, daß ich nur gar
Zu kurze Zeit bei ihm gewesen.

**Nathan.**

Wißt

Ihr denn nicht wenigstens, was für Geschlechts
Die Mutter war? — War sie nicht eine Stauffin?

**Klosterbruder.**

Wohl möglich! — Ja, mich dünkt.

### Nathan.

Hieß nicht ihr Bruder
3100 Konrad von Stauffen? — und war Tempelherr?

### Klosterbruder.

Wenn mich's nicht trügt. Doch halt! Da fällt mir ein,
Daß ich vom sel'gen Herrn ein Büchelchen
Noch hab'. Ich zog's ihm aus dem Busen, als
Wir ihn bei Askalon verscharrten.

### Nathan.

Nun?

### Klosterbruder.

3105 Es sind Gebete drin. Wir nennen's ein
Brevier. — Das, dacht' ich, kann ein Christenmensch
Ja wohl noch brauchen. — Ich nun freilich nicht —
Ich kann nicht lesen —

### Nathan.

Thut nichts! — Nur zur Sache.

### Klosterbruder.

In diesem Büchelchen stehn vorn und hinten,
3110 Wie ich mir sagen lassen, mit des Herrn
Selbsteigner Hand die Angehörigen
Von ihm und ihr geschrieben.

### Nathan.

O erwünscht!
Geht! lauft! holt mir das Büchelchen. Geschwind!
Ich bin bereit mit Gold es aufzuwiegen;
3115 Und tausend Dank dazu! Eilt! lauft!

### Klosterbruder.

Recht gern!
Es ist Arabisch aber, was der Herr
Hineingeschrieben. (Ab.)

### Nathan.

Einerlei! Nur her! —
Gott! wenn ich doch das Mädchen noch behalten,
Und einen solchen Eidam mir damit
3120 Erkaufen könnte! — Schwerlich wohl! — Nun, fall'
Es aus, wie's will! — Wer mag es aber denn
Gewesen sein, der bei dem Patriarchen
So etwas angebracht? Das muß ich doch
Zu fragen nicht vergessen. — Wenn es gar
3125 Von Daja käme?

---

### Achter Auftritt.

#### Daja und Nathan.

**Daja** (eilig und verlegen).

Denkt doch, Nathan!

### Nathan.

Nun?

#### Daja.

Das arme Kind erschrak wohl recht darüber!
Da schickt . . .

### Nathan.

Der Patriarch?

#### Daja.

Des Sultans Schwester,
Prinzeſſin Sittah . . .

### Nathan.

Nicht der Patriarch?

#### Daja.

Nein, Sittah! — Hört Ihr nicht? — Prinzeſſin Sittah
3130 Schickt her, und läßt ſie zu ſich holen.

### Nathan.

Wen?
Läßt Recha holen? — Sittah läßt sie holen? —
Nun; wenn sie Sittah holen läßt, und nicht
Der Patriarch . . .

### Daja.

Wie kommt Ihr denn auf den?

### Nathan.

So hast du kürzlich nichts von ihm gehört?
3135 Gewiß nicht? Auch ihm nichts gesteckt?

### Daja.

Ich? ihm?

### Nathan.

Wo sind die Boten?

### Daja.

Vorn.

### Nathan.

Ich will sie doch
Aus Vorsicht selber sprechen. Komm! — Wenn nur
Vom Patriarchen nichts dahinter steckt. (Ab.)

### Daja.

Und ich — ich fürchte ganz was anders noch.
3140 Was gilt's? die einzige vermeinte Tochter
So eines reichen Juden wär' auch wohl
Für einen Muselmann nicht übel? — Hui,
Der Tempelherr ist drum. Ist drum: wenn ich
Den zweiten Schritt nicht auch noch wage; nicht
3145 Auch ihr noch selbst entdecke, wer sie ist! —
Getrost! Laß mich den ersten Augenblick,
Den ich allein sie habe, dazu brauchen!
Und der wird sein — vielleicht nun eben, wenn
Ich sie begleite. So ein erster Wink
3150 Kann unterwegens wenigstens nicht schaden.
Ja, ja! Nur zu! Jetzt oder nie! Nur zu! (Ihm nach.)

# Fünfter Aufzug.

## Erster Auftritt.

(Szene: das Zimmer in Saladins Palaste, in welches die Beutel
mit Geld getragen worden, die noch zu sehen.)
Saladin und bald darauf verschiedene Mamelucken.

### Saladin (im Hereintreten).

Da steht das Geld nun noch! Und niemand weiß
Den Derwisch aufzufinden, der vermutlich
Uns Schachbrett irgendwo geraten ist,
3155 Das ihn wohl seiner selbst vergessen macht; —
Warum nicht meiner? — Nun, Geduld! Was giebt's?

### Ein Mameluck.

Erwünschte Nachricht, Sultan! Freude, Sultan! . . .
Die Karawane von Kahira kommt;
Ist glücklich da! mit siebenjährigem
3160 Tribut des reichen Nils.

### Saladin.

· Brav, Ibrahim!
Du bist mir wahrlich ein willkommner Bote! —
Ha! endlich einmal! endlich! — Habe Dank
Der guten Zeitung.

### Der Mameluck (wartend).

(Nun? nur her damit!)

### Saladin.

Was wart'st du? — Geh nur wieder.

### Der Mameluck.

Dem Willkommnen
3165 Sonst nichts?

**Saladin.**

Was denn noch sonst?

**Der Mameluck.**

Dem guten Boten
Kein Botenbrot? — So wär' ich ja der erste,
Den Saladin mit Worten abzulohnen,
Doch endlich lernte? — Auch ein Ruhm! — Der erste,
Mit dem er knickerte.

**Saladin.**

So nimm dir nur
3100 Dort einen Beutel.

**Der Mameluck.**

Nein, nun nicht! Du kannst
Mir sie nun alle schenken wollen.

**Saladin.**

Trotz! —
Komm her! Da hast du zwei. — Im Ernst? er geht?
Thut mir's an Edelmut zuvor? — Denn sicher
Muß ihm es saurer werden, auszuschlagen,
3175 Als mir zu geben. — Ibrahim! — Was kommt
Mir denn auch ein, so kurz vor meinem Abtritt
Auf einmal ganz ein andrer sein zu wollen? —
Will Saladin als Saladin nicht sterben? —
So mußt' er auch als Saladin nicht leben.

**Ein zweiter Mameluck.**

Nun, Sultan! . . .

**Saladin.**

Wenn du mir zu melden kommst . .

**Zweiter Mameluck.**

Daß aus Ägypten der Transport nun da!

**Saladin.**

Ich weiß schon.

**Zweiter Mameluck.**

Kam ich doch zu spät!

**Saladin.**

Warum

Zu spät? — Da nimm für deinen guten Willen
Der Beutel einen oder zwei.

**Zweiter Mameluck.**

Macht drei!

**Saladin.**

3185 Ja, wenn du rechnen kannst! — So nimm sie nur.

**Zweiter Mameluck.**

Es wird wohl noch ein dritter kommen, — wenn
Er anders kommen kann.

**Saladin.**

Wie das?

**Zweiter Mameluck.**

Je nu;

Er hat auch wohl den Hals gebrochen! Denn
Sobald wir drei der Ankunft des Transports
3190 Versichert waren, sprengte jeder frisch
Davon. Der Vorderste, der stürzt; und so
Komm' ich nun vor, und bleib' auch vor bis in
Die Stadt; wo aber Ibrahim, der Lecker,
Die Gassen besser kennt.

**Saladin.**

O der Gestürzte!
3195 Freund, der Gestürzte! — Reit' ihm doch entgegen.

**Zweiter Mameluck.**

Das werd' ich ja wohl thun! — Und wenn er lebt:
So ist die Hälfte dieser Beutel sein. (Geht ab.)

### Saladin.

Sieh, welch ein guter edler Kerl auch das! —
Wer kann sich solcher Mamelucken rühmen?
3200 Und wär' mir denn zu denken nicht erlaubt,
Daß sie mein Beispiel bilden helfen? — Fort
Mit dem Gedanken, sie zu guter Letzt
Noch an ein andres zu gewöhnen! . . .

### Ein dritter Mameluck.

Sultan, . . .

### Saladin.

Bist du's, der stürzte?

### Dritter Mameluck.

Nein. Ich melde nur, —
3205 Daß Emir Mansor, der die Karawane
Geführt, vom Pferde steigt . . .

### Saladin.

Bring' ihn! geschwind! —
Da ist er ja!

———

## Zweiter Auftritt.

### Emir Mansor und Saladin.

### Saladin.

Willkommen, Emir! Nun,
Wie ist's gegangen? — Mansor, Mansor, hast
Uns lange warten lassen!

### Mansor.

Dieser Brief
3210 Berichtet, was dein Abulkassem erst
für Unruh' in Thebais dämpfen müssen:
Eh' wir es wagen durften abzugehen.
Den Zug darauf hab' ich beschleuniget
So viel, wie möglich war.

### Saladin.

Ich glaube dir! —
3215 Und nimm nur, guter Manfor, nimm sogleich...
Du thust es aber doch auch gern?... nimm frische
Bedeckung nur sogleich. Du mußt sogleich
Noch weiter; mußt der Gelder größern Teil
Auf Libanon zum Vater bringen.

### Manfor.
Gern!
3220 Sehr gern!

### Saladin.

Und nimm dir die Bedeckung ja
Nur nicht zu schwach. Es ist um Libanon
Nicht alles mehr so sicher. Hast du nicht
Gehört? Die Tempelherrn sind wieder rege.
Sei wohl auf deiner Hut! — Komm nur! Wo hält
3225 Der Zug? Ich will ihn sehn; und alles selbst
Betreiben. — Ihr! ich bin sodann bei Sittah.

---

### Dritter Auftritt.

(Scene: die Palmen vor Nathans Hause, wo der Tempelherr
auf= und niedergeht).

### Tempelherr.

Ins Haus nun will ich einmal nicht. — Er wird
Sich endlich doch wohl sehen lassen! — Man
Bemerkte mich ja sonst so bald, so gern! —
3230 Will's noch erleben, daß er sich's verbittet,
Vor seinem Hause mich so fleißig finden
Zu lassen. — Hm! — ich bin doch aber auch
Sehr ärgerlich. — Was hat mich denn nun so
Erbittert gegen ihn? — Er sagte ja:
3235 Noch schlüg' er mir nichts ab. Und Saladin

Hat's über ſich genommen, ihn zu ſtimmen. —
Wie? ſollte wirklich wohl in mir der Chriſt
Noch tiefer niſten, als in ihm der Jude? —
Wer kennt ſich recht? Wie könnt' ich ihm denn ſonſt
3240 Den kleinen Raub nicht gönnen wollen, den
Er ſich's zu ſolcher Angelegenheit
Gemacht, den Chriſten abzujagen? — Freilich;
Kein kleiner Raub, ein ſolch Geſchöpf! — Geſchöpf?
Und weſſen? — Doch des Sklaven nicht, der auf
3245 Des Lebens öden Strand den Block geflößt,
Und ſich davon gemacht? Des Künſtlers doch
Wohl mehr, der in dem hingeworfnen Blocke
Die göttliche Geſtalt ſich dachte, die
Er dargeſtellt? — Ach! Rechas wahrer Vater
3250 Bleibt, trotz dem Chriſten, der ſie zeugte — bleibt
In Ewigkeit der Jude. — Wenn ich mir
Sie lediglich als Chriſtendirne denke,
Sie ſonder alles das mir denke, was
Allein ihr ſo ein Jude geben konnte: —
3255 Sprich, Herz, — was wär' an ihr, das dir gefiel'?
Nichts! Wenig! Selbſt ihr Lächeln, wär' es nichts
Als ſanfte ſchöne Zuckung ihrer Muskeln;
Wär', was ſie lächeln macht, des Reizes unwert,
In den es ſich auf ihrem Munde kleidet: —
3260 Nein; ſelbſt ihr Lächeln nicht! Ich hab' es ja
Wohl ſchöner noch an Aberwitz, an Tand,
An Höhnerei, an Schmeichler und an Buhler,
Verſchwenden ſehn! — Hat's da mich auch bezaubert?
Hat's da mir auch den Wunſch entlockt, mein Leben
3265 In ſeinem Sonnenſcheine zu verflattern? —
Ich wüßte nicht. Und bin auf den doch launiſch,
Der dieſen höhern Wert allein ihr gab?
Wie das? warum? — Wenn ich den Spott verdiente,
Mit dem mich Saladin entließ! Schon ſchlimm

3270 Genug, daß Saladin es glauben konnte!
Wie klein ich ihm da scheinen mußte! wie
Verächtlich! — Und das alles um ein Mädchen? —
Kurt! Kurt! das geht so nicht. Lenk' ein! Wenn vollends
Mir Daja nur was vorgeplaudert hätte,
3275 Was schwerlich zu erweisen stünde? — Sieh,
Da tritt er endlich, in Gespräch vertieft,
Aus seinem Hause! — Ha! mit wem! — Mit ihm?
Mit meinem Klosterbruder? — Ha! so weiß
Er sicherlich schon alles! ist wohl gar
3280 Dem Patriarchen schon verraten! — Ha!
Was hab' ich Querkopf nun gestiftet! — Daß
Ein einz'ger Funken dieser Leidenschaft
Doch unsers Hirns so viel verbrennen kann! —
Geschwind entschließ dich, was nunmehr zu thun!
3285 Ich will hier seitwärts ihrer warten; — ob
Vielleicht der Klosterbruder ihn verläßt.

---

### Vierter Auftritt.

Nathan und der Klosterbruder.

**Nathan** (im Näherkommen).

Habt nochmals, guter Bruder, vielen Dank!

**Klosterbruder.**

Und Ihr desgleichen!

**Nathan.**

Ich? von Euch? wofür?
Für meinen Eigensinn, Euch aufzudringen,
3290 Was Ihr nicht braucht? — Ja, wenn ihm Eurer nur
Auch nachgegeben hätt'; Ihr mit Gewalt
Nicht wolltet reicher sein, als ich.

**Klosterbruder.**

Das Buch
Gehört ja ohnedem nicht mir; gehört
Ja ohnedem der Tochter; ist ja so
3295 Der Tochter ganzes väterliches Erbe. —
Je nu, sie hat ja Euch. — Gott gebe nur,
Daß Ihr es nie bereuen dürft, so viel
Für sie gethan zu haben!

**Nathan.**

Kann ich das?
Das kann ich nie. Seid unbesorgt!

**Klosterbruder.**

Nu, nu!
3300 Die Patriarchen und die Tempelherren...

**Nathan.**

Vermögen mir des Bösen nie so viel
Zu thun, daß irgend was mich reuen könnte:
Geschweige, das! — Und seid Ihr denn so ganz
Versichert, daß ein Tempelherr es ist,
3305 Der Euern Patriarchen hetzt?

**Klosterbruder.**

Es kann
Beinah kein andrer sein. Ein Tempelherr
Sprach kurz vorher mit ihm; und was ich hörte,
Das klang darnach.

**Nathan.**

Es ist doch aber nur
Ein einziger jetzt in Jerusalem.
3310 Und diesen kenn' ich. Dieser ist mein Freund.
Ein junger, edler, offner Mann!

**Klosterbruder.**

Ganz recht;

Der nämliche! — Doch was man ist, und was
Man sein muß in der Welt, das paßt ja wohl
Nicht immer.

#### Nathan.

        Leider nicht. — So thue, wer's
3315 Auch immer ist, sein Schlimmstes oder Bestes!
Mit Eurem Buche, Bruder, troß' ich allen;
Und gehe graden Wegs damit zum Sultan.

#### Klosterbruder.

Viel Glücks! Ich will Euch denn nur hier verlassen.

#### Nathan.

Und habt sie nicht einmal gesehn? — Kommt ja
3320 Doch bald, doch fleißig wieder. — Wenn nur heut
Der Patriarch noch nichts erfährt! — Doch was?
Sagt ihm auch heute, was Ihr wollt.

#### Klosterbruder.

                      Ich nicht.
Lebt wohl! (Geht ab.)

#### Nathan.

        Vergeßt uns ja nicht, Bruder! — Gott!
Daß ich nicht gleich hier unter freiem Himmel
3325 Auf meine Kniee sinken kann! Wie sich
Der Knoten, der so oft mir bange machte,
Nun von sich selber löset! — Gott! wie leicht
Mir wird, daß ich nun weiter auf der Welt
Nichts zu verbergen habe! daß ich vor
3330 Den Menschen nun so frei kann wandeln, als
Vor dir, der du allein den Menschen nicht
Nach seinen Thaten brauchst zu richten, die
So selten seine Thaten sind, o Gott! —

### Fünfter Auftritt.

Nathan und der Tempelherr, der von der Seite auf ihn zukommt.

**Tempelherr.**

He! wartet, Nathan; nehmt mich mit!

**Nathan.**

Wer ruft? —

3335 Seid Ihr es, Ritter? Wo gewesen, daß
Ihr bei dem Sultan Euch nicht treffen laßen?

**Tempelherr.**

Wir sind einander fehlgegangen. Nehmt's
Nicht übel.

**Nathan.**

Ich nicht; aber Saladin ...

**Tempelherr.**

Ihr wart nur eben fort ..

**Nathan.**

Und spracht ihn doch?

3340 Nun, so ist's gut.

**Tempelherr.**

Er will uns aber beide
Zusammen sprechen.

**Nathan.**

Desto besser. Kommt
Nur mit. Mein Gang stand ohnehin zu ihm. —

**Tempelherr.**

Ich darf ja doch wohl fragen, Nathan, wer
Euch da verließ?

**Nathan.**

Ihr kennt ihn doch wohl nicht?

**Tempelherr.**

3345 War's nicht die gute Haut, der Laienbruder,
Des sich der Patriarch so gern zum Stöber
Bedient?

**Nathan.**

Kann sein! Beim Patriarchen ist
Er allerdings.

**Tempelherr.**

Der Pfiff ist gar nicht übel:
Die Einfalt vor der Schurkerei voraus
3350 Zu schicken.

**Nathan.**

Ja, die dumme; — nicht die fromme.

**Tempelherr.**

An fromme glaubt kein Patriarch.

**Nathan.**

Für den
Nun steh' ich. Der wird seinem Patriarchen
Nichts Ungebührliches vollziehen helfen.

**Tempelherr.**

So stellt er wenigstens sich an. — Doch hat
3355 Er Euch von mir denn nichts gesagt?

**Nathan.**

Von Euch?
Von Euch nun namentlich wohl nichts. — Er weiß
Ja wohl auch schwerlich Euern Namen?

**Tempelherr.**

Schwerlich.

**Nathan.**

Von einem Tempelherren freilich hat
Er mir gesagt . . .

#### Tempelherr.

Und was?

#### Nathan.

Womit er Euch
3360 Doch ein= für allemal nicht meinen kann!

#### Tempelherr.

Wer weiß? Laßt doch nur hören.

#### Nathan.

Daß mich einer
Bei seinem Patriarchen angeklagt . . .

#### Tempelherr.

Euch angeklagt? — Das ist, mit seiner Gunst —
Erlogen. — Hört mich, Nathan! — Ich bin nicht
3365 Der Mensch, der irgend etwas abzuleugnen
Imstande wäre. Was ich that, das that ich!
Doch bin ich auch nicht der, der alles, was
Er that, als wohlgethan verteid'gen möchte.
Was sollt' ich eines Fehls mich schämen? Hab'
3370 Ich nicht den festen Vorsatz ihn zu bessern?
Und weiß ich etwa nicht, wie weit mit dem
Es Menschen bringen können? — Hört mich, Nathan!
Ich bin des Laienbruders Tempelherr,
Der Euch verklagt soll haben, allerdings. —
3375 Ihr wißt ja, was mich wurmisch machte! was
Mein Blut in allen Adern sieden machte!
Ich Gauch! — ich kam, so ganz mit Leib und Seel'
Euch in die Arme mich zu werfen. Wie
Ihr mich empfingt — wie kalt — wie lau — denn
3380 Ist schlimmer noch als kalt; wie abgemessen
Mir auszubeugen Ihr beflissen wart;
Mit welchen aus der Luft gegriffnen Fragen
Ihr Antwort mir zu geben scheinen wolltet:

Das darf ich kaum mir jetzt noch denken, wenn
3385 Ich soll gelassen bleiben. — Hört mich, Nathan! —
In dieser Gährung schlich mir Daja nach,
Und warf mir ihr Geheimnis an den Kopf,
Das mir den Aufschluß Eures rätselhaften
Betragens zu enthalten schien.

### Nathan.
Wie das?

### Tempelherr.

3390 Hört mich nur aus! — Ich bildete mir ein,
Ihr wolltet, was Ihr einmal nun den Christen
So abgejagt, an einen Christen wieder
Nicht gern verlieren. Und so fiel mir ein,
Euch kurz und gut das Messer an die Kehle
3395 Zu setzen.

### Nathan.
Kurz und gut? und gut? — Wo steckt
Das Gute?

### Tempelherr.

Hört mich, Nathan! — Allerdings:
Ich that nicht recht! — Ihr seid wohl gar nicht schuldig. —
Die Närrin Daja weiß nicht was sie spricht —
Ist Euch gehässig — Sucht Euch nur damit
3400 In einen bösen Handel zu verwickeln —
Kann sein! kann sein! — Ich bin ein junger Laffe,
Der immer nur an beiden Enden schwärmt;
Bald viel zu viel, bald viel zu wenig thut —
Auch das kann sein! Verzeiht mir, Nathan.

### Nathan.
Wenn
3405 Ihr so mich freilich fasset —

### Tempelherr.
Kurz, ich ging
Zum Patriarchen! — hab' Euch aber nicht

Genannt. Das ist erlogen, wie gesagt!
Ich hab' ihm bloß den Fall ganz allgemein
Erzählt, um seine Meinung zu vernehmen. —
3410 Auch das hätt' unterbleiben können: ja doch! —
Denn kannt' ich nicht den Patriarchen schon
Als einen Schurken? Konnt' ich Euch nicht selber
Nur gleich zur Rede stellen? — Mußt' ich der
Gefahr, so einen Vater zu verlieren,
3415 Das arme Mädchen opfern? — Nun, was thut's?
Die Schurkerei des Patriarchen, die
So ähnlich immer sich erhält, hat mich
Des nächsten Weges wieder zu mir selbst
Gebracht. — Denn hört mich, Nathan; hört mich aus! —
3420 Gesetzt; er wüßt' auch Euern Namen: was
Nun mehr, was mehr? — Er kann Euch ja das Mädchen
Nur nehmen, wenn sie niemands ist, als Euer.
Er kann sie doch aus Euerm Hause nur
Ins Kloster schleppen. — Also — gebt sie mir!
3425 Gebt sie nur mir; und laßt ihn kommen. Ha!
Er soll's wohl bleiben lassen, mir mein Weib
Zu nehmen. — Gebt sie mir; geschwind! — Sie sei
Nun Eure Tochter, oder sei es nicht!
Sei Christin, oder Jüdin, oder keines!
3430 Gleich viel! gleich viel! Ich werd' Euch weder jetzt
Noch jemals sonst in meinem ganzen Leben
Darum befragen. Sei, wie's sei!

**Nathan.**

                              Ihr wähnt
Wohl gar, daß mir die Wahrheit zu verbergen
Sehr nötig?

**Tempelherr.**

          Sei, wie's sei!

**Nathan.**

                    Ich hab' es ja

3435 Euch — oder wem es sonst zu wissen ziemt —
Noch nicht geleugnet, daß sie eine Christin,
Und nichts als meine Pflegetochter ist. —
Warum ich's aber ihr noch nicht entdeckt? —
Darüber brauch' ich nur bei ihr mich zu
3440 Entschuldigen.

**Tempelherr.**

Das sollt Ihr auch bei ihr
Nicht brauchen. — Gönnt's ihr doch, daß sie Euch nie
Mit andern Augen darf betrachten! Spart
Ihr die Entdeckung doch! — Noch habt Ihr ja,
Ihr ganz allein, mit ihr zu schalten. Gebt
3445 Sie mir! Ich bitt' Euch, Nathan; gebt sie mir!
Ich bin's allein, der sie zum zweitenmale
Euch retten kann — und will.

**Nathan.**

Ja — konnte! konnte!
Nun auch nicht mehr. Es ist damit zu spät.

**Tempelherr.**

Wie so? zu spät?

**Nathan.**

Dank sei dem Patriarchen ..

**Tempelherr.**

3450 Dem Patriarchen? Dank? ihm Dank? wofür?
Dank hätte der bei uns verdienen wollen?
Wofür? wofür? .

**Nathan.**

Daß wir nun wissen, wem
Sie anverwandt; nun wissen, wessen Händen
Sie sicher ausgeliefert werden kann.

**Tempelherr.**

3455 Das dank' ihm — wer für mehr ihm danken wird!

#### Nathan.

Aus diesen müßt Ihr sie nun auch erhalten;
Und nicht aus meinen.

#### Tempelherr.

   Arme Recha! Was
Dir alles zustößt, arme Recha! Was
Ein Glück für andre Waisen wäre, wird
3460 Dein Unglück! — Nathan! — Und wo sind sie, diese
Verwandte?

#### Nathan.

 Wo sie sind?

#### Tempelherr.

    Und wer sie sind?

#### Nathan.

Besonders hat ein Bruder sich gefunden,
Bei dem Ihr um sie werben müßt.

#### Tempelherr.

     Ein Bruder?
Was ist er, dieser Bruder? Ein Soldat?
3465 Ein Geistlicher? — Laßt hören, was ich mir
Versprechen darf.

#### Nathan.

   Ich glaube, daß er keines
Von beiden — oder beides ist. Ich kenn'
Ihn noch nicht recht.

#### Tempelherr.

 Und sonst?

#### Nathan.

    Ein braver Mann!
Bei dem sich Recha gar nicht übel wird
3470 Befinden.

**Tempelherr.**

Doch ein Christ! — Ich weiß zuzeiten
Auch gar nicht, was ich von Euch denken soll: —
Nehmt mir's nicht ungut, Nathan. — Wird sie nicht
Die Christin spielen müssen, unter Christen?
Und wird sie, was sie lange g'nug gespielt,
3475 Nicht endlich werden? Wird den lautern Weizen,
Den Ihr gesä't, das Unkraut endlich nicht
Ersticken? — Und das kümmert Euch so wenig?
Dem ungeachtet könnt Ihr sagen — Ihr? —
Daß sie bei ihrem Bruder sich nicht übel
3480 Befinden werde?

**Nathan.**

Denk' ich! hoff' ich! — Wenn
Ihr ja bei ihm was mangeln sollte, hat
Sie Euch und mich denn nicht noch immer?

**Tempelherr.**

Oh!
Was wird bei ihm ihr mangeln können! Wird
Das Brüderchen mit Essen und mit Kleidung,
3485 Mit Naschwerk und mit Putz, das Schwesterchen
Nicht reichlich g'nug versorgen? Und was braucht
Ein Schwesterchen denn mehr? — Ei freilich: auch
Noch einen Mann! — Nun, nun; auch den, auch den
Wird ihr das Brüderchen zu seiner Zeit
3490 Schon schaffen; wie er immer nur zu finden!
Der Christlichste der Beste! — Nathan, Nathan!
Welch einen Engel hattet Ihr gebildet,
Den Euch nun andre so verhunzen werden!

**Nathan.**

Hat keine Not! Er wird sich unsrer Liebe
3495 Noch immer wert genug behaupten.

**Tempelherr.**

Sagt

Das nicht! Von meiner Liebe sagt das nicht!
Denn die läßt nichts sich unterschlagen; nichts.
Es sei auch noch so klein! Auch keinen Namen! —
Doch halt! — Argwohnt sie wohl bereits, was mit
3500 Ihr vorgeht?

**Nathan.**

Möglich; ob ich schon nicht wüßte,
Woher?

**Tempelherr.**

Auch eben viel; sie soll — sie muß
In beiden Fällen, was ihr Schicksal droht,
Von mir zuerst erfahren. Mein Gedanke,
Sie eher wieder nicht zu sehn, zu sprechen,
3505 Als bis ich sie die Meine nennen dürfe,
Fällt weg. Ich eile . . .

**Nathan.**

Bleibt! wohin?

**Tempelherr.**

Zu ihr!

Zu sehn, ob diese Mädchenseele Manns genug
Wohl ist, den einzigen Entschluß zu fassen
Der ihrer würdig wäre!

**Nathan.**

Welchen?

**Tempelherr.**

Den:

3510 Nach Euch und ihrem Bruder weiter nicht
Zu fragen —

**Nathan.**

Und?

**Tempelherr.**

Und mir zu folgen; — wenn

Sie drüber eines Muselmannes Frau
Auch werden müßte.

#### Nathan.

Bleibt! Ihr trefft sie nicht.
Sie ist bei Sittah, bei des Sultans Schwester.

#### Tempelherr.

3515 Seit wann? warum?

#### Nathan.

Und wollt Ihr da bei ihnen
Zugleich den Bruder finden: kommt nur mit.

#### Tempelherr.

Den Bruder? welchen? Sittahs oder Rechas?

#### Nathan.

Leicht beide. Kommt nur mit! Ich bitt' Euch, kommt!
(Er führt ihn fort.)

---

### Sechster Auftritt.

(Scene: in Sittahs Harem).

Sittah und Recha in Unterhaltung begriffen.

#### Sittah.

Was freu' ich mich nicht deiner, süßes Mädchen! —
3520 Sei so beklemmt nur nicht! so angst! so schüchtern! —
Sei munter! sei gesprächiger! vertrauter!

#### Recha.

Prinzessin, ...

#### Sittah.

Nicht doch! nicht Prinzessin! Nenn'
Mich Sittah, — deine Freundin, — deine Schwester.
Nenn' mich dein Mütterchen! — Ich könnte das

3525 Ja schier auch sein. — So jung! so klug! so fromm!
Was du nicht alles weißt! nicht alles mußt
Gelesen haben!

**Recha.**

Ich gelesen? — Sittah,
Du spottest deiner kleinen albern Schwester.
Ich kann kaum lesen.

**Sittah.**

Kannst kaum, Lügnerin!

**Recha.**

3530 Ein wenig meines Vaters Hand! — Ich meinte,
Du sprächst von Büchern.

**Sittah.**

Allerdings! von Büchern.

**Recha.**

Nun, Bücher wird mir wahrlich schwer zu lesen! —

**Sittah.**

Im Ernst?

**Recha.**

In ganzem Ernst. Mein Vater liebt
Die kalte Buchgelehrsamkeit, die sich
3535 Mit toten Zeichen ins Gehirn nur drückt,
Zu wenig.

**Sittah.**

Ei, was sagst du! — Hat indes
Wohl nicht sehr unrecht! — Und so manches, was
Du weißt ..?

**Recha.**

Weiß ich allein aus seinem Munde.
Und könnte bei dem meisten dir noch sagen,
3540 Wie? wo? warum? er mich's gelehrt.

### Sittah.

So hängt
Sich freilich alles beffer an. So lernt
Mit eins die ganze Seele.

### Recha.

Sicher hat
Auch Sittah wenig oder nichts gelefen!

### Sittah.

Wie fo? — Ich bin nicht ftolz aufs Gegenteil. —
3545 Allein wie fo? Dein Grund! Sprich dreift. Dein Grund?

### Recha.

Sie ift fo fchlecht und recht; fo unverfünftelt;
So ganz fich felbft nur ähnlich ...

### Sittah.

Nun?

### Recha.

Das follen
Die Bücher uns nur felten laffen: fagt
Mein Vater.

### Sittah.

O was ift dein Vater für
3550 Ein Mann!

### Recha.

Nicht wahr?

### Sittah.

Wie nah er immer doch
Zum Ziele trifft!

### Recha.

Nicht wahr? — Und diefen Vater —

### Sittah.

Was ift dir, Liebe?

#### Recha.

Diesen Vater —

#### Sittah.

Gott!

Du weinst?

#### Recha.

Und diesen Vater — Ah! es muß
Heraus! Mein Herz will Luft, will Luft...
(Wirft sich, von Thränen überwältigt, zu ihren Füßen).

#### Sittah.

Kind, was
3555 Geschieht dir? Recha?

#### Recha.

Diesen Vater soll —
Soll ich verlieren!

#### Sittah.

Du? verlieren? ihn?
Wie das? — Sei ruhig! — Nimmermehr! — Steh auf!

#### Recha.

Du sollst vergebens dich zu meiner Freundin,
Zu meiner Schwester nicht erboten haben!

#### Sittah.

3560 Ich bin's ja! bin's! — Steh doch nur auf! Ich muß
Sonst Hilfe rufen.

#### Recha (die sich ermannt und aufsteht).

Ah! verzeih! vergieb! —
Mein Schmerz hat mich vergessen machen, wer
Du bist. Vor Sittah gilt kein Winseln, kein
Verzweifeln. Kalte, ruhige Vernunft
3565 Will alles über sie allein vermögen.
Wes Sache diese bei ihr führt, der siegt!

**Sittah.**

Nun denn?

**Recha.**

Nein; meine Freundin, meine Schwester
Giebt das nicht zu! Giebt nimmer zu, daß mir
Ein andrer Vater aufgedrungen werde!

**Sittah.**

3570 Ein andrer Vater? aufgedrungen? dir?
Wer kann das? kann das auch nur wollen, Liebe?

**Recha.**

Wer? Meine gute böse Daja kann
Das wollen, — will das können. — Ja; du kennst
Wohl diese gute böse Daja nicht?
3575 Nun, Gott vergeb' es ihr! — belohn' es ihr!
Sie hat mir so viel Gutes, — so viel Böses
Erwiesen!

**Sittah.**

Böses dir? — So muß sie Gutes
Doch wahrlich wenig haben.

**Recha.**

Doch! recht viel,
Recht viel!

**Sittah.**

Wer ist sie?

**Recha.**

Eine Christin, die
3580 In meiner Kindheit mich gepflegt; mich so
Gepflegt! — Du glaubst nicht! — Die mir eine Mutter
So wenig missen lassen! — Gott vergelt'
Es ihr! — Die aber mich auch so geängstet!
Mich so gequält!

### Sittah.

Und über was? warum?

3585 Wie?

### Recha.

Ach! die arme Frau, — ich sag' dir's ja —
Ist eine Christin; — muß aus Liebe quälen; —
Ist eine von den Schwärmerinnen, die
Den allgemeinen, einzig wahren Weg
Nach Gott, zu wissen wähnen!

### Sittah.

Nun versteh' ich!

### Recha.

3590 Und sich gedrungen fühlen, einen jeden,
Der dieses Wegs verfehlt, darauf zu lenken. —
Kaum können sie auch anders. Denn ist's wahr,
Daß dieser Weg allein nur richtig führt:
Wie sollen sie gelassen ihre Freunde
3595 Auf einem andern wandeln sehn, — der ins
Verderben stürzt, ins ewige Verderben?
Es müßte möglich sein, denselben Menschen
Zur selben Zeit zu lieben und zu hassen. —
Auch ist's das nicht, was endlich laute Klagen
3600 Mich über sie zu führen zwingt. Ihr Seufzen,
Ihr Warnen, ihr Gebet, ihr Drohen hätt'
Ich gern noch länger ausgehalten; gern!
Es brachte mich doch immer auf Gedanken,
Die gut und nützlich. Und wem schmeichelt's doch
3605 Im Grunde nicht, sich gar so wert und teuer,
Von wem's auch sei, gehalten fühlen, daß
Er den Gedanken nicht ertragen kann,
Er müss' einmal auf ewig uns entbehren!

### Sittah.

Sehr wahr!

**Recha.**

Allein — allein — das geht zu weit!
3610 Dem kann ich nichts entgegensetzen; nicht
Geduld, nicht Überlegung; nichts!

**Sittah.**
Was? wem?

**Recha.**

Was sie mir eben jetzt entdeckt will haben.

**Sittah.**

Entdeckt? und eben jetzt?

**Recha.**
Nur eben jetzt!
Wir nahten, auf dem Weg hierher, uns einem
3615 Verfallnen Christentempel. Plötzlich stand
Sie still; schien mit sich selbst zu kämpfen; blickte
Mit nassen Augen bald gen Himmel, bald
Auf mich. Komm, sprach sie endlich, laß uns hier
Durch diesen Tempel in die Richte gehn!
3620 Sie geht; ich folg' ihr, und mein Auge schweift
Mit Graus die wankenden Ruinen durch.
Nun steht sie wieder; und ich sehe mich
An den versunknen Stufen eines morschen
Altars mit ihr. Wie ward mir? als sie da
3625 Mit heißen Thränen, mit gerungnen Händen,
Zu meinen Füßen stürzte ...

**Sittah.**

Gutes Kind!

**Recha.**

Und bei der Göttlichen, die da wohl sonst
So manch Gebet erhört, so manches Wunder
Verrichtet habe, mich beschwor; — mit Blicken

3630 Des wahren Mitleids mich beschwor, mich meiner
Doch zu erbarmen! — Wenigstens, ihr zu
Vergeben, wenn sie mir entdecken müsse,
Was ihre Kirch' auf mich für Anspruch habe.

### Sittah.

(Unglückliche! — Es ahnte mir!)

### Recha.

                    Ich sei
3635 Aus christlichem Geblüte; sei getauft;
Sei Nathans Tochter nicht; er nicht mein Vater! —
Gott! Gott! Er nicht mein Vater! — Sittah! Sittah!
Sieh mich aufs neu' zu deinen Füßen ...

### Sittah.

                    Recha!
Nicht doch! steh auf! — Mein Bruder kommt! steh auf!

---

### Siebenter Auftritt.

#### Saladin und die Vorigen.

### Saladin.

3640 Was giebt's hier, Sittah?

### Sittah.

          Sie ist von sich! Gott!

### Saladin.

Wer ist's?

### Sittah.

    Du weißt ja ...

### Saladin.

          Unsers Nathans Tochter?

Was fehlt ihr?

**Sittah.**

Komm doch zu dir, Kind! — Der Sultan ...

**Recha**
(die sich auf den Knien zu Saladins Füßen schleppt, den Kopf zur Erde gesenkt).

Ich steh' nicht auf! nicht eher auf! — mag eher
Des Sultans Antlitz nicht erblicken! — eher
3645 Den Abglanz ewiger Gerechtigkeit
Und Güte nicht in seinen Augen, nicht
Auf seiner Stirn bewundern ...

**Saladin.**

Steh ... steh auf!

**Recha.**

Eh' er mir nicht verspricht ...

**Saladin.**

Komm! ich verspreche ...
Sei was es will!

**Recha.**

Nicht mehr, nicht weniger,
3650 Als meinen Vater mir zu lassen; und
Mich ihm! — Noch weiß ich nicht, wer sonst mein Vater
Zu sein verlangt; — verlangen kann. Will's auch
Nicht wissen. Aber macht denn nur das Blut
Den Vater? nur das Blut?

**Saladin** (der sie aufhebt).

Ich merke wohl! —
3655 Wer war so grausam denn, dir selbst — dir selbst
Dergleichen in den Kopf zu setzen? Ist
Es denn schon völlig ausgemacht? erwiesen?

**Recha.**

Muß wohl! Denn Daja will von meiner Amm'
Es haben.

**Saladin.**

Deiner Amme!

**Recha.**

Die es sterbend
3660 Ihr zu vertrauen sich verbunden fühlte.

**Saladin.**

Gar sterbend! — Nicht auch faselnd schon? — Und wär's
Auch wahr! — Ja wohl: das Blut, das Blut allein
Macht lange noch den Vater nicht! macht kaum
Den Vater eines Tieres! giebt zum höchsten
3665 Das erste Recht, sich diesen Namen zu
Erwerben! — Laß dir doch nicht bange sein! —
Und weißt du was? Sobald der Väter zwei
Sich um dich streiten: — laß sie beide; nimm
Den dritten! — Nimm dann mich zu deinem Vater!

**Sittah.**

3670 O thu's! o thu's!

**Saladin.**

Ich will ein guter Vater,
Recht guter Vater sein! — Doch halt! mir fällt
Noch viel was Beffers bei. — Was brauchst du denn
Der Väter überhaupt? Wenn sie nun sterben?
Beizeiten sich nach einem umgesehn,
3675 Der mit uns um die Wette leben will!
Kennst du noch keinen? . . .

**Sittah.**

Mach' sie nicht erröten!

**Saladin.**

Das hab' ich allerdings mir vorgesetzt.
Erröten macht die Häßlichen so schön:
Und sollte Schöne nicht noch schöner machen? —

3680 Ich habe deinen Vater Nathan; und
Noch einen — einen noch hierher bestellt.
Errätst du ihn? — Hierher! Du wirst mir doch
Erlauben, Sittah?

### Sittah.

Bruder!

### Saladin.

Daß du ja
Vor ihm recht sehr errötest, liebes Mädchen!

### Recha.

3685 Vor wem? erröten? . . . .

### Saladin.

Kleine Heuchlerin!
Nun so erblasse lieber! — Wie du willst
Und kannst! —

(Eine Sklavin tritt herein, und nahet sich Sittah.)

Sie sind doch etwa nicht schon da?

### Sittah.

Gut! laß sie nur herein. — Sie sind es, Bruder!

———

### Letzter Auftritt.

#### Nathan und der Tempelherr zu den Vorigen.

### Saladin.

Ah, meine guten lieben Freunde! — Dich,
3690 Dich, Nathan, muß ich nur vor allen Dingen
Bedeuten, daß du nun, sobald du willst,
Dein Geld kannst wieder holen lassen! . . .

### Nathan.

Sultan! . .

### Saladin.

Nun steh' ich auch zu deinen Diensten...

### Nathan.

· Sultan! ..

### Saladin.

Die Karawan' ist da. Ich bin so reich
3695 Nun wieder, als ich lange nicht gewesen. —
Komm, sag' mir, was du brauchst, so recht was Großes
Zu unternehmen! Denn auch ihr, auch ihr,
Ihr Handelsleute, könnt des baren Geldes
Zuviel nie haben!

### Nathan.

Und warum zuerst
3700 Von dieser Kleinigkeit? — Ich sehe dort
Ein Aug' in Thränen, das zu trocknen, mir
Weit angelegner ist. (Geht auf Recha zu.) Du hast geweint?
Was fehlt dir? — bist doch meine Tochter noch?

### Recha.

Mein Vater! ..

### Nathan.

Wir verstehen uns. Genug! —
3705 Sei heiter! Sei gefaßt! Wenn sonst dein Herz
Nur dein' noch ist! Wenn deinem Herzen sonst
Nur kein Verlust nicht droht! — Dein Vater ist
Dir unverloren!

### Recha.

Keiner, keiner sonst!

### Tempelherr.

Sonst keiner? — Nun! so hab' ich mich betrogen.
3710 Was man nicht zu verlieren fürchtet, hat
Man zu besitzen nie geglaubt, und nie
Gewünscht. — Recht wohl! recht wohl! — Das ändert,
                            · Nathan,

Das ändert alles! — Saladin, wir kamen
Auf dein Geheiß. Allein, ich hatte dich
3715 Verleitet: jetzt bemüh' dich nur nicht weiter!

**Saladin.**

Wie gach nun wieder, junger Mann! — Soll alles
Dir denn entgegen kommen? alles dich
Erraten?

**Tempelherr.**

Nun du hörst ja! siehst ja, Sultan!

**Saladin.**

Ei wahrlich! — Schlimm genug, daß deiner Sache
3720 Du nicht gewisser warst!

**Tempelherr.**

So bin ich's nun.

**Saladin.**

Wer so auf irgend eine Wohlthat trotzt,
Nimmt sie zurück. Was du gerettet, ist
Deswegen nicht dein Eigentum. Sonst wär'
Der Räuber, den sein Geiz ins Feuer jagt,
3725 So gut ein Held, wie du!
(Auf Recha zugehend, um sie dem Tempelherrn zuzuführen.)
Komm, liebes Mädchen,
Komm! Nimm's mit ihm nicht so genau. Denn wär'
Er anders; wär' er minder warm und stolz:
Er hätt' es bleiben lassen, dich zu retten.
Du mußt ihm eins fürs andre rechnen. — Komm!
3730 Beschäm' ihn! thu', was ihm zu thun geziemte!
Bekenn' ihm deine Liebe! trage dich ihm an!
Und wenn er dich verschmäht; dir's je vergißt,
Wie ungleich mehr in diesem Schritte du
Für ihn gethan, als er für dich ... Was hat
3735 Er denn für dich gethan? Ein wenig sich

Beräuchern laſſen! iſt was Recht's! — ſo hat
Er meines Bruders, meines Aſſad, nichts!
So trägt er ſeine Larve, nicht ſein Herz.
Komm, Liebe ...

**Sittah.**

Geh! geh, Liebe, geh! Es iſt
3740 für deine Dankbarkeit noch immer wenig;
Noch immer nichts.

**Nathan.**

Halt Saladin! halt Sittah!

**Saladin.**

Auch du?

**Nathan.**

Hier hat noch einer mit zu ſprechen ...

**Saladin.**

Wer leugnet das? — Unſtreitig, Nathan, kommt
So einem Pflegevater eine Stimme
3745 Mit zu! Die erſte, wenn du willſt. — Du hörſt,
Ich weiß der Sache ganze Lage.

**Nathan.**

Nicht ſo ganz! —
Ich rede nicht von mir. Es iſt ein andrer;
Weit, weit ein andrer, den ich, Saladin,
Doch auch vorher zu hören bitte.

**Saladin.**

Wer?

**Nathan.**

3750 Ihr Bruder!

**Saladin.**

Rechas Bruder?

**Nathan.**

Ja!

**Recha.**

Mein Bruder?

So hab' ich einen Bruder?

**Tempelherr.**

(Aus seiner wilden, stummen Zerstreuung auffahrend).

Wo? wo ist

Er, dieser Bruder? Noch nicht hier? Ich sollt'
Ihn hier ja treffen.

**Nathan.**

Nur Geduld!

**Tempelherr** (äußerst bitter).

Er hat

Ihr einen Vater aufgebunden: — wird
3755 Er keinen Bruder für sie finden?

**Saladin.**

Das

hat noch gefehlt! Christ! ein so niedriger
Verdacht wär' über Assads Lippen nicht
Gekommen. — Gut! fahr nur so fort!

**Nathan.**

Verzeih

Ihm! — Ich verzeih' ihm gern. — Wer weiß, was wir
3760 An seiner Stell', in seinem Alter dächten!

(Freundschaftlich auf ihn zugehend.)

Natürlich, Ritter! — Argwohn folgt Mißtrau'n! —
Wenn Ihr mich Euers wahren Namens gleich
Gewürdigt hättet . . .

**Tempelherr.**

Wie?

**Nathan.**

Ihr seid kein Stauffen!

**Tempelherr.**

Wer bin ich denn?

**Nathan.**

Heißt Kurt von Stauffen nicht!

**Tempelherr.**

3765 Wie heiß' ich denn?

**Nathan.**

Heißt Leu von Filnek.

**Tempelherr.**

Wie?

**Nathan.**

Ihr stutzt?

**Tempelherr.**

Mit Recht! Wer sagt das?

**Nathan.**

Ich; der mehr,
Noch mehr Euch sagen kann.  Ich straf' indes
Euch keiner Lüge.

**Tempelherr.**

Nicht?

**Nathan.**

Kann doch wohl sein,
Daß jener Nam' Euch ebenfalls gebührt.

**Tempelherr.**

3770 Das sollt' ich meinen! — (Das hieß Gott ihn sprechen!)

**Nathan.**

Denn Eure Mutter — die war eine Stauffin.
Ihr Bruder, Euer Ohm, der Euch erzogen,
Dem Eure Eltern Euch in Deutschland ließen,
Als, von dem rauhen Himmel dort vertrieben,
3775 Sie wieder hier zu Lande kamen: — der

Hieß Kurt von Stauffen; mag an Kindesstatt
Vielleicht Euch angenommen haben! — Seid
Ihr lange schon mit ihm nun auch herüber
Gekommen? Und er lebt doch noch?

#### Tempelherr.

Was soll
3780 Ich sagen? — Nathan! — Allerdings! So ist's!
Er selbst ist tot. Ich kam erst mit der letzten
Verstärkung unsers Ordens. — Aber, aber —
Was hat mit diesem allen Rechas Bruder
Zu schaffen?

#### Nathan.

Euer Vater . . .

#### Tempelherr.

Wie? auch den
3785 Habt Ihr gekannt? Auch den?

#### Nathan.

Er war mein Freund.

#### Tempelherr.

War Euer Freund? Ist's möglich, Nathan! . . .

#### Nathan.

Nannte
Sich Wolf von Filnek; aber war kein Deutscher . . .

#### Tempelherr.

Ihr wißt auch das?

#### Nathan.

War einer Deutschen nur
Vermählt; war Eurer Mutter nur nach Deutschland
3790 Auf kurze Zeit gefolgt . . .

#### Tempelherr.

Nicht mehr! Ich bitt'
Euch! — Aber Rechas Bruder? Rechas Bruder . . .

**Nathan.**

Seid Ihr!

**Tempelherr.**

Ich? ich ihr Bruder?

**Recha.**                         Er mein Bruder?

**Sittah.**

Geschwister!

**Saladin.**

Sie Geschwister!

**Recha** (will auf ihn zu).

Ah! mein Bruder!

**Tempelherr** (tritt zurück).

Ihr Bruder!

**Recha** (hält an, und wendet sich zu Nathan).

Kann nicht sein! nicht sein! — Sein Herz
3795 Weiß nichts davon! — Wir sind Betrüger! Gott!

**Saladin** (zum Tempelherrn).

Betrüger? — wie? Das denkst du? kannst du denken?
Betrüger selbst! Denn alles ist erlogen
An dir: Gesicht und Stimm' und Gang! Nichts dein!
So eine Schwester nicht erkennen wollen! Geh!

**Tempelherr** (sich demütig ihm nahend).

3800 Mißdeut' auch du nicht mein Erstaunen, Sultan!
Verkenn' in einem Augenblick, in dem
Du schwerlich deinen Assad je gesehen,
Nicht ihn und mich!
                    (Auf Nathan zueilend).
                    Ihr nehmt und gebt mir, Nathan!
Mit vollen Händen beides! — Nein! Ihr gebt

3805 Mir mehr, als Ihr mir nehmt! unendlich mehr!
(Recha um den Hals fallend).
Ah meine Schwester! meine Schwester!

### Nathan.
Blanda

Von Filnek!

### Tempelherr.
Blanda? Blanda? — Recha nicht?
Nicht Eure Recha mehr? — Gott! Ihr verstoßt
Sie! gebt ihr ihren Christennamen wieder!
3810 Verstoßt sie meinetwegen! — Nathan! Nathan!
Warum es sie entgelten lassen? sie!

### Nathan.
Und was? — O meine Kinder! meine Kinder! —
Denn meiner Tochter Bruder wär' mein Kind
Nicht auch, — sobald er will?
(Indem er sich ihren Umarmungen überläßt, tritt Saladin mit
unruhigem Erstaunen zu seiner Schwester).

### Saladin.
Was sagst du, Schwester?

### Sittah.
3815 Ich bin gerührt...

### Saladin.
Und ich, — ich schaudere
Vor einer größern Rührung fast zurück!
Bereite dich nur drauf, so gut du kannst.

### Sittah.
Wie?

### Saladin.
Nathan, auf ein Wort! ein Wort! —
(Indem Nathan zu ihm tritt, tritt Sittah zu den Geschwistern,
ihnen ihre Teilnahme zu bezeigen; und Nathan und Saladin
sprechen leiser).

Hör'! hör' doch, Nathan! Sagtest du vorhin
3820 Nicht —?

#### Nathan.
Was?

#### Saladin.
Aus Deutschland sei ihr Vater nicht
Gewesen; ein geborner Deutscher nicht.
Was war er denn? Wo war er sonst denn her?

#### Nathan.
Das hat er selbst mir nie vertrauen wollen.
Aus seinem Munde weiß ich nichts davon.

#### Saladin.
3825 Und war auch sonst kein Frank'? kein Abendländer?

#### Nathan.
O! daß er der nicht sei, gestand er wohl. —
Er sprach am liebsten Persisch . . .

#### Saladin.
Persisch? Persisch?
Was will ich mehr? — Er ist's! Er war es!

#### Nathan.
Wer?

#### Saladin.
Mein Bruder! ganz gewiß! Mein Assad! ganz
3830 Gewiß!

#### Nathan.
Nun, wenn du selbst darauf verfällst: —
Nimm die Versichrung hier in diesem Buche!
(Ihm das Brevier überreichend.)

#### Saladin (es begierig aufschlagend).
Ah! seine Hand! Auch die erkenn' ich wieder!

### Nathan.

Noch wissen sie von nichts! Noch steht's bei dir
Allein, was sie davon erfahren sollen!

### Saladin (indes er darin geblättert.)

3835 Ich meines Bruders Kinder nicht erkennen?
Ich meine Neffen — meine Kinder nicht?
Sie nicht erkennen? ich? Sie dir wohl lassen?

(Wieder laut.)

Sie sind's! sie sind es, Sittah, sind's! Sie sind's!
Sind beide meines ... deines Bruders Kinder!

(Er rennt in ihre Umarmungen.)

### Sittah (ihm folgend).

3840 Was hör' ich! — Konnt's auch anders, anders sein! —

### Saladin (zum Tempelherrn.)

Nun mußt du doch wohl, Trotzkopf, mußt mich lieben!

(Zu Recha.)

Nun bin ich doch, wozu ich mich erbot?
Magst wollen, oder nicht!

### Sittah.

Ich auch! ich auch!

### Saladin (zum Tempelherrn zurück).

Mein Sohn! mein Assad! meines Assads Sohn!

### Tempelherr.

3845 Ich deines Bluts! — So waren jene Träume,
Womit man meine Kindheit wiegte, doch —
Doch mehr als Träume! (Ihm zu Füßen fallend).

**Saladin** (ihn aufhebend).

Seht den Bösewicht!
Er wußte was davon, und konnte mich
Zu seinem Mörder machen wollen! Wart!

(Unter stummer Wiederholung allseitiger Umarmungen fällt der
Vorhang).

# NOTES

L.M. = The edition of Lessing's works by Lachmann, newly revised by Muncker.

M.H.G. = Middle High German.—N.H.G. = New or Modern High German.

**Title.**—In the story of Boccaccio from which the Ring Parable is taken the Jew's name is Melchisedec. Lessing may have changed the name to Nathan for several reasons. It is better adapted to the verse. Besides, in the ninety-third Novel of the *Decameron*, Boccaccio treats of a rich and very liberal Jew whose name is Nathan; but more than that, Nathan is to be to the opposing theologians what the prophet Nathan (2. Sam. XII, I ff.) was to David, a relentless monitor of their wrongs.

The Motto was interpolated into the *Noctes Atticae* of Aulus Gellius by Phil. Beroaldus (Bologna, 1503). It is a translation of the words εἶναι γὰρ καὶ ἐνταῦθα θεούς, put by Aristotle (*De Partibus Animalium* I, 5) into the mouth of Heraclitus when some friends, come to visit him, hesitated to enter a stable where he was warming himself (Buchheim).

1. **doch endlich einmal.** doch and einmal give additional emphasis to the impatience which Daja expresses in endlich.

3. **Daja.** In the prose version her name is Dinah. On the back of the title page Lessing had written: "N. B. instead of Dinah rather Daja. I see from the *Excerptis ex Abulfeda*, concerning the life of Saladin, Daja means *Nutrix*, nurse."

7. **seitab** = abseits, *off the direct road*. Digressions were necessary possibly on account of the disturbed condition of the country, the time of action being during the third Crusade, about 1192-93. Babylon had, however, even at that time, lost all its commercial importance. Trade with India was carried on rather by way of Bagdad on the Tigris River (cp. v. 43, and 734-735). The distance from Jerusalem to Babylon is about one hundred and forty German miles or nearly seven hundred English. In the prose version Lessing wrote gute hundert Meilen.

11. **von der Hand schlagen** = *to make short work of.* Cp. „Es geht ihm leicht von der Hand" = *he is apt in doing anything.*

12. **elend, elend.** In the first draft, which was written in prose, except in a few places, we have: „Wie unglücklich hättet Ihr

283

indeß hier werden können." The change was made for the sake of
the meter; similar cases are very numerous in our play.

16. **leicht.** We should expect faſt or beinahe. The first draft
has: „Das ganze Haus hätte abbrennen können." Possibly Lessing
means to convey precisely this idea here, equivalent to hätte leicht
von Grund aus abbrennen können; — von Grund aus = *to the
ground;* note the difference; also Germ. bis auf den Boden.

18. **Schon wahr** = *That's true enough!* Concessive.

24. The prose version has: „Sage es nur vollends heraus, —
ſage es nur heraus." The omission of the es is quite unusual; the
reason for it here is evidently the meter; a contraction to ſag's would,
however, not have been impossible.

27. Daja is usually supposed to imply that she would have perished
in the attempt to rescue Recha, or that she would not have ventured
to inform Nathan of the calamity; the latter with more justice, ·
because we do not learn that Daja in person made any attempt to
rescue Recha.

29. It seems a little forced for Daja to single out the possessive,
unless Nathan laid stress on the meine; and he had a good reason to
do so. Recha's narrow escape from the fire reminded him of the
death of his sons, the price at which she became his. Cp. ll. 3037-
3066. That Lessing meant to have the possessive meine stressed is
pretty clearly shown from the fact that in a sketch, partly prose,
partly verse, found among his writings, the word is capitalized. O
Meine Rachel! just as Lessing regularly capitalizes the numeral Ein
for emphasis; see *Lachmann-Muncker Edition*, vol. 3, p. 494.

32. **viel Rechte** is a little unexpected. Usually either both
forms are without inflectional ending, mit eben ſo viel Recht, or both
are inflected, mit eben ſo vielem Rechte.

35-36. Cp. ll. 3037-3066. For danken we have now more commonly verdanken in this meaning. Lessing wrote danken also in the
prose version. ·

38. Kindness, if not shown for its own sake, is no kindness.
Nathan is so kind to Daja, partly at least, because he desires to quiet
her conscience about conniving in keeping secret the mystery of
Recha's personality. This is at least Daja's view. We should rather
ascribe Nathan's action to pure generosity. If a few lines farther on
he tells Daja to keep the secret, he does this fully assured of his better insight and his pure motives; and there was no better way of ap-
peasing Daja than by practical deeds of kindness, for which she had
more understanding than for subtle theories.

42. Babylon had once been famous for its manufacture of silk and woolen stuffs.  Damascus has still a fair reputation among jewelers.

44. **und mit Geſchmack ſo reich** = *rich, and yet not gaudy, not violating good taste.*

54. With **zweifeln** the negative particle is commonly omitted now. Its origin is probably to be found in the Latin and Romance usage in similar clauses; cp. Latin *non dubito quin.*

56. **Gelt,** really a pres. subj. of **gelten,** is no longer felt as such; in early Modern High German it began to be used as a mere particle equivalent to **nicht wahr;** its use is confined to questions expecting an affirmative answer.

57. What she meant to say, we can infer from ll. 2318–21.  We have no reason to suppose that Daja was dishonest in her solicitude about Recha's condition, and if she had been able to analyze her apprehensions, she would probably have found that Nathan's „**Doch bin ich nur ein Jude**" accurately expressed them.

61. **Komm über Euch** reminds of Matt. XXVII, 25.

64. Daja's question is probably intended to convey the same idea, which she expresses in the prose sketch in these words: „**Sie weiß es, daß Ihr da ſeid, und weiß es vielleicht auch nicht.**"

74. **ſelbſt,** adverb, = **ſogar,** i. e. **nicht nur das Nahen der Kamele, ſondern ſelbſt ſeine Stimme höre ich.**

75. **Brach ſich,** more commonly not reflexive = *to stare aimlessly,* used especially of dying persons. — **Haupt** is the antecedent of **ſeines,** l. 76.

84. With plural forms **wenig** is more commonly inflected.

87–89. As a matter of history, Saladin not infrequently pardoned his enemies, both Templars and lay warriors, and from the position he holds throughout our play Nathan's surprise at his clemency to the Templar seems hardly justified.  To be sure, we are told in ll. 231 f., that Saladin never spared a Templar, and the poet had a right to assume this; but this severity does not at all seem to correspond to the Sultan's character as it appears in our play.  Cp., however, for faithlessness on the part of the Templars, and a justification of Saladin's severity, ll. 647 f.

88. See 210 ff.

90. **Gewinſt** = *the prize promised the winner in races, lotteries,* etc. ; less frequently it is used for **Gewinn,** in the sense of gain through an ordinary effort.

91. In vivid narration the Preterite Ind. is sometimes used for the more common Plup. Subj.: cp.: „**Trotz eurer Spürkunſt war Maria**

Stuart | Noch heute frei, wenn ich es nicht verhindert." Sch. *Mar. St.* „Wir Engelländer, waren wir allein, | Bei Gott, wir hätten Orleans nicht verloren." Sch. *Jungfr. v. Orl.* „Mit diesem zweiten Pfeil durchschoß ich Euch, | Wenn ich mein liebes Kind getroffen hätte." Sch. *Wilh. Tell.* Similarly Goethe, Lessing, Heine, even Wolfram v. Eschenbach, *Parzival* 1, 51 and 52, and others. — frisch = *unhesitatingly.*

98. **alle.** e is not an inflectional ending, but an inorganic addition to the uninflected form. Notice alle die Kundschaft, Gen., alle der Kundschaft. It is supposed to have been added for euphony, but the changes for euphony must be taken with some reserve. We have a similar excrescent e in many other forms: Lessing has ein Sinn= gedichte, Narre, Eremite, Glücke, Gerichte, sanfte, süße, dicke, helle, zurücke, ofte, etc.; in Goethe, too, we find similar forms mostly in poetry however. In case of adverbs this may go back to regular usage of M. H. G.

99. The position of the genitive between the pronominal or indef. adjective, or the article and the noun modified, common in M. H. G., is now altogether unusual. In M. H. G. this genitive could not have an article. — Kundschaft = Kenntnis, more commonly used with von and the dative.

100. **vorgespreiztem,** *spread out before* — for the purpose of shielding from smoke and fire.

113. **erhob** = *extolled;* entbot (with the acc. ihn understood) = *summoned, invited;* beschwor = *implored, conjured.*

117. **zu unserer Bitte taub,** more commonly, unserer Bitte gegenüber, or gegen unsere Bitte, or für unsere Bitte.

119. **Nichts weniger** = Eng., *anything but that;* lit., *there is nothing that could be less the case than that;* als das is readily sup. plied. The phrase is very common in German.

120. **antreten,** for the more common jemanden angehen (cp. 1054) = *to importune some one;* cp. Eng. *to approach some one for a favor.*

125. In the first edition of 1779 we have seines Auferstandenen; the change was naturally made; it is not necessary, however, to lay any stress on the unsers, as Düntzer, Buchheim, and others, suggest.— Auferstandene = *the risen Lord.*

133–34. If the heart predominates, Schwermut = *heaviness of heart;* if the head predominates, Menschenhaß = *misanthropy will carry the day.* If Recha reflects, and finds that gratitude is useless, she will incline to misanthropy. If she fosters the feeling of personal neglect, she will be melancholy.   Both states of mind are likely to predominate alternately.   Clearness of understanding is the only safeguard in the search for truth.   The fanatic, the dreamer supplements his perceptions by fancies and feelings.   See Appendix.

144. **Keines Jrdiſchen.**   Imitation of a construction common in Greek; equivalent to **keines Jrdiſchen Sohn.**

147 ff.   The meaning of the lines would probably be clearer for a slight rearrangement of the words: **Der Engel einer ſei aus ſeiner Wolke, in die verhüllt er ſonſt, — auch noch im feuer, — um ſie geſchwebt,** i. e., *enveloped in which he had at other times, and even during the fire, been hovering about her.*   **ſei** forms a tense with **hervorgetreten; verhüllt** is a postpositive participial adjective agreeing with **er;** with **geſchwebt, habe** might be supplied.

153.   The **„Wahn"** had its origin with Daja; cp. ll. 1577 f.   In a note taken from Marin, Lessing says: **„Die Kreuzbrüder, die ſo unwiſſend als leichtgläubig waren, ſtreuten oft aus, daß ſie Engel in weißen Kleidern, mit blitzenden Schwertern in der Hand, und inſonderheit den heiligen Georg zu Pferde in voller Rüſtung hätten vom Himmel herabkommen ſehen, welche an der Spitze ihrer Kriegsvölker geſtritten hätten."** — L. M. III, p. 149.   Cp. Tasso, *Jerusalem Delivered,* various places.

156. **launig** = **launenhaft;** the more common form in this sense is **launiſch.**

158. **hienieden wallen** is a sanctimonious phrase with a delicate tinge of irony; **wallen** means to be on a pilgrimage; the phrase suggests that, as an angel, the Templar could not have the earth as his permanent biding place and had probably ere this ended his pilgrimage among us, his special mission being ended.

159.   The chivalry of the Templar is called **ungeſittet,** *unmannerly,* because he so obstinately refuses to accept the gratitude of Recha.

169.   Cp. ll. 63 and 64. — Having escaped so great a danger, Recha is doubly anxious to see her father as soon as possible, and in the following expresses her surprise at the delay after she had heard his voice.

191.   For an explanation of this and the following lines cp. Note to l. 153.

195.   The prose sketch reads: **„Gott war es, der einen ſichtbaren Engel herabſchickte, deſſen weißer fittig die flammen verwehte, deſſen ſtarker Arm mich durch das feuer tragen mußte."**   From this it is evident that the phrase **„von ſeinem fittige verweht"** is meant to modify **feuer;** grammatically it would more naturally be

taken with the subject er, or the object mich; the construction, as it stands, can hardly be justified even in poetry.

200. The only explanation doing justice, or giving reasonable sense at any rate, to these two lines, is that by Ammer: „Dem Engel oder Euch —," i.e. "Are you flattering me, whom you call an angel (in making me like the angel), or yourself, as the father of this angel."

204. Nathan had applied in Recha's education the principles laid down by Lessing in his „Erziehung des Menschengeschlechts." Nathan allowed her to adopt the current conception of angels (cp. Hebrews 1, 14), until he thought her to be sufficiently mature to accept a purely rational view, which he proceeds to expound to her in the following verses. This view considers everything looking like a miracle to be planned from all eternity, i.e. in the whole economy of nature. We can hardly suppose that Recha understands even now all that is implied. See App. 211. This entire discussion of miracles bears directly on the controversy with Goeze.

235. From Marin 1, 249, Lessing made a note. „Daß die gefangenen Tempelherrn für ihre Loskaufung nichts geben durften, als cingulum et cultellum, Dolch und Gürtel."

237. schließt, somewhat unusual in the sense of, to prove, to argue in favor of someone. Cp. for a similar use of the word a review of March 23, 1751, in the Berl. privilegierte Zeitung L. M. IV, 299. The contents are, at the same time, interesting in connection with verses 2514 f.: „Die vornehmste Ursache (warum der Verfasser auf hundert Fragen, die seiner ersten Anzeige entgegengesetzt waren, zur Zeit noch nicht geantwortet habe) ist, weil sich dieser Gegner unter einem falschen Namen genannt, und der Herr Doktor durchaus denjenigen erst persönlich kennen will, welchen er widerlegen soll. Die Wahrheit zu gestehen; wir sehen das Schließende dieser Ursache nicht ein." Again Laokoon XVII, L. M. IX, 101.

251. viele zwanzig Jahre, some twenty, or rather, close to thirty years; einige zwanzig Jahre exactly corresponds to the English expression.

260. Geschwister was formerly a neuter singular collective noun, and is so used here. It is now commonly used in the plural.

262 f. The meaning of the following lines seems to be this: It is not an uncommon thing for two faces, even of strangers, to bear some general resemblance to each other. Thus the face of the Templar might well have reminded the Sultan of some features of his long lost brother. These features had once been the concrete object of the Sultan's

deep affection, and now, though born by a stranger, kindled this same
love : similar cause : similar effect; das Nämliche : das Nämliche.

269. **Glauben** in this line has for Nathan probably the same
meaning as for the Fragmentist. See App. 211, last quotation.

270. **Weil du meiner spottest.** In telling Nathan, 247–255,
that too many circumstances militate against his "natural miracle,"
she is trifling with him (spotten in a slightly modified sense).

274. **Spiel** and **Spott** are probably best considered nominatives,
rather loosely modifying **Entschlüsse.** — Goeze had emphasized (*e. g.*
*Strschr.*, p. 6) that with Lessing's demands on the documents of
religion „würde die menschliche Freiheit völlig zugrunde gehen, und
es würde alsdann heißen : entweder Christ oder in Dolhaus!" Cp.
App. 385; also 211, first quotation.

283. In his *Dramaturgie* Lessing insists that for all the actions
of a dramatic character there must be a sufficient motive. If here he
indicates that the Sultan, in sparing the Templar's life, was apparently
influenced by a mere nothing, he disregards his own rules for higher
purposes. He means to show that what in the eyes of the thoughtless masses becomes a miracle, is by a competent, rational man readily
reduced to natural causes.

284. **wilden** has here probably the sense of *barbarous, uncivil,*
referring probably to 120 f.

286. **wundersüchtig,** coined by Lessing : *intent upon miracles
where there are none;* similarly **Engelschwärmerin** (166), *angel-visionary.*

298. See App. 211. **dürft'** = brauchte. Quite common in this
sense in Lessing, less so in Schiller, Goethe, and later writers.

300. **Unsinn,** if Daja, without having thought on the subject,
considers this and similar absurd "miracles" as belonging to the plans
of Providence; **Gotteslästerung,** if she, with premeditation, asserts
that God's plans can not be realized but by means of such arbitrary
interferences with the established course of nature. The miracles, in
Nathan's sense, have been arranged for from the beginning.

311 f. A man engaging in such devotions enjoys the satisfaction .
afforded by genuine charity; the „Nächster," the *neighbor* in the
biblical sense, is benefitted as the object of this charity.

312. **deucht,** old form for dünkt.

318. Daja makes a last attempt to uphold her angel theory in
suggesting that the self-sufficiency of the Templar exceeded all human
measure.         .

323. **Vergnügsam** = genügsam.

329. **schad't,** see Note to 670, *d.*

334. **Franke** was in the Orient a general designation for members of any western nation. The greater number of crusaders were either French or under the general leadership of the French.

340. **Zusprach = Zuspruch** = *comfort, consolation.*

343. **es war ein Mensch,** *i.e.* for the Templar it was enough that a human being was in danger; narrower, clannish considerations had no weight with him. His utter disinterestedness as to the personality of the recipient of his kindness is also indicated in the use of the neutre pronoun **was,** 345; **ihm,** 346, refers to **was** as antecedent.

355. Cp. the familiar Hymn „**Was Gott thut, das ist wohlgethan.**" In one of the stanzas are these verses:

> „Der Herr, mein Arzt, der heilen kann,
> Wird mir nicht Gift einschenken
> für Arzenei: Gott ist getreu,
> Drum will ich auf ihn bauen
> Und seiner Güte trauen."

360. See App.

364. **dürfen,** see 298.

376. The character of the dervish Al Hafi was modeled in part after a contemporary of Lessing whom he met occasionally in the house of Moses Mendelssohn. Zelter wrote to his friend Goethe: "The mathematician Abram Wulff served Lessing as a model for his Al Hafi. He was an expert in figures, but very eccentric. . . . Lessing prized him for his wit and his native cynicism." **Derwisch,** from a Persian word meaning a poor man. **Hafi** is a title of honor, like the biblical "scribe," a man versed in the Koran. The dervishes are a religious Mohammedan order, corresponding to the Catholic mendicant friars. Our dervish is by birth and profession a Mohammedan, but by choice and conviction a Parsee, that is, an adherent of the old Persian religion of Zoroaster. The Parsees were also called **Gheber,** *i.e.* "infidels" or "unbelievers," because after the overthrow of the Persian government by the Arabs they remained faithful to their own religion. To Lessing this title may have appealed for other reasons. (See Appendix 2537.) In India also some Parsees are found, who emigrated from their old home in Persia on account of some religious differences. It seems, however, that Lessing confused these Parsees, who were very thrifty merchants in many cases, with the Gymnosophists, or naked philosophers, belonging to the Brahmanic religion, and living mostly as hermits. Their severe penitential exercises are said to be interrupted only for the purpose of playing chess, a game of Indian origin.

380 f. Nathan means to say that the genuine dervish — the Mohammedan monk — is too much inclined to idle contemplation to be

of any real use to the world. It is worth while noticing in this connection, that not only is the dervish not a genuine dervish; Saladin also is no genuine Mohammedan, Nathan is no genuine Jew, and — possibly the good friar excepted — there is certainly no genuine Christian portrayed in the drama. On this ground alone, a comparison of the three nominally represented religions, as to their relative merits, cannot have been Lessing's purpose, as is often wrongly assumed.

385. This line is very often quoted, and has regularly a meaning assigned to it that directly opposes Lessing's and Nathan's views. Cp. *Modern Language Notes*, Vol. XI, 220 f. Also Introduction § 68, and Appendix.

394. **drauf,** *i.e.* on the security presented in the assumption that at heart he is still the old dervish. Leave it untranslated.

396. **Was wär ich an Eurem Hofe?** *Supposing you were sultan, what position would you assign me?*

399. He hints at Nathan's frugality; a cook would not have sufficient practice to keep up in his trade; and for a cupbearer or waiter there would be still less to do.

401. Ironical.

406. **ift von feinem Haufe** = gehört feinem Haufe an. The phrase is unusual; probably an imitation of the French: *est de sa maison.*

409. **Strumpf und Stiel,** now Stumpf und Stiel; *root and branch.*

411. **trotz einem. Trotz** is used in an older sense: *vying with some one* (here in poverty), *a beggar as much as any one.* Cp. 1067.

419. In his prose sketch, L. M. III, 477, Lessing says: „Die Maxime, welche die Araber dem Ariftoteles beilegen: es fei beffer, daß ein Fürft ein Geier fei unter Äfern, als ein Aas unter Geiern."

422. **Ihr habt gut reden;** possibly an imitation of the French *il a beau dire, beau faire,* etc.: *Certainly, it is easy for you to talk.*

432. **Scheidebrief.** The same expression is used a number of times in the Bible; cp. Matt. v, 31.

437. **Ihr fchüttelt,** supply den Kopf; the omission is unusual; possibly due to analogy with the opposite nicken.

440. **Was ich vermag,** *anything within my power;* cp. Vermögen = *wealth.*

441. **Defterdar,** a Persian word for treasurer, but derived from

the Greek διφϑέρα, 'skin,' 'parchment'; so that it really means 'scribe,' 'bookkeeper.'

453. Cp. Act II, Sc. 9; also 3152 f.

456. **Den reichſten Bettler,** meaning, very likely, himself.

477. **Pfeiſe,** *decoy whistle,* with which the fowler caught the **Gimpel,** *bullfinch.* **Gimpel** has about the same figurative meaning as the English colloquial 'sucker.'

482. **ausmergeln,** etymologically connected with **Marſ,** *marrow; to drain, to plunder.*

485. Cp. Matt. v, 45.

510. Nathan once more taunts Daja with her angel theory and shows from the actions enumerated in the following verses how absurdly she herself contradicts her former claims.

520. **ſchlägt,** *turns;* probably from **ſich in die Büſche ſchlagen, einen Weg einſchlagen,** expressions which seem to have originated in times and under circumstances when paths were literally *hewn* into forests.

524. **Abſein = Abweſenheit.**

528. **Kommt Euch nicht,** stronger than **Kommt nicht zu Euch,** nearly equal to *will not come near you.*

534. The 'brothers' (*fratres*) or 'lay brothers' were a kind of monastic servants. They were bound by certain vows, but were not in holy orders. Persons properly consecrated as priests were called 'Fathers' (*patres*).

535. **zu dienen** denotes respectful assent, about equivalent to 'if you please.'

541. The use of **der Herr** instead of a pronoun, as a sign of submission, is still quite common in some parts of Germany; *e.g.* Leipzig.

549. Lessing had read of this evil effect of dates in Baumgarten's *General History.*

555. **auf den Zahn fühlen,** *to feel one's pulse,* figuratively.

562. The **Einfalt** of the Friar has more "method in it" than the Templar is at first aware.

567. **neubegierig = neugierig;** archaic form.

570. **das rote Kreuz auf weißem Mantel.** The white mantle, decorated on the left side with an octagonal red cross and worn over the armor, was the sign of the templars. In the year 1118 Hugo de Payens and nine other French knights formed a league for the protection of pilgrims. They took the vows of chastity, obedience, and poverty before the patriarch of Jerusalem. They made

their home in a part of Baldwin's palace, supposed to be built on the ancient site of the temple, whence their name.

577. **Selbzwanzigſter**, lit., *myself the twentieth*, i. e. 'with *nineteen others.*'

591. **Patriarche** for **Patriarch**. The Templar was not wholly ignorant in the matter. See 3845 f.

593. **aufbehalten** = aufbewahren. The term sounds biblical.

595. In prose the article **den** would not be omitted with Sinai.

598. **ſelbſt der Patriarch**, for **der Patriarch ſelbſt**. **Selbſt** is here the intensive pronoun, not the adverb. The odd position is due to metrical considerations.

611. **ſagt der Patriarch**, see 712, Note.

615. The figure is of biblical origin; cp. 2d Timothy IV, 8; 1st Peter V, 4. Lessing emphasizes in various places that good ought to be done for its own sake, not with a gross view to reward. — It is well to call to mind the fact, that in the patriarch Lessing meant to exhibit certain traits of his antagonist Goeze. In justice to Goeze it must be said, however, that, though he was not very liberal in his views, his ideas have none of the grossness of those held by the patriarch, and his conduct was on the whole honest and manly.

622. **ſich beſehen**, more commonly **ſich umſehen**.

645. **um** with the infinitive regularly denotes purpose. This clause is clearly intended for a result clause, and is due to a contamination of two constructions. Aside from the construction with **um zu** and the infinitive, purpose is expressed in **damit** or **daß** clauses with the subjunctive (often replaced by the indicative). But result clauses are also introduced by **daß**, and coincide then in form with purpose clauses having the indicative. By a sort of analogy, we have here **um zu** with the infinitive in a result clause, a rare construction; cp. Schiller, *Tell*, 1. 645. (Cp., for similar contamination, „**Lag er nun ſo auf dem Bette und zählte die langen Stunden; . . . dann war es oft ſein einziges Labſal, an die Vaterſtadt zurückzudenken.**" The interrogative clause (**Lag**, etc.) originally used in conditional sentences, has here temporal force.) Our sentence is clear thus: . . . **ob die Gefahr denn gar ſo groß, ſo daß man den Waffenſtillſtand wieder herſtellen müſſe; d. h. ob es nicht zu wagen ſei, den Krieg wieder anzufangen.** Cp. *Historical Summary*, in the Introduction.

653. **ergründen können**, supply **hättet**. Lessing ventures much farther in the omission of the finite form of auxiliaries than *good* usage allows at present.

661. **ausgattern** is said to denote 'spying out, by looking through bars,' a Gatter, or Gitter. — hiernächst, *moreover*.

670. **Des Saladins.** Generally the genitive of proper names preceded by the article has no inflectional s. Buschmann gives the following list of the more noticeable grammatical peculiarities found in *Nathan*:

*a*) Proper names, even if preceded by a pronominal word or article, sometimes have an s in the genitive: des Saladins, but also des Saladin, unsers Nathans.

*b*) Adjectives ending in -er, when used in neutre nouns, lose the inflectional e: Abgeschmackters, Bessers, Unglaublichers, Wichtigers. — Adjectives in -eln, -ern sometimes drop an additional inflectional en: albern for albernen, ledern, silbern, einzeln.

*c*) Metrical considerations occasioned forms such as feu'r, eu'r, Neu'ste, kürz'ste, beteu'rte, reb't, reb'te, schad't, also more colloquial forms and contractions such as: mit jemand übern (for über den) Fuß gespannt sein; untern (for unter den) Palmen; even in (for in'n = in den) Sack, in (for in den) Kopf.

*d*) The omission of the auxiliaries haben and sein is frequent, both in relative clauses, and in subordinate clauses introduced by a conjunction; the auxiliary is regularly omitted in these cases, if the following clause begins with an auxiliary.

*e*) There are a number of antiquated words and forms in *Nathan*, *e.g.* Strumpf (now Stumpf) und Stiel; Neubegier, neubegierig, Rachbegier, blutbegierig (now Neugier, neugierig, etc.); ängsten (commonly ängstigen), begnaden (begnadigen), beschönen (beschönigen), erkunden (erkundigen); annoch (noch), allwo (wo), vors erste (fürs erste), fördersamst (zunächst), zum mindsten (contraction from mindesten).

*f*) A number of colloquial expressions deserve to be noticed, *e.g.* herausschmeißen; ersaufen; nu, nu; nur zu; bei einem Haare; die alte Leier (= das alte Lied); Knall und Fall; mir nichts, dir nichts; mach (= beeile dich); drum sein (= etwas verloren haben); einen sitzen lassen; mit jemanden übern Fuß gespannt sein; auf dem Trocknen sein (= ohne Mittel sein); zu Rande (= zu Ende) sein; einem etwas an den Kopf werfen (= ihm ein Geheimnis aufdrängen); sein Näschen in alles stecken; von jemandes Mache (= Art) sein; einem den Garaus machen. — Colloquial is also the rather frequent omission of the pronominal subject: Weiß nicht, versteht sich; gilt nicht; muß doch wohl; laufe nichts; wünsch' Euch Glück; wird schon noch kommen; ist wahr; taugt nichts;

wår' nicht mein Mann; biſt doch meine Tochter noch; and even: wo geweſen?

673. **Maroniten** are the remaining adherents of the Monotheletes, a Christian sect in the mountains of Lebanon, who insist that in spite of his twofold nature Christ was of one will, his human will having been wholly supplanted by the divine.   In 1182 they recognized the authority of the pope and took some part in the crusades with the ardor of first love.   They are called Maronites after their first abbot, Maro.

675. **Stück** = **Streich**.

676. **Hätt' erſehn**, potential subjunctive. — "Can it be possible that the patriarch chose me to be this gallant man also," would nearly give the meaning.

678. **Ptolemais** (now called *Acre, Accho* or *St. Jean d'Acre*), the most important harbor north of Mt. Carmel, was held by the Christians from 1104–1187, and was recaptured by Richard the Lion-hearted and Philip Augustus II, in 1191, remaining in the possession of the Johannite order till 1291.

680. **Verbindlichkeit dem Saladin**: more commonly **gegen-über** would be added.

683. **Ja, das wär' ſchon gut**. — **Ja** and **ſchon**, both have concessive force. — It is worthy of notice with what fine discrimination Lessing uses the preterite and the present subjunctive and tenses of the indicative in indirect discourse throughout this entire interview. If modes and tenses are here roughly confused by the reader, he is sure to miss the fine shades of meaning which Lessing meant to express.   A few examples: 605, future with potential force; potential subj. wäre, 609; in indirect discourse regularly present subj. 611–629; 642–49; wüßte, 630, optative.   wär', 653, not merely indir. disc. subj., but preterite with potential, so-called polite force; notice the following verses; similarly hätt', 676; wär', 683; wär' and raubt', 688, 689; also bliebe, 689, is a potential subjunctive with an almost fiendish suggestiveness.

698. **wolle** has here, as in many similar phrases with an impersonal subject, almost lost its meaning; cp., as common report *will have it*.

701. **eingeleuchtet** = etwas ſeinem Bruder Ähnliches er-ſchienen ſei.

703. From here to the end of 710 the Templar seems almost to overlook the presence of the friar.   wäre is probably an optative, possibly a potential subjunctive.   In view of the dash after doch, we are

justified in referring the demonstrative pronoun **das**, 703, not to the same antecedent as **dieses** in 702, but to something which the Templar carries with him as a precious secret and mentions only in 3845.

705. Studies in physiognomy were popular in Lessing's day, and somewhat later. The Templar is convinced of a perfect parallelism between body and mind, both being the work of God (710).

712 f. In spite of the friar's frequent „**sagt der Patriarch**," and his avowal of implicit obedience, it is evident that the Patriarch could not have anticipated all of the Templar's reasons for refusal; and yet we cannot say that his "simple" representative wronged him with the sophistries which he ascribed to him.

717. **Patet.** The phrase is surely an imitation of the French "*risquer le paquet*" = *to venture*. The phrase "*risquons donc le paquet*" is found in some remarks accompanying Lessing's unfinished French translation of his *Laokoon*.

718. **Sprichwort.** Just in this form the proverb seems to be unknown generally. There is a proverb running: **Die Weiber sind des Teufels Krallen. wohl**, here not expressive of doubt as ordinarily; it might be rendered by: "Now tell me, the adage lies, etc." — Notice the loquaciousness of Daja and, in contrast, the Templar's curt answers. A somewhat similar scene is enacted by Just and the landlord in Lessing's *Minna von Barnhelm*, I, I.

721. **Was seh ich?** Daja means to act as if she merely happened to come this way and were surprised to see the Templar.

730. **so öfters; öfters**, adverbial **s** added to the common comparative **öfter**; with **so** the positive is commonly used, as one would naturally expect.

734. **Spezereien**, particularly herbs valued for their fragrance.

736. **Sina,** Arabian form for China.

737. **Kaufe nichts,** a rather sharp and yet an appropriate answer to Daja's enumeration of Nathan's wealth, which was evidently intended to make a favorable impression on the Templar.

738. **als,** now we should use **wie**; Daja does not mean to say, they honor him *as* a prince, but as they would a prince, *like* a prince.

741. Cp. 1. 1805 f., and notes.

747. **Ei!** Ironical surprise: *Indeed!*

748. **Wie schnell ein Augenblick vorüber ist, soll ich sehen?** He means to say, if Nathan was generous indeed, this noble impulse was surely limited to the moment in which he heard of the Templar's deed. Compare for a pretty close parallel Shakespeare's *Richard III*, Act IV, Scene 4. To Richard, enumerating all the honors

which he is about to bestow on the daughter of the queen, whose sons
he had killed, the queen answers:

> "Be brief, lest that the process of thy kindness
> Last longer telling than thy kindness' date."

752. For Daja, Christianity is, as a matter of course, superior to
Judaism, or any other religion, and the mere fact of her bearing the
name of Christian makes her correspondingly better.

752. **Auch mir ward's vor der Wiege nicht gesungen** = *From the nature of my environment it could not be expected*,
etc. The expression evidently arose from the belief that prophecies
of fairies or wise women, made at the birth of a child, — over the
cradle, — were sure to be fulfilled.

757. **Ein edler Knecht** (Knecht in the older significance of
the word) = *squire;* a man not bound to common service in the army,
but, as the English equivalent really signifies, a man for service on
horseback.

761. **erjaufen,** vulgar and rough for ertrinken. Cp. for a
similar thrust of a man bored by too frequent repetition of the same
story, *Minna von Barnhelm* I, 12. — See also Note to 570.

765 ff. Cp. Introduction, § 74, *b*, I.

777. **vom Halfe,** a figure probably taken from the yoke placed
on the neck of oxen and other animals = *Don't bother me with the
girl's father*.

782. She has reference to Recha's birth and religious affiliation.

787. **Muß.** A number of editors seem to prefer dürfen in this
place. Müssen is here used quite as the English *must*, and, in parts
of North Germany at least, it is still so used, both in positive and
negative sentences.

789. **Für mich, und kaum,** admits of two interpretations.
Sittah may mean, that for her, being a less skillful player, Saladin
plays well enough, and even for her but hardly well enough. — More
likely she means that he is playing well for her, *i. e.* so that the
game will turn out in her favor. Yet hardly to her advantage either
(cp. 804-5; 809-11; 1457-8); because if he plays carelessly, so that
she wins, he has no occasion to comfort her with a present larger
than the stakes.

791. **In die Gabel ziehen** or **gehen,** *to fork*, i.e. 'to
make a move by which two pieces are at once endangered.'

793. **Ich setze vor,** *I cover it; I interpose.*

794. **Klemme,** *difficulty, strait.*

795. **Buße,** *fine, loss;* ordinarily 'repentance'; from the same stem as Engl. 'better.'

800. **Was gilt's,** *I'll bet.*

801. **Vermuten,** from older **vermutend.** In certain parts of North Germany the present participle, losing its final **d,** has become identical with the present infinitive. Lessing (*Emilia Galotti* IV, 3 and II, 7) and Schiller (*Don Carlos* IV, 14) have retained this **d**: **ver= mutend.** Similarly **anmuten = anmutend** in **jemand etwas an= muten sein.** The use of **sein** with present participle was rare even in Middle High German.

805. **Dinar,** a gold coin adopted from the Byzantine empire, worth about two dollars in modern money. **Naserinchen,** the smallest Turkish silver coin, worth much less than a cent. **meine tausend Dinar.** The **meine** indicates that a thousand dinars was the customary amount played for, and won by Sittah, which is an additional argument in favor of the second, and as distinctly against the first interpretation of „**gut für mich**" (789).

806. **Mit Fleiß,** *intentionally.*

821. **Abschach.** The queen having been threatened, a new move endangers also the king, so that the queen must be sacrificed. But by the loss of this most movable piece the conclusion of the game is prepared. **Abschach,** or **Abzugsschach,** is nearly equivalent to **doppelt Schach** in line 820.

826. **Bloß mit dem Steine.** Most commentators see in this a jesting allusion to Saladin's unhappy relations with his queens. It seems doubtful, at least rather far-fetched. Why not take **dem** as a demonstrative pronoun, not the article? In line 828 Sittah probably alludes to some experiences of Saladin with other queens. Marin, Lessing's authority on Saladin, mentions a number of cases. He granted the wives of princes fighting against him safe conduct to visit their husbands, and even went so far as to restore a fortress to the enemy at the request of the sister of Saleh, son of Sultan Nurreddin, on whom Saladin had been making war.

833. **Matt,** abbreviation for **Schach matt.** The word is the Persian *mâta,* meaning *dead;* **Schach matt,** *the king is dead,* i. e. *the play is lost.*

835. **Gleichviel.** *It does not matter much, in the end you must lose anyway.*

836. The command is given to some slave in attendance.

837. **war zerstreut.** The cause of his distraction is mentioned in lines 902 ff.

839. **Und dann.**  An additional cause for his lack of attention was given by the smooth chessmen.  The *Koran* interprets the first commandment of the Mosaic law literally, and forbids any carved or graven image.  Accordingly, strict Mohammedans, in playing chess, use smooth, though painted or numbered geometrical figures.  Person. ally, the Saladin of our play had outgrown this narrowness of his creed, though he might use smooth pieces, if he played with the Imam, the Mohammedan priest.

849. **Zerstreuung — nicht!**  In view of the exclamation point by Lessing's hand I take the line to be intended ironically, though good-natured.  **Zerstreuung** means here not, as it often does, and from its composition might be expected to mean, the quality or state of being distracted, but rather the cause of the distraction.  Sittah thinks this cause is, as a matter of course, the impending war, the thought of which had diverted also her attention.

854. **Stillestand = Waffenstillstand.**

857. **das,** demonstrative pronoun, *i.e.* a good man.  This mar. riage of Sittah to Richard's brother is an invention of the poet.  It is a matter of history, however, that a marriage between Melek al Adhel, a brother of Saladin, and a sister of Richard was contemplated. Melek was to have the kingdom of Jerusalem and share his throne with Joan, the widow of William of Sicily, on condition that she would bring him Ptolemais or Acre as a dowry (cp. ll. 678 and 892). But Richard's sister would not give her consent, unless Melek would profess Christianity (cp. l. 880 f.).  Saladin expresses his view of the real cause, l. 889 ff.

867. **Du kennst die Christen nicht.**  Cp. Appendix. Sittah's harsh judgment has primarily reference to the crusaders, whom she judges quite in accordance with the prevalent but hardly just views of the eighteenth century.  On the principle of the man living in the glass house, she ought to have been more charitable to the fanaticism of the crusaders, because, of all religions, probably not one was ever so zealously propagated by means of fire and sword as Mohammedanism.

878. **schänden.**  I should think some emphasis ought to be put on **Menschen.**  She means, evidently, that the name of Christian is applied to so many unworthy subjects that a *good man* must be ashamed to bear it.

882. Voltaire's Zaïre, though a Christian, ardently desires to unite with Orosman, a Mohammedan, and. is prevented from doing so by Christian priests and friends.  Cp. particularly *Zaïre*, Act IV, Sc. I.

886. **Männin.**  Cp. *Genesis*, II, 23 : „Man wird sie Männin

heißen, darum daß fie vom Manne genommen ift."   Lessing probably means to point out, by using this term, that conjugal love ante-
dates all differences of creed.

**887 ff.**   Saladin distinguishes two elements in the Templars: that
of the soldier and that of the monk or Christian.   As a matter of
fact, the movement did not remain as pure, in the course of time, as
its originators had meant it to be.   Often the crusaders made their
religion a pretext for gaining advantages which would otherwise have
been denied them.

**897. ob vielleicht,** etc., supply um zu fehen, or some such
phrase.   gelänge is not merely subjunctive of indirect discourse.
Lessing would probably have used the present subjunctive for that
purpose.   Gelänge has, besides, optative force.   Cp. l. 574.

**903. irrte, könnte,** polite subj.: irren, here used as in M.H.G.,
in the sense of ftören, *to trouble, perplex.*

**908.** Freely, *He can not make ends meet; there is trouble on all*
   *s.*

**915**                        had received the summons, and supposes that he
had been called to dispose of the money expected from Egypt.

**917. fein** is used in North German dialects much the same as
fchön, which is common also in Middle and South Germany.   It
corresponds closely to the colloquial English 'nice,' except that fein or
fchön is used as adverb with an adjective: fein viel; es ift heute
fchön warm; while in English we use it as an adjective: *It is nice
and warm to-day.*

**921. was = etwas,** common in spoken language, and not infrequently found in literature: *That is instead of something (as I expected), less than nothing, a minus quantity.*

**925. Was gönnen?** Was used adverbially.   *What use is
it to talk of grudging?*   Wenn —, supply the ellipsis from l. 966 ff.
Sittah is anxious to have the play considered finished and won by
her, in order that her generosity may still be concealed from Saladin.
Hence her impatient exclamation (l. 932), when she sees her secret
endangered by Al Hafi's words.

**941. Ja fo!** *Is that the way matters stand!*   You want to be
counted the loser, and therefore consider you are.   *Like play, like
pay.   She will be paid as she has won.*

**943. er fträubt fich gern,** *he likes to be urged.*

**947.** Important testimonial for Sittah.

**953. Die Mummerei —,** *this farce.*

**958. Befcheiden,** in an older sense of the word, still common in the eighteenth century, literally equal to belehrt, informed of all the conditions, and hence *considerate, discreet.* Cp. Beſcheid; also abſchläglich beſcheiden = *to give an unfavorable reply;* similarly l. 1416, Beſcheidenheit = *discretion.*

962. ſich verbitten. Saladin assumes that Sittah had put herself under some obligation to Al Hafi rather than to himself, and he wonders what it could be that she would rather ask the dervish not to disclose than her brother. verbitten = *deprecate;* 'ask, *not* to do something.'

965. näher treten, *let not a trifle trouble you more than it ought.* Cp. l. 2553, das geht mir nah.

976. auswerfen, or ausſetzen, *to set apart; to make a special allowance.*

983. Aufwand, Ausgaben.

989. Ich arm? Der Bruder arm? The brother of a sister as noble as Sittah is showing herself cannot be called poor. Der bears some stress.

990. Cp. Appendix. In his Collectanea for *Nathan* Lessing has this note from *Marin* and Dapper's *Delitiae orientales,* p. 180: „Saladin hatte nie mehr als ein Kleid, nie mehr als ein Pferd in ſeinem Stall. Mitten unter Reichtümern und Überfluß freute er ſich einer völligen Armut. Ein Kleid, ein Pferd, einen Gott!"

1002. Abbrechen, einziehen, *to curtail, to limit one's self in his expenses.*

1005. machen, *avail.*

1012. ſpießen was considered a more disgraceful way of executing than droſſeln = erdroſſeln. ſpießen = *impale;* erdroſſeln = *strangle.*

1015. Embezzlement would have been less dangerous, under the circumstances, than a surplus. Not to be taken too seriously.

1021. Auf dem Crocknen, nautical, = *to be stranded.*

1022. Das fehlte noch! fehlte, potential subj., *That alone is wanting to complete matters. That would cap the climax.*

1029. wuchern, ordinarily to be guilty of taking usury; here, *to bring in large interest.*

1032. Al Hafi is *startled* (betroffen). He at once sees some apparent danger for Nathan and tries to avert it; cp. l. 1427 f.

1035. Mich denkt. The impersonal with either dative or accusative of person is somewhat more common with gedenken = ich erinnere mich. Instances are found also in Schiller and Gleim, but the construction is hardly used now.

**1047 f.**   Al Hafi intimates that, according to a current rumor, Nathan's affairs are in so precarious a state that he was hardly expected to return.

**1050. erſchallt,** supply von dem Gerede darüber . . .

**1054. angehen,** cp. l. 120.

**1055. Da kennt Ihr ihn.**   Ironical.

**1066. Den Armen giebt er zwar,** etc.   Mendelssohn answered a recension of Lessing's *Die Juden,* adversely in some particulars, in a letter to a friend.   Lessing afterwards published this letter. In it we find these words: „Überhaupt ſind gewiſſe menſchliche Tugenden den Juden gemeiner, als den meiſten Chriſten . . . Wie mitleidig ſind ſie nicht gegen alle Menſchen, wie milde gegen die Armen beider Nationen?   Und wie hart verdient das Verfahren der meiſten Chriſten gegen ihre Armen genannt zu werden?   Es iſt wahr, ſie treiben dieſe beiden Tugenden faſt zu weit.   Ihr Mitleiden iſt allzu empfindlich, und hindert beinah die Gerechtigkeit, und ihre Mildigkeit iſt beinah Verſchwendung.   Allein, wenn doch alle, die ausſchweifen, auf der guten Seite ausſchweifeten!"

**1067. trotz Saladin;** trotz in its older meaning = er wetteifert mit Saladin im Geben.

**1077 f. euch,** ethical dative. auf's Geben eiferſüchtig; ordinarily eiferſüchtig as well as neidiſch are followed by auf and an accusative of a person.   'He is so jealous, so envious of every opportunity to give!'   „Lohn von Gott," an abridged phrase used by beggars to express their gratitude = Es werde Euch (or Ihnen) Lohn von Gott.   A more common phrase in South and Middle Germany is: „Vergelt's Gott!"   In North Germany: „Gott lohn's!"

**1081. Milde,** now commonly equal to *kindness.*   For the special form of kindness known as charity, we use now more commonly Mildthätigkeit.   Im Geſetz = im moſaiſchen Geſetz.   Al Hafi represents Nathan's charity as springing from entirely selfish, at any rate from very narrow motives, in obedience to a command, not for its own sake. — Possibly, some of the charity mentioned by Mendelssohn in his letter quoted above may be due to such considerations. — Accordingly, Al Hafi calls Nathan also „den ganz gemeinen Juden," *"the very ordinary Jew"; ordinary* with the same tinge as gemein.

**1086. Über'n Fuß geſpannt,** *on bad terms.*   Taken from wrestling, where each participant endeavors to make his opponent fall over his leg, to trip him.   More common: „Mit jemand auf geſpanntem Fuß ſein or ſtehen."

**1103.** Josephus, *Jewish Antiquities,* relates that Solomon buried large treasures with his father David's body.   The high priest Hyrcanus and King Herod were believed to have opened the grave and to have enriched themselves with the buried valuables.   This circumstance was also related by Baumgartner in his *General History*, from which Lessing probably drew.

**1111 f. ℜarren,** if they buried their treasures with themselves thoughtlessly; **Böſewichter,** if with the malicious intent to deprive posterity of their use.

**1116. Saumtier.**   The first part of the compound is derived from the Greco-Latin *sagma* = *cover* or *saddle*, or also *the load*. Saumtier, accordingly = **Laſttier,** *beast of burden*.   **treibt,** ordinarily transitive, here = **zieht.**

**1125. eingeſtimmt,** *attuned to, in harmony with.*

**1130.**   Cp. l. 2434.   Nathan's unwillingness to lend was ascribed by Al Hafi to religious narrowness.

**1135. mehr als ein Jud'** = 'a *man* free from religious‚ prejudice and national faults;' **weniger als ein Jud'** = 'making of these faults a virtue,' as Al Hafi intimated.   Cp. l. 1751 ff.

**1141. Schwäche.**   The sentence is not as clear to the average reader as it seems to be to the commentators generally.   Probably there is a play on the word.   In the fourth scene of the third act we see what weapon she means to employ, and both she and Saladin express the opinion that this cunning is peculiar to women.   **Schwäche** has the same meaning, in this place, as the English *weakness* at times, *i.e. a predisposition.*   **die Schwachen = das schwache Geſchlecht,** *the weaker vessels.*   Hence: '*What other resources does a woman need but her cunning.*'

**1162.**   The **„ganz etwas andres,"** supposed to be agitating her soul, cannot very well be anything but love for the Templar, though judging from her question, Recha seems to be unaware of it; but cp. ll. 1183 and 1186.

**1167.**   Why exact this promise?   Is it mere fatherly interest?   Or does Nathan, as yet unacquainted with the Templar, think of obstacles that might seem to be in the way of a union on account of Recha's supposed Judaism?   On the other hand, even if these were removed, the Templar would still be bound by his vows; cp. l. 1388.

**1179. Was gilt's?**   *What is the wager?* — without any tinge of vulgarity.

**1191. ſcheuen** is commonly construed with **vor** and the dative.

**1192. rauhe Tugend,** oxymoron; cp. ll. 156 and 159; **rauh** = *rude, rough.*

1194. Nathan wonders that he, being a *man*, like the Templar, should be perplexed by his actions.

1196. **drallen Gang**, *elastic step*.

1198. **Wo ſah ich**, etc., spoken aside.    Nathan at once detects familiar features in the Templar.

1199. **Franke**, see l. 334. — In his impatience the Templar does not wait for Nathan even to begin speaking.   His **Was** is much the same as if Nathan had said: 'I beg your pardon, sir' — and he had at once interrupted: 'What for?'

1202. **Verſieht** reminds of the Bible and is used instead of „bleibt," probably to give some oriental coloring.

1203. **vorübereilen** commonly takes an and the dative.

1218. **Schanze**, from French *chance*, i. e. *to put at stake*.

1219. The dash shows that the clause following is an afterthought, not as rudely meant as it sounds.   To the Templar religious differences, were of no importance.   He merely wanted to get rid of Nathan, possibly for the quiet of his own soul.   Cp. Introd., § 74, b, 1–3. A passage from the first draft, L. M. III, 483, corroborates these views: Wenn ihm Nathan, auf dem Wege zum Sultan, begegnet iſt; ſo kann es leicht ſein, daß er ſeinen Beſuch verſchieben zu müſſen glaubt. — Rachel: Wieſo?   Iſt er bey uns allein nicht ſicher? Dinah: Liebe Unſchuld!   Wo ſind Leute ſicher, die ſich ſelbſt nicht trauen dürfen?   Und wer darf ſich ſelbſt weniger trauen, als der unnatürliche Gelübde auf ſich genommen hat?

1227. Nathan excuses himself for having offered to the Templar some of his wealth.

1231. Cp. 741.   In his answer, Nathan disregards the Templar's insinuations as to the wealth of the Jews, and only reminds him that, other things being equal, wealth is surely better than poverty, and in so many words places his wealth at the young knight's disposal.

1240. **Seht**, etc.   The Templar's suspicious nature crops out on all occasions, in spite of his own disavowal, l. 2714.   Cp. ll. 533, 2721.

1245. **bekam** must be stressed, not **das**.   He means to show the justice of his claim on Nathan.

1252. **der Tropfen.**   der is a demonstrative; *i.e.* 'more tears than these have fallen on the mantle.'   It can hardly be inferred that the Templar refers to his own tears.   He was not in the mood to confess to so much emotion.

1257. **Eure Kniee ſelber.**   Literally, *your knees themselves.* The meaning is clear.

1259. The numerous dashes show that the Templar is perplexed. The change from Jude to Nathan indicates a kindlier feeling.

1267. It would have been quite improper for Recha to receive the Templar in the absence of her father.    The Templar indicates in l. 1270 that his motives were less noble.    Cp. Introduction, § 74, b, 1.

1273. Cp. Appendix.    Also Goethe, *Iphigenie*, verses 1937–42.

1277 f. The line refers directly back to l. 1274; *i.e.* 'some countries have a larger number of good men than others.'    Nathan does not agree, great men are everywhere scarce.

1278. **Mit diesem Unterschied ist's nicht weit her.** *That difference is of little importance.*

1283. **mäteln,** *to find fault.*

1284. **Knorr, Knubben.**    Both excrescences on the tree; *i.e.* both are faulty, imperfect, and neither has the right to inveigh against the other for its faults.

1285. **ein.**    Probably meant for the numeral; some little top of the tree must not be so presumptuous as to imagine that it alone is of nobler origin than other branches.

1288. **Das diese Menschenmätelei —.**    *That first practiced this invidious discrimination.*    (Buchheim).

1293. See Appendix, also Introduction.    **entbrechen** = *to refrain from.*    Lessing uses this word repeatedly in his writings.    It is not common now.    Cp. also Cardanus, *De subtilitate*, Book 11, translated in part by Lessing in his *Rettung des Cardanus*, L. M. 5, p. 313 f.

1302. **Schuppen.**    Cp. Acts IX, 18: Und alsobald fiel es von seinen Augen wie Schuppen und er ward wieder sehend.    hier, jetzt, of course, in Palestine, at the time of the crusades.    Cp. 2289 f.

1309. Cp. Appendix.    The same view as Sittah's and Saladin's, l. 881.

1312. **Mensch,** with Lessing, meant much the same as „ein ganzer Kerl" or „ein Kerl," later with Goethe in his younger years, and his contemporaries.    Cp. an interesting study on the word „Übermensch," by R. M. Meyer, *Zeitschrift für deutsche Wortforschung*, 1, p. 3 f.

1321. It is difficult exactly to determine the meaning of this verse. It seems unnatural for Nathan to cherish any matrimonial project so early, or even earlier (l. 1165).    But so the Templar understood him (l. 2730 f.) and verses 1388–89 seem to point in the same direction.

Sittah's plot is about to be carried out.    A messenger must have been sent after Al Hafi's departure.    Act II, Sc. 3.

1343. Saladin has been called, in Lessing's own words, "the

poetic ideal of the real character ascribed by history to the man bearing that name." Majestic greatness, magnanimity, liberality find
their counterpart in almost ascetic frugality in his personal habits; and
his tenderness as shown to his kin and his friends are historical, as
well as his warlike savagery and cruelty, which are also mentioned in
the play. His tolerance alone is much idealized. He saw his calling in fighting relentlessly against the enemies of the prophet, and it
is related that a philosopher who ventured too far in heterodox speculation was without much ado seized and strangled. His humaneness
and his religiosity were never reconciled in him. In liberality Walther
von der Vogelweide sets him up as a model for German princes,
especially for Philip:

> "Denk an den milten Salatîn:
> der jach daz küneges hende dürkel solten sîn:
> sô wurden sie erforht und ouch geminnet."

**1346. Sparung** sounds biblical. In the Bible **sparen** is used in
the sense of the more modern **schonen**.

**1349.** Cp. l. 3075.

**1350 f. verändert.** Cp. the interview with Al Hafi, particularly l. 439 f.

**1367. Nach wessen Willen.** The Templar elaborates on this
thought, with evident sophistry, l. 2135 f.

**1369. Auf Euch kommen,** *to mention you.*

**1374.** The Templar starts to give his real name, but changes his
mind, and gives the name later adopted; for reasons which will become clear later. With what justice he uses the new name, is indicated in l. 1378, where the same man is first called **Oheim,** and then
**Vater.**

**1378. faulen.** A rude expression, when used of the dead; the
motive of the Templar for choosing it is not apparent; he is naturally
not so vulgar.

**1386. Kundschaft.** Now commonly **Bekanntschaft.**

**1388 f. Ist es doch,** etc. That indicates that Nathan is not well
pleased with the discovery which he is about to make; that he had
plans even at this early date, which were threatened by the family
relations of the Templar.

**1391.** Cp. l. 3787.

**1403. Das Herz drücken.** Probably made in analogy to **etwas
auf dem Herzen haben, schwer was auf dem Herzen haben.**

**1405. mir will.** Possibly due to French influence; commonly
**wollen** is constructed with **von** and the dative.

**1413.** In view of ll. 1388 and 1389 we can hardly assume that Nathan thought definitely of matrimony between Recha and the Templar. But he hoped that the Templar would either as her husband or as her brother affect the life of Recha, and, restoring her nominally to her faith, would appease Daja's conscience.

**1416. Beſcheidenheit.** Cp. l. 958.

**1418. erinnern** commonly takes an and accusative.

Al Hafi does not know that a messenger from Saladin had been sent to Nathan before him, and when he learns of the fact, he thinks Nathan knows for what purpose Saladin wants him.

**1434.** Cp. l. 450.

**1436. Ein Nackter.** Here, *a man without any baggage.*

**1445. aushöhlen bis auf die Zehen** means *to drain completely.* In Sebastian Frank's *Collection of Proverbs* Lessing found the colloquial expression „hohl bis an die Zehen," of which he made a note.

**1447 Der weiſen Milde.** Probably possessive genitive. It might possibly be taken as a dative, in which case it would mean that to wise charity Nathan would never refuse a loan.

**1449. die eingebornen Mäuslein** must mean the persons having the first right to Nathan's charity.

**1459. verloren** is to be taken both with „glaubte" and „ge=geben hatte."

**1463. durfte,** in its older meaning, = brauchte, *i.e.* he had only to move his king close to the pawn to avoid her check.

**1466. Denn,** etc. By moving the king, as stated above, the castle gained room to move. Roche = Turm; from Persian *rukh,* an elephant with a turret, from which also English *rook.*

**1470. in Klumpen** = über den Haufen. In this scene, just as in I, 3, Nathan speaks in a light tone with Al Hafi; cp. Introduction, § 68.

**1474. taube Nuß,** Nuß ohne Kern, *a trifle.*
**Geld hin, Geld her** = Geld iſt das wenigſte.

**1489.** Cp. Note to l. 376.

**1491. Das Werkzeug beider,** *i.e.* ich brauche mich zu keinem von beiden, weder zum Betteln noch zum Borgen, als Werkzeug brauchen laſſen.

**1492.** Notice here again the pregnant signification of the word Menſch.

**1495. ihm.** Dative of interest. Plunder = *rubbish.* Money has no inherent value for Al Hafi; cp. l. 910 f.

**1497. Placerei,** *annoyance.*

**1498. ſchaff'** = verſchaffe.    **Delk.** In a letter to his brother Lessing says: „Delk, welches im Arabiſchen der Name des Kittels eines Derwiſch iſt."

**1499-1500. dächte, blieb'.** Polite subj., *i.e* it is time enough to go to the desert, when I am really deprived of all of my possessions.

**1505. dürfen.** Here probably in the modern sense, hence, nicht dürfen = *to be prevented;* cp. l. 1518.

**1506. Knall und Fall,** *suddenly;* a term taken from hunting in which the *report* and the *fall* seem simultaneous. **ihm.** In M. H. G. and later, cases of the personal pronoun were used for the reflexive of the third person in the dative.

**1507. andrer Sklav'.** An older, and in poetry still common construction for als Sklave anderer. Cp. Schiller's *Don Carlos:*

„Das Jahrhundert
Iſt meinem Ideal nicht reif. Ich lebe
Ein Bürger derer, welche kommen werden." III, 10.

**1510. ſelbſt das Deine berichtigen.** The ſelbſt is not meant to indicate that Al Hafi, and no other, is expected to settle his accounts, but rather, that in doing so he himself will be detained, just as Nathan needs time to settle his business with the sultan.

**1515.** Cp. l. 456 f.

**1519. noch ſo bald,** *ever so soon;* noch ſo is common in con- cessive and other subordinate clauses, rare as used here: „während der noch ſo kurzen Friſt." „wenn er mich auch noch ſo ſehr bitten ſollte."

**1524. er,** i.e. der Augenblick.

**1525.** In M. H. G. a genitive of cause was common with inter- jections. It is now confined to poetic diction. Prose: O über, etc.

**1544. Bild** must be stressed, being in contrast with the realities within Recha's reach.

**1547. Sich ſperren** = *to resist, be obstinate.*

**1548.** *Isaiah,* LV, 8: „Denn meine Gedanken ſind nicht eure Ge- danken, und eure Wege ſind nicht meine Wege."

**1556. Wem eignet Gott** (uncommon) = wem gehört Gott als beſonderes Eigentum? — Recha, the too apt pupil of her father, had made God a mere intellectual abstraction. Cut off the imagery to which a devout heart, not only of the unlearned, resorts in its con- templation of the divine being, and all the rich sources of religious art, and of many spontaneous, and by no means entirely worthless ex- pressions of religious devotion are at once clogged. And yet Daja's faith was indeed too much burdened by flowers, *i.e.* fruitless form-alism.

**1562. immer,** *i.e.* Daja had repeatedly touched upon this sub-ject.    The infinitives **vorzuspiegeln** and **mischen** are grammatically justifiable if we supply an ellipsis which easily suggests itself : **Was that er dir, daß du Grund zu haben glaubst,** etc.

**1564.** Cp. *Matt.,* XIII, 24 f.

**1577. zuschlagen,** *to be of benefit, to be conducive to one's well-being.*

**1582. Wenn ich nur reden dürfte!** - If she could speak, she would point out in her way the dealings of Providence, intended to draw Recha and the Templar to the Savior ; cp. l. 2280 f.  Recha does not grasp the hidden meaning in Daja's words.

**1588 f.** See Appendix.

**1589.** See Appendix.  Just what Nathan means by this „**Wähnen über Gott"** is not easily determined.   We know that love, filial de-votion, not fear of the law, characterizes his relation to God, who is to him a father in the Christian sense far more than the lord and judge of Judaism.   Again, we have seen how he extirpated Recha's angel fancy and held decided opinions concerning the providential dis-pensations of God.   And so his „**Wähnen über Gott"** must have reference to less essential things.   Probably the phrase means the same as Lessing's assertion in other connections : „**Ich habe noch im-mer die besten Christen unter denen gefunden, die von der Theologie am wenigsten verstanden."**   In these verses Schiller found the entire spiritual content of *Nathan* expressed.

**1594.** It is worth while to take due notice of these lines, in view of the general total lack of appreciation for Daja.

**1600. ob auch er . . .**   Probably : **frei denkt wie mein Vater, oder, wie von einem Tempelherrn wohl zu erwarten wäre, deine Ansichten teilt.**

**1604. bloß** is really to be taken with the preceding infinitive. **Und doch —** the ellipsis is clear from Recha's answer ; probably : **bleibt's mir jetzt nicht erspart.**

**1610. mir nichts, dir nichts —** **ohne weiteres.**   Recha re-iterates what the Templar had said to Daja.   Cp. l. 1623 f.

**1614. so wie ein Funken auf seinem Mantel** might in-dicate that to Daja also, the Templar had mentioned the „**garst'gen Fleck"** (l. 1243).   **ungefähr = von ungefähr.**

**1617. Herausschmiß.**   Commentators generally find this word vulgar and excuse it in Recha's mouth as a quotation.   It *is* vulgar in its origin, but, like many other words, has lost every objectionable tinge, at least in North Germany ; not so in the South.

1618. **Jn Europa.** Not that wine acts differently in Asia, but the Templar, with whom these words originated, had probably been impressed with the abstinence enjoined upon the Mohammedans by the Koran.

1621. **jugelernte.** Since the sixteenth century lernen occasionally occurs in the sense of lehren. Similar confusion in English between *teach* and *learn ;* cp. also the English participle 'learned,' going back to the older use of the word *learn.*

1625. **einen übel anlaffen.** The origin of this phrase has not been explained ; the meaning is *"to treat one harshly."* It is not often used at present.

1627. **Das hieß sich,** etc.    That was taking too cruel revenge.

1633. He had been unwilling to share his trouble with any one, but ready to risk his life even for a stranger.    Cp. l. 1215.

1636. Cp. Introduction, § 74, b, 1.

1641. Stage direction : **Dergleichen,** i.e. **Pause, unter der er in Anschauung ihrer sich wie verliert,** plainly not she was staring at him, as some explain, but his eye was fixed on her.    This is evident from the remainder of the stage direction as well as from the surprised **Nun,** and v. 1643-44.    **dürft = wäre es auch nötig.**

1646. **folltet fein gewesen.**    This somewhat unusual construction instead of **wo Jhr nicht hättet fein follen,** is probably occasioned by the form of the Templar's answer : **wo ich nicht follte fein.**    Colloquially the construction is occasionally found ; in M. H. G. and earlier in N. H. G. it was common.    The Templar's answer has reference to his vows.

1655. Notice the dash at the end of the verse, denoting also Recha's confusion.    The meaningless question said merely for the sake of saying something, was probably suggested to Lessing by a passage from Breuning von Buchenbach's *Oriental Journey.*    It is there related that the descent from Sinai in a specific instance, was more difficult than the ascent, owing to the fact that in ascending a party made use of more or less regular steps, while they descended on the other side of the mountain, down the rough slope.

1670 f. Every commentator seems to have his own interpretation for the verses.    Niemeyer thinks it is Recha's roguishness (Schalkheit) that appears in what she says or does not say.    Peters thinks it is Recha's deistic, liberal views.    Buchheim : "Her lofty mind and deep intelligence."    Primer practically agrees with Buchheim.    He overlooks in his interpretation the dash at the end of 1655. Buschmann, Brandt and Ammer: "Her affection for him." The Templar would be less likely „unter einer Pauſe in Anſchauung ihrer ſich wie zu verlieren" (l. 1640, stage direction), if he were to be assured merely of her intellectual superiority; nor would, with this assumption, the words „Ich bin — wo ich vielleicht nicht ſollte ſein" have much point. I should understand the lines to mean that Recha by her behavior tells the Templar how modest, how genuinely womanly, how sensible withal she is; speaking through her silence what the Templar had heard from Nathan's words, — that she is surpassingly lovely. We must not leave out of consideration that Nathan had said his „Kennt ſie nur erſt," before he had heard the Templar's name. He would *then*, no doubt, have welcomed him as a suitor; but cp. ll. 1167, 1388 and 1680 f. The significance of the Templar's strange conduct Daja points out in the next scene.

1694. **ankommen.** *What is troubling, disturbing him?*

1699. **Nun iſt's an Euch.** *Now it's your turn.*

1706 f. Daja thinks that Recha's composure is due to the assurance that the Templar loves her and is greatly agitated on her account. Most commentators see in this scene a sudden change in Recha's feeling for the Templar, clearly for the purpose of reconciling themselves with the final outcome. She herself, quite like one of Lessing's female characters, asserts she finds no less delight in seeing a beloved object with some composure. Cp. Introduction, § 74.

1714. **Thun.** Most editors substitute, with Lachmann, **Ton** for **Thun.** **Thun** has here probably the meaning which it has often in Low German, viz. *the whole behavior and bearing of a man.*

1733. Nathan had been somewhat delayed by the Templar and Al Hafi. See Act II, Sc. 6–9. But it seems quite characteristic of him not to hasten.

1735. **Schweſter! Schweſter!** Not so much expressive of reproach as of apprehensiveness, as appears from Sittah's reply.

1736. **vorſtehen,** for the more common **bevorſtehen.**

1738. **ſtellen,** in the sense of **verſtellen.** Cp. er ſtellt ſich, als ob er Wahrheit wollte. **beſorgen laſſen,** *make apprehensive, intimidate;* **auf Glatteis führen,** *to lead one into slippery places.*

1743. **abbangen.** A word made for the occasion = *extort.*

1755. **Schon unſer, ohne Schlinge.** Rather optimistic, in view of l. 440 ff.

1759. **die Netze vorbei —.** Commonly, an den Netzen ſich vorbei winden. The construction with the simple accusative may be of Low German origin, where it is common.

1771. **Traun**, *indeed.*

1774. **beschönen.** Commonly beschönigen.

1775. Read: „beſorg ich' nur" as a parenthetic expression, and the order is normal.

1779. **Ich tanze**, as if he were a trained bear.

1780. **Und könnt'.** He whould prefer to have even less aptitude for his task.

1786. Cp. Lessing's *Fable of the Lion and the Ass.* The Lion and the ass were hunting together, it being the task of the latter to stir up the animals by his horrible voice. A crow taunted the lion with his disreputable company. But the lion answered: If I can make use of any one, I can well afford to grant him a place at my side.

1794. **beſtehn.** Used regularly of examinations; here quite appropriately in view of l. 1790.

1798. **Die bleibe deinem Feinde!** Die, demonstrative pronoun, *i.e.* 'fear.'

1799. **Du nennſt dich Nathan** may mean: *You call yourself, and you are called*, hence Nathan's answer.

1800. Lessing wrote: **Wohl! nennſt du dich nicht; nennt dich das Volk.** Every school edition, so far as I have seen, has changed the semicolon to a comma, and thus made a conditional clause of the two elliptical clauses. Saladin means: *Of course; you do not call yourself "the Wise"; but the people do.*

1803. Cp. l. 1071.

1805 f. Cp. 442. If in the estimation of the people *shrewd and wise*, „klug und weiſe," were the same, and he only is shrewd who can enhance his real advantage, then the most selfish would be at the same time the most shrewd and the most wise; because, thinking only of his *real* advantage, he could never enrich himself at the expense of others, but in enhancing his own happiness he would necessarily also bless his fellow-men, provided, of course, that they too are able to distinguish real from imaginary blessings. See Appendix for Lessing's conception of happiness.

1811. **was du widerſprechen willſt**, i.e. *that the people were right in calling him "the Wise."* widerſprechen now governs the dative; in M. H. G. frequently the accusative.

1819. **trockene Vernunft**, *sober, plain reason.* **ekeln**, *is disgusting.*

1822. Nathan acts as if he supposed the Sultan wished to buy of his goods.  Saladin's admonition: „aufrichtig" justified him in his assumption, in spite of Al Hafi's warning,

1827.  Schachern = *to barter, to drive a shrewd bargain;* applied to Jews particularly.   This rather harsh term is chosen as a thrust for Sittah, supposed to be listening.

1835.  auf etwas gesteuert sein, *to aim at.*   Lessing uses the phrase repeatedly in his writings.

1837.  heischen = fordern.   Unterricht = Auskunft.

1842.  See Appendix.

1845.  See Appendix.

1852.  die Wahl (acc., object of wissen); die (acc., object of bestimmt [haben]); diese Gründe, nom., subject.

1855.  wägst mich mit dem Auge.   Contamination of two expressions: auf der Hand wägen, and mit dem Auge messen or mustern; resulting phrase: mit dem Auge wägen.   Nathan had several reasons for being surprised.   Saladin seems to have some appreciation of the truth and the value of truth, and yet confesses that he has not found time to think about it and is ready to receive it on Nathan's recommendation, instead of working for it himself.

1868.  bar, blank; often applied to coins: *cash and bright;* referring here to truth, better probably: *sharp and clear.*

1873.  darf = braucht; *i.e.* modern coin is taken at sight, at its face value.   Earlier, money was weighed, and its content, not its face, determined its value.   So it must be with truth.   It cannot be transferred from one to the other without effort.

1874.  in Sack, for in'n Sack, for in den Sack.

1875.  See Appendix.   Jude, i.e. *the man eager to acquire something without giving any equivalent.*

1881.  Mit der Thüre so ins Haus, *to blunder out, to ask abruptly.*   Nathan was unknown to Saladin, and it was surely strange that the Sultan demanded his opinion on matters so important without first finding out whether his views were worth listening to.

1885.  Stockjude, *fanatic Jew.*

1888.  Das war's!  Referring to a plan which he had just then conceived.

1889.  See Appendix.  abspeisen, *to satisfy one in the easiest way possible,* as a child is appeased with almost any kind of food.

Cp. Friedrich Paulsen's *Kant's Verhältnis zur Metaphysik,* Vaihinger's *Kantstudien,* IV, p. 413 ff; also Brigg's "Christianity," *Popular Science Monthly,* February, 1900, on this whole scene.

**1891. das Feld rein,** *the coast clear,* i.e. *Sittah is not lis-*
*tening.*

**1892. Zu Rande = zu Ende.**

**1900. Ja! Ja!** More than likely, Lessing had here in mind
the repeated demand of Goeze to reveal the name of the Fragmentist.
He persistently answered, the name of the author had nothing to do
with the contents of his work, and, he being dead, there was no call
for exposing his relatives to the hatred of fanatics. See Appendix,
ll. 1900 and 2546.

**1901.** Lessing has the following note from *Marin*, II, 120: „Unter
den Citeln, deren sich Saladin bediente, war auch „Besserer der
Welt und des Gesetzes.''

**1911. Vor grauen Jahren,** *long, long ago.* — Grau being
synonymous with alt, it is used figuratively for periods long since
passed. We speak also of „graue, nebelhafte Ferne,'' where „gran''
evidently is expressive of the indistinctness due to long distance.
Possibly it might have been transferred from local to temporal relations,
as in case of so many other adverbs. — Jn Osten, now im Osten.
See Introduction, §§ 49–54, for a discussion of the parable.

**1914. spielte:** in which a hundred beautiful colors were blended.

**1933. sich entbrechen,** see l. 1293.

**1936. ergießend Herz;** ordinarily used with a reflexive pronoun; *overflowing with love.*

**1945. in geheim,** now either im Geheimen or insgeheim.

**1949. Vollkommen gleich.** To my knowledge, no one has
ever laid any stress on these words. And yet they seem clearly intended to be stressed. If the new rings were vollkommen gleich,
in *every way like* the original ring, they must also have had the same
secret virtue, for the father at least. Hence the version of Boccaccio,
according to which the ring could *hardly* be distinguished by the
father, was changed, and the ring could *not* be distinguished. And
now the father can „froh und freudig'' give to each one of his sons
a ring. True religion is something depending on the growth of the
individual, on his conscious effort. Hence, to speak with Hebler, ''the
wise father, in one sense, did not bequeath the genuine ring at all,
because he could not bequeath it, because that which made the ring
genuine and gave it its secret power can not be transferred and be-
queathed. Nevertheless he gave to each of his sons a ring, because
he knew that it would be helpful to the owner in gaining, by earnest
effort, the genuine ring. And so the judge, afterwards, appropriately
admonishes the sons that each should consider his ring an incentive

for striving to realize through their own efforts the promise attached to the genuine ring."

1957. The curt **wird's** has ordinarily a tinge of impatience, which would here be quite inappropriate in view of the repetition of the „höre," and after the „nur" in the imperative sentence; this tinge must on that account be obviated by the tone in which the word is read.

1973. See l. 1276. **Speife und Trank** refer to the limitations placed upon the Jews and the Mohammedans regarding certain foods and drinks.

1974. Sée Appendix.

1978. Cp. ll. 1845-48. Nathan has reference to the ceremonial rather than to the essentials of religion. With regard to these, he would surely agree with Saladin. Cp. also verses 3538-40.

1983-84. Possibly Nathan thought of the deception he had been obliged to practice upon Recha. Cp. l. 3325 f.

2006. **bezeihen,** *accuse.* Now commonly zeihen.

2019-25. The dash in this and the following line, and the indicated confusion of the brothers at the question of the judge, point to the fact that the practical side of their religion had been quite forgotten, that for them the rings were indeed all false. They had based their claims on the visible signs, not on the secret virtue of their possessions. See Appendix, l. 2025.

2053. **Sprechen** = Recht sprechen, *judge.*

2060. Saladin had been so impressed by Nathan's parable that he for some time apparently forgot the purpose for which he had called him. And now, when reminded by Nathan's question, he is ashamed to make even a request for money.

2061. **hätte,** potential subjunctive: *And is there no other business, possibly?*

2070. **wo damit hin** — wo ich damit hin foll.

2077. **freierdings,** made in analogy with allerdings, fchlechter= dings, platterdings. *Of your own accord.* — Ein Argwohn? Feigned surprise. Cp. l. 1876 ff.

2081. **Un mich fuchen,** in analogy with Jch habe ein An= fuchen, eine Bitte, an dich. Ordinarily, um etwas bei einem an= fuchen.

2085. **Poft** = Poften, 'a sum of money intended for some definite purpose'; here *debt, obligation.* Cp. l. 1233 ff.

2087. Notice that Saladin regards the Templars as his worst enemies.

2090. **fparen,** cp. l. 1346, also l. 1361.

2094. **für ihn** goes with **Gnade** : **Gnade für ihn.**

2095. Cp. ll. 90, 1347-48 ; also l. 1217.

2101. **den fie nicht gekannt.** It is worth while, possibly, to note a little inconsistency. The brother left Saladin, probably but a few years before Recha's birth. In l. 3524 Sittah states she might almost be Recha's mother ; here we learn that she did not know her brother. Cp. ll. 251 and 2971.

2103. **Gebar fie auch fchon bloße Leidenfchaft.** A concessive clause, admitting that the real goodness or merit in saving the Templar's life is of little consequence, because the deed was the result of mere impulse. Cp. Appendix, l. 867.

2111. **Opfertier,** *victim,* a significant appellation. The Templar had, against his will, been drawn into his present difficulty. Take notice of the dashes in this monologue.

2113. **wittern,** *to scent; to have a premonition ; to divine.*

2116. We should now place a comma after the **nun,** important in this case. Lessing almost always omits the comma after **nun.**

2117. Notice the tense of the verb: **war gefallen.** Ordinarily we should have the preterite. The pluperfect may be intended to indicate that the blow had been dealt, before the victim had time to think of his safety. **ausbeugen,** more correct form **ausbiegen.** **beugen** is really a factitive verb = **biegen machen,** from the same stem as **biegen.**

2119-20. Cp. Introduction, pp. 65 f. The lines have ordinarily been interpreted as meaning that the Templar had avoided Recha, because he despised her as a common Jewess, as he at first pretended, especially to Daja ; a number of passages, mentioned in the Introduction, make it much more plausible that he refused to "submit to the blow," because he was in love with Recha from the first moment he saw her, and tried to avoid the danger threatening his vows.

2123. **That** and **litt** are in a sense opposites. **That,** *action;* **litt,** etc., *I was passive, did not attempt to act, hence cannot speak of resolution.* **litt'** and **litte** are not subjunctives, as the final **e** would now indicate. Even in M. H. G. some strong preterites took a final **e** in the first and third singular indicative by analogy to weak preterites. Probably the most common instance is **fahe** for **fah,** though Lessing, as well as Schiller and Goethe, has also a number of other similar forms. **fchiene,** l. 2773, might be taken for one ; it might, however, possibly be meant for an optative subjunctive.

**2124. Das Gefühl.** Notice the nice use of words: incapable of any resolution, the Templar was conscious of a deep feeling only.

**2125. An sie verstrickt — verwebt,** *to be intertwined, interwoven with her.*

**2130. freilich** has concessive force: *to be sure.* Templars took the three vows of poverty, obedience, and celibacy.

**2132. gelobt,** in this verse participle of **geloben,** *to promise, to vow;* in the next of **loben,** *to praise.* I see no way of imitating the play on the word in English. — It is worth while noticing that the Templar explicitly states that he had rid himself of other prejudices, one of which was that against other creeds. Cp. l. 1295, and Introduction, § 74, *b*, 2. **drum** anticipates the following verse.

**2135. will.** *What does my order amount to?*

**2136. ihm = meinem Orden.** He was dead to his order, because to be captured by Saladin was synonymous with being dead. — His sophistry and its purpose are apparent.

**2142. väterlichen Himmel,** *paternal sky.* The first indication that the Templar was aware of his Oriental parentage. The following lines show that they had talked quite plainly to the young man about his father's affairs. Why should they not have mentioned his sister also? Cp. Introduction, § 74, *a.*

**2148. Gefahr laufen,** cp. English *run the risk;* both probably due to French influence: *courir risque.* — It is not clear on what ground the Templar could say of himself that he was merely *in danger of stumbling,* where his father *fell,* unless **straucheln** is here to be taken as equivalent to **fallen.** It is frequently used in very nearly the same sense, especially with figurative significance. But cp. l. 2175, note.

**2154. mehr** is here to be considered an adverb, in view of the punctuation: *his encouragement rather than his approval can not fail me.* Cp. ll. 1321–22.

**2156.** Implicitly the Templar states here that Nathan is not merely a Jew, but something more.

**2157. glüht heit're Freude,** commonly: **glüht vor heiterer Freude.**

**2163. steht seinen Ruhm,** *is equal to his reputation.* The phrase is probably formed in analogy with **seinen Mann stehen.** This construction has not been satisfactorily explained. It should not be confused with **seinem Mann stehen.** There is another phrase, **meinen Mann stellen,** i.e. *to be the man for any given task.* **stehen,** particularly in early N. H. G., sometimes had the meaning of ſtellen and the construction may originate here. — Rede ſtehen, l. 2567, is of different origin. A kindred form is zur Rede ſtehen, i.e. *stand, for the sake of, for the purpose of a defense.* Rede, l. 2567, is probably an old genitive, denoting cause.

2166. **ungeſäumt,** *undelayed.* ſäumen was transitive in M.H.G. and even with Luther. The participial adverb must start from this meaning.

2170. The word order due to poetic license.

2175. **nie! nie! nie!** — Could it be possible that this threefold „nie," spoken with consideration, as indicated by the dash after wie= derſehen, expresses the sober judgment of the Templar, and that the conditional clause added is expressive, rather of his impulse, his feeling? In that case l. 2149 would find its explanation, taking ſtraucheln in its ordinary signification. — zur Stelle = auf der Stelle.

2178. **Junger Mann!** 2179. **Lieber junger Mann!** 2184. **Lieber, lieber Freund!** The increasing tenderness in these appellations are to indicate to the Templar that Nathan loves him and does not wantonly refuse him.

2181-82. **Banden,** *bonds;* Feſſeln, *fetters;* notice the nice dis- tinction; also the pregnant signification of Menſch. Cp. ll. 1311-13, and note.

2186-87. **Erkenntlichkeit — Liebe.** *Gratitude* had smoothed the way upon which *love* was about to enter Recha's heart, and now, beide (l. 2189), *gratitude* and *love* were waiting for the signal at which to melt into one.

2192. **Euern eigenen Gedanken.** Cp. ll. 1310-13, and ll. 1320-22. verkennen may mean *to mistake some one* (l. 1316) as well as *to misconstrue, to deny something,* the one without, the other with purpose. Here the latter.

2198. **Neubegier** = Neugier(de).

2202. A more common abbreviation for Konrad is Kunz.

2208. There is no apparent reason why the Templar should go so far in concealing his perfectly honorable origin, whereby he is surely taxing Nathan's liberality to the utmost, except his unwillingness to own that he had twice told half a truth, ll. 1374 and 2202. Lessing discusses the difference in meaning between Baſtard and Ban- kert in his *Wörterbuch zu Logau,* L. M. vii, l. 361. Baſtard with him meant probably a child born in wedlock, but of a mother inferior in rank. Bankert is a coarse term for an illegitimate child.

2210. **Schlag** = Menſchenſchlag, *race, tribe.* Cp. the first speech of Edmund in *King Lear*, 1, 2; also Schiller's *Jungfrau*, the speech of Dunois, Bastard von Orleans, 1, 2, end, v. 531 ff.

**2211. Entlaßt mich immer meiner Ahnenprobe —** *Yet, nevertheless, release me from giving a proof of my ancestry, from producing my pedigree.* The bitterness of the Templar exhibited in these verses is to be ascribed to the fact that he thinks Nathan has suddenly forgotten his noble sentiments of judging a man by his own merits. Hence he scornfully reminds him in the following verses that he is nothing but a common Jew.

**2214. Stammbaum,** literally *genealogical tree*, hence l. 2215: **Blatt vor** (= für) **Blatt.**

**2229. Schon mehr als g'nug** refers to l. 2226 f.

**2231. Taugt nichts,** cp. l. 3281. A bad state of affairs, if the human mind is absorbed, distracted, no matter with what.

**2233. aufgedunsen,** a figure taken from rising dough, suggested by the word **voll**; *i.e.* the mind soon reduces to its proper shape whatever in the storm of passion has assumed inordinate proportions; here his love and the consequent irritation. This work of the mind begins (l. 2235) only to be rudely interrupted by Daja.

**2253. versichert,** old participial adverb, now **sicher** or **sicherlich.**

**2256. abfragen,** *to find out by cross-questioning.*

**2257. vertrauet,** see l. 2248.

**2261.** There are traces of the infinitive with the accusative, similar to the common usage in the classical languages, in the oldest stages of German as well as in Gothic, also in instances where classic influence is not probable. The construction practically died out, however, and instances in modern writers are probably attributable to classic example. „Von dem wir oft selbst nicht wissen, daß wir es haben."

**2266. sich aus dem Staube machen,** *to escape suddenly;* figure probably taken from fugitives escaping from the dust of battle.— **jemand sitzen lassen,** *to desert some one.*

**2271. Geflattre,** ordinarily **Geflatter;** the form **Geflattre** denotes a more confused *anxious fluttering,* cp. a striking example from Immermann, *Münchhausen:* „Das ist euch ein Gerutsche, Gebrumme, Gepoltre, Gedusele, Gedudele, Geschreite, Gewinsele und ein Gerumore durcheinander." Or Lessing's *Emilia Galotti:* wo ich das Gequieke, das Gekreische hörte."

**2276. den Unsinn,** i. e. den Unsinn zuzugeben; *I'll release you from admitting the madness.*

**2282. uns** must be Recha; and yet **der Kluge** would be much more suitable for the Templar.

2286. **Vorficht = Vorfehung.** The Templar would not admit a personal, direct interference of the Savior or God, in the affairs of men, but he believes that they have been wisely ordered by Providence.

2289. **Das Land der Wunder.** Das Wunderbare is that which seems like a miracle to children, but would not be called a miracle by a thinking person. Cp. l. 220 f.

2297. **hier** = *this world;* **dort** = *yonder world;* 'for time and eternity.'

2305. **Er muß nicht müffen.** Commentators have quibbled about this line as much as they have about l. 385. — The first müffen is used in an entirely different sense from the second. It would be more exact, but not more usual, to substitute for it follen, particularly in negative clauses. Cp. Storm's *Immensee:* „Du mußt auch nicht immer dasfelbe erzählen"; or, the common prohibition to children: „Du mußt mir nicht fortlaufen." Translate: "*I do not want him to be forced.*" — „So muß er wollen." "*Then he must show himself willing, and even anxious.*" Daja uses müffen, just as we do *must* in the translation, in the sense of: "it will be necessary for him"; she can thus combine müffen and wollen, owing to the condition implied in fo. The Templar disregards this fo, and hence calls attention to the apparent contradiction.

2308. **diefe Saite ihm** (= in ihm) **anfchlagen:** "*I tried to strike this chord in him.*" — The figure is kept up in the following lines: einfallen, *chime in;* Mißlaut, *discordant note.*

2312. **den Schatten ihm blicken laffen.** We should now have two accusatives. In the eighteenth century laffen ordinarily took an accusative subject with a dependent infinitive. Only in cases where an accusative object depended on the infinitive, as here, the subject was often changed to the dative, possibly due to French influence. Cp. also l. 3581.

2320. **Daß er doch,** etc., elliptical. *What a pity that,* etc.

2322. **kurz und gut** = ohne Umfchweif, *without any ado.*

2327. **etwas zu verfchweigen,** viz.: his secret, and her own secret.

2330. Whenever the Templar is vexed he verges dangerously near the vulgar; so here. Converting a soul has frequently been called giving it birth for heaven. (Cp. Nicodemus' interview with Christ.) Hence the Templar's scornful congratulation as upon the physical birth of a child, and his other indelicate allusions. His bitterness is explained in l. 2338: von Eurer Mache, *of your making.*

2339. **So** (to be stressed) **versteht Jhr's?** Etc. *If your scorn is directed against my particular type of Christianity, very well* (**so mags gelten**).

2341. **zu werden verdorben;** characteristic testimony : Recha is too firmly established in her views ever to be converted to Christianity; happily she is a Christian against her will and wishes.

2347. **weinen machen** = **hat weinen machen.**

2350. The first sign of the Templar's mean distrust of Nathan crops out in the **sich.**

2352. Now commonly **als was geboren; als Christin, nicht als Jüdin.** The omission of **als** is now confined to poetry.

2360. **Ergießung eines Herzens.** Figure taken from a river : *the trend or course of the heart.*

2361. **lassen,** now **überlassen. verlenken** = *pervert.* Cp. l. 3470, as to the Templar's zeal for Christianity.

2366. **Was mir zu thun** [**gut ist**]; or, = **was für mich zu thun ist.**

2374. **den letzten Druck dem Dinge:** *the final impulse to the affair,* i.e. a union between the Templar and Recha.

2379. **schon,** concessive : *I must admit.*

2382. **so aufgetragen:** *what he has seen fit to trust me with.* The exact meaning of **so** in this connection is hard to define, an approximate equivalent would be : *I have not been very successful, if he has at any time seen fit to trust me with missions of the kind.* From this sentence the **auch** in the next is to be explained. It expresses the parallelism between cause and result, but has, in sentences of this kind, almost the force of an excuse. *I have been unsuccessful: he also gives me unsuccessful things;* the implication: *so I am blameless.*

2384. **fein** = *sly.*

2385. **Näschen, Händchen.** Curiosity and forwardness such as the Patriarch expects of him are fit for children, hence the diminutives, expressive of disgust.

2396. **sauer,** *disagreeable. hard.*

2397. **verbunden sein,** *to be obliged, (to do something).*

2400. **so rund von Euch wies't** = *refused flatly (squarely).*

2403. **nachwirken,** a medical term, denoting : *to have an after-effect, to work, to operate.*

2411. **mit Fleisch und Blut erwogen. Fleisch und Blut,** the sordid, carnal nature, as used in the Bible. Cp. *Matt.* XVI, 17, and elsewhere.

2412. **wieder**; *i.e.* not that he had offered his services once before; once he had refused his services, cut loose from the Patriarch; now he offers his services, is willing to establish his connection *again.*

2423. **pfaff(e)** was originally the designation of any priest. Since the Reformation the word has been a term of reproach for priests; no English word corresponds. Buchheim suggests *monk*, and for pfäffifch, *monkish.*

2427. **fich vergehn,** *to err.* The privilege of erring cannot be explained on the ground of the Jesuite principle that the end sanctifies the means, which would be applicable to the Templar as well as to the Patriarch. The Templar has reference to the doctrine of the infallibility of the church, and its ministers as its representatives. Cp. l. 2481. The inconsistency in his own action the Templar indicates by saying that this infallibility is nothing enviable, and more clearly in l. 3410.

2432. A thoroughly vicious principle from an ethical view point; sophistry on the part of the Templar.

2435. **partei** = parteifache.

2436. **drob** = darob, poetic for darüber, *with regard to it*, i.e. to *religion.*

2438. **Die Stange halten** means *to take the part of some one.* The figure is taken from persons fighting with swords or some other weapon. Cp. Lessing in another place: „Auch will ich mir nicht herausnehmen, bei diesem Kampfe Wärtel (that is the officer, acting as arbiter between the combatants) zu sein und meine Stange dazwischen zu werfen, wenn von der einen oder andern Seite ein gar zu hämischer und unedler Streich geführt würde." Wird's fo wohl recht fein: a reminiscence of Pope's "*Whatever is, is right,*" which Lessing, years before, had proved to be thoroughly unphilosophic in his essay, *Pope, ein Metaphysiker?* But cp. also Appendix, l. 2439.

2441. The sudden resolve of the Templar to take advice from the Friar seems to indicate that he came not for peremptory command, but for honest advice; and, yet, he had come to see the Patriarch (not the Friar) for the purpose of putting Nathan to the knife (l. 3394), and fully aware that the Patriarch was a scoundrel, l. 3411. It is worth while to notice the unsettled state of the Templar. Cp. note to l. 3512.

2451. **einer Sorge,** to that of his eternal salvation.

2454 ff. The Patriarch of Jerusalem shortly before the time of our play was Heraclius, notorious throughout the Orient and Europe for his immorality and total lack of conscience. At the time of our play he was probably dead; at all events he was not in Jerusalem, as Lessing himself knew very well from Marin. He says, L. M. III, 491: „So hat der Patriarch Heraklius gewiß nicht in Jerusalem bleiben dür= fen, nachdem Saladin es eingenommen. Gleichwohl nahm ich ohne Bedenken ihn daselbst noch an, und bedaure nur, daß er in meinem Stücke noch bei weitem so schlecht nicht erscheint, als in der Ge= schichte." — He could not very well retain all his worst features, if he was at all to remind of Goeze. See Appendix, l. 2454.

2455. **dick, rot, freundlich,** *stout, ruddy, well-satisfied.*

2457. **sich erheben,** indicative of the pretentious bombast of the Patriarch. The term is archaic, biblical; cp. *Matt.* XIX, 1.

2459. Cp. l. 990.

2465–66. **eher noch, was weniger.** Buchheim, following a hint of Niemeyer, thinks these lines are to indicate the Templar's purpose of leaving his order. If we are not to see a bit of society small talk in these words, they are difficult to explain.

2469. **blühn und grünen.** The Patriarch maintains the sermonizing tone throughout; cp. *Isaiah,* XXVII, 6: „Es wird dennoch dazu kommen, daß Jakob wurzeln, und Israel blühen und grünen wird."

2471. **dem reifen Rate:** a reminder of the Templar's disobedience; Act I, Scene 5.

2476 f. In the following verses virtually the whole quarrel about the *Fragments* is once more fought out, particularly in its more objectionable features. See Appendix.

2487. **Willkür,** *arbitrary dictates, free choice.* See Appendix.

2490. **Herrlichkeit des Himmels,** *i.e.* God.

2493. **unsern Rat:** *pluralis majestaticus.*

2494. **der Herr,** instead of the pronoun, was in the eighteenth century employed to show greater respect; cp. l. 541. It is still common in some parts of Germany.

2495. **es sei,** hortative; *let us suppose,* or *say.*

2511 f. The demand of the Patriarch to know the name of the offender before passing any judgment on the offense is clearly a reminder of Goeze's attitude in the quarrel about the *Fragments.* He, too, insisted on knowing the name of the author, and Lessing, like the Templar, refused to comply with his wish. See Appendix.

2516. See Appendix.

2522. The mentioning of the theater — quite against Lessing's own advice in the *Dramaturgie*, Article 42 — is an anachronism, in a sense. These lines again contain a thrust at Goeze.    See Appendix.

2531 f. See Appendix.    **mit, now: an.**    Possibly contamination with **vornehmen,** regularly construed with **mit.**

2537. About apostasy and heresy Lessing had his peculiar views, of which at the time of the publication of *Nathan* people were probably reminded by these lines.    See Appendix.

2542. See Appendix.

2544. **Erbarmte,** preterite indicative, instead of pluperf. subj. ; cp. note to l. 91.

2552. See Appendix.

2555 f.  See Appendix.

2560. **dieserwegen,** ordinarily **deswegen.**

2567. **Rede stehen,** see note to l. 2163.

2574. **unserer allerheiligsten Religion** recalls the title of one of Goeze's pamphlets: *Etwas Vorläufiges gegen Lessings mittelbare und unmittelbare feindselige Angriffe auf unsere allerheiligste Religion.*

2579. It is customary to recall, in connection with these verses, the "intolerant bigotry" of Goeze, who saw in religion, or rather in the Christian religion, an indispensable condition of all civic order. He was by no means alone in this view, and it may be of interest to his revilers to know that a man no less liberal than the philosopher Wolff was of the same opinion, and many others could be mentioned. See Appendix.

2582. **darf = braucht.** — As a matter of history, the articles of capitulation contained none of the conditions alluded to by the Patriarch.

2584. **Sermon,** rather contemptuous for **Predigt.**

2586. Notice the four dashes in this verse, indicative of the Patriarch's sudden fear and confusion, which is shown still more clearly in the following verses.

2592. See Appendix.

2600. **Bruder Bonafides = der Klosterbruder.**

2602. **Des Dings,** indicative of Saladin's contempt of money; cp. ll. 910 and 1745.    These were the purses sent by Nathan.

2609. **abzuzwacken,** *to extort.*

2611. **das Urmut,** now **die Urmut.**    The neuter was formerly used occasionally, if the noun was used in a collective sense.

2612. As a matter of history, Saladin not only released pilgrims from the tax which he had the right to claim at the Holy Sepulcher, but also gave alms to the poorer ones among them. Lessing's purpose in mentioning the fact is evident.

2634. **Blieb weg,** euphemistically used, particularly of sailors, for **ſterben**; Saladin probably does not exactly mean to convey this idea (cp. 2636 f), but Sittah understands him thus. And in the next line he takes up her thought: *"he never returned."* — *"Never mind! sooner or later we all go and never return."*

2638. **das Ziel verrücken**; literally, *to misplace, to move the aim, the mark.*—*"It is not death alone that crosses the path of youths such as he was."*

2639. **der Stärkſte erliegt dem Schwächſten.** Saladin had heard some rumor of his brother's fate, and alludes by the word **dem Schwächſten** to the woman who conquered the strong young knight.

2640. **Sei wie ihm ſei.** The dative has crept into this construction probably from such expressions as **mir iſt wohl**; and these in turn are probably formed by analogy with **mir wird wohl, mir wird etwas.**

2668. **Ginniſtan.** Lessing explained **Ginniſtan** to his brother as **feenland** = *fairyland*, and **Div** as **fee,** *fairy.*

2677. — **Nun mags!** Expressive of a sad resignation. The Templar would in every way pass as his brother, — if Saladin did not also see himself, and this tells him that he can not be the lost brother; this reminds him of his loss. I should translate: *"But, then —!"*

2680. **es zufrieden.** **es** is really an old genitive, denoting the source or cause. It is now felt as an accusative.

2684. **um mir**; **um** . with the dative was rarely used even in the older stages of the language. Occasionally we find it down to the eighteenth century.

2685. **Im weißen Mantel** = *as a Templar;* **im Jamer‐ lonk,** according to Lessing's note, „**das weiße Oberkleid der Araber,**" i.e. *as a Mohammedan.* **Culban** or **Curban; filz** = **Hut.**

2687. **Ich habe nie verlangt,** etc. The lines have a deeper significance than is ordinarily ascribed to them. Differences of creed are not only something external in the eyes of Saladin, *i.e.* the Saladin of our play, but also a spontaneous growth, like the bark of a tree. See Appendix.

2690. Saladin had compared men to trees: the Templar continues the figure; Saladin was forced by circumstances to excel in valor, in the art of war; by choice he would rather foster and cherish the trees (*i.e.* men) in God's orchard.

2693. **Ein Wort, ein Mann,** is a proverbial expression: *a man must be, or is, as good as his word.* — **Empfange mehr,** etc. Saladin could deprive him of only a more or less aimless, half-hearted life: he now gives himself heart and soul. Cp. l. 1215; also l. 730 and notes.

2704 f. The Templar is thinking of the apparent inconsistency in Nathan, who is wise and tolerant in words, and bigoted in deed — according to Daja's revelation.

2712. An apt characterization of the historical Saladin.

2714. Cp. *Minna von Barnhelm*, II, I: „**Man spricht selten von der Tugend, die man hat, aber desto öfter von der, die uns fehlt.**"

2715. **Es mit jemand haben,** *to be quarreling with some one.*

2721. The Templar had concluded from Daja's information that Nathan refused to give him Recha, because of religious prejudice.

2726. Cp. l. 1210; but also Introduction, § 74, *b*, I.

2730-32. Cp. l. 1320 f.

2737. **auf . . . hin:** *relying upon.*

2740. **Tropf,** *fool, blockhead.*

2741. Notice that the two **ich** are spaced.

2743. **platterdings** = **geradezu,** *flatly.*

2755. The Templar calls all creeds **Überglauben,** *superstition,* and compares them to chains. Cp. l. 2182 and note; l. 2434 f; l. 1979; l. 3511.

2762. **Dem,** demonstrative, = **dem seinigen Überglauben,** *to one's own superstition.* **vertrauen,** next line, = **anvertrauen,** *intrust, commit to.* **blöde** = *weak,* in any part · of the body, but it is now rarely used, except of eyes in this sense. He admits here that Nathan is sincere when he says, all creed differences are matters of little importance. But if humanity in its blindness cannot do without creeds, he is anxious to make converts for the very creed which he himself outgrew.

2767. **Ausbund,** really the *skein of wool* which is tied on the outside of a package to indicate the quality of the whole. Owing to the depravity of the dealers, the best **Bund** was placed on the outside (**aus**); hence anyone excelling in any way, more commonly now in bad qualities, is called **Ausbund.**

2769. **suchte.** The L.-M. text has **suche,** which is probably a mistake. But see also the present subjunctive **könne,** l. 2943, where the preterite subjunctive would be more natural.

2772. **körnen** = mit **Körnern locken,** *to hold out as a bait, as* *grain to birds.*   deren, a sort of objective genitive; more commonly, Hoffnung auf welche.

2773. **ſchiene,** cp. Note to l. 2124.

2776. **verzettelt,** literally, *to scatter, as scraps of paper;* hence, *to get into wrong places, as loose slips of paper;* here, *an apostate Christian child.*

2777. **wollte,** not preterite indicative, but potential subjunctive.

2779. **tolerante Schwätzer,** *tolerant babbler;* cp. Act II, Sc. 5.

2780. Cp. *Matt.* VII, 15.

2783. Having just now so bitterly accused Nathan of being tolerant in words only, the word **Chriſt,** spoken with admonishing emphasis, could hardly fail to gain the Templar's attention.

2785. **auf . . . beſtehen,** if the Jew and Mohammedan turn out Jew and Mohammedan.

2787. **Des Vorwurfs Laſt,** which was, that he made himself guilty of the very crime which he had laid to Nathan's charge: that of forgetting the broader human interests over the prejudices of creed.

2790. **genommen** = benommen.

2793. **mit einem Worte,** *i.e.* in readily admitting his wrong, ll. 2786–87.

2795. **ſich in jemand finden** = *to understand some one.*

2798. **weiſen** = raten.

2799. **den Schwärmern deines Pöbels,** *to the vulgar Christian fanatics.*   It seems as if Saladin used the word Pöbel (*rabble*) to indicate that within a creed there is some room for noble-minded enthusiasm.

2800. Cp. l. 2570 f. and Note.

2804. **zum Troß** = *to spite a Jew or a Mohammedan.*

2811. Saladin means to say that this fear of the Templar, indicative of his appreciation of his wrong, and his regret, is a quality which he is quite willing to recognize as one of Assad's.

2820. Cp. l. 3268; l. 1276; l. 1973 f.

2830. Sittah, somewhat shocked by the rather insidious and not altogether delicate suggestion of her brother, exclaims, ironically (and I should read it in a deep voice) Das machſt du gut!   I should substitute for it, or translate it, if you please, by: *Well, I beg of you!* — Saladin seeks to hold his ground in the next lines.

2833. **erpicht.** Auf etwas erpicht ſein, lit. *to be held, attracted by something,* as a bird to a trap in which it is held by *pitch.*

2842. **Wer,** etc., i.e. *the Templar;* cp. l. 2544 f; l. 3243 f; as to the relative claims of Nathan and the Templar.

**2848. Die liebe Neubegier** = *mere curiosity, common to my sex.*

**2860. Silberstoff,** *silver-gray cloth.*

**2861. noch.** In early N. H. G. noch was sometimes used to express a double degree of some quality; this use is now replaced by noch einmal: noch einmal so groß. In concessive clauses we have remnants of the old usage: es sei noch so klein. By analogy with this use with adjectives, noch is also used with nouns, as here, particularly with nouns having a pregnant signification: *that I call a bridal robe, I tell you.*

**2871. witzelst,** *what are you driving at?* — sinnbildern = *to whose bridal dress do these learned allegories have reference?*

**2879. Siebensachen.** Due to biblical influence, the number seven has always played an important part. Meine sieben Sachen, or Siebensachen, with shift of stress, meant, possibly, *all that I have,* seven being the 'perfect number.' It is now applied to insignificant trifles.

**2881. Nicht rühr an!** The verb is surely in the imperative, second singular, not the indicative, as many seem to suppose. I should supply: Nicht rühr an! heißt es bei mir, or, mahnt mich das Gewissen.

**2888. doch einmal,** cp. l. 2.

**2891. wird wieder, was sie ist,** d. h. eine Christin.

**2894. Feuerkohlen,** cp. *Rom.* XII, 20. The situations here and in *Romans* are not quite parallel. Nathan is supposed to have caused himself pangs of conscience by his good deeds, while in *Romans* one having suffered an injury is to cause remorse in the offender by good deeds.

**2896. Die alte Leier,** etc. The figure cannot well be kept in English. Translate: *Harping the same old tune? Only on a new string; but that is out of tune, and may snap.*

**2904. Was wird er wollen?** Daja is as sure of the Friar's business as the Templar was; cp. l. 533.

**2919. annoch,** archaic for noch; similarly allwo, l. 2942.

**2920. Je nu;** *why, of course.*

**2930. zur Buße,** related to baß, besser, English *better;* hence really *bettering.* *Let me give you, to make amends,* etc.

**2936. Quarantana,** according to tradition the mountain on which Christ, being tempted, fasted for forty days. It used to be occupied by many hermits.

**2944. Ich steh' auf Kohlen:** *I am sitting on needles; on thorns.*

2947. **Siedelei** = **Einsiedelei, auf Tabor**; Mount Tabor on which Christ was transfigured,

2955. **Ins Ohr setzen,** cp. the English colloquial *to put a flee in one's ear; to tell secretly.*

2961. **ob,** for **über,** archaic, and now used only in higher diction, and then more commonly with the dative.

2963. **Sünde wider den heil'gen Geist,** cp. *Matt.* XII, 31. A thrust at the fruitless controversies of the contemporary theologians; cp. also *St.Mark* III, 29; *St.Luke* XII, 10. The tone of these verses, rather pungent, seems hardly in accord with the Friar as we have learned to know him. The sin against the Holy Ghost is generally understood to be the wilful resistance to well-recognized divine truth, — a resistance which, according to Lessing's view, is impossible; cp. Appendix, l. 2439.

2979. **Gaz(z)a** was an important commercial city in the land of the Philistines, between Damascus and Egypt. **Darun** was a hamlet near Gaza.

2987. **Wohl sonst. — sonst** in the sense of "in other respects" will hardly do here. The word had another meaning in early N. H. G.; „**so schon**", which I should like to claim for it here; in l. 2885 the Friar expresses his regret for having lost his good master all too soon; l. 2986 : "soon afterward he fell at Ascalon, and, as it was, he was a dear, kind lord." — **sonst,** or *"as it was"* implying, that his untimely death made him all the more dear.

2993. The dash at the end of the verse designates a pause, in which Nathan might have had time to answer. He is perplexed, hence the Friar's reassuring words in the next verses. **Laßt's lieber,** etc.: *You need not say she died!*

2995. **gute Wege haben :** here *there is no reason for any apprehension.*

2997 f. The argument of the friar is not very clear. See Appendix for a similar thought from an earlier work of Lessing; but the situations are not quite parallel. In *Alcibiades* the good deeds of an ambitious (that is a selfish) man are judged. Does the Friar mean to cast doubt upon all good deeds which we perform, fully conscious of their being good? Cp. *Matt.* XXV, 37 f.

3007. **so belohnet,** *i.e.* with the punishment threatened by the Patriarch.

3008. **ein** = einleuchten, *"I do not see the justice."*

3009. **klüger :** notice that the Friar does not say **weiser.** Klugheit in *Nathan* always implies more or less selfishness; cp. ll. 443; 1805 f, and the notes; also ll. 3012-13.

3024. See Appendix.

3025. **Fürſprach** = ordinarily **Fürſprecher**, or possibly **Für·** **ſprech**.

3032. **fromme Einfalt**; cp. l. 3348 f.

3039. **Gath** used to be one of the cities of the Philistines, north-west of Jerusalem. That the crusaders were often cruel to the Jews as well as to the Mohammedans, is quite likely. Systematic persecutions in Europe were common enough, but I am unaware of any having been inaugurated by the crusaders in the Holy Land.

3046. **in Aſch' und Staub** = *dust and ashes* were a common sign of mourning among the Jews; cp. *Job*, and also Jonah's mission to Nineveh.

3048. **rechten**, really *to call to account;* ordinarily *to find fault.*

3053. **Und doch iſt Gott!** *i.e.* in spite of this overwhelming trouble, God is, as I have always believed him to be, provident, wise, and kind.

3055. **Übe,** etc. The relation between theory and practice has often been dwelt on by Lessing. Cp. Appendix, l. 35; l. 360; l. 867, first quotation.

3059. **Ich will! Willſt du nur, daß ich will!** *i.e.* I can not form a resolution, if God does not permit me. Cp. l. 385 and notes. — With regard to Nathan's action as described in the next lines, it is to be observed that the little girl was the daughter of a friend who had often shielded him from violence, not that of any enemy who had murdered his dear ones. On the other hand observe also that Nathan vowed to God: *I will,* before he knew what God might demand of him.

3063. **Vergeſſen:** not entirely: he knew who Recha's father was, and probably also her Christian name; cp. l. 3806.

3065. **auf,** here *toward.*

3067 f. See Appendix. The Friar has some right to his words, as to the difference in the views of Judaism and those of Christianity; cp. also *Matt.* v, 38–48.

3069. **das macht Euch mir zum Juden,** *i.e.* they were one in the principle of love, by which they guided their lives; but none the less Nathan saw no reason to abandon the faith of his fathers, and if the community of spirit induced the Friar to see in Nathan a Christian, the same made Nathan to see in him a Jew; cp. the Introduction, § 55, as to the justice in this position.

3077. **ich gehorche!** These words may well be called express-ive of the height of Nathan's virtue and character. Nowhere else does his implicit faith in Providence so clearly manifest itself. See Appendix.

**3078. Nun vollends!** is evidently elliptical. It is probably best to supply muß ich Euch für einen Chriſten halten. — bedacht' ich mich ſo viel, *I hesitated so long,* — not because he was too stupid to find the proper words — there is method in his madness — but because he knew what it must cost Nathan to act on any suggestion of this kind.

**3081. der erſte beſte** = *the first one coming along.* The phrase has no doubt arisen from: der erſte iſt der beſte, *i.e.* I want some thing or some man for any purpose, and am willing to forego all privilege of choosing; hence der erſte beſte, *just any one.*

**3084. zum minſten,** older and correct form for zum mindeſten, now more usual.

**3088. als Sippe verwandt,** *related in any other way.* Sippe formerly could mean either a male or female relative; so here.

**3093. deſſen,** now desſelben.

**3102. ſel'ger Herr** = *deceased master.*

**3104. verſcharren** is ordinarily used of animals only. The friar wants to indicate that, owing to the needs of the hour, the funeral rites had to be neglected.

**3106. Chriſtenmenſch,** familiar for Chriſt, *Christian.*

**3108. ˉJch kann nicht leſen.** The art of reading was, to be sure, quite rarely found among Christian knights of the time; and yet this statement is significant in another direction. The only man who could lay just claim to being a Christian could not read. Cp. Appendix, l. 2445. — Lessing transfers the good old German custom of inscribing the names of a family in the family Bible to the Orient.

**3126. wohl recht** = wohl mit Recht.

**3133. nicht der Patriarch.** Nathan mentions the Patriarch repeatedly, in order to sound Daja.

**3135. ihm nichts geſteckt?** *You did not whisper anything to him?* The expression has a history. The messengers designated by the Holy Feme, the ancient secret tribunal, particularly in Westphalia, to announce to one accused his summons before the tribunal, had the right *to fasten* (ſtecken) this summons in a groove which they cut in a draw-bridge or some other accessible place, in case they could not obtain a personal interview. — A reminder of this custom is to be found also in the word Steckbrief.

**3136. Die Boten, d. h. von Sittah.**

3142. **Hui, der Tempelherr ift drum.** *Before I know it, the Templar will have lost her.*

3145. The dash ending the preceding verse designates her hesitation. Hence, **Getroft!** encouraging herself: *Never mind!* Cp. l. 3151.

3150. **unterwegens,** more commonly, in literary German at least, **unterwegs.**

**Mamelucken,** (stage direction) *slaves,* generally highly educated, and often of high parentage, on one side at least.

3152. **das Geld.** Cp. l. 2603.

3155. Cp. ll. 452–53.

3159. **Kahira** = Kairo.

3163. **der guten Zeitung,** genitive of cause; more common für die gute **Nachricht.** **Zeitung** in its older sense of the English *tidings.* — (**Nun? nur her damit!**) to be spoken aside; *Well? hand it out!* i.e. *the customary fee,* das **Botenbrot,** of l. 3166.

3176. **Abtritt** = *departure;* he is speaking of his death; cp. the historical summary in the Introduction.

3183. **Warum zu fpät?** Saladin has returned to his accustomed liberality.

3187. **wenn . . . anders,** used in clauses making a provision; *provided.*

3188. **auch,** cp. Note on l. 2382. *O well! It's just as likely he broke his neck.*

3193. **Der Lecker,** *the rogue,* good-naturedly.

3201. **bilden helfen,** for habe bilden helfen.

3202. **zu guter Letzt,** *the last minute,* from M. H. G. **Letze** = **Abfchied, Abfchiedsgefchenk, Abfchiedstrunk. Letze** fell into disuse; and as **zu guter Letze** designated the end of a visit, the last of a visit, the farewell, **Letzte** and **Letzt** were readily substituted for it.

3205. **Emir,** title of Mohammedan rulers and chieftains.

3210. **Abulkaffem.** The name of the ruler of Egypt, as well as the revolt mentioned is invented by the poet.

3211. **Thebais** (three syllables), designated southern or upper Egypt; named after Thebes, its capital; now Saīd.

3217. **Bedeckung,** *escort.*

3225. **der Zug** = die Karawane.

3226. — **Ihr! ich bin fodann bei Sittah,** is addressed to some slaves standing in waiting.

3229. Significant. Cp. Introduction, § 74, *b,* 1. The Templar is carrying out Saladin's order, l. 2815.

3230. **Will** rather denotes here futurity, as commonly **werden** does.

3235. Cp. l. 2219.

3236. **ihn ſtimmen**, *get him into tune*, or *get him into line*.

3241. **es ſich zur Angelegenheit machen** = es ſich ange‧legen ſein laſſen, *to take pains*.

3242. **abjagen**, *to wrest from some one*.

3244. Cp. ll. 3653–54; and l. 3662. — **Doch des Sklaven nicht**, etc. The father to whom Recha owes her physical existence is likened to a slave floating a block of marble to some shore and then abandoning it; Nathan was the artist who saw in the abandoned block the divine form and features, which he released.

3259. **es** = *what makes her smile; if it were unworthy of the charm, in which it is clothed on her lips*, etc.

3261. **Überwitz**, *buffoonery;* **Tand**, *frivolity;* **Höhnerei**, *scoff‧ing, mockery;* **Schmeichler**, *flatterers;* **Buhler**, *coquettes, paramours.*

3265. **ſeinem Sonnenſchein** = des Lächelns Sonnenſchein.

3268. Cp. ll. 2819–21.

3273. **Lenk ein!** *Hold back!*

3275. **ſtünde:** ſtehen is used in a few set phrases in the same sense as ſein.

3281. **Querkopf**, *madcap*.

3285. **ihrer warten**, commonly auf ſie warten.

3287. **Habt Dank!** for bringing the breviary.

3290. **Was Ihr nicht braucht** — *i.e.* money. — **Eurer** = Euer Eigenſinn; cp. l. 3114.

3292. **reicher;** cp. ll. 456–57.

3296. **Je nu!** reassuring after the rather sad thought of the pre‧ceding verse. nu, older and now familiar form for nun.

3301 f. Cp. l. 358, and notes.

3305. **hetzen**, hunting term, *to spur on, to incite.*

3313. Cp. l. 3329 f.

3318. **Viel Glücks;** the genitive was formerly always used with viel; cp. l. 3283.

3324. **daß** — elliptical; supply wie ſchade. — From these words of Nathan some commentators have concluded that he was conscious of some guilt, assumed in taking and keeping Recha as his child. The assumption is absurd on its face. The wrong is not with Nathan, but with the fanaticism of men, which did not permit him to walk as openly before them as he could before his God.

3333. **ſeine** must be stressed; *i.e.* the deeds of a man often have their source in circumstances rather than in man's own choice: *e.g.* that Nathan concealed Recha's parentage.

3339. It must be assumed that Nathan had been a second time at Saladin's palace.

3342. **ſtand** = war ... gerichtet; cp. l. 3275.

3343. **ja doch wohl**, *I presume.*

3345. **Die gute Haut**; Haut for Menſch, denotes *guilelessness,* almost *simplicity.*

3346. **Stöber** = Spürhund, *a setter,* here *spy.*

3348. **Pfiff,** *trick;* cp. the more common pfiffig.

3350. **dumme, fromme Einfalt;** notice the same double meaning in English *simplicity.*

3356. **namentlich** = ſo daß der Name genannt wurde.

3363. **Euch** must be stressed. **mit ſeiner Gunſt** = mit ſeiner Erlaubnis; *if you please.*

3369. **eines Fehls,** eines Fehltritts.

3371. **mit dem** = mit dieſem Dorſat.

3375. **wurmiſch** = ärgerlich; cp. das wurmt.

3377. **Gauch,** down to the sixteenth century the common name for the *cuckoo,* considered a stupid bird. Hence, even in O. H. G., also in the sense of *simpleton, fool.*

3380. **lau : kalt.** Cp. *Revel.* III, 15, 16. **abgemeſſen,** etc., *with what premeditated effort you tried to elude me.*

3382. **aus der Luft gegriffen,** *manufactured for the occasion; groundless.*

3394. **kurz und gut,** an idiomatic expression, meaning *without much ado.* Nathan analyzes it, hence his question. We might translate: *I decided to make short and good work of it, and put you to the knife.* Cp. l. 2322.

3401. **Laffe** = Gauch.

3402. **an beiden Enden ſchwärmen,** *i.e.* an den äußerſten Enden; *"whose thoughts are always wandering in extremes."*

3405. **ſo mich faſſet,** *if you approach me in that way,* i.e. begging forgiveness.

3413. **zur Rede ſtellen,** cp. l. 2163, notes.

3417. **ſo ähnlich ſich erhält** = *is always the same.*

3423. **Euerm,** must be stressed.

3430. **Gleichviel,** cp. l. 3512, and note.

3434. **ſehr nötig —.** Cp. l. 3316.

3435. **oder wem es ſonſt zu wiſſen ziemt —** implies the rather sharp rebuke for the Templar, that he is meddling in affairs that do not concern him.

3455. **wer für mehr ihm danken wird! —** *i.e.* the devil.

**Das.** — **Danken** used to be construed with the genitive.   Owing to
the contamination of some genitive and accusative forms in the pro-
nouns, the genitive was gradually replaced by the accusative throughout.

3456. **diesen** = diesen Händen.

3459. **Was ein Glück,** etc., *viz.:* to find her relatives, why?
Cp. l. 3472 f.

3475. **den lautern Weizen.**   Cp. l. 1564 f.   Notice how little
the Templar makes of the creed which he professes.

3484. **Brüderchen — Schwesterchen,** ironical terms of en-
dearment.

3493. **verhunzen,** possibly formed from **Hund,** as erzen, ihrzen
from er, ihr; it would mean then first, *to call or treat some person as
a dog;* then *to debase;* thence *to spoil.*   It is not a very delicate term.

3494. **Er** = der Engel.

3497. **unterschlagen,** ordinarily *to embezzle,* here *to be deprived of.*

3507. **Manns genug;** genitive with **genug;** *enough of a man,
courageous enough;* rarely said of women.

3512. See Appendix.
In the prose sketch Lessing has this note on our scene: „Sittah
findet an Rahel nichts, als ein unschuldiges Mädchen, ohne alle geoffenbarte Religion, wovon sie kaum die Namen kennt, aber voll
Gefühl des Guten und Furcht vor Gott."   L. M. III, 489.

3520. **angst** was originally a noun, and is even now rarely used
as a predicate objective.   Commonly: mir ist angst.

3524. Cp. l. 2101.

3525. Cp. with the above quotation another from a letter of Lessing
to his brother Karl, referring to the character of his *Emilia Galotti:*
„Ich kenne an einem unverheirateten Mädchen keine höhere Tugenden als Frömmigkeit und Gehorsam."

3534. **Die kalte Buchgelehrsamkeit.**   It may be that we
are to see an Oriental feature in Nathan's pedagogical methods; it may
possibly be an approval of Rousseau's and Pestalozzi's ideas.   But,
more likely, it is another reference to the quarrels preceding the publication of *Nathan.*   See Appendix.

3546. **schlecht und recht;** only in this phrase schlecht has its
earlier meaning of schlicht, *plain;* cp. schlechthin, schlechtweg, schlechterdings; similarly recht has here its older meaning, *straight: plain
and natural;* cp. in die Richte gehen, l. 3619.

3554. **will Luft,** *needs to give vent to its care.*

3563. **gelten,** used primarily of coins: *to have value, to count.*

3565. **will... vermögen,** a somewhat odd use of wollen, probably analogous to such expressions as: „Ein verzweifeltes Übel will eine verwegene Arznei," in which case wollen indicates that the nature of the *impersonal* subject makes something else necessary.

3569. **aufdringen;** aufgedrungen is really intransitive; aufdrängen, aufgedrängt are transitive; cp. also ll. 3289 and 3590.

3576. **Gutes** = *kindness;* **Böses** = *cruelty.*

3591. Some indications of Daja's missionary efforts we have seen in Act III, Sc. I. **verfehlen** is now ordinarily construed with the accusative.

3611. **Überlegung,** *reflection.* She had excused Daja's efforts, reflecting on her motives, and the other grounds enumerated in l. 3603 f.

3612. **entdeckt will haben;** *what she claimed to be a fact which she revealed to me.*

3624. **Wie ward mir?** *What feeling came over me?*

3627. **der Göttlichen,** d. h. der heiligen Jungfrau.

3630. Observe: **des wahren Mitleids;** Daja acted from pure motives, at least.

3639. **Mein Bruder kommt!** It will be observed, as a matter of dramaturgical technique, that the closing words of most scenes introduce a new-comer of the following scene; cp. l. 3226.

3640. **von sich,** *beside herself.* Cp. the opposite in l. 3642: „Komm doch zu dir, Kind!"

3648. **Eh' er mir nicht verspricht.** We now omit the negative. Throughout the eighteenth century a negative was frequently used in a dependent clause, expressing once more the negative idea contained in the main clause: *Tell:* „Verhüt' es Gott, daß ich nicht Hilfe brauche!" — Similarly after main clauses with a comparative, as in this instance.

3661. **faselnd,** rather indelicate term for *"being delirious";* due to Saladin's impatience with Daja's procedure.

3666. **Erwerben;** how? Cp. l. 3246 f.

3674. **umgesehen,** participle used imperatively.

3675. **um die Wette leben,** *who will vie with you in living;* i.e. is as young as you. Notice the **uns,** which is another expression of the easy familiarity with which Saladin is trying to reassure Recha.

3683. **Bruder!** a slight reproach, implying probably *How can you ask? Of course, they may come!*

3690. The repetition of **Dich** is probably due to metrical considerations; similarly auch ihr, l. 3697.

3703. **— bist doch meine Tochter noch?** Nathan surmises

the cause of Recha's tears, and, half comforting, half anxious asks his question.

3705 f. Cp. l. 1161 f.　He refers to her possible love for the Templar, of course.　The double negative, l. 3707, was once good German as well as English.　To conclude from Recha's answer that she had no love for the Templar, would be just as *hasty* (gach = jach = jäh[e]), and hence just as much open to censure, as the Templar's conduct.

3715. **Bemüh dich nicht**; cp. l. 2816 f.

3716. **Entgegenkommen, erraten.**　Saladin knew that Nathan had, in a sense, refused the Templar's request for Recha's hand, and surmised that the Templar had since then not seen Recha, and so had not made her acquainted with his wishes.　Could not Recha on that ground say that she was threatened with no other loss?

3727. **nicht genau nehmen**, *to make allowance.*

3728. **warm = hitzig**, *fiery, impulsive.*

3729. **eins fürs andere**, *i.e.* you must balance his readiness to abandon you now, with his noble deed in your behalf at the time of the fire.

3731. **sich antragen**, *to offer one's self.*

3736. **ist was Recht's**, *that's something great!*

3737. **meines Bruders**; nichts (M. H. G. niht) was formerly regularly construed with a partitive genitive; now ordinarily with **von** and the dative.

3738. **Larve**, *empty appearance.*

3743 f. Apparently slightly sarcastic, or in a tone of superiority, which Nathan ably retaliates.

3754. **aufbinden**, *foist upon one.*

3756. **Christ**, again in its pregnant meaning of l. 2786.　It is hardly the Christian, however, or religious fanaticism, which is at the bottom of this low suspicion.　Cp. l. 3512, and note.　Nathan understands his motives better.

3761. **Argwohn** (*base suspicion*) and **Mißtraun** (*lack of confidence*) come from the same source.

3767. **einen einer Lüge** (genitive of cause) **strafen**, *to accuse one of a lie.*

3770. **Das hieß Gott ihn sprechen** always implies a threat: *lucky for him, he said that!*

3775. **hier zu Lande** ordinarily means *in this country;* here, *to this country.*　It is now commonly written hierzulande.

3790. Here, at last, appears the reason which the Templar had for concealing his real name: he did not look on his father's conduct with favor, in spite of his much boasted liberality.    See Introduction, § 75. Notice the punctuation in these lines.*

3793. **Sie Geſchwiſter!** This relationship may have been suggested by Diderot's play *Le Fils naturel* = „**Der natürliche Sohn, oder die Proben der Tugend,**" which Lessing translated. As to the fitness of the ending see Introduction, §§ 74 and 75, also for the rest of the scene.

3794. **Ihr Bruder!** The kind of emotion expressed in these words may easily be misunderstood; be sure to take notice of l. 3800 f.

3795. **Wir** (mein Vater und ich) **ſind Betrüger,** *i. e.* in the Templar's eyes.

3797. **alles iſt erlogen an dir :** *you are made up of deception; deception your face,* etc.

3799. **erkennen** = anerkennen; cp. l. 3835.

3810. **Verſtoßt ſie meinetwegen,** *disown her on my account,* i. e. for the wrong I have once more committed against you. This is plainly the meaning, as appears from **entgelten laſſen** (l. 3811): *why let her pay the penalty.* Nathan's forgiveness is simply expressed in **Und was?** *penalty, for what?*

3825. **Frank',** cp. l. 334, note. **Abendländer** = *a native of the Occident.*

3833. In view of l. 2835, it was well for Nathan to leave it with the Sultan, whether he wished to acknowledge the Templar and Recha as relatives, or regard them as friends.

3836. **Neffen,** stretching the term to include Recha as well as the Templar.

3842. Cp. ll. 3523–24; l. 3669.

---

* A word must be said about the punctuation of the text. Lessing considered it an important item. In a letter to his brother Carl (Jan. 17, 1779), who was supervising the printing, he urged that no arbitrary changes be made, and that particularly the difference between the dash (—) and the dots (. . .) be observed, which he calls an essential point of his new punctuation for actors. Dots indicate an interruption by the speaker himself, or by the listener; the dash indicates a pause for the actor. Kuno Fischer justly says: "Lessing's punctuation is so eloquent, so freighted with meaning, so significant; every comma, every semicolon has its meaning. Some authors place dashes in want of thought; with Lessing a dash always denotes that there were too many thoughts crowding in on him. They denote a most eloquent silence."

# APPENDIX

**34.** Was Nathan unter Tugend versteht, geht hervor aus den *Gedanken über die Herrnhuter*, L. M. XIV, 160:* "Man stelle sich vor, es stünde zu unsern Zeiten ein Mann auf... dessen Ermahnungen und Lehren auf das einzige zielten, was uns ein glückliches Leben verschaffen kann, auf die Tugend. Er lehrte uns, des Reichtums entbehren, ja ihn fliehen. Er lehrte uns, unerbittlich gegen uns selbst, nachsehend gegen andere sein. Er lehrte uns, das Verdienst, auch wenn es mit Unglück und Schmach überhäuft ist, hochachten und gegen die mächtige Dummheit verteidigen. Er lehrte uns die Stimme der Natur in unserm Herzen lebendig empfinden. Er lehrte uns, Gott nicht nur glauben, sondern was das Vornehmste ist, lieben. Er lehrte uns endlich, dem Tode unerschrocken unter die Augen gehen, und durch einen willigen Abtritt von diesem Schauplatze beweisen, daß man überzeugt sei, die Weisheit würde uns die Maske nicht ablegen heißen, wenn wir unsere Rolle nicht geendigt hätten." Dieser Mann wäre der wahre Philosoph, ganz einerlei, wie wenig er sonst von den zu diesem Namen berechtigenden Kenntnissen hätte. Siehe auch Appendix, 867.

**136.** Vgl. dazu, was Lessing am 1. August 1759 in einer Rezension über Schwärmer sagt, L. M. VIII, 133. Der *Nordische Aufseher* hatte behauptet, die Sprache sei zu arm, alles was wir denken, in Worten auszudrücken, und fährt dann fort: "Wofern man imstande wäre, aus dem Gedränge dieser schnell fortgesetzten Gedanken, dieser Gedanken von so genauen Bestimmungen (d. h. mit feinen Gefühlsnüancen—T. D.) einige mit Kaltsinn auszunehmen, und sie in kurze Sätze zu bringen: was für neue Wahrheiten von Gott würden oft darunter sein!"—"Keine einzige neue Wahrheit!"—sagt Lessing. "Die Wahrheit läßt sich nicht so in dem Taumel unserer Empfindungen *haschen*. Ich verdenke es dem Verfasser sehr, daß er sich bloßgegeben, so etwas auch nur vermuten zu können. Er steht an der wahren Quelle, aus welcher alle fanatische und enthusiastische Begriffe von Gott geflossen sind. Mit wenig deutlichen Ideen von Gott und den

---

* Lessing's theologische Schriften, worin auch die *Fragmente* einbegriffen, sind einem weiteren Leserkreise leicht zugänglich gemacht durch Christian Gross, *Lessings Theologische Schriften*, 4 Teile in 2 Bd. Berlin, Hempel.

göttlichen Vollkommenheiten setzt sich der Schwärmer hin, überläßt sich ganz seinen Empfindungen, nimmt die Lebhaftigkeit derselben für Deutlichkeit der Begriffe, wagt es, sie in Worte zu kleiden, und wird — ein Böhme, ein Pordage (zwei bedeutende Mystiker des Mittelalters)." Vgl. dazu: Zeller, Von Sybel's *Historische Zeitschrift*, XXIII, S. 347 f., wie Lessing sich in dieser Ansicht mit Leibniz und Wolff begegnet.

153. Aus Marin's *Geschichte Saladins* hatte Lessing sich aufgezeichnet: "Die Kreuzbrüder, die so unwissend als leichtgläubig waren, streuten oft aus, daß sie Engel in weißen Kleidern, mit blitzenden Schwertern in der Hand, und insonderheit den heiligen Georg zu Pferde in voller Rüstung hätten vom Himmel herabkommen sehen, welche an der Spitze ihrer Kriegsvölker gestritten hätten." (L. M. III, 491.) Vgl. auch Tasso, *Gerusalemme liberata*, wo ähnliche Erscheinungen mehrfach erwähnt werden

Zu Zeile 199 ff. vgl. Rousseau *Émile*, IV (*Édition stéréotype, d'après le procédé de Firmin Didot, tome* II, *p.* 271): "*Pourquoi mon âme est-elle soumise à mes sens, et enchaînée à ce corps qui l'asservit et la gêne? Je n'en sais rien: suis-je entré dans les décrets de Dieu? Mais je puis, sans témérité, former de modestes conjectures. Je me dis: Si l'esprit de l'homme fût resté libre et pur, quel mérite auroit-il d'aimer et suivre l'ordre qu'il verroit établi, et qu'il n'auroit une intérêt à troubler? Il seroit heureux, il est vrai; mais il manqueroit à son bonheur le degré le plus sublime, la gloire de la vertu et le bon témoignage de soi; il ne seroit que comme les anges, et sans doute l'homme vertueux sera plus qu'eux.*"

211. Was Lessing und mit ihm Nathan unter Wundern versteht, geht aus mehreren Stellen deutlich hervor. Für sprunghafte, unmotivierte Eingriffe in den Gang der Natur ist in der Welt kein Raum. In der Rettung des Cochläus, L. M. v, 366 f., heißt es z. B.: "Der Ausgang der Kinder Israel aus Egypten ward durch einen Totschlag, und man mag sagen, was man will, durch einen strafbaren Totschlag veranlaßt; ist er aber deswegen weniger ein Werk Gottes und weniger ein Wunder? — Ich weiß wohl, daß es auch eine Art von Dankbarkeit gegen die Werkzeuge, wodurch unser Glück ist befördert worden, giebt, allein ich weiß auch, daß diese Dankbarkeit, wenn man sie übertreibt, zu einer Idolatrie wird (wie zum Beispiel die Dankbarkeit Rechas gegen den Tempelherrn. T. D.).... Ein neuer Schriftsteller hatte vor einiger Zeit einen witzigen Einfall; er sagte, die Reformation sei in Deutschland ein Werk des Eigennutzes, in England ein Werk der Liebe, und in dem liederreichen Frankreich das Werk eines

Gassenhauers gewesen. Man hat sich viel Mühe gegeben, diesen Einfall zu widerlegen; als ob ein Einfall widerlegt werden könnte? Man
kann ihn nicht anders widerlegen, als wenn man ihm den Witz nimmt,
und das ist hier nicht möglich. Er bleibt witzig, er mag nun wahr
oder falsch sein. Allein ihm sein Gift zu nehmen, wenn er anders
welches hat, hätte man ihn nur so ausdrücken dürfen: In Deutschland hat die ewige Weisheit, welche alles zu ihrem Zwecke zu lenken
weiß, die Reformation durch den Eigennutz, in England durch die
Liebe, und in Frankreich durch ein Lied gewirkt. Auf diese Weise
wäre aus dem Tadel der Menschen ein Lob des Höchsten geworden!
Doch wie schwer gehen die Sterblichen an dieses, wenn sie ihr eigenes
nicht damit verbinden können." (Vgl. *Nathan*, 293 ff.) Ganz ähnliche
Ansichten fand Lessing vertreten von Rousseau *Émile*, IV (*Édition
stéréotype, d'après le procédé de Firmin Didot, tome II, p.* 284):
*"C'est l'ordre inaltérable de la nature qui montre le mieux la sage
main qui la régit; s'il arrivoit beaucoup d'exceptions, je ne saurois
plus, qu'en penser; et pour moi je crois trop en Dieu pour croire à
tant de miracles si peu dignes de lui."* — Der unmittelbare Vorgänger
Lessings in dieser Ansicht war aber Reimarus, der Fragmentist.
Namentlich was er Vers 220 ff. sagt, findet eine weitere Ausführung
im zweiten *Fragment* (L. M. XII, 355). Nachdem zunächst die Kriterien für die Echtheit der Weissagungen festgestellt sind, fährt der Ungenannte fort: "Bei den Wundern hat man zu beobachten, ob sie von
den Gegenwärtigen ohne Widerspruch für Wunder gehalten sind?
(Man bemerke, daß Daja den Ritter bald Tempelherr, bald Engel sein
läßt. T. D.) Ob dieselben das Geschick gehabt, das Natürliche und
die Kunstgriffe von übernatürlichen Wirkungen zu unterscheiden? Ob
die Wunder so erzählet sind, daß man aus der Erzählung selbst ein
geübtes Urteil des Schreibers, und die Merkmale, daß es ein Wunder,
und nichts Natürliches oder Betrug gewesen, schließen kann? Ob die
Wunder selbst so beschaffen sind, daß die Umstände mit einander
übereinstimmen oder sich widersprechen? Ob sie der Art sind, daß
sie nicht allein Gottes Macht, sondern auch seine Weisheit und Güte
beweisen, oder ob sie vielmehr diesen Vollkommenheiten Gottes ent-
gegenlaufen, und bloß die Ordnung und den Lauf der Natur stören
und aus der Welt einen Traum machen? Letztlich ist sehr darauf
zu sehen, was sie für einen Zweck gehabt, und was denn eigentlich
durch diese Wunder Gutes und Herrliches ausgerichtet worden."
Nachdem er dann im dritten *Fragment* diese Kriterien auf die bibli-
schen Wunder angewandt, kommt er zu dem Schluß (S. 368): "Sehet,
so wenig Verstand und Nachdenken kostet es, Wunder zu machen!

So wenig ist auch nötig (d. h. mehr darf man auch nicht haben, T.D.), sie zu glauben!" (Vgl. Vers 269.)

269. Harnack, *Dogmengesch.* I, 59, Anm. 2: "Der Historiker ist nicht imstande, mit einem Wunder als einem sicher gegebenen geschichtlichen Ereignis zu *rechnen;* denn er hebt damit die Betrachtungsweise auf, auf welcher alle geschichtliche Forschung beruht. Jedes einzelne Wunder bleibt geschichtlich völlig zweifelhaft, und die Summation des Zweifelhaften führt niemals zu einer Gewißheit. Überzeugt sich der Historiker trotzdem aber, daß Jesus Christus Außerordentliches, im strengen Sinn Wunderbares gethan hat, so schließt er von dem einzigartigen Eindruck, welchen er von dieser Person gewonnen hat, auf eine übernatürliche Macht derselben. Dieser Schluß gehört selbst dem Gebiet des religiösen Glaubens an. Übrigens kommen nach strenger geschichtlicher Prüfung überhaupt nur die Heilungswunder Jesu in Betracht. Diese lassen sich allerdings aus den geschichtlichen Berichten nicht eliminieren, ohne diese Berichte bis auf den Grund zu zerstören. Allein wie ungeeignet sind sie an und für sich, um dem, dem sie beigelegt werden, nach 1800 Jahren irgend welche besondere Bedeutung zu sichern! Daß er mit sich selber konnte wie er wollte, daß er ein Neues schuf, ohne das Alte zu stürzen, daß er die Menschen für *sich* gewann, indem er von seinem *Vater* kündete, daß er ohne Schwärmerei begeisterte, ohne Politik ein Reich aufrichtete, ohne Askese von der Welt befreite, ohne Theologie ein Lehrer war, inmitten einer Zeit der Schwärmerei und Politik, der Askese und Theologie, das ist das große Wunder seiner Person, und daß er, der die Bergpredigt gesprochen, sich im Hinblick auf sein Leben und Sterben als den Erlöser und Richter der Welt verkündete, ist das Ärgernis und die Thorheit, welche aller Vernunft spotten."

358-9. *Dramaturgie,* 12. Stück, L. M. IX, 231: "Wenn daher die *Semiramis* des Herrn Voltaire weiter kein Verdienst hätte, als dieses, worauf er sich so viel zu gute thut, daß man nämlich daraus die höchste Gerechtigkeit verehren lerne, die, außerordentliche Lasterthaten zu strafen, außerordentliche Wege wähle: so würde *Semiramis* in meinen Augen nur ein sehr mittelmäßiges Stück sein. Besonders, da diese Moral selbst nicht eben die erbaulichste ist. Denn es ist ohnstreitig dem weisesten Wesen weit anständiger, wenn er dieser außerordentlichen Wege nicht bedarf, und wir uns die Bestrafung des Guten und Bösen in die ordentliche Kette der Dinge von ihr mit eingeflochten denken." — Für Recha werden die Worte kaum mehr als ziemlich unbedeutende Trostworte gewesen sein. Für Nathan enthielten sie eine tiefe Wahrheit.

360 ff.  In den *Gedanken über die Herrnhuter*, L. M. XIV, 154 ff. erörtert Lessing die These: "Der Mensch ward zum Thun, und nicht zum Vernünfteln erschaffen." Er zeigt, wie sich nach und nach Philosophie und Religion in Förmlichkeiten verloren und auf der praktischen Seite ganz verkümmerten. (159): "Was hilft es, recht zu glauben, wenn man unrecht lebt? Wie glücklich, wenn ihr uns ebenso viel fromme als gelehrte Nachfolger gelassen hättet! Der Aberglaube fiel. Aber eben das, wodurch ihr ihn stürztet, die Vernunft, die so schwer in ihrer Sphäre zu erhalten ist, die Vernunft führte euch auf einen andern Irrweg, der zwar weniger von der Wahrheit, doch desto weiter von der Ausübung der Pflichten eines Christen entfernt war. — Und jetzo, da unsere Zeiten — soll ich sagen so glücklich? oder so unglücklich? — sind, daß man eine so vortreffliche Zusammensetzung von Gottesgelahrtheit und Weltweisheit gemacht hat, worinne man mit Mühe und Not eine von der andern unterscheiden kann, worinne eine die andere schwächt, indem diese den Glauben durch Beweise erzwingen, und jene die Beweise durch den Glauben unterstützen soll; jetzo, sage ich, ist durch diese verkehrte Art, das Christentum zu lehren, ein wahrer Christ weit seltener, als in den dunklen Zeiten geworden. Der Erkenntnis nach sind wir Engel und dem Leben nach Teufel. — Ich will es dem Leser überlassen, mehr Gleichheiten zwischen den Schicksalen der Religion und der Weltweisheit aufzusuchen. Er wird durchgängig finden, daß die Menschen in der einen wie in der anderen nur immer haben vernünfteln, niemals handeln wollen."

385. Es ließen sich eine ganze Menge Stellen anführen, um Lessings Determinismus, seine Ansicht von der Willensfreiheit, oder vielmehr der Willens-Gebundenheit klarzulegen. Eine einzige muß genügen. "Der dritte Aufsatz (Jerusalems *Über die Freiheit*) zeiget, wie wohl der Verfasser ein System gefaßt hatte, das wegen seiner gefährlichen Folgerungen so verschrieen ist, und gewiß weit allgemeiner sein würde, wenn man sich so leicht gewöhnen könnte, diese Folgerungen selbst in dem Lichte zu betrachten, in welchem sie hier erscheinen. Tugend und Laster *so* erklärt, Belohnung und Strafe, *hierauf* eingeschränkt: was verlieren wir, wenn man uns die Freiheit abspricht? Etwas — wenn es etwas ist — was wir nicht brauchen, was wir weder zu unserer Thätigkeit hier, noch zu unserer Glückseligkeit dort brauchen. Etwas, dessen Besitz weit unruhiger und besorgter machen müßte, als das Gefühl seines Gegenteils nimmermehr machen kann. — Zwang und Notwendigkeit, nach welchen die Vorstellung des Besten wirkt, wie viel willkommener sind sie mir als kahle Vermögenheit, unter den nämlichen Umständen bald so, bald anders handeln zu kön-

nen! Ich danke dem Schöpfer, daß ich *muss*, das *Beste* muß. Wenn
ich, in diesen Schranken selbst, so viel Fehltritte noch thue, was
würde geschehen, wenn ich mir ganz allein überlassen wäre? einer
blinden Kraft überlassen wäre, die sich nach keinen Gesetzen richtet,
und mich darum nicht minder dem Zufall unterwirft, weil dieser Zufall sein Spiel in mir selbst hat? — Also von der Seite der Moral ist
dieses System geborgen." L. M. XII, 298. — In den *Gesprächen für
Freimaurer*, L. M. XIII, 353 heißt es: "Der Weise *kann* nicht sagen,
was er besser 'verschweigt." Grillparzer (*Des Meeres und der Liebe
Wellen*, 1. Aufzug, Cotta'sche Ausgabe, S. 24) spricht genau aus, was
auch Nathan und Al-Hafi sagen wollen:

> "Die freie Wahl ist schwacher Thoren Spielzeug;
> Der Tücht'ge sieht in jedem *Soll* ein *Muss*,
> Und Zwang, als erste Pflicht, ist ihm die·Wahrheit."

**867 ff.** Allgemein wäre zu diesen Versen zu vergleichen, was
Lessing schon im Jahre 1756 an Mendelssohn schreibt: "Ich gehe
noch weiter und gebe Ihnen zu überlegen, ob die tugendhafte That,
die ein Mensch aus bloßer Nacheiferung ohne deutliche Erkenntnis
thut, wirklich eine tugendhafte That ist und ihm als eine solche zu-
gerechnet werden kann."

Ferner in der *Rettung des Cardanus* (L. M. v, 316) läßt Cardanus den Christen sagen: "Der dritte Grund [für die Echtheit des
christlichen Glaubens] wird von den Geboten Christi hergenommen,
welche nichts enthalten, was mit der Moral oder mit der natürlichen
Philosophie streitet. Was sein Leben anlangt, darinne kann es ihm
niemand gleich thun, und wenn er auch der allerbeste wäre; aber es
nachahmen kann ein jeder. Was? *können* sag ich? Ja, so viel du
dich von seinem Exempel entfernst, soviel Gottlosigkeit nimmst du
an." — Bedeutsamer ist, was Lessing dann, als Verteidiger der Mohammedaner dem Cardan erwidert: L. M. v, 325: "Man sieht es wohl,
mein guter Cardan, daß du ein Christ bist, und daß dein Vorsatz nicht
sowohl gewesen ist die Religionen zu vergleichen, als die christliche,
so leicht als möglich, triumphieren zu lassen. Gleich anfangs bin ich
schlecht mit dir zufrieden, daß du die Lehren unsers Mahomets in
eine Klasse setzest, in welche sie gar nicht gehören. Das, was der
Heide, der Jude, der Christ seine Religion nennet, ist ein Wirrwar
von Sätzen, die eine gesunde Vernunft nie für die ihrigen erkennen
wird. Sie berufen sich alle auf höhere Offenbarungen, deren Möglichkeit noch nicht einmal erwiesen ist. Durch diese wollen sie Wahrheiten überkommen haben, die vielleicht in einer andern möglichen
Welt, nur nicht in der unsrigen, Wahrheiten sein können. Sie erken-

nen es selbst und nennen sie daher Geheimnisse; ein Wort, das seine Widerlegung gleich bei sich führet. Ich will sie dir nicht nennen, sondern ich will nur sagen, daß eben sie es sind, welche die allergröbsten und sinnlichsten Begriffe von allem was göttlich ist, erzeugen; daß sie es sind, die nie dem gemeinen Volk erlauben werden, sich seinen Schöpfer auf eine anständige Art zu denken; daß sie es sind, welche den Geist zu unfruchtbaren Betrachtungen verführen und ihm ein Ungeheuer bilden, welches ihr den Glauben nennet. Diesem gebt ihr die Schlüssel des Himmels und der Höllen; und Glücks genug für die Tugend, daß ihr sie mit genauer Not zu einer etwannigen Begleiterin desselben gemacht! Die Verehrung heiliger Hirngespinster macht bei Euch ohne Gerechtigkeit selig; aber nicht diese ohne jene. Welche Verblendung!"

Endlich sagt Lessing in seinen *Gegensätzen zu den Fragmenten:* (L. M. XII, 429): "Die Religion ist nicht wahr, weil die Evangelisten und Apostel sie lehrten, sondern sie lehrten sie, weil sie wahr ist. Aus ihrer innern Wahrheit müssen die schriftlichen Überlieferungen erklärt werden, und alle schriftliche Überlieferungen können ihr keine innere Wahrheit geben, wenn sie keine hat."

990. Es scheint etwas unnatürlich, daß Saladin seiner Schwester gegenüber die *Einheit* seines Gottes betonen sollte. Es wird eine versteckte Anspielung auf einen Ausdruck des Fragmentisten darin enthalten sein. Er sagt im *II. Fragment:* L. M. XII, 342 (auch 340): "Der Jude ist im Gesetze Mosis aufs schärfste gewarnet, er soll nicht mehrere Götter anerkennen, es sei nur *ein* Gott. Er kann aber doch die Lehre, daß Jesus sowohl Gott sei wie der Vater, und der heilige Geist sowohl Gott sei wie Vater und Sohn, nicht anders einsehen als eine Lehre von vielen Göttern; er denkt wie seine Vorfahren, das sei eine Gotteslästerung, daß sich Jesus selbst zum Gott gemacht." Und auch im *Cardanus* läßt Lessing den Mohammedaner dem Christen gegenüber geltend machen, daß sie an nur *einen einzigen* Gott glauben. Und im ersten Stück seiner *Dramaturgie* verdenkt es Lessing einem Schauspieldichter, "daß er eine Religion überall des Polytheismus schuldig macht, die fast mehr als jede andere auf die Einheit Gottes dringt."

1273. Im *Freigeist* sagt Lessing: "Ich bin es nur allzuwohl überzeugt, daß alle ehrliche Menschen einerlei denken." L. M. II, 58.

1293. Lessing sucht in seinen *Gegensätzen*, L. M. XII, 436, zu erweisen, daß die göttliche Offenbarung bei den Juden vor allen Völkern in gute Hände geraten sei. "Dieses unendlich mehr verachtete als verächtliche Volk ist doch in der ganzen Geschichte

schlechterdings das erste und einzige, welches sich ein Geschäft daraus gemacht, seine Religion mitzuteilen und auszubreiten. Wegen des
Eifers, mit welchem die Juden dieses Geschäft betrieben, bestrafte sie
schon Christus, verlachte sie schon Horaz. Alle anderen Völker waren
mit ihren Religionen entweder zu geheim und zu neidisch, oder viel
zu kalt gegen sie gesinnt als daß sie für derselben Ausbreitung sich
der geringsten Mühwaltung hätten unterziehen sollen. Die christlichen Völker, die den Juden in diesem Eifer hernach gefolgt sind,
überkamen ihn bloß, insofern sie auf den Stamm des Judentums gepfropft
waren."
　　Interessant ist es in Verbindung mit dieser Zeile eine auch auf
die ganze Tendenz des Stücks bezügliche Stelle aus der *Dramaturgie*
(7. Stück, 22. Mai 1767) L. M. IX, 210–11. zu vergleichen: "Es war
von dem Herrn von Cronegk ein wenig unüberlegt, in einem Stück,
dessen Stoff aus den unglücklichen Zeiten der Kreuzzüge genommen
ist, die Toleranz predigen, und die Abscheulichkeiten des Geistes der
Verfolgung an den Bekennern der mohamedanischen Religion zeigen
zu wollen. Denn diese Kreuzzüge selbst, die in ihrer Anlage ein poli-
tischer Kunstgriff der Päpste waren, wurden in ihrer Ausführung die
unmenschlichsten Verfolgungen, deren sich der christliche Aberglaube
jemals schuldig gemacht hat; die meisten und blutgierigsten Ismenors hatte damals die wahre Religion; und einzelne Personen, die
eine Moschee beraubt haben, zur Strafe ziehen, kommt das wohl
gegen die unselige Raserei, welche das rechtgläubige Europa entvöl-
kerte, um das ungläubige Asien zu verwüsten." Diese Ansicht von
den Kreuzzügen war dem Aufklärungsjahrhundert ganz geläufig. Das
neunzehnte Jahrhundert hat in manchem dies Urteil gemildert.
　　**1309 ff.** *Ernst und Falck, Gespräche für Freimaurer*, L. M.
XIII, 358 f. *Falck:* Wenn die bürgerliche Gesellschaft auch nur das
Gute hätte, daß allein in ihr die menschliche Vernunft angebauet werden kann, ich würde sie auch bei weit größeren Übeln noch segnen. —
*Ernst:* Wer des Feuers genießen will, sagt das Sprichwort, muß sich
den Rauch gefallen lassen. — *Falck:* Allerdings! — Aber weil der
Rauch bei dem Feuer unvermeidlich ist, dürfte man darum keinen
Rauchfang erfinden? Und der den Rauchfang erfand, war der darum
ein Feind des Feuers? — Sieh, dahin wollt ich. — *Ernst:* Wohin?
ich verstehe dich nicht. — *Falck:* Das Gleichnis war doch sehr pas-
send. — — Wenn die Menschen nicht anders in Staaten vereinigt
werden konnten als durch jene Trennungen, werden sie darum gut,
jene Trennungen? — *Ernst:* Das wohl nicht. — *Falck:* Werden sie
darum heilig, jene Trennungen?... *Falck:* Ich dächte [es wäre]

recht sehr zu wünschen, daß es in jedem Staate Männer geben
möchte, die über die Vorurteile der Völkerschaft hinweg wären und
genau wüßten, wo Patriotismus Tugend zu sein aufhört. —— Recht
sehr zu wünschen, daß es in jedem Staate Männer geben möchte, die
dem Vorurteil ihrer angeborenen Religion nicht unterlägen, nicht
glaubten, daß alles notwendig gut und wahr sein müsse, was sie für
gut und wahr erkennen. —— Recht sehr zu wünschen, daß es in
jedem Staate Männer geben möchte, welche bürgerliche Hoheit nicht
blendet, und bürgerliche Geringfügigkeit nicht ekelt, in deren Gesellschaft der Hohe sich gern herabläßt und der Geringe sich dreist er-
hebt." — Aber übereilen soll man sich mit Reformen auch nicht:
"Der Freimaurer erwartet ruhig den Aufgang der Sonne und läßt die
Lichter brennen, so lange sie wollen und können. — Die Lichter aus-
löschen, und, wenn sie ausgelöscht sind, erst wahrnehmen, daß man
die Stumpe doch wieder anzünden oder wohl gar andere Lichter wieder aufstecken muß, das ist der Freimaurer Sache nicht."

1588. "Cardan läßt bei diesem Beweise (für die Glaubwürdigkeit der chr. Lehre) nichts weg, als das, was ich wünschte, daß man
es immer weggelassen hätte. Das Blut der Märtyrer nämlich, welches
ein sehr zweideutiges Ding ist. Er war in ihrer Geschichte ohne
Zweifel allzuwohl bewandert, als daß er nicht sehr viele unter ihnen
bemerken sollte, die eher Thoren und Rasende genannt zu werden
verdienen als Blutzeugen. Auch kannte er ohne Zweifel das menschliche Herz zu gut, als daß er nicht wissen sollte, eine geliebte Grille
könne es eben so weit bringen, als die Wahrheit in allem ihren
Glanze. Kurz, er ist nicht allein ein starker Verfechter des christlichen Glaubens, sondern auch ein vorsichtiger; zwei Dinge, die nicht
immer beisammen sind." (L. M. V, 321.)

1589 ff. Ganz im selben Geist sagt Lessing in seinen *Gegensätzen zu den Fragmenten*, L. M. XII, 428: "Wie vieles läßt sich
noch auf alle diese Einwürfe und Schwierigkeiten antworten! Und
wenn sich auch schlechterdings nichts darauf antworten ließ: was
dann? Der gelehrte Theolog könnte am Ende darüber verlegen sein,
aber auch der Christ? Der gewiß nicht. Jenem höchstens könnte es
zur Verwirrung gereichen, die Stützen, welche er der Religion unterziehen wollen, so erschüttert zu sehen, die Strebepfeiler so niedergerissen
zu finden, mit welchen er, wenn Gott will, sie so schön verwahret hatte.
Aber was gehen dem Christen dieses Mannes Hypothesen und Erklärun-
gen und Beweise an? Ihm ist es doch einmal da, das Christentum,
welches er so wahr, in welchem er sich so selig *fühlet*. Wenn der
Paralytikus die wohlthätigen Schläge des elektrischen Funkens *erfährt*,

was kümmert es ihn, ob Nollet oder ob Franklin, oder ob keiner von beiden recht hat?"

1805. Vgl. dazu die *Dramaturgie*, xx. St., L. M. ix, 265. "Dorimond (in *Cenie*, von Frau Françoise de Graffigny) hat dem Mericourt eine ansehnliche Verbindung nebst dem vierten Teil seines Vermögens zugedacht. Aber das ist das wenigste, worauf Mericourt geht (d. h. das ist ihm lange nicht genug). Er verweigert sich dem großmütigen Anerbieten und will sich ihm aus Uneigennützigkeit verweigert zu haben scheinen. 'Wozu das?' sagt er. 'Warum wollen Sie sich Ihres Vermögens berauben? Genießen Sie Ihrer Güter selbst, sie haben Ihnen Gefahr und Arbeit genug gekostet.' *J'en jouirai, je vous rendrai tous heureux*, läßt die Graffigny den lieben gutherzigen Alten antworten. "Ich will ihrer genießen, ich will euch alle glücklich machen." Vortrefflich! Hier ist kein Wort zu viel! Die wahre nachlässige Kürze, mit der ein Mann, dem Güte zur Natur geworden ist, von seiner Güte spricht, wenn er davon sprechen muß! Seines Glückes genießen, andere glücklich machen: beides ist ihm nur eines; das eine ist ihm nicht bloß eine Folge des andern, ein Teil des andern; das eine ist ihm ganz das andere: und so wie sein Herz keinen Unterschied darunter kennt, so weiß auch sein Mund keinen darunter zu machen."

1815. Vgl. *Duplik*, L. M. XIII, S. 23-24. "Nicht die Wahrheit, in deren Besitz irgend ein Mensch ist, oder zu sein vermeinet, sondern die aufrichtige Mühe, die er angewandt hat, hinter die Wahrheit zu kommen, macht den Wert des Menschen. Denn nicht durch den Besitz, sondern durch die Nachforschung der Wahrheit erweitern sich seine Kräfte, worin allein seine immer wachsende Vollkommenheit besteht. Der Besitz macht ruhig, träge, stolz.

Wenn Gott in seiner Rechten alle Wahrheit, und in seiner Linken den einzigen immer regen Trieb nach Wahrheit, obschon mit dem Zusatze, mich immer und ewig zu irren, verschlossen hielte, und spräche zu mir: Wähle! Ich fiele ihm mit Demut in seine Linke und sagte: "Vater gieb! die reine Wahrheit ist ja doch nur für dich allein." — Goeze, S. 84 ff. ereifert sich sehr über diese Stelle, und nennt das Ganze Unsinn. Es ist interessant, damit zu vergleichen, was der unzweifelhaft fromme und christgläubige Karl Gerock dazu sagt. Die betreffende Stelle findet sich in seinem Büchlein *Ideale und Illusionen*, S. 26: "Kein philosophisches System beut uns die volle und fertige Wahrheit; aber eine Wahrheit giebt es darum für den Idealgesinnten doch, und statt mit Pilatus blasiert zu fragen: 'Was ist Wahrheit?!' hält er es mit dem tapferen Lessing, der das rastlose Forschen nach Wahrheit dem ruhigen Besitz derselben vorzieht."

Ich finde zu den Worten Lessings in Erich Schmidts *Lessing*, Bd. II, 2. Aufl., S. 244, die folgende Anmerkung: "Adolf Harnack schreibt mir (d. h. Erich Schmidt): Vielleicht interessiert es Sie und Ihre Leser, daß ein alter Kirchenvater, ja, der erste kirchliche Theologe im strengen Sinne des Worts, Clemens Alexandrinus (gest. um 202), ein Dilemma gebildet hat, das dem Lessing'schen sehr verwandt ist. Er sagt in seinen *Stromateis*, IV, 22, 136: 'Gesetzt, es schlüge jemand dem christlichen Denker (τῷ γνωστικῷ, im Sinn und Sprachgebrauch des Clemens: dem Idealchristen) vor, er möge zwischen der Erkenntnis Gottes und der ewigen Seligkeit wählen — angenommen die beiden Güter wären getrennt, während sie in Wahrheit streng identisch sind — so würde sich der christliche Denker keinen Augenblick besinnen und die Erkenntnis Gottes wählen.' Es ist mir wahrscheinlich, daß der patristisch so ausgezeichnet belesene Lessing diese Stelle gekannt und geradezu aus ihr die Anregung geschöpft hat, aus dem ersten Dilemma ein noch feineres zweites zu entwickeln. Das ist ganz seine Art, sich durch eine geistvolle Bemerkung zu einer noch tieferen anregen zu lassen. Ist die Clementinische Stelle der Grundtext für Lessings Parabel, so tritt die Eigenart und Feinheit seines Geistes sowohl in der Form der Erzählung als in den Nebenzügen und dem neuen Acumen besonders deutlich hervor." — Kettner dagegen macht auf eine Stelle bei Leibniz (*Nouveaux essais* L. II, § 36; *Op. philos.* ed. Erdmann, p. 258) aufmerksam, die dem Lessingschen Wort noch näher kommt: "*Je trouve que l'inquiétude est essentielle à la félicité des créatures, laquelle ne consiste jamais dans une parfaite possession, qui les rendroit insensibles et comme stupides, mais dans un progrès continuel*" etc.

Vgl. auch *Anti-Goeze*, L. M. XIII, 164: "Nun ist die letzte Absicht des Christentums nicht unsere Seligkeit, sie mag herkommen woher sie will, sondern unsere Seligkeit vermittelst unserer Erleuchtung."

Vgl. auch Schiller, *Ideal und Leben:*

> "Ach, kein Weg will dahin führen,
> Ach, der Himmel über mir
> Will die Erde nie berühren,
> Und das Dort ist niemals hier."

Ferner, *Bibliolatrie* (in der neuen L.M. noch nicht erschienen): "Ich hatte es längst für meine Pflicht gehalten, mit eigenen Augen zu prüfen, *quid liquidum sit in causa Christianorum.*"

1842. "Ich bin ein Jud'." — Man hat es Lessing sehr verübelt, daß er gerade einen Juden zum Repräsentanten der Idee seines Gedichtes gemacht hat. Abgesehen davon, daß er in seiner Vorlage beim Boccaz den Juden fand, wäre er darin wohl auch aus inneren Gründen zu rechtfertigen, und könnte sich zudem auf das Beispiel Christi berufen, der, wenn er den *Juden* ihre Pflicht ins Gedächtnis rufen wollte, ihnen öfters einen Andersgläubigen als Beispiel hinstellte, so im Gleichnis vom guten Samariter (*Lukas* X, 30 ff.), bei der Reinigung der zehn Aussätzigen (*Lukas* XVII, 15–18), im Gleichnis vom Pharisäer und Zöllner (*Lukas* XVIII, 10–14). Aber wie Christus sicher nicht andeuten wollte, daß die betreffenden Tugenden nur außerhalb des Judentums zu finden seien, so ist es auch sicher nicht Lessings Absicht, die Tugend einzig ins Judentum zu verlegen. Vielmehr umgekehrt in beiden Fällen; die Tugend, die man vor allem im Juden- resp. Christentum suchen und erwarten sollte, wenn die jeweiligen Bekenner mit dem Herzen dabei gewesen wären, diese Tugend erscheint in um so hellerem Glanze, wenn sie von weniger begnadeten Personen geübt wird. Es wird ja niemand leugnen wollen, daß das Gebot der Bruderliebe ein *neu* Gebot ist, das erst mit dem Christentum der Welt verkündet wurde. — Zudem bemerkt sicher Beyschlag ganz richtig, daß Lessing, wenn er im *Nathan* nur die gegenseitige Duldung der verschiedenen Religionen hätte lehren wollen, uns drei wirklich gläubige Repräsentanten der drei positiven Religionen hätte vorführen müssen, die trotz ihrer Überzeugungen den andern gegenüber Duldung hätten beweisen müssen (*Lessings Nathan der Weise und das positive Christentum*, S. 10). Nathan ist ein Jude freilich übrigens, wie's nicht viel Juden giebt, d. h. er ist nur dem Namen nach Jude, und dasselbe gilt von den andern Charakteren. (Vgl. auch Spielhagen, *Faust und Nathan*, S. 21). Nathan ist als vorchristlicher Jude kaum denkbar. Der Klosterbruder, unzweifelhaft der ehrwürdigste Christ im Stück, hat gar nicht so unrecht, wenn er auch Nathan einen Christen nennt: seinem Leben nach ist er es sicher.

1845. Vgl. dazu *Cardanus*, L. M. v, 319. "Was ist nötiger, als sich von seinem Glauben zu überzeugen, und was ist unmöglicher als Überzeugung, ohne vorhergegangene Prüfung? Man sage nicht, daß die Prüfung seiner eigenen Religion schon zureiche; daß es nicht nötig sei, die Merkmale der Göttlichkeit, wenn man sie an dieser schon entdeckt habe, auch an anderen aufzusuchen. Man bediene sich des Gleichnisses nicht, daß, wenn man einmal den rechten Weg wisse, man sich nicht um die Irrwege zu bekümmern brauche. — — Man lernt nicht diese durch jenen, sondern jenen durch diese kennen. Und benimmt man sich nicht, durch die Anpreisung dieser einseitigen Untersuchung, selbst die Hoffnung, daß die Irrgläubigen aus Erkenntnis unsere Brüder werden können? Wenn man dem Christen befiehlt, nur die Lehren Christi zu untersuchen, so befiehlt man auch dem Mohammedaner, sich nur um die Lehre des Mohammed zu bekümmern. Es ist wahr, jener wird darüber

in Gefahr kommen, einen besseren Glauben für einen schlechteren fahren
zu lassen ; allein dieser wird auch die Gelegenheit nicht haben, den
schlechteren mit einem besseren zu verwechseln.  Doch was rede ich von
Gefahr?  Der muß ein schwaches Vertrauen auf die ewigen Wahrheiten
des Heilandes setzen, der sich fürchtet, sie mit Lügen gegeneinander zu
halten." — Damit steht in gewissem Widerspruch, was Nathan 1974 ff.
sagt.  Der Weise, wenn er stehen bleibt, wo der Zufall der Geburt ihn
hingeworfen, bleibt aus Einsicht, Gründen, Wahl des Bessern, sagt der
Sultan.  Nathan dagegen sagt, die Religionen sind nur von Seiten ihrer
Gründe nicht zu unterscheiden.  Denn alle sollen sich auf Geschichte,
geschrieben oder überliefert, gründen ; und Geschichte ist auf Treu und
Glauben hinzunehmen.  Und doch macht Lessing in seinen *Gegensätzen
zu den Fragmenten* darauf aufmerksam (L. M. XII, 429), daß "die Religion nicht wahr ist, weil die Evangelisten und Apostel sie lehrten (d. h.
weil sie geschichtlich wohl verbürgt sein mag), sondern sie lehrten sie,
weil sie wahr ist.  Aus ihrer inneren Wahrheit müssen die schriftlichen
Überlieferungen erklärt werden, und alle schriftliche Überlieferungen
können ihr keine innere Wahrheit geben, wenn sie keine hat." — Und
seinem Vater gegenüber nimmt Lessing schon als Zwanzigjähriger für
sich das Recht in Anspruch, mit eigenen Augen zuzusehen, wie es um
seine Religion stehe.  Auch hier kann Nathan-Lessing nicht wollen, daß
man blindlings seiner Väter Religion dem inneren Kern nach annehme.
Auch hier, ja hier vor allem gilt Goethes Wort:

> "Was du ererbt von deinen Vätern hast,
> Erwirb es, um es zu besitzen."

Nathan hat sicher weniger auf den *Kern* der Religion, als auf die
Äußerlichkeiten der verschiedenen Konfessionen Bezug.  Ich glaube,
der Arzt in Auerbachs *Auf der Höhe* (II. Buch, 4. Kap., Bd. 1, S. 131),
spricht ihm aus der Seele, wenn er sagt: "Majestät, verharren wir in
unserer angestammten Religion, so können wir in ihr frei sein, das
heißt in unserm Denken über sie hinausgehen ; kein Ketzergericht hat
mehr Gewalt über uns.  Bekennen wir aber eine neue Religion, so haben
wir kein Recht mehr, frei zu sein ; wir haben die Pflicht, sie zu bekennen!  Ein geborener Adeliger kann sich zur bürgerlichen Freiheit
bekennen; einer, der sich adeln läßt, kann das nicht.  Und, Majestät,
lassen Sie mich noch eins sagen : ich betrachte es als ein Glück für die
Menschheit und für unser deutsches Vaterland besonders, daß es keine
Konfessionseinheit giebt; dadurch allein ist die Humanität gewahrt, denn
wir müssen lernen, daß es verschiedene Formen und Seelensprachen für
ein und dasselbe giebt.  In der Vielfältigkeit der Konfessionen liegt eine

Bürgschaft gegen den Fanatismus, wie weiter hinaus eine Bestätigung, daß die äußere Religionsform gleichgültig, ich meine, daß man in jeder Religion ein rechtschaffener Mensch sein könne, und sogar ohne äußere Religion."

Auch der Fragmentist (L. M. XII, 320) macht einem Menschen einen Vorwurf daraus, wenn er nicht unparteiisch zu Werke geht und gleich die väterliche und großväterliche Religion als eine gute Erbschaft antritt oder für bare göttliche Offenbarung hält.

1875. Locke schrieb in einem Essay unter dem Titel *Error*, nach Fox Bourne (*Life of Locke*, Vol. I, p. 306), ungefähr im Jahr 1672: "*The great division among Christians is about opinions. Every sect has its set of them and that is called orthodoxy; and he that professes his assent to them, though with an implicit faith and without examining is orthodox and in the way to salvation; but, if he examines and thereupon questions any one of them, he is presently suspected of heresy, and, if he oppose them or hold the contrary, he is presently condemned as in a damnable error, and in the sure way to perdition. Of this one may say, that there is nor can be nothing more wrong. For he that examines and upon a fair examination embraces an error for a truth, has done his duty more than he who embraces the profession of the truth (for the truths themselves he does not embrace) without having examined whether it be true or no. For, if it be our duty to search after truth, he certainly that has searched after it, though he has not found it, in some points has paid a more acceptable obedience to the will of his Maker than he that has not searched at all, but professes to have found truth when he has neither searched nor found it; for he that takes up the opinions of any church in the lump, without examining them, has truly neither searched after nor found truth, but has only found those that he thinks have found truth, and so receives what they say with an implicit faith, and so pays them the homage that is due only to God.*"

Noch eine andere bedeutsame Stelle in demselben Essay ist wohl des Anführens wert. Sie bildet zugleich einen weiteren Kommentar zu *Nathan*, 360 und 1587 ff. Locke macht es zunächst einem jeden zur Pflicht, sich nicht zum Richter über die Handlungen anderer Menschen aufzuwerfen, sondern für sein Teil gut zu leben und seiner besonderen Pflicht zu genügen, und fährt dann fort: "*I lay it down as a principle of Christianity that the right and only way to saving orthodoxy (i.e. orthodoxy that will save) is the sincere and steady purpose of a good life. — Here we may see the difference between the orthodoxy required by the several sects or, as they are called, churches of Christians. The orthodoxy required by the several sects is a profession of believing the whole*

*bundle of their respective articles set down in each church's system, with-*
*out knowing the rules of every one's particular duty, or requiring a*
*sincere or strict obedience to them. But it is to be observed that this is*
*much better fitted to get and retain church members than the other way,*
*inasmuch as it is easier to make profession of believing a certain collection*
*of opinions that one never perhaps so much as reads, and several whereof*
*one could not perhaps understand if one did read and study (for no more*
*is required than a profession to believe them, expressed in an acquiescence*
*that suffers one not to question or contradict any of them), than it is to*
*practice the duties of a good life in a sincere obedience to those precepts*
*of the gospel wherein his actions are concerned—precepts not hard to be*
*known by those who are ready and willing to obey them."*

Bourne sagt über Locke: "*Locke had his own opinions about the truths*
*of Christianity, opinions which some may think unwarranted and others may*
*regard as altogether incomplete. But he maintained that his own opinions*
*and other people's opinions on all matters of faith must be separated*
*from the plain and fundamental and sufficient rule of Christianity, the*
*sincere and steady purpose of a good life.*"

Ähnlich sagt Mendelssohn: "Dogmatisch in dem strengsten Verstande
in Absicht auf mich, habe ich, was die wichtigsten Punkte der Religion
und Sittenlehre betrifft, meine Partei genommen... bin aber eben so skep-
tisch, wenn ich meinen Nächsten richten soll. Ich räume einem jeden
das Recht ein, das ich mir anmaße, und setze das größte Mißtrauen
in meine Kräfte, irgend jemanden, der auch Partei genommen hat, von
meiner Meinung überführen zu können." (Kettner, S. 23, A.)

In der *Erziehung des Menschengeschlechts*, § 76 ff. (L. M. XIII, 432),
besteht Lessing darauf, daß das Recht, die geoffenbarten Wahrheiten in
Vernunftwahrheiten zu verwandeln, nicht beanstandet werden dürfe.
Die dazu nötigen Spekulationen allein können uns zu jener völligen
Aufklärung gelangen lassen, uns diejenige Reinigkeit des Herzens hervorzubringen befähigen, die uns die Tugend um ihrer selbst willen zu
lieben fähig macht, wozu der Mensch bestimmt ist. — Daß zur Er-
reichung der Wahrheit ernstes Streben notwendig ist, deutet Lessing
in noch vielen andern Stellen an. Ich führe nur noch eine an aus
seiner *Vorrede, etc., zu Jerusalems philosophischen Aufsätzen*, L. M. XII,
293 ff. "Und dazu lernte ich ihn eigentlich nur von *einer* Seite kennen.
— Allerdings zwar war das gleich diejenige Seite, von der sich meines
Bedünkens so viel auf alle übrige schließen läßt. Es war die Neigung,
das Talent, mit der sich alle gute Neigungen so wohl vertragen, welches
kein einziges Talent ausschließt; nur daß man bei ihm so viele andere
Talente lieber nicht haben mag und, wenn man sie hat, vernach-

lässiget. Es war die Neigung zu deutlicher Erkenntnis, das Talent,
die Wahrheit bis in ihre letzte Schlupfwinkel zu verfolgen. Es war
der Geist der kalten Betrachtung. Aber ein warmer Geist und so viel
schätzbarer, der sich nicht abschrecken ließ, wenn ihm die Wahrheit
auf seinen Verfolgungen öfters entwischte, nicht an ihrer Mitteilbarkeit
verzweifelte, weil sie sich in Abwege vor ihm verlor, wohin er
schlechterdings ihr nicht folgen konnte."

1889. Goeze geht oft mit Lessings Märchen und Gleichnissen arg
ins Gericht, so S. 8: "Ich will die Sache mit einem Bilde aufklären.
Herr L. wird solches um so viel weniger an mir tadeln, da seine
größeste Stärke in dem Gebrauche dieser Methode bestehet." S. 48:
Goeze fordert von Lessing, daß er ein Glaubensbekenntnis ablege:
"eine Forderung, die ihm sehr ungelegen fallen, und welche er bald
mit einem höhnenden Gleichnisse abweisen wird." S. 53: "Gleich
anfangs übertrifft Herr L. sich selbst in der Kunst, schwachen Lesern
durch Bilder über Bilder einen blauen Dunst vorzumachen und ihnen
gefärbte Brillen aufzusetzen." — Lessing wehrt natürlich gelegentlich
solche Angriffe spitzig ab.

1900. Ja, ja, wenns nötig ist und nützt: Ähnlich *Dramaturgie*,
1. Stück, L. M. IX, 187: "Die zweite Anmerkung betrifft das
christliche Trauerspiel insbesondere. Die Helden desselben sind meh-
renteils Märtyrer. Nun leben wir zu einer Zeit, in welcher die Stimme
der gesunden Vernunft zu laut erschallet, als daß jeder Rasende, der
sich mutwillig, ohne alle Not, mit Verachtung aller seiner bürgerlichen
Obliegenheiten, in den Tod stürzet, den Titel eines Märtyrers sich an-
maßen dürfte. Wir wissen itzt zu wohl, die falschen Märtyrer von den
wahren zu unterscheiden; wir verachten jene eben so sehr, als wir
diese verehren, und höchstens können sie uns eine melancholische
Thräne über die Blindheit und den Unsinn auspressen, deren wir die
Menschheit überhaupt in ihnen fähig erblicken." Vgl. auch die Anmerkung zu 1588.

1974 ff. Sehr viele Stellen ließen sich als Parallelen zu den hier
vertretenen Ansichten anführen. So sagt der Ungenannte in dem
zweiten *Fragment* (L. M. XII, 316 ff.), das sich durchweg mit der Offenbarung beschäftigt, auf Seite 352: "Wir haben aber noch die wich-
tigste und allerschwerste Untersuchung übrig. - Soll ein Buch als die
göttliche Offenbarung, als der Grund des Glaubens und der Seligkeit
angenommen werden, so muß ja wohl ein Mensch erst recht klar und
deutlich überführt sein, daß die Schrift Gottes Wort sei, und daß die
Verfasser, welche sonst ohnstreitig sündliche Menschen gewesen wie
andere, dieses voraus gehabt, daß ihnen Gott alles eingeflößet, und

daß sie sich darin weder selbst betrogen, noch andere betrügen wollen...
Es ist artig, wie diese schwere und wichtige Sache denen Leuten er-
leichtert wird.  Die Kinder lernen ein halb Dutzend Sprüche aus der
Bibel, darin gesagt wird, daß die Bibel Gottes Wort sei ; so sind sie
darnach ihr ganzes Leben hindurch mit Hilfe ihres Gedächtnisses im
Christentume vortrefflich gegründet und wider allen Zweifel und An-
fechtung bewahret.  Die Offenbarung hat denn allein das Vorrecht, sich
*per petitionem principii* zu erweisen: Die Schreiber sind von Gott getrieben, denn sie sagen es; Beweis genug! nur schade, daß denn doch
allein die wahre Offenbarung solch Vorrecht haben kann, die falschen
aber nicht, und daß folglich die Ungewißheit bleibt, welche die wahre
Offenbarung sei, mithin die Nötigkeit solcher Untersuchung aus besseren
Gründen bestätiget wird."
    Ähnlich Lessings : *Beweis des Geistes und der Kraft* (L. M. XIII,
1 f.) Auch im *Cardanus*, L. M. V, 321 : "Cardan hätte es bei den
historischen Gründen können bewenden lassen.  Denn wer weiß nicht,
daß, wenn diese nur ihre Richtigkeit haben, man sonst alle Schwierigkeiten unter das Joch des Glaubens zwingen müsse ?  Allein er ist zu
klug, diese Aufopferung der Vernunft, so gerade hin, zu fordern.  Er
behauptet vielmehr, daß die ganze Lehre Christi nichts enthalte, was
mit der Moral und mit der natürlichen Weltweisheit streite, oder mit
ihr in keine Einstimmung könne gebracht werden." —
    Recht stark kommt Lessings Zweifel in Bezug auf historisch über-
lieferte Beweise in seinen *Gesprächen für die Freimaurer* zum Ausdruck.
*Falck* hat erwiesen, daß trotz vieler gegenstreitender Behauptungen der
Name Freimaurer nicht vor dem Beginn seines Jahrhunderts gebräuch-
lich gewesen.  *Ernst* antwortet darauf (L. M. XIII, 404) : "Und das
hätten sie so lange ungerügt vor den Augen der Welt treiben dürfen?
— *Falck:* Warum nicht?  Der Klugen sind viel zu wenig, als daß sie
allen Geckereien gleich bei ihrem Entstehen widersprechen könnten.  Genug, daß bei ihnen keine Verjährung stattfindet. — Freilich
wäre es besser, wenn man vor dem Publico ganz und gar keine
Geckereien unternähme; denn gerade das Verächtlichste ist, daß sich
niemand die Mühe nimmt, sich ihnen entgegenzustellen, wodurch sie
mit dem Laufe der Zeit das Ansehen einer sehr ernsthaften, heiligen
Sache gewinnen.  Da heißt es dann über tausend Jahre: Würde man
denn so in die Welt haben schreiben dürfen, wenn es nicht wahr gewesen wäre?  Man hat diesen glaubwürdigen Männern damals nicht
widersprochen, und Ihr wollt ihnen jetzt widersprechen? — *Ernst :*
O Geschichte ! O Geschichte ! Was bist du ?"
    In den *Gegensätzen zu den Fragmenten* sagt Lessing (L. M. XII,

435): "Aber beider (der Chiromantie und der Offenbarung) Beweise sind doch aus der nämlichen Klasse, sie gründen sich beide auf Zeugnisse und Erfahrungssätze. Und das Abstechende der stärksten Beweise dieser Art gegen Beweise, die aus der Natur der Dinge fließen, ist so auffallend, daß alle Kunst, dieses Auffallende zu vermindern, dieses Abstechende durch allerlei Schattierungen sanfter zu machen, vergebens ist."

1895. S. auch Appendix, 1309. Zu Adam Neuser bemerkt Lessing, L. M. XII, 267 : "Als Neuser so weit gekommen war, daß er sich kein Bedenken machte, zur mohammedanischen Religion überzutreten, war er doch vermutlich kein Phantast, der sich von der Wahrheit der mohammedanischen Religion als geoffenbarter Religion, vorzüglich vor der christlichen, überzeugt fühlte, sondern er war ein Deist, der *eine* geoffenbarte Religion für so erdichtet hielt als die andere und den nur die äußerste Verfolgung zu einem Tausch brachte, an den er nie würde gedacht haben, wenn er irgendwo in der Christenheit die Duldung zu finden gewußt hätte, auf welcher unser Unbekannte für solcher Art Leute dringt." Das hieße also, nicht aus Überzeugung, sondern aus Gleichgültigkeit verharrt man in der angestammten Religion. — Namentlich aber der Fragmentist hat für unsere Stelle wieder das Vorbild gegeben, wie auch Gross hervorhebt. Er sagt I. M. XII, 325: "Zuweilen wird schon in den Ehepakten der Eltern den Kindern, die noch sollen geboren werden, ihr Glaube als ein Erbgut, als ihre väterliche oder mütterliche Portion bestimmt: die Knaben bekommen etwa den katholischen, die Mädchen den lutherischen Glauben. Und siehe, sie nehmen ihn, wie alle übrigen Religionen und Sekten, nach den Ehepakten, nach dem Willen und Bestimmung ihrer Eltern, nach dem Exempel ihrer Vorfahren getrost an und können nicht anders handeln. Wer kann von solchen Kindern eine Fähigkeit fordern, daß sie die Wahrheit dessen, was sie lernen, beurteilen und, so sie im Irrtume wären, eine bessere Religion suchen und finden sollten? Wer kann ihnen verdenken, daß sie bei dem Vertrauen, bei dem Gehorsame, so sie ihren Eltern schuldig sind, auch derselben ihre Religion für wahr und für die beste halten?" — Über den Wert der Tradition vom Vater auf das Kind sagt aber der Ungenannte L. M. XII, 320: "Wie viel muß nicht ferner in so manchen Jahrhunderten die Glaubwürdigkeit abnehmen, wenn einer, der dergleichen zu seiner Zeit von einem andern für wahr hält, solches seinen Kindern, die Kinder wieder seinen Enkeln, die Enkel seinen Urenkeln und so weiter erzählen! Da wird aus der allergrößten Glaubwürdigkeit eine Wahrscheinlichkeit, dann eine Sage und zuletzt ein Märlein."

Ganz denselben Gedanken finden wir aber auch in Rousseaus *Émile*, wie überhaupt sich beim Vicaire Savoyard recht viele Gedanken finden, die man in den *Fragmenten* und bei Lessing wieder antrifft.   Die betr. Stelle, Rousseau, *Émile* IV (*Édition stéréotype, d'après le procédé de Firmin Didot, tome* II, *p.* 301) lautet: "*Voulez-vous mitiger cette méthode, et donner la moindre prise à l'autorité des hommes? à l'instant vous lui rendez tout; et si le fils d'un chrétien fait bien de suivre, sans un examen profond et impartial, la religion de son père, pourquoi le fils d'un Turc feroit-il mal de suivre de même la religion du sien? Combien d'hommes sont à Rome très bons catholiques, qui, par la même raison, seroient très bons musulmans s'ils fussent nés à la Mecque! et réciproquement que d'honnêtes gens sont très bons Turcs en Asie, qui seroient très bons chrétiens parmi nous! Je défie tous les intolérants du monde de répondre à cela rien qui contente un homme sensé.*"

2025.   "Eure Ringe sind alle drei nicht echt." Über die Entstehung der geoffenbarten Religion, L. M. XIV, 313: "Die Unentbehrlichkeit einer positiven Religion, vermöge welcher die natürliche Religion in jedem Staate nach dessen natürlicher und zufälliger Beschaffenheit modifiziert wird, nenne ich die innere Wahrheit derselben, und diese innere Wahrheit derselben ist bei einer so groß als bei der andern. — Alle positiven und geoffenbarten Religionen sind folglich gleich wahr und gleich falsch. — Gleich wahr, insofern es überall gleich notwendig gewesen ist, sich über verschiedene Dinge zu vergleichen, um Übereinstimmung und Einigkeit in der öffentlichen Religion hervorzubringen. Gleich falsch, indem nicht sowohl das, worüber man sich verglichen, neben dem Wesentlichen besteht, sondern das Wesentliche schwächt und verdrängt. — Die *beste* geoffenbarte oder positive Religion ist die, welche die wenigsten konventionellen Zusätze zur natürlichen Religion enthält, die guten Wirkungen der natürlichen Religion am wenigsten einschränkt." — Ich meine, man müßte demnach unter dem *echten* Ring die natürliche Religion verstehen, welchem sich die andern Ringe, je nach ihrer *Wirksamkeit* mehr oder weniger nähern.   Oder aber *die* positive Religion, welche die guten Wirkungen der natürlichen Religion am wenigsten einschränkt.   Ich glaube, man darf es wohl für festgestellt erachten, daß auch Lessing von den drei in Frage kommenden Religionen in dieser Beziehung dem Christentum den Vorrang giebt, d. h. natürlich dem Christentum nach seinem inneren Kern.   In einer Rezension vom Jahr 1755 (L. M. VII, S. 1) sagt Lessing: "Das stärkste innere Kennzeichen, woran man die einige wahre Religion erkennen kann, ist ohne Zweifel dieses, daß sie eine

vollkommene Richtschnur des sittlichen Lebens der Menschen lehren
und zugleich einen überzeugenden Unterricht erteilen muß, wie man,
in Ansehung der Abweichungen von derselben, Gnade und Vergebung
erlangen könne.   Da nun aber die christliche Religion die einzige ist,
der man diese Eigenschaft zugestehen muß, so wird man auch zugestehen müssen, daß ihre Wahrheit von dieser Seite über alle Einwürfe
hinweg gesetzt sei." — Es liegt aber nahe anzunehmen, daß Lessing
schon hier unter der chr. Religion die Religion verstand, die er sonst
im Gegensatz als die Religion Christi bezeichnete, von welcher er sowohl als der Ungenannte meinte, sie enthalte nichts, was sich mit den
Grundsätzen der natürlichen Religion nicht vereinen lasse.   Daß es
nicht das orthodoxe Christentum seiner Zeit gewesen sein kann, ließe
sich aus unzähligen Stellen beweisen.   So sagt Lessing in einem Brief
an Mendelssohn (9. Jan. 1771): "Noch mehr aber bitte ich Sie, wenn
Sie darauf (d. h. auf Lavaters neue Bekehrungsversuche) antworten, es
mit aller möglichen Freiheit, mit allem nur ersinnlichen Nachdrucke
zu thun.   Sie allein dürfen und können in dieser Sache so sprechen
und schreiben und sind daher unendlich glücklicher als andere ehrliche Leute, die den Umsturz des abscheulichsten Gebäudes von Unsinn nicht anders als unter dem Vorwande es neu zu unterbauen,
befördern können." (Das war sicher auch der Zweck, den Lessing in
seinen *Gegensätzen zu den Fragmenten* verfolgte). — Gegen die Annahme, daß die natürliche Religion unter dem echten Ring zu verstehen sei, spricht scheinbar v. 2035-6; denn bei ihr dürfte doch von
einer Tyrannei nicht die Rede sein.   Man könnte versucht sein zu
glauben, daß zwar Nathan nicht, wohl aber Lessing mit dem echten
Ring die christliche Religion, oder, wie er lieber will, die Religion
Christi, gemeint habe.   Auch in der *Erziehung des Menschengeschlech-
tes* wird angedeutet, daß mit dem Kommen Christi neue, edlere Ele-
mente in die jüdische Religion eingeführt wurden.   Ein wichtiges
Zeugnis für diese Annahme wäre auch aus dem *Cardanus* zu ent-
nehmen (L. M. v, 321): "Endlich sehe man auch, wie gründlich er von
dem Beweise der Fortpflanzung der christlichen Religion redet.   Er
berührt nichts davon, als was wirklich eine schließende Kraft* hat
... und bemerkt auch etwas, was ich nur von wenigen bemerkt finde.
Dieses nämlich, daß unsere Religion auch alsdann nicht aufgehört hat,
sich die Menschen unterwürfig zu machen, da sie von innerlichen
Sekten zerrissen und verwirret war.   Ein wichtiger Umstand!   Ein
Umstand, welcher notwendig zeigt, daß in ihr etwas sein müsse, welches unabhängig von allen Streitigkeiten seine Kraft zu allen Zeiten

---

* Vgl. sprachlich: das *schliesst* für mich, Zeile 237.

äußert. Und was kann dieses anders sein, als die immer siegende Wahrheit?" Das sind Lessings, nicht Cardans Worte.

2439. "Will es denn *eine* Klasse von Leuten nie lernen, daß es schlechterdings nicht wahr ist, daß jemals ein Mensch wissentlich und vorsätzlich sich selbst verblendet habe? Es ist nicht wahr, sag' ich; aus keinem geringern Grunde, als weil es nicht möglich ist." *Duplik*, L. M. XIII, 23. Goeze, *Streitschr.*, S. 6, sagt dagegen: "Das innere Zeugnis des heiligen Geistes, welches sich durch die Kraft der heil. Schrift an den Seelen derer offenbaret, welche der Wahrheit nicht mutwillig widerstreben (vielleicht ist dieses dem Herrn L. lächerlich? auf seine Gefahr!) muß hier notwendig die Ehre behaupten, unser Herz in der Wahrheit Gottes fest zu machen."

2445. Vgl. dazu *Axiomata*, L. M. XIII, 135–6: "Sollen denn, müssen denn alle Christen zugleich Theologen sein? Ich habe noch immer die besten Christen unter denen gefunden, die von der Theologie am wenigsten wußten." Ähnlich der Philosoph, den Lessing in seinem Aufsatz über die Herrnhuter auftreten läßt. Vgl. Appendix 35.

2454. Zum Patriarchen wäre zu vergleichen, was Lessing über Ismenor, den Priester in Cronegks *Olint und Sophronia*, sagt. Die Stelle findet sich im 2. Stück der *Dramaturgie* (L. M. IX, 192): "Ich weiß wohl, die Gesinnungen müssen in dem Drama dem angenommenen Charakter der Person, welche sie äußert, entsprechen; sie können also das Siegel der absoluten Wahrheit nicht haben; genug, wenn sie poetisch wahr sind, wenn wir gestehen müssen, daß dieser Charakter, in dieser Situation, bei dieser Leidenschaft, nicht anders als so habe urteilen können. Aber auch diese poetische Wahrheit muß sich, auf einer andern Seite, der absoluten wiederum nähern, und der Dichter muß nie so unphilosophisch denken, daß er annimmt, ein Mensch könne das Böse, um des Bösen wegen, wollen, er könne nach lasterhaften Grundsätzen handeln, das Lasterhafte derselben erkennen, und doch gegen sich und andere damit prahlen. Ein solcher Mensch ist ein Unding, so gräßlich als ununterrichtend, und nichts als die armselige Zuflucht eines schalen Kopfes, der schimmernde Tiraden für die höchste Schönheit des Trauerspieles hält. Wenn Ismenor ein grausamer Priester ist, sind darum alle Priester Ismenors? Man wende nicht ein, daß von Priestern einer falschen Religion die Rede sei. So falsch war noch keine in der Welt, daß ihre Lehrer notwendig Unmenschen sein müssen. Priester haben in den falschen Religionen, so wie in der wahren, Unheil gestiftet, aber nicht weil sie Priester, sondern weil sie Bösewichter waren, die, zum Behuf ihrer schlimmen Neigungen, die Vorrechte auch eines jeden andern Standes gemiß.

braucht hätten."—Brief an C. A. Schmid, 23. Mai 1770: "Als ob man
nicht in jeder Kirche sehr rechtgläubig sein und dennoch ein ärger-
liches Leben führen könnte?"

2476 f. In dem ersten Fragment (L. M. XII, 311) greift Reimarus
die Theologen an, weil sie von den Laien fordern, "daß sie ihre Vernunft gefangen nehmen müssen unter dem Gehorsam des Glaubens."
Er weist nach, daß in der betreffenden Stelle (II. Cor. x, 4–5) Paulus
nicht von der Vernunft, sondern von Vernunftschlüssen redet, die sehr
wohl falsch sein können. "Aber die Vernunft selbst, mit ihren ewigen
Grundregeln, ist nicht zu widerlegen, und wir müssen sie auch nimmer
fahren lassen, wo wir uns nicht in unvernünftige Irrtümer stürzen
wollen. Warum heißt man uns denn die Vernunft selbst gefangen
nehmen? Kann dies wohl einen andern Verstand erwecken, . . . . als
daß die Leute ihre Vernunft, da sie doch von Dingen, die des Gottes
sind, nichts versteht, immer bei sich unterdrücken, und gänzlich un-
gebraucht lassen müssen, wenn sie gute Christen sein wollen." — Paulus
widerlegte die Vernunftschlüsse der Corinther und gewann sie so für
den christlichen Glauben. Das thun aber unsere Theologen nicht.
"Das ist nicht der rechte Weg: erst die Kinder in der Wiege *par force*
zu Christen zu taufen und ihnen dabei einen christlichen Glauben und
Verlangen nach der Taufe anzudichten: sie darnach, vor dem Gebrauche
der Vernunft, ohne alle vernünftige Religion, zu einem blinden Glauben an die Bibel und deren Lehre anzuführen, und solchen Glauben
durch Furcht und Hoffnung, durch Himmel und Hölle, tief in die
zarten Gemüter einzuprägen: endlich aber, wenn die Jahre der Überlegung und Prüfung des Glaubens kommen sind, sie vor dem Gebrauch der blöden und verdorbenen Vernunft sorgfältig zu warnen, und
von ihnen zu verlangen, daß sie ihre Vernunft zum Voraus gefangen
nehmen sollen unter dem Gehorsam desjenigen Glaubens, der ihnen
bloß durch ein kindliches Vorurteil eingeflößet war." Vgl. den ganzen
Aufsatz: "Von Verschreiung der Vernunft von den Kanzeln."
L. M. XII, 304 f.

Fast noch schärfer drückt sich der Fragmentist in dem Aufsatz
*Von Duldung der Deisten* aus. L. M. XII, 260: "Die Wahrheit
muß durch Gründe ausgemacht werden, und sie stehet ihren Gegnern
kein Verjährungsrecht zu . . . Sind die Theologi allein privilegiert,
daß sie keine Rede und Antwort geben dürfen (= brauchen) von den
Sätzen, welche sie andern zu glauben aufbürden?"

2487. Appendix 385. An anderer Stelle deutet Lessing an, daß
Gott als das vollkommenste Wesen in seinem Handeln durchaus ge-
bunden ist; und all sein Handeln ist gut; der Patriarch dagegen deutet

in den auf 2487 folgenden Versen an, daß das, was nach den kleinen Regeln einer eiteln Ehre schlecht — in diesem Fall den Saladin
verräterisch und meuchlings zu ermorden — vor Gott gut sein kann.
Vgl. dazu eine der Hauptregeln der Jesuiten, die natürlich auch für
den Patriarchen gilt.    "Auf die innere Beschaffenheit der Handlung
kann es natürlich nicht ankommen, da sie in dem hohen Zwecke ihre
Berechtigung und Heiligung findet; daher wird selbst die Handlung,
welche, abgesehen von diesem Zwecke, eine Todsünde oder ein Verbrechen sein würde, zur Tugend." Ed. Niemeyer, *Commentar zu Nathan.*

2511.  "Folget aus dem bloß möglichen Fall nicht eben das, was
aus dem wirklichen folgen würde?" fragt Lessing den Pastor Goeze,
als dieser in seinen *Streitschriften* für ein von Lessing erzähltes Histör-
chen den Beweis verlangte, daß es wirklich geschehen sei.    Und im
zehnten Anti-Goeze, L. M. XIII, 201: "Wenn der Herr Hauptpastor
unter diese neugierigen spielenden Kinder nicht selbst gerechnet werden will, so sage er doch nur, in welcher ernsthaften Absicht sonst, er
gern den Namen meines Ungenannten wissen möchte.    Kann er seine
Asche noch einmal zu Asche brennen lassen?    Sollen seine Gebeine in
der Erde, welche sie willig aufnahm, nicht länger ruhen?"

2516.  Rousseau, *Émile,* IV, p. 280 f: "*Ou toutes les religions
sont bonnes et agréables à Dieu, ou, s'il en est une qu'il prescrive aux
hommes et qu'il les punisse de méconnoître, il lui a donné des signes
certains et manifestes pour être distinguée comme pour la seule véri-
table: ces signes sont, de tous les temps et de tous les lieux, également
sensibles à tous les hommes grands et petits, savants et ignorants,
Européens, Indiens, Africains, sauvages.    S'il étoit une religion sur la
terre hors de laquelle il n'y eût que peine éternelle, et qu'en quelque
lieu du monde un seul mortel de bonne foi n'eût pas été frappé de son
évidence, le Dieu de cette religion seroit le plus inique et le plus cruel
de tyrans.*"

Ähnlich wird auch im zweiten *Fragment* (L. M. XII, 313 f) zu erweisen gesucht, daß alle anderen Fähigkeiten des Menschen ihrem Zweck
entsprechen, also nicht verdorben sein können, und es ist auch kein
Grund, die menschliche Vernunft allein zu verachten und ihren Gebrauch zu untersagen.    In der That untersagen die Herren Theologi denselben auch nur andern; selbst aber widerlegen sie einander eben mit
Vernunftschlüssen.    (S. 305): "Sondern man schreckt vielmehr diejenigen, welche nun Lust bekommen möchten, nachzudenken und auf den
Grund ihres bisherigen blinden Glaubens zu forschen, von dem Gebrauche ihrer edelsten Naturgabe, der Vernunft, ab.    Die Vernunft
wird ihnen als eine schwache, blinde, verdorbene und verführerische

Leiterin abgemalt, damit die Zuhörer, welche noch nicht einmal recht
wissen, was Vernunft oder vernünftig heiße, jetzt bange werden, ihre
Vernunft zur Erkenntnis göttlicher Dinge anzuwenden, weil sie dadurch leicht zu gefährlichen Irrtümern gebracht werden möchten."
In seinen *Gegensätzen*, L. M. XII, 433, giebt Lessing dem Fragmentisten zum guten Teil recht, namentlich darin, daß die Vernunft an
sich nicht verderbt sei.    An anderer Stelle geht der Fragmentist gar
so weit, zu behaupten, daß "die gesunde Vernunft und das Naturge-
setz die eigentliche Quelle aller Pflichten und Tugenden sei, woraus
Christus selbst und die Apostel ihre Vorschriften geschöpft haben."

2522. Vgl. Goeze, *Streitschriften*, 7 und 8: "So viel kann ich
zum Voraus sagen: werde ich in diesen Blättern eben die Logik finden, welche Herr L. in den übrigen, die Fragmente betreffenden
Schriften gebraucht hat; so ist er keiner Antwort würdig.    Denn
Sophismen, Equivocen, Fallacien, falsche, und schwache Leser blen-
dende Bilder, statt der Gründe; Schlüsse und Axiomen, aus vieldeuti-
gen, und von ihm nicht bestimmten Worten, Hohn und Naserümpfen
über die Gegner, haben in der gelehrten Welt eben den Wert, den
falsche Würfel in der bürgerlichen haben.    Die Theaterlogik, und die
Logik, welche in theologischen Streitigkeiten, insonderheit in denen,
welche die Wahrheit der christlichen Religion entscheiden sollen, gebraucht werden muß, sind himmelweit unterschieden.    Die erste kann
auf die Zuschauer große Wirkung thun, und diejenige, welche Goethe
in seiner schändlichen *Stella* gebraucht hat, um die Hurerei und Viel-
weiberei zu rechtfertigen, hat öfters den Zuschauern ein lautes Jauchzen und ein heftiges Klatschen abgelocket.    Allein alle Rechtschaffene
verabscheuen solche auf dem theologischen Kampfplatze, so wie sie in
juristischen Streitigkeiten die Chicane verabscheuen.    In der Theaterlogik ist Herr L. ein großer Meister, aber er hat von derselben in seinen bisherigen, in ein ganz anderes Feld gehörigen Schriften beständig
Gebrauch gemacht . . . Allein es werden sich Männer finden, die seinen
Fechterstreichen mit gehörigem Nachdruck zu begegnen wissen, und
die ihm zeigen, daß er mit seiner Übertragung der Theaterlogik auf
den theologischen Kampfplatz selbst, die vom Aristoteles so hoch ver-
botene μεταβασιν εἰς ἀλλο γενος begehe, mit welcher der Verfasser
des Bogens: *Über den Beweis des Geistes und der Kraft*, den Herrn
Dir. Schumann, aber zu seiner eigenen Schande, zu verwirren gesucht
hat." — S. 97: "Doch von einem Heterogeneo auf das andere, oder
von dem Stocke im Winkel auf den morgenden Regen zu schließen,
das verstattet seine Theaterlogik."

Es ist schade, daß wir nicht auch Lessings launige Antwort ganz hersetzen können. Sie findet sich im zweiten *Anti-Goeze*, L. M. XIII, 148 f., und ist zugleich ein vortreffliches Urteil über Lessings Stil. Wir müssen uns mit einem kleinen Auszug begnügen: "Aber, Herr Hauptpastor, das ist mein Stil, und mein Stil ist nicht meine Logik.— Doch ja! Allerdings soll auch meine Logik sein, was mein Stil ist: eine Theaterlogik. So sagen Sie. Aber sagen Sie, was Sie wollen: die gute Logik ist immer die nämliche, man mag sie anwenden, worauf man will. Sogar die Art, sie anzuwenden, ist überall die nämliche. Wer Logik in einer Komödie zeigt, dem würde sie gewiß auch zu einer Predigt nicht entstehen: so wie der, dem sie in einer Predigt mangelt, nimmermehr mit ihrer Hilfe auch eine nur erträgliche Komödie zustande bringen würde, und wenn er der unerschöpflichste Spaßvogel unter der Sonne wäre."

2531. Ähnliche Intoleranz hatte schon der Fragmentist den Christen zur Last gelegt. Lessing sagt darüber in seinen Zusätzen zum Fragment *Von Duldung der Deisten,*—L. M. XII, 267: "Neuser war ein Deist, der *eine* geoffenbarte Religion für so erdichtet hielt als die andere, und den nur die äußerste Verfolgung zu einem Tausche brachte, an den er nie würde gedacht haben, wenn er irgendwo in der Christenheit die Duldung zu finden gewußt hätte, auf welche unser Unbekannte für solcher Art Leute dringet."

2537. Vgl. *Berengarius*, L. M. XI, 62: "Das Ding, was man Ketzer nennt, hat eine sehr gute Seite. Es ist ein Mensch, der mit seinen eigenen Augen *wenigstens* sehen *wollen*. Die Frage ist nur, ob es gute Augen gewesen, mit welchen er selbst sehen wollen. Ja, in gewissen Jahrhunderten ist der Name Ketzer die größte Empfehlung, die von einem Gelehrten auf die Nachwelt gebracht werden können: noch größer als der Name Zauberer, Magus, Teufelsbanner; denn unter diesen läuft doch mancher Betrüger mit unter."

2542. Vgl. *Von Duldung der Deisten*, L. M. XII, 258: "Was ist also an der Heuchelei so vieler bedrückten Vernünftigen anders schuld, als der mit so manchem zeitlichen Unglück verknüpfte Glaubenszwang, welchen die Herren Theologi und Prediger, vermöge ihrer Schmähungen und Verfolgungen, den Bekennern einer vernünftigen Religion bis in den Tod anlegen?"

"Wahrlich, solch Verfahren ist auf alle Weise zu mißbilligen. Ein Mensch, der ohne sein Wissen in der ersten Kindheit mit Gewalt zum Christen getaufet ist, und dem man den Glauben teils fälschlich andichtet, teils in den unverständigen Jahren ohne Vernunft eingeprägt hat, kann nach keinem göttlichen oder menschlichen Rechte gehalten sein, sobald er andere Einsichten von der Wahrheit bekommt, eben dasselbe zu glauben, was er als ein Kind in Einfalt zu glauben gelehrt war."

2552. Der Fragmentist führt aus, daß es sehr von Umständen abhängt, ob jemand dem Christentum oder einer anderen Religion sich äußerlich anschließt.    Und da der Mensch über die Umstände meist keine Macht hat, wäre es ungerecht von Gott, ihn dafür verantwortlich zu machen.    L. M. XII, 326: "Gott handelt gewiß anders im Leiblichen.    Was den Menschen, und besonders auch den Kindern, zum Leben notwendig ist, das reicht er durch die Natur im Überflusse dar, daß es sich allen und jeden von selbst anbietet; und giebt wiederum jedem das Vermögen, sich dessen zu bedienen.    Wie kann er die Mittel zu dem geistlichen und ewigen Leben und Wohlfahrt so sehr über das Vermögen der Menschen gesetzt haben, daß sie (d. h. die Mittel) teils unmöglich sind, teils dem Zufall überlassen werden?"

2555 f.    Vgl. den Fragmentisten, L. M. XII, 259: "Zieht der Priester auf die Ungläubigen los, so denkt der gemeine Mann, dessen ganze Religion im Glauben besteht, daß es Leute sind, die gar keine Religion haben, die weder Gott noch Teufel, weder Himmel noch Hölle glauben.    Denn er urteilt nach sich selbst: wenn bei ihm der Glaube wegfiele, so bliebe gar keine Religion übrig.    Unchristen klingen in des Pöbels Ohren als ruchlose, lasterhafte Bösewichter." — An anderer Stelle: "Der Pöbel glaubt so kräftig, daß er sich wohl auf seinen Glauben totschlagen ließe, und andere gern totschlüge, die das nicht glauben, was er glaubt."

2579.    Paulsen, *Einleitung in die Philosophie*, S. 310: "Die natürliche Theologie war dem achtzehnten Jahrhundert die Grundlage seines ganzen Denkens, ja schien ihm die Grundlage des ganzen Lebens zu sein; sie antasten hieß alle göttliche und menschliche Ordnung auf den Kopf stellen.    Man höre einen so frei denkenden Mann wie Wieland (*Über den Gebrauch der Vernunft in Glaubenssachen*, 1788): "Der Glaube an Gott nicht nur als die erste Grundursache aller Dinge, sondern auch als unumschränkten und höchsten Gesetzgeber, Regenten und Richter der Menschen macht nebst dem Glauben an einen künftigen Zustand nach dem Tode die ersten Grundartikel der Religion aus.    Diesen Glauben auf alle mögliche Weise zu bekräftigen und zu unterstützen ist eines der würdigsten und nützlichsten Geschäfte der Philosophie, in Rücksicht der Unentbehrlichkeit desselben sogar Pflicht; ihn anzufechten und durch alle Arten von Zweifeln und Scheingründen in den Gemütern der Menschen wankend zu machen oder sogar umzustoßen, kann nicht nur zu gar nichts helfen, sondern ist im Grunde um gar nichts besser, als ein öffentlicher Angriff auf

die Grundverfassung des Staates, wovon die Religion einen wesentlichen Teil ausmacht, und auf die öffentliche Ruhe und Sicherheit,
deren Stütze sie ist. Ich trage also kein Bedenken, meinem unmaß-
geblichen Rat an den König oder Fürsten, der mich (wider alles Vermuten) nach 50 Jahren etwa über diese Dinge um Rat fragen sollte,
noch diesen Artikel hinzuzusetzen: daß das ungereimte und ärgerliche
Disputieren gegen das Dasein Gottes *oder gegen die angenommenen Beweise desselben*, wenn man keine bessere zu geben hat, imgleichen das
öffentliche Bestreiten der Lehre von der Unsterblichkeit der Seele für
ein Attentat gegen die Menschheit und gegen die bürgerliche Gesellschaft erklärt und durch ein ausdrückliches Strafgesetz verboten werden sollte." "

Ganz im Sinne Wielands widersetzte sich das Consistorium von Bres-
lau den von Friedrich dem Großen angebahnten Schulreformen mit
den Worten, "der Unterthan sei der beste, welcher am meisten (*sic!*)
glaube und der der schlechteste, welcher am meisten raisonniere."
Vgl. Ziegler, *Geschichte der Pädagogik*, S. 238. — Und es ist wohl zu
beachten, daß selbst der Fragmentist von einem guten Staatsbürger
verlangt, daß er Religion habe; nur erklärt er seine vernünftige Religion für mindestens so gut als jede andere. Vgl. *Von Duldung der
Deisten*, L. M. XII, 258: "Was haben die Herren Theologi für Recht,
daß sie diejenigen, *die doch eine wahre Religion haben und ausüben*,
sonst aber nichts wider den Staat und ihre Nebenmenschen, oder in
besonderen Tugendpflichten verbrechen, öffentlich vor dem gemeinen
Haufen beschimpfen und verhaßt machen?"

Die Stelle, auf welche wohl Lessing besonders anspielt, findet sich
in Goeze's *Streitschriften*, S. 70–71: "Woher entspringt die Sicherheit
unserer Monarchen und die Treue, welche sie von ihren Kriegern erwarten, und wirklich bei ihnen finden? Daher, weil solche Christen
sind. Sind sie es gleich nicht alle im schärfsten Verstande; so sind
doch die Grundgesetze der christlichen Religion von dem Rechte der
Obrigkeit, und von der Pflicht der Unterthanen, zu tief in ihre Herzen geprägt, als daß es ihnen so leicht, als den Heiden, werden sollte,
solche daraus zu vertilgen. Werden sie aber Christen bleiben? Wird
nicht mit der Ehrerbietung gegen die heil. Schrift und Religion, auch
zugleich die Bereitwilligkeit ihren Oberherren den schuldigen Gehorsam zu leisten, und der Abscheu gegen Rebellion in ihren Herzen aus-
gelöschet werden, wenn es jedem Witzlinge und Narren freistehet, mit
der christlichen Religion und mit der Bibel vor den Augen des ganzen
christlichen Publici das tollkühnste Gespötte zu treiben? Ich habe
die Hoffnung zu Gott, daß die Zeit nahe sei, welche diesem unsinni-

gen Unfuge ein Ende machen wird, und daß große Herren, um ihrer
eigenen Sicherheit willen, oder wenigstens zu verhüten, daß sie, als
Gottes Statthalter, als Liebhaber des Lebens, nicht nötig haben
mögen, Schwert und Rad, zur Rache über die Übelthäter gebrauchen
zu dürfen, solchen Thoren und den verwegenen Ausbrüchen ihres Un-
sinns, Grenzen setzen werden."

2592. Goeze hatte Lessing und andern wegen ihrer Schriften Gottes Strafgericht angekündigt. Lessing antwortet darauf im dritten
*Anti-Goeze*, L. M. XIII, 154: "Warum sollte er also nicht, *trotz* seines
fleißigen Verdammens . . . selig zu werden hoffen? Ich bilde mir ein,
daß er selbst *durch* dieses Verdammen selig zu werden hoffet."

2687. Vgl. *Ernst und Falk*. L. M. XIII, 357: *Ernst:* Denn allen-
falls dächte ich doch, so wie du angenommen hast, daß alle Staaten
einerlei Verfassung hätten, daß sie auch wohl alle einerlei Religion
haben könnten. Ja, ich begreife nicht, wie einerlei Staatsverfassung
ohne einerlei Religion auch nur möglich ist. — *Falk:* Ich eben so
wenig. — Auch nahm ich jenes nur an, um deine Ausflucht abzu-
schneiden. Eines ist zuverlässig eben so unmöglich als das andere.
Ein Staat: mehrere Staaten. Mehrere Staaten: mehrere Staatsverfassungen. Mehrere Staatsverfassungen: mehrere Religionen.

2997. *Alcibiades*, L. M. III, 399: *Susamithres:* Das weiß ich,
mein Vater ist ehrgeizig. — *Alcibiades:* Und wessen ist ein Ehrgeizi-
ger nicht fähig; wie der größten Tugenden, so der schändlichsten
Laster, mit dem Unterschiede nur, daß diese Laster ganz unfehlbare
Laster, und jene Tugenden sehr zweifelhafte Tugenden sind. — Wie
spät habe ich das erkennen lernen! Daß ich es nicht eher erkannt,
lag an dir nicht, göttlicher Sokrates. Mit welcher liebenden Hart-
näckigkeit verfolgtest du meine Jugend, um mich zur Kenntnis meiner
selbst, meiner eignen Unwürdigkeit zu bringen, um den Stolz in mir
zu unterdrücken.

3024. Vgl. den Fragmentisten, *Vom Zwecke Jesu und seiner
Jünger*, L. M. XIII, 227: "Ich kann nicht umhin, einen gemeinen
Irrtum der Christen zu entdecken, welche aus der Vermischung der
Lehre der Apostel mit der Lehre Jesu sich einbilden, daß Jesu Absicht in seinem Lehramte gewesen, gewisse zum Teil neue und unbekannte Glaubensartikel und Geheimnisse zu offenbaren, und also ein
neues Lehrgebäude der Religion aufzurichten . . . Allein in allen
Lehren, Reden und Gesprächen Jesu kann ich davon nicht die ge-
ringste Spur finden. Er trieb nichts als lauter sittliche Pflichten,
wahre Liebe Gottes und des Nächsten: darin setzet er den ganzen Inhalt des Gesetzes und der Propheten: und darauf heißet er die Hoff-

nung zu seinem Himmelreich und zur Seligkeit bauen. Übrigens war er ein geborener Jude und wollte es auch bleiben: er bezeuget, er sei nicht gekommen, das Gesetz abzuschaffen, sondern zu erfüllen: er weiset nur, daß das Hauptsächlichste im Gesetze nicht auf die äußerlichen Dinge ankäme." Moses Mendelssohn war derselben Ansicht; und Heinr. Heine — der übrigens auf religiösem Gebiet kaum zu einem Urteil berechtigt sein dürfte — nennt die Christen sowohl als die Hebräer Juden, nur mit dem Unterschiede, daß die einen getauft, die andern ungetauft seien.

3053. Vgl. *Über die Entstehung der geoffenbarten Religion*, L. M. XIV, 312: "Einen Gott erkennen, sich die würdigsten Begriffe von ihm zu machen suchen, auf diese würdigsten Begriffe bei allen unseren Handlungen und Gedanken Rücksicht nehmen: ist der vollständigste Inbegriff aller natürlichen Religion. Zu dieser natürlichen Religion ist ein jeder Mensch, nach dem Maße seiner Kräfte, aufgelegt und verbunden."

3067. Vgl. dazu Lessings Definition eines Christen in den *Axiomata*, L. M. XIII, 125: "Ehe ich weiter erzähle, Herr Pastor: waren diese guten Leutchen wohl Christen, oder waren sie keine? Sie glaubten sehr lebhaft, daß es ein höchstes Wesen gebe; daß sie arme sündige Geschöpfe wären; daß dieses höchste Wesen demohngeachtet, durch ein anderes eben so hohes Wesen, sie nach diesem Leben ewig glücklich zu machen, die Anstalt getroffen. — Herr Pastor; waren diese Leutchen Christen, oder waren sie keine?" Dieselbe Frage wiederholt er im achten *Anti-Goeze*. Vgl.: *Das Testament Johannis*, L. M. XIII, 16. Hier fragt Lessing seinen Gegner: "Aber ich versteh' Sie auch wohl nicht. — So ist die christliche Liebe nicht die christliche Religion?"

3077. Mendelssohn schrieb in der 15. *Morgenstunde* — was ich aus Kettner anführe —: "Hauptsächlich, was die Lehre von der Vorsehung und Regierung Gottes betrifft, kenne ich keinen Schriftsteller, der diese großen Wahrheiten in derselben Lauterkeit, mit derselben Überzeugungskraft und mit demselben Interesse dem Leser ans Herz gelegt hätte, als Lessing in seinem Meisterstücke (d. h. *Nathan*) ... Es kommt mir so vor, als wenn er die Absicht gehabt hätte in seinem *Nathan* eine Art von "Anti-Candide" zu schreiben. Der französische Dichter strengte alle außerordentlichen Talente, die ihm die Vorsehung gegeben, an, um auf diese Vorsehung selbst eine Satire zu verfertigen. Der Deutsche that ebendies, um sie zu rechtfertigen und um sie den Augen der Sterblichen in ihrer reinsten Verklärung zu zeigen."

3512. Frick und Gaudig bemerken zu diesem Verse: "Damit ist

der letzte Rest des Fanatismus überwunden und ausgebrannt" (Düntzer, *Erläuterungen zu Nathan*, S. 249), "aber auch — des Charakters. Ein Tempelherr, der das Christentum einem Juden gegenüber herabsetzt (wird den lautern Weizen, den Ihr gesät, das Unkraut endlich nicht ersticken?) und der die Möglichkeit setzt, daß er ebensogut auch ein Muselmann werden könne, ist kein Charakter mehr." — Wir haben in der Einleitung auszuführen gesucht, daß der Tempelherr vielmehr *noch* kein Character *sei*, aber sich auf dem Wege befinde, einer zu *werden*.

3534. Im XI. Band der Lachmannschen Ausgabe (nicht der neuen Lachmann-Munckerschen), S. 747, findet sich folgendes Bekenntnis Lessings: "Ich bin nicht gelehrt — ich habe nie die Absicht gehabt, gelehrt zu werden — ich möchte nicht gelehrt sein, und wenn ich es im Traume werden könnte. Alles, wonach ich ein wenig gestrebt habe, ist, im Fall der Not ein gelehrtes Buch brauchen zu können. — Der aus Büchern erworbene Reichtum fremder Erfahrung heißt Gelehrsamkeit. Eigne Erfahrung ist Weisheit. Das kleinste Kapital von dieser ist mehr wert, als Millionen jener." Von größerer Wichtigkeit ist wohl eine Stelle aus den *Axiomata*, L. M. XIII, 120: "Noch kann ich mich über eine Frage nicht genug wundern, die der Herr Pastor mit einer Zuversicht thut, als ob nur *eine* Antwort darauf möglich wäre. "Würde," fragt er, "wenn die neutestamentlichen Bücher nicht geschrieben, und bis auf uns gekommen wären, wohl eine Spur von dem, was Christus gethan und gelehrt hat, in der Welt übrig geblieben sein?" — Gott behüte mich, jemals so klein von Christi Lehren zu denken, daß ich diese Frage so geradezu mit Nein zu beantworten wagte. Nein; dieses *Nein* spräche ich nicht nach, und wenn mir es ein Engel vom Himmel vorsagte. Geschweige, da mir es nur ein Lutherscher Pastor in den Mund legen will. — Alles, was in der Welt geschieht, ließe Spuren in der Welt zurück, ob sie der Mensch gleich nicht immer nachweisen kann: und nur deine Lehren, göttlicher Menschenfreund, die du nicht aufzuschreiben, die du zu predigen befahlest, wenn sie auch *nur* gepredigt worden, sollten nichts, gar nichts gewirket haben, woraus sich ihr Ursprung erkennen ließe? Deine Worte sollten erst, in tote Buchstaben verwandelt, Worte des Lebens geworden sein? Sind die Bücher der einzige Weg, die Menschen zu erleuchten, und zu bessern? Ist mündliche Überlieferung nichts?"

CPSIA information can be obtained
at www.ICGtesting.com
Printed in the USA
BVHW04*1203240818
525521BV00006B/114/P

9 780266 620525